⑧

Love & Lies

LOVE and LIES by MUSAWO

CONTENTS

Chapter 30: A Normal Sort of Love

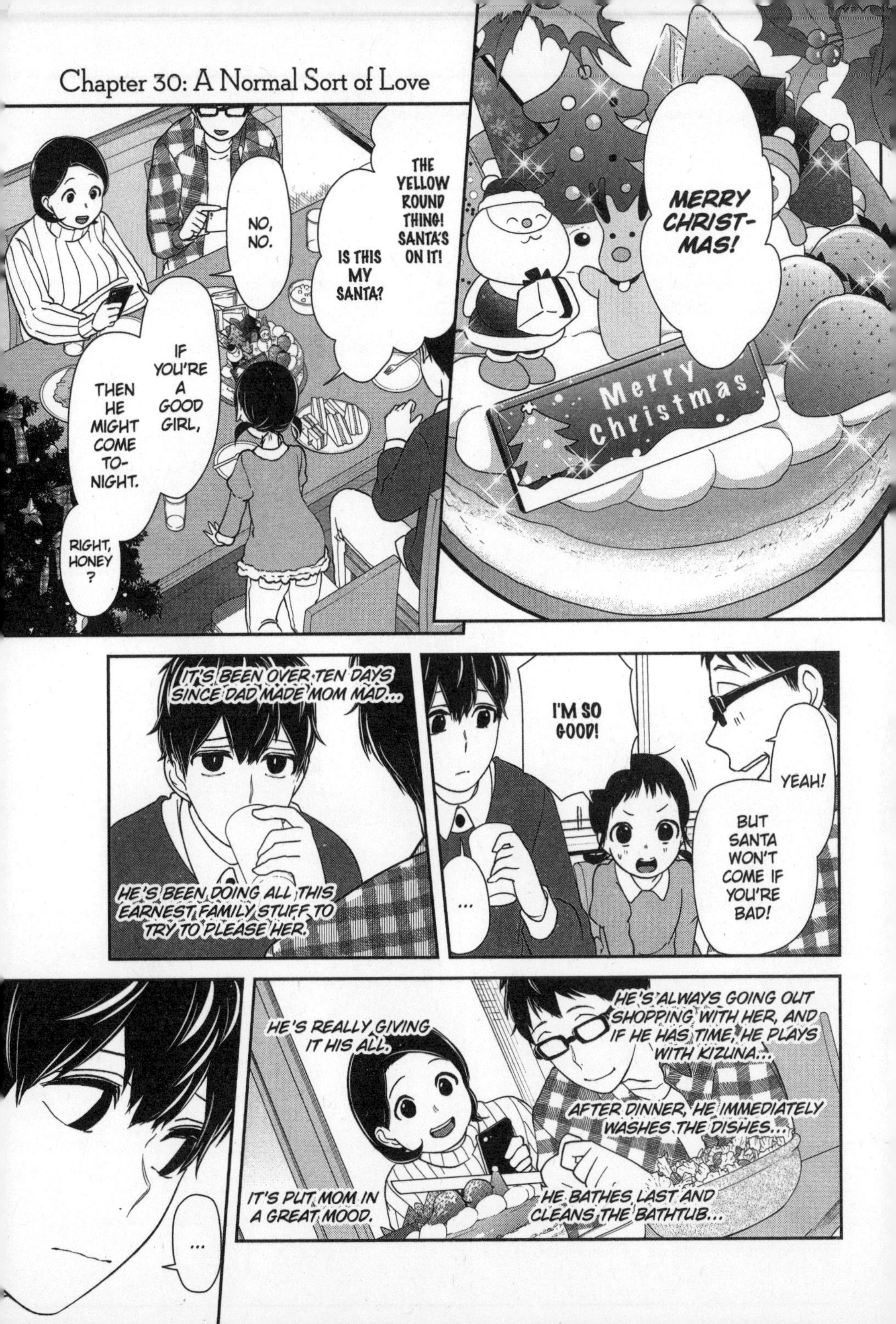

MERRY CHRISTMAS!
Merry Christmas
THE YELLOW ROUND THING! SANTA'S ON IT!
IS THIS MY SANTA?
NO, NO.
IF YOU'RE A GOOD GIRL,
THEN HE MIGHT COME TONIGHT.
RIGHT, HONEY?
YEAH!
BUT SANTA WON'T COME IF YOU'RE BAD!
I'M SO GOOD!
...
IT'S BEEN OVER TEN DAYS SINCE DAD MADE MOM MAD...
HE'S BEEN DOING ALL THIS EARNEST FAMILY STUFF TO TRY TO PLEASE HER.
HE'S ALWAYS GOING OUT SHOPPING WITH HER, AND IF HE HAS TIME, HE PLAYS WITH KIZUNA...
HE'S REALLY GIVING IT HIS ALL.
AFTER DINNER, HE IMMEDIATELY WASHES THE DISHES...
HE BATHES LAST AND CLEANS THE BATHTUB...
IT'S PUT MOM IN A GREAT MOOD.
...

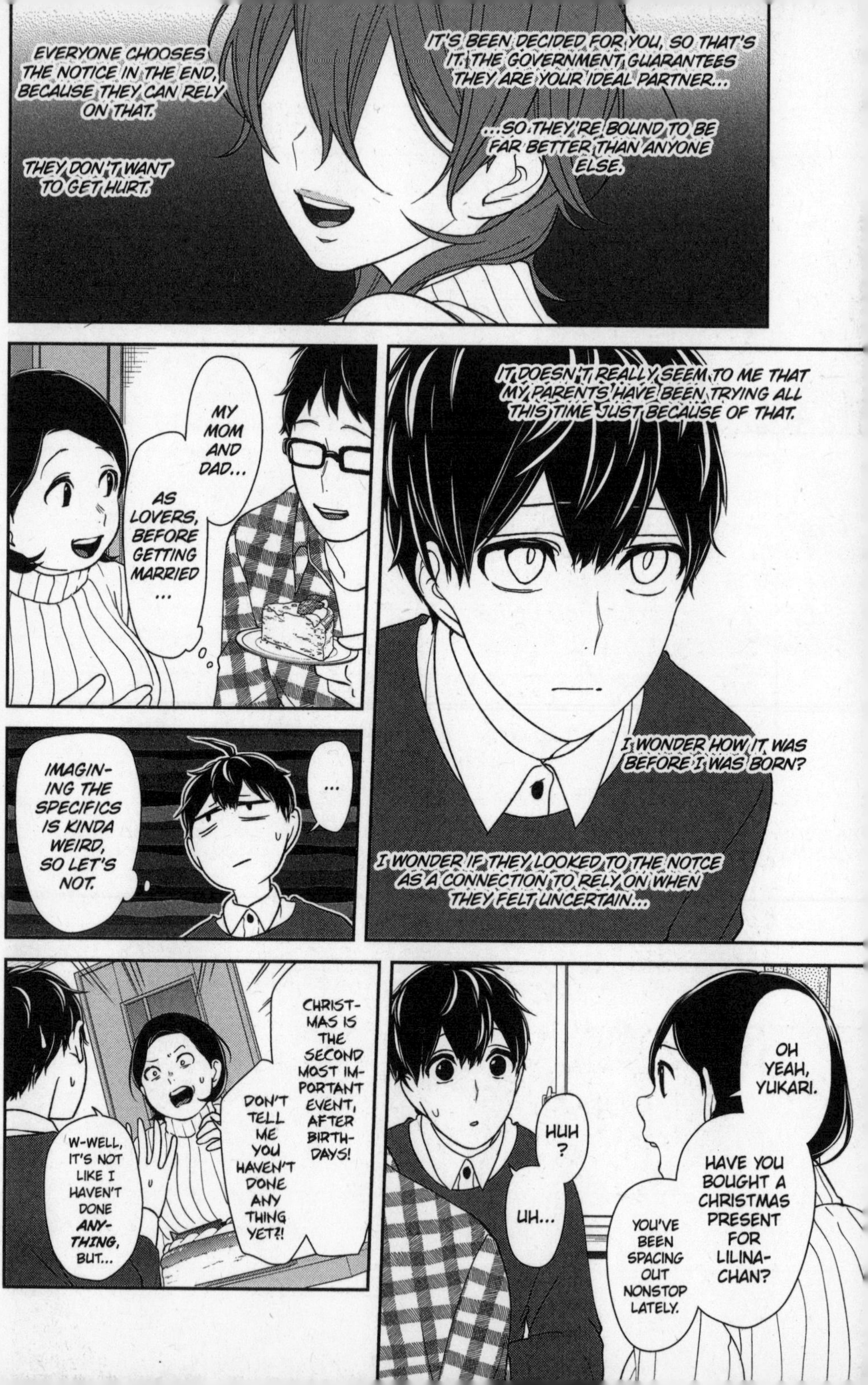
IT'S BEEN DECIDED FOR YOU, SO THAT'S IT. THE GOVERNMENT GUARANTEES THEY ARE YOUR IDEAL PARTNER...
...SO THEY'RE BOUND TO BE FAR BETTER THAN ANYONE ELSE.
EVERYONE CHOOSES THE NOTICE IN THE END, BECAUSE THEY CAN RELY ON THAT.
THEY DON'T WANT TO GET HURT.
IT DOESN'T REALLY SEEM TO ME THAT MY PARENTS HAVE BEEN TRYING ALL THIS TIME JUST BECAUSE OF THAT.
I WONDER HOW IT WAS BEFORE I WAS BORN?
I WONDER IF THEY LOOKED TO THE NOTCE AS A CONNECTION TO RELY ON WHEN THEY FELT UNCERTAIN...
MY MOM AND DAD...
AS LOVERS, BEFORE GETTING MARRIED...
...
IMAGINING THE SPECIFICS IS KINDA WEIRD, SO LET'S NOT.
OH YEAH, YUKARI.
HAVE YOU BOUGHT A CHRISTMAS PRESENT FOR LILINA-CHAN?
HUH?
YOU'VE BEEN SPACING OUT NONSTOP LATELY.
UH...
CHRISTMAS IS THE SECOND MOST IMPORTANT EVENT, AFTER BIRTHDAYS!
DON'T TELL ME YOU HAVEN'T DONE ANY THING YET?!
W-WELL, IT'S NOT LIKE I HAVEN'T DONE ANYTHING, BUT...

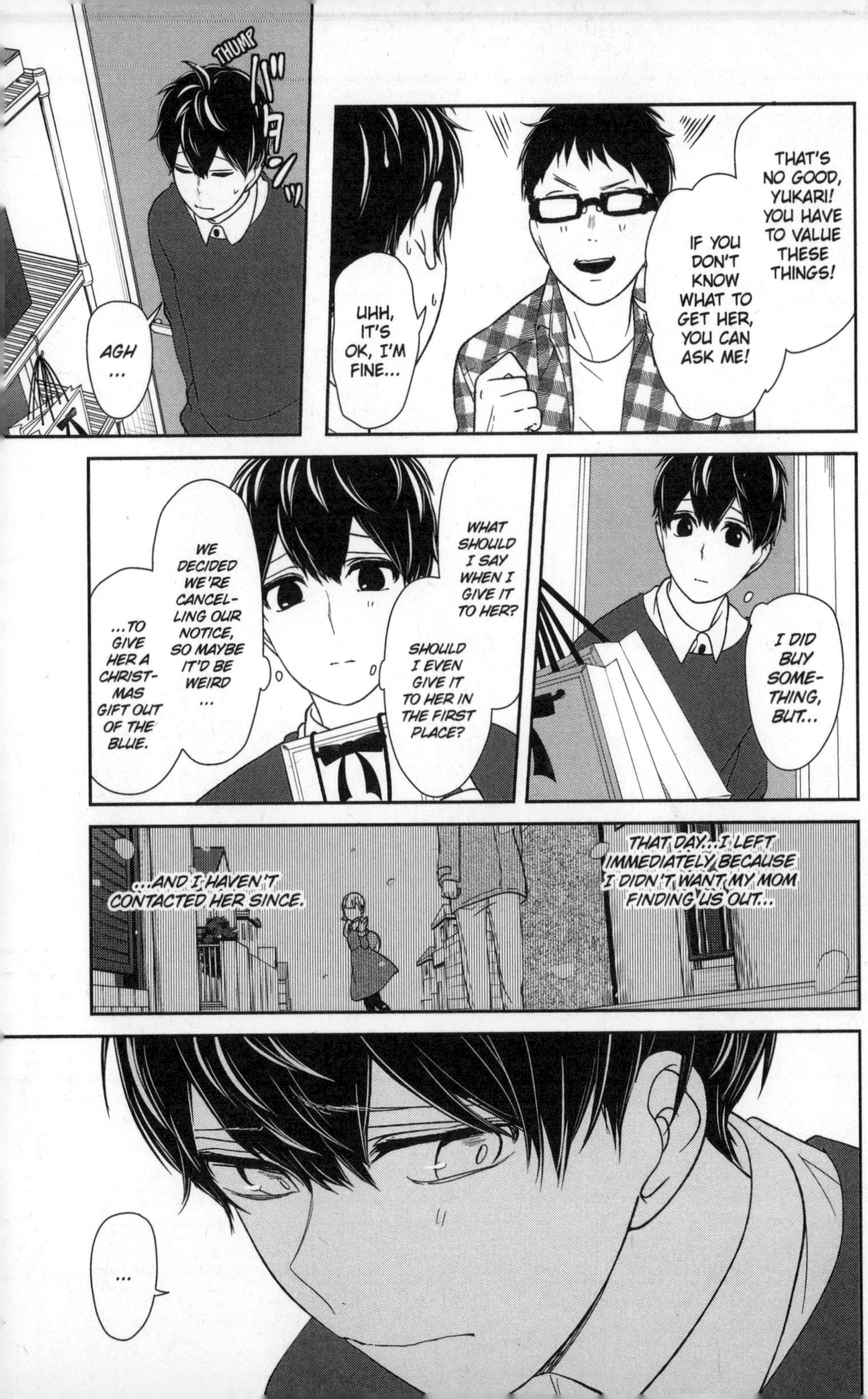
THAT'S NO GOOD, YUKARI! YOU HAVE TO VALUE THESE THINGS!
IF YOU DON'T KNOW WHAT TO GET HER, YOU CAN ASK ME!
UHH, IT'S OK, I'M FINE...
THUMP
AGH ...
I DID BUY SOMETHING, BUT...
WHAT SHOULD I SAY WHEN I GIVE IT TO HER?
SHOULD I EVEN GIVE IT TO HER IN THE FIRST PLACE?
WE DECIDED WE'RE CANCEL-LING OUR NOTICE, SO MAYBE IT'D BE WEIRD ...
...TO GIVE HER A CHRIST-MAS GIFT OUT OF THE BLUE.
THAT DAY... I LEFT IMMEDIATELY BECAUSE I DIDN'T WANT MY MOM FINDING US OUT...
...AND I HAVEN'T CONTACTED HER SINCE.
...

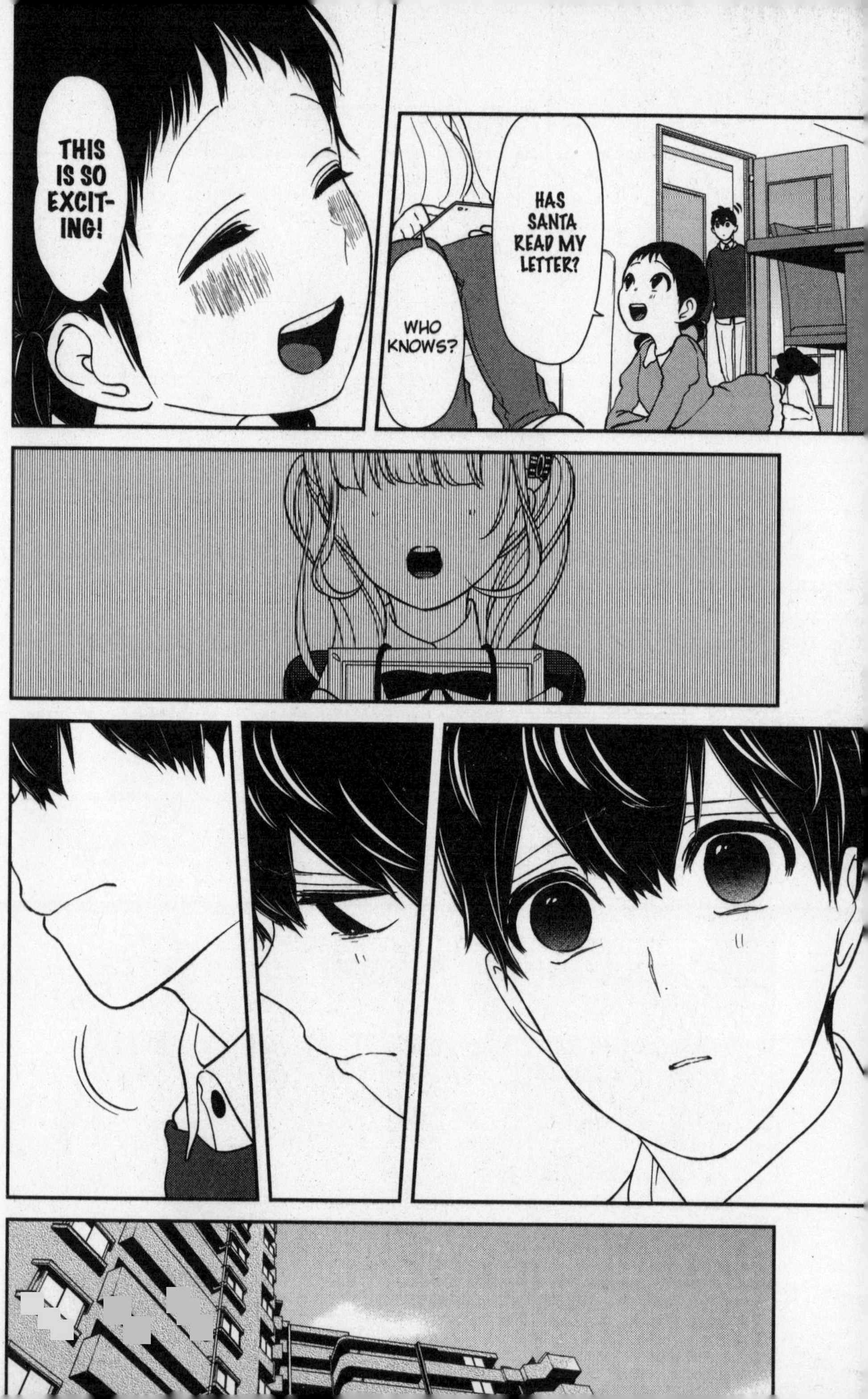
HAS SANTA READ MY LETTER?
WHO KNOWS?
THIS IS SO EXCIT-ING!

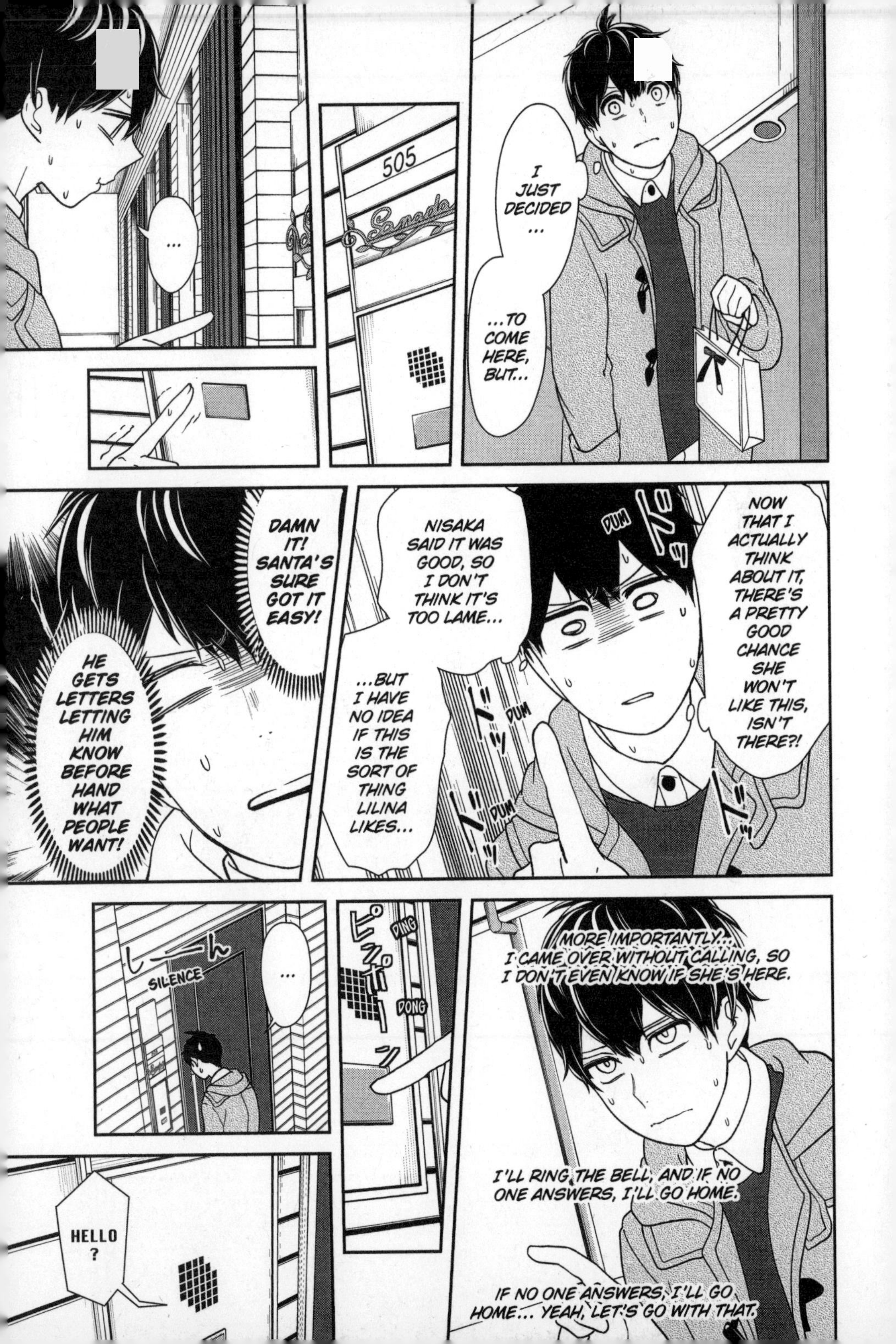
I JUST DECIDED...
...TO COME HERE, BUT...
505
...
NOW THAT I ACTUALLY THINK ABOUT IT, THERE'S A PRETTY GOOD CHANCE SHE WON'T LIKE THIS, ISN'T THERE?!
DUM
NISAKA SAID IT WAS GOOD, SO I DON'T THINK IT'S TOO LAME...
...BUT I HAVE NO IDEA IF THIS IS THE SORT OF THING LILINA LIKES...
DUM
DUM
DAMN IT! SANTA'S SURE GOT IT EASY!
HE GETS LETTERS LETTING HIM KNOW BEFORE HAND WHAT PEOPLE WANT!
MORE IMPORTANTLY... I CAME OVER WITHOUT CALLING, SO I DON'T EVEN KNOW IF SHE'S HERE.
I'LL RING THE BELL, AND IF NO ONE ANSWERS, I'LL GO HOME.
IF NO ONE ANSWERS, I'LL GO HOME... YEAH, LET'S GO WITH THAT.
DING
DONG
SILENCE
...
HELLO?

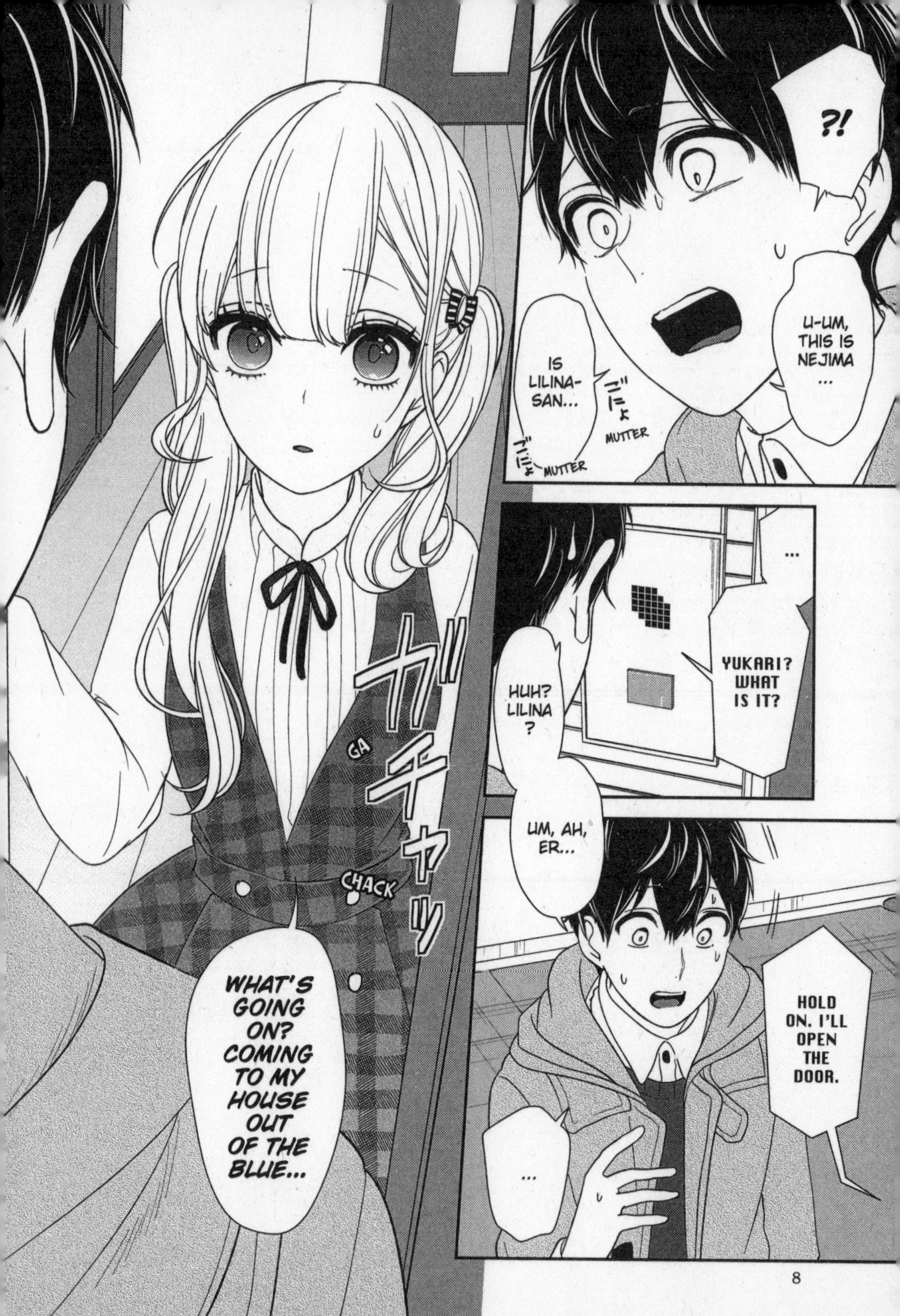
?!
U-UM, THIS IS NEJIMA ...
IS LILINA-SAN...
ごにょ MUTTER
ごにょ MUTTER
...
YUKARI? WHAT IS IT?
HUH? LILINA ?
UM, AH, ER...
HOLD ON. I'LL OPEN THE DOOR.
...
ガチャッ GA CHACK
WHAT'S GOING ON? COMING TO MY HOUSE OUT OF THE BLUE...

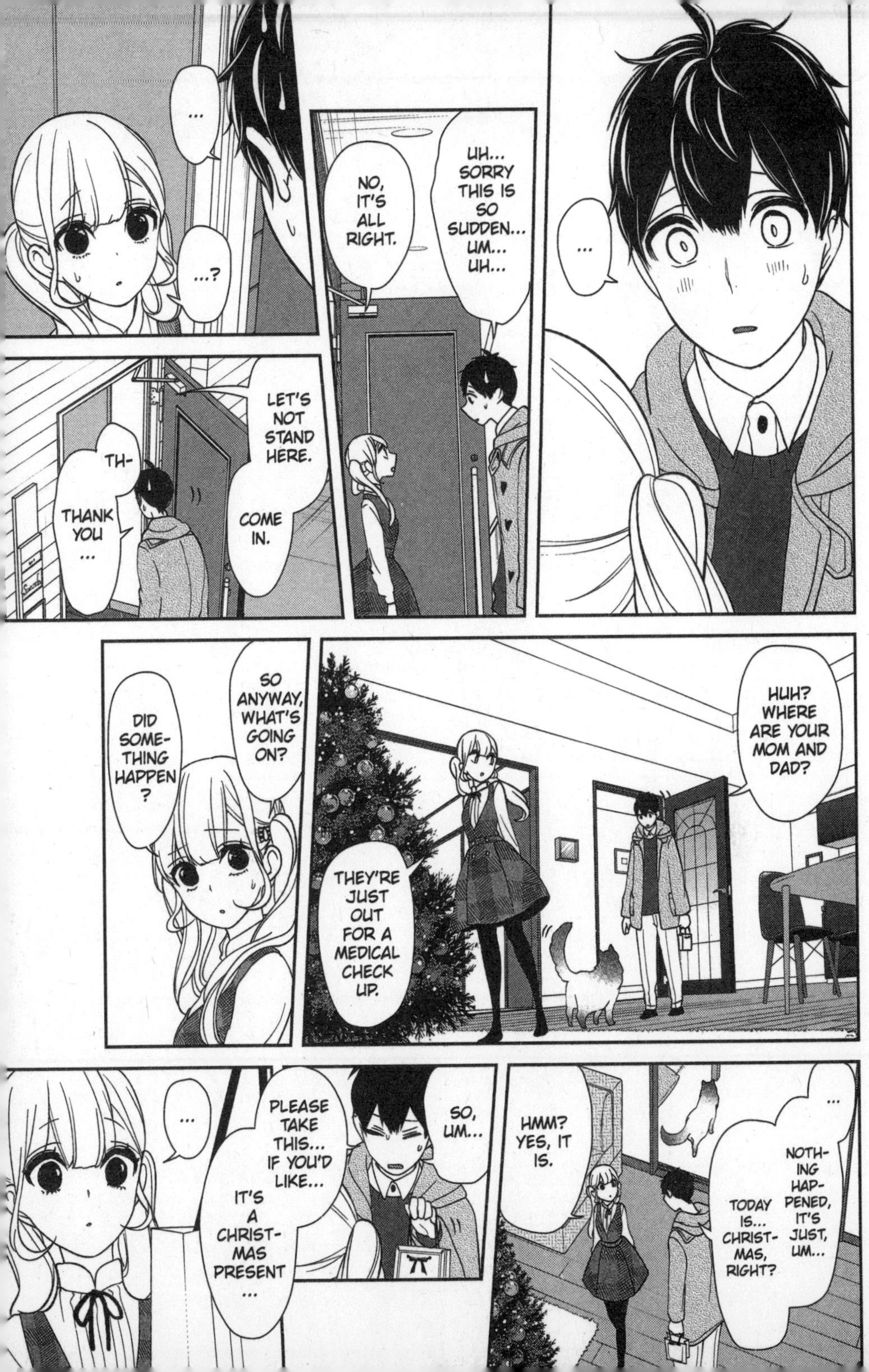
...
UH... SORRY THIS IS SO SUDDEN... UM... UH...
NO, IT'S ALL RIGHT.
...
...?
LET'S NOT STAND HERE. COME IN.
TH- THANK YOU ...
HUH? WHERE ARE YOUR MOM AND DAD?
THEY'RE JUST OUT FOR A MEDICAL CHECK UP.
SO ANYWAY, WHAT'S GOING ON?
DID SOMETHING HAPPEN?
...
NOTHING HAPPENED, IT'S JUST, UM...
TODAY IS... CHRISTMAS, RIGHT?
HMM? YES, IT IS.
SO, UM...
PLEASE TAKE THIS... IF YOU'D LIKE...
IT'S A CHRISTMAS PRESENT ...
...

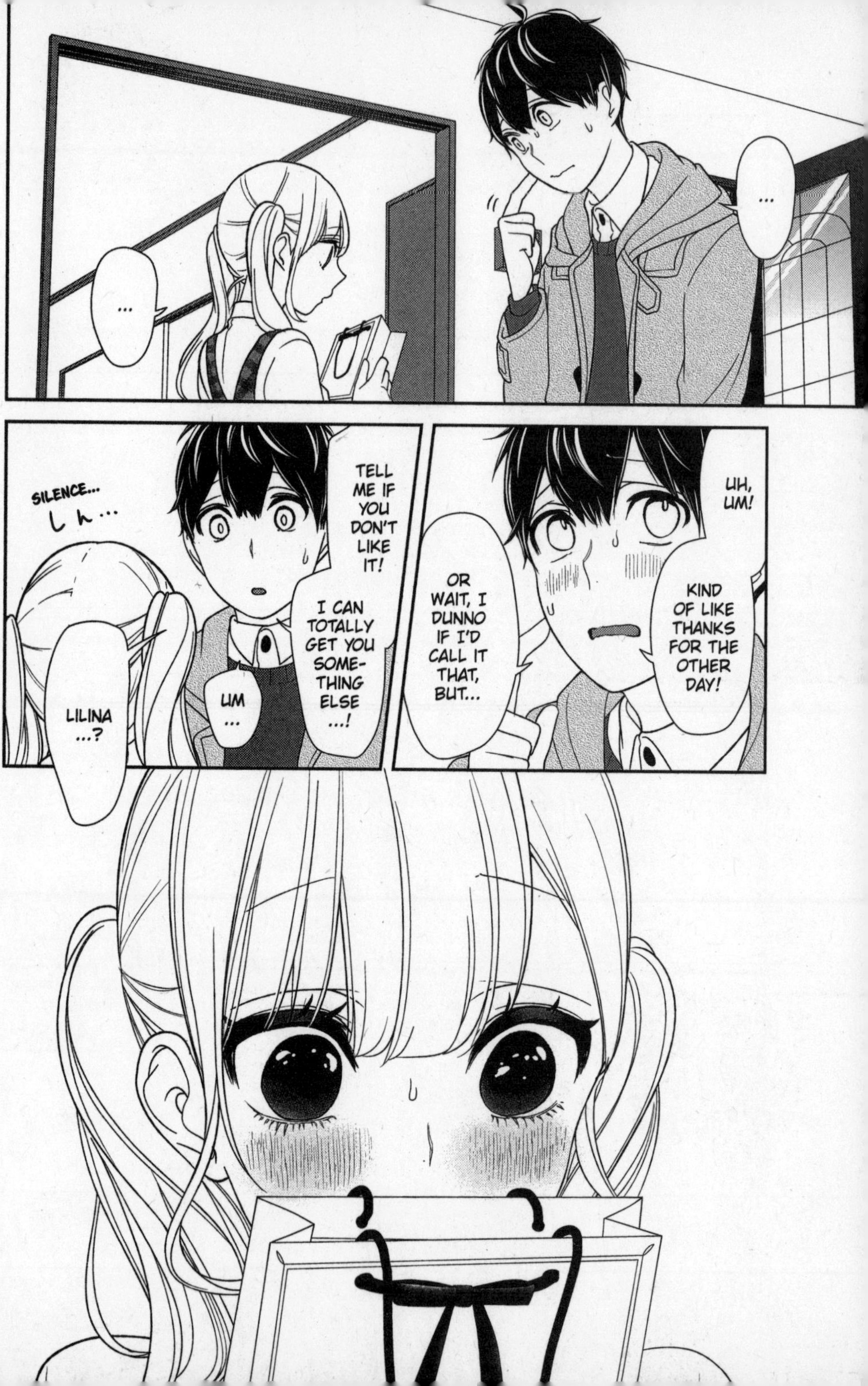
...
...
UH, UM!
KIND OF LIKE THANKS FOR THE OTHER DAY!
OR WAIT, I DUNNO IF I'D CALL IT THAT, BUT...
TELL ME IF YOU DON'T LIKE IT!
I CAN TOTALLY GET YOU SOME-THING ELSE ...!
SILENCE...
しん…
UM ...
LILINA ...?

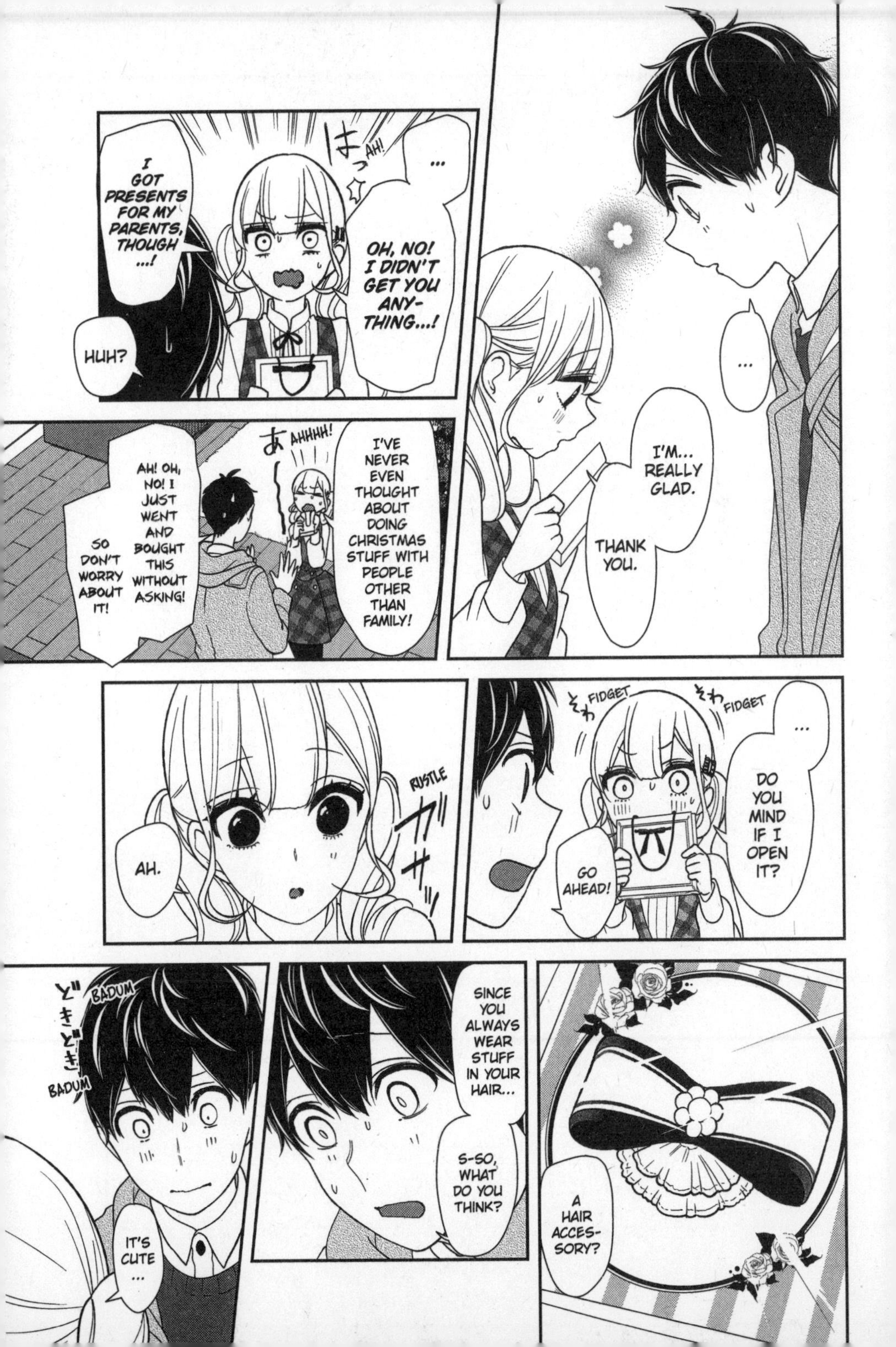
...
I'M... REALLY GLAD.
THANK YOU.
...
はっ AH!
OH, NO! I DIDN'T GET YOU ANYTHING...!
I GOT PRESENTS FOR MY PARENTS, THOUGH...!
HUH?
I'VE NEVER EVEN THOUGHT ABOUT DOING CHRISTMAS STUFF WITH PEOPLE OTHER THAN FAMILY!
あ AHHHH!
AH! OH, NO! I JUST WENT AND BOUGHT THIS WITHOUT ASKING!
SO DON'T WORRY ABOUT IT!
そわ FIDGET
そわ FIDGET
...
DO YOU MIND IF I OPEN IT?
GO AHEAD!
RUSTLE
AH.
A HAIR ACCESSORY?
SINCE YOU ALWAYS WEAR STUFF IN YOUR HAIR...
S-SO, WHAT DO YOU THINK?
BADUM
BADUM
IT'S CUTE...

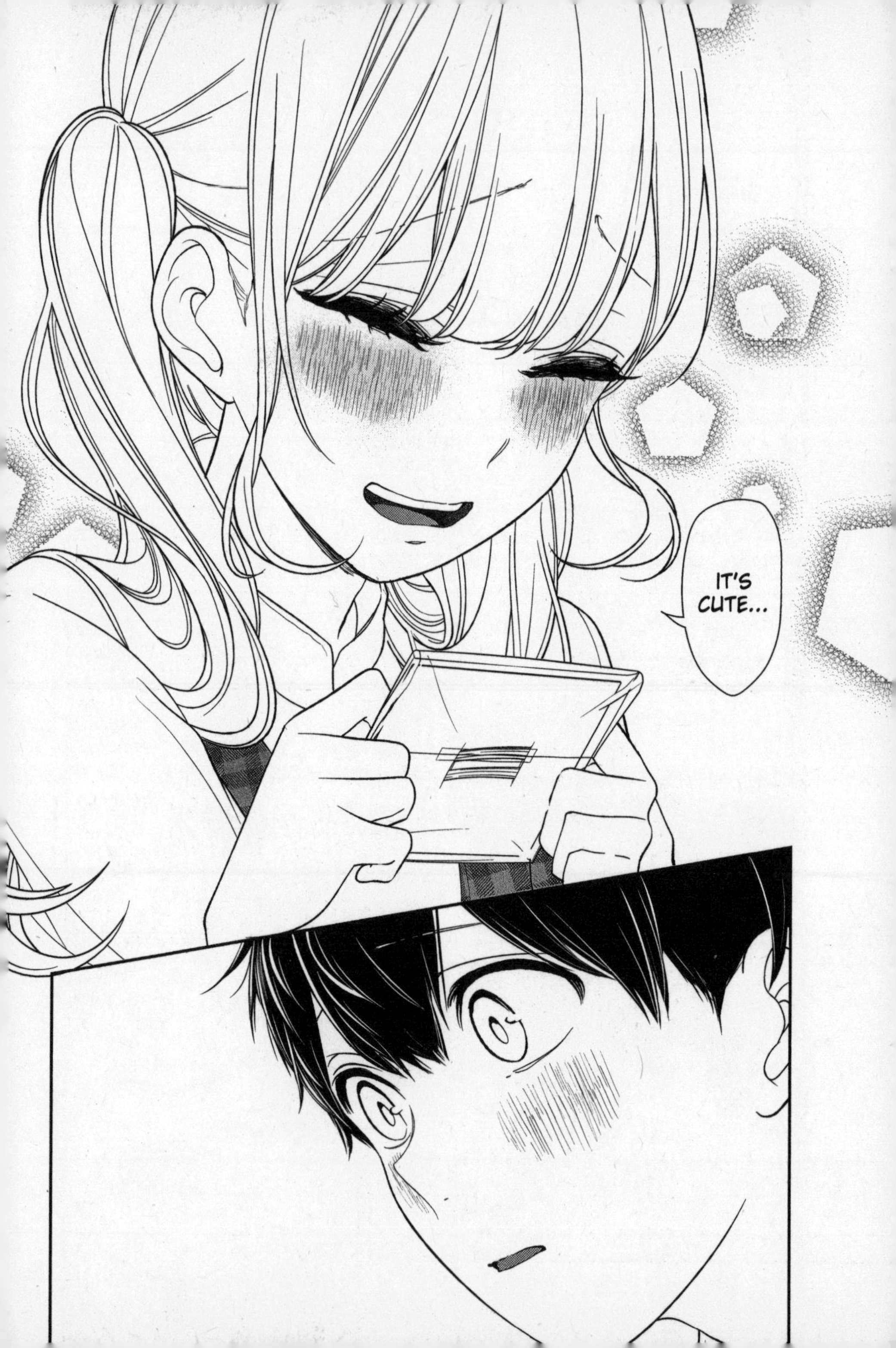
IT'S CUTE...

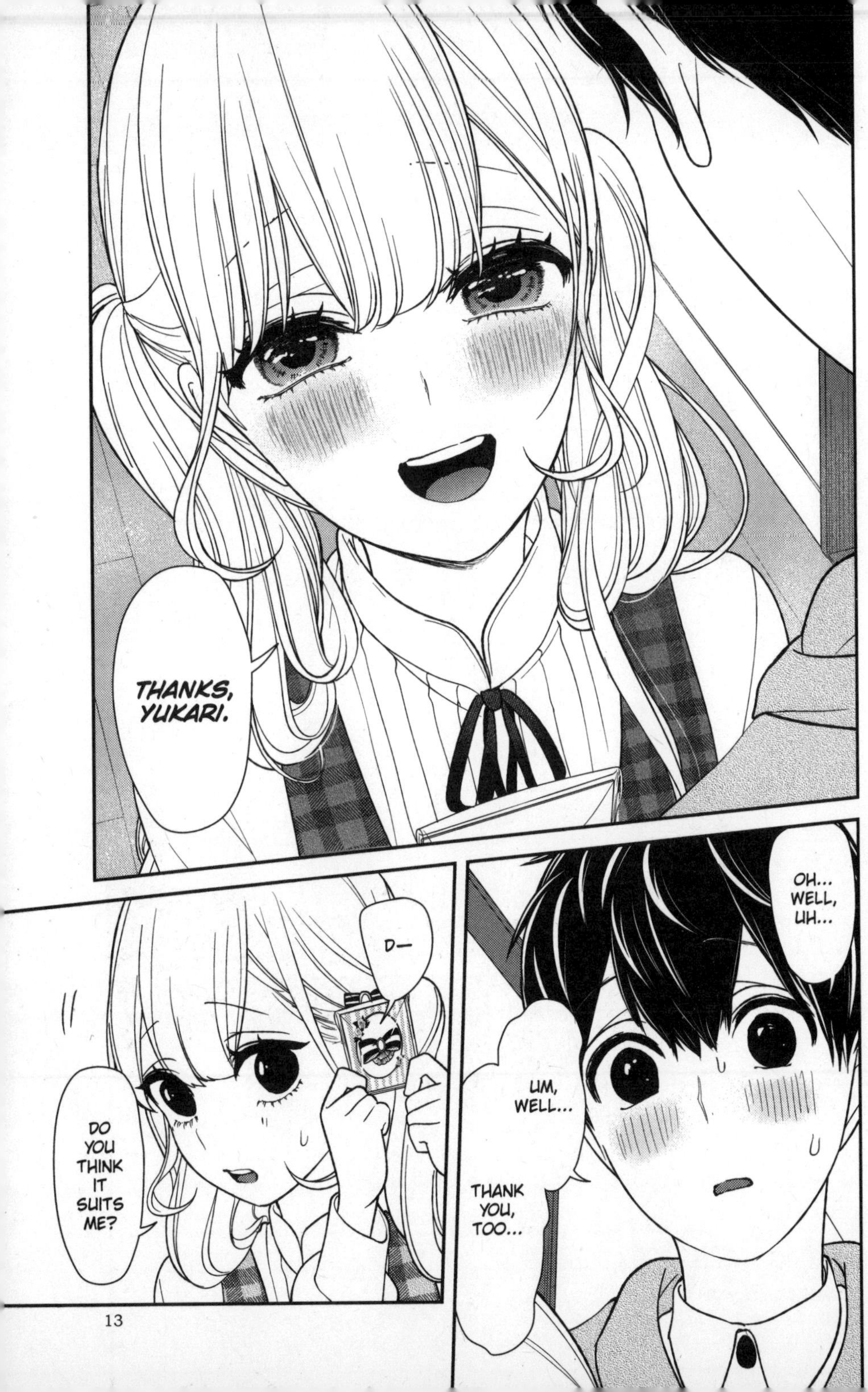
THANKS, YUKARI.
OH... WELL, UH...
UM, WELL...
THANK YOU, TOO...
D—
DO YOU THINK IT SUITS ME?

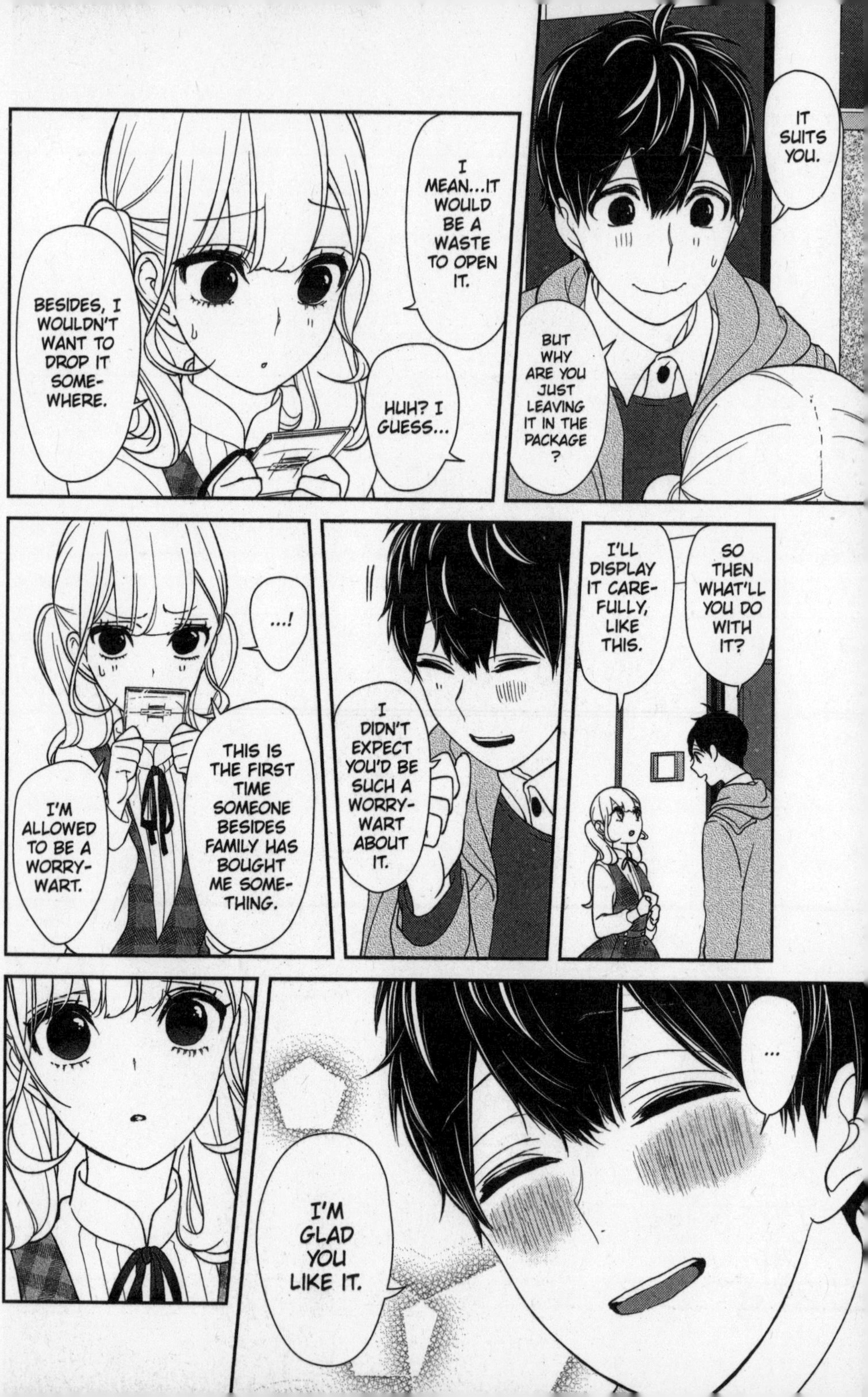
IT SUITS YOU.
BUT WHY ARE YOU JUST LEAVING IT IN THE PACKAGE?
I MEAN...IT WOULD BE A WASTE TO OPEN IT.
HUH? I GUESS...
BESIDES, I WOULDN'T WANT TO DROP IT SOME-WHERE.
SO THEN WHAT'LL YOU DO WITH IT?
I'LL DISPLAY IT CARE-FULLY, LIKE THIS.
I DIDN'T EXPECT YOU'D BE SUCH A WORRY-WART ABOUT IT.
...!
THIS IS THE FIRST TIME SOMEONE BESIDES FAMILY HAS BOUGHT ME SOME-THING.
I'M ALLOWED TO BE A WORRY-WART.
...
I'M GLAD YOU LIKE IT.

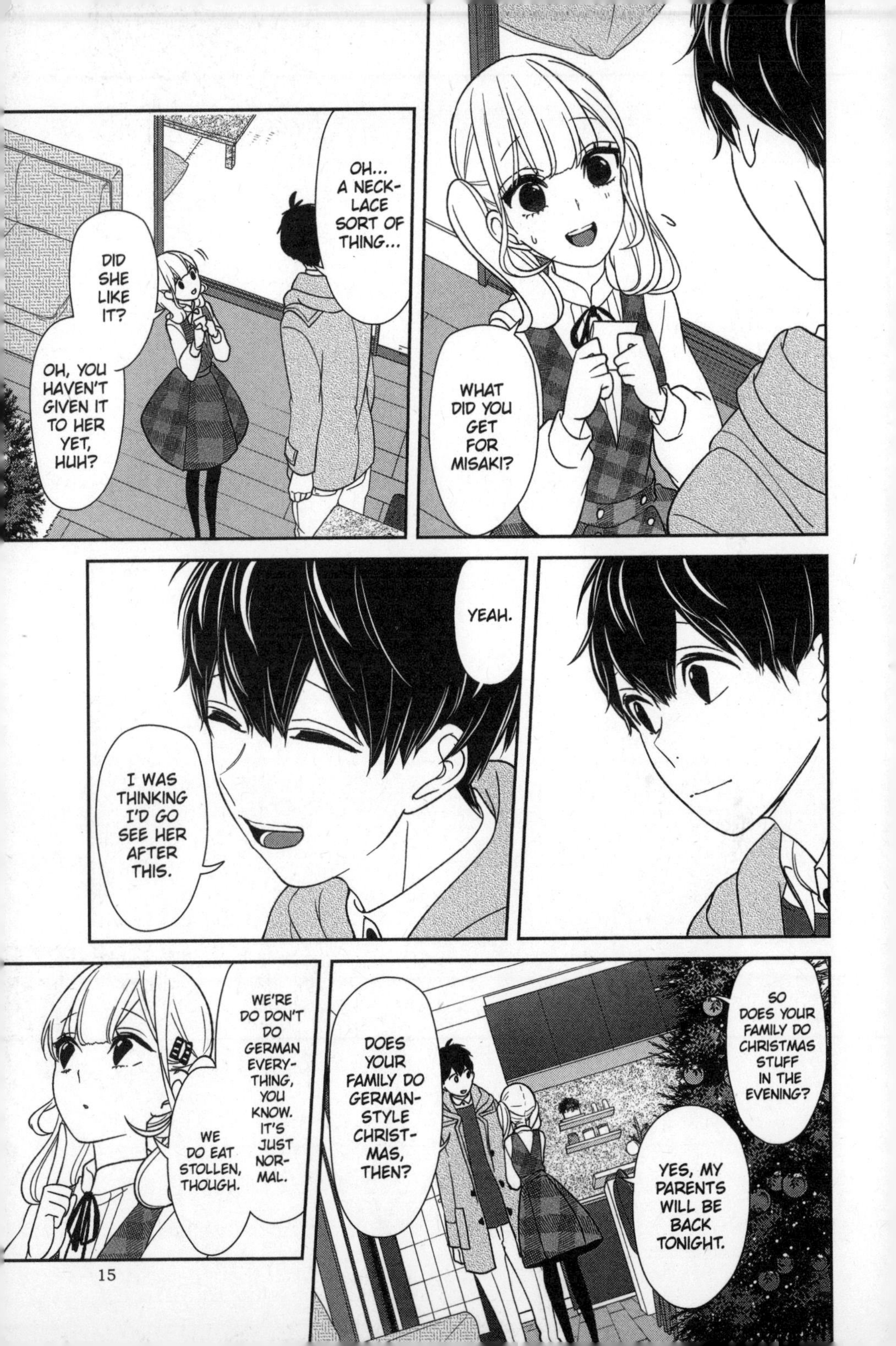
WHAT DID YOU GET FOR MISAKI?
OH... A NECK-LACE SORT OF THING...
DID SHE LIKE IT?
OH, YOU HAVEN'T GIVEN IT TO HER YET, HUH?
YEAH.
I WAS THINKING I'D GO SEE HER AFTER THIS.
SO DOES YOUR FAMILY DO CHRISTMAS STUFF IN THE EVENING?
YES, MY PARENTS WILL BE BACK TONIGHT.
DOES YOUR FAMILY DO GERMAN-STYLE CHRIST-MAS, THEN?
WE'RE DO DON'T DO GERMAN EVERY-THING, YOU KNOW. IT'S JUST NOR-MAL.
WE DO EAT STOLLEN, THOUGH.

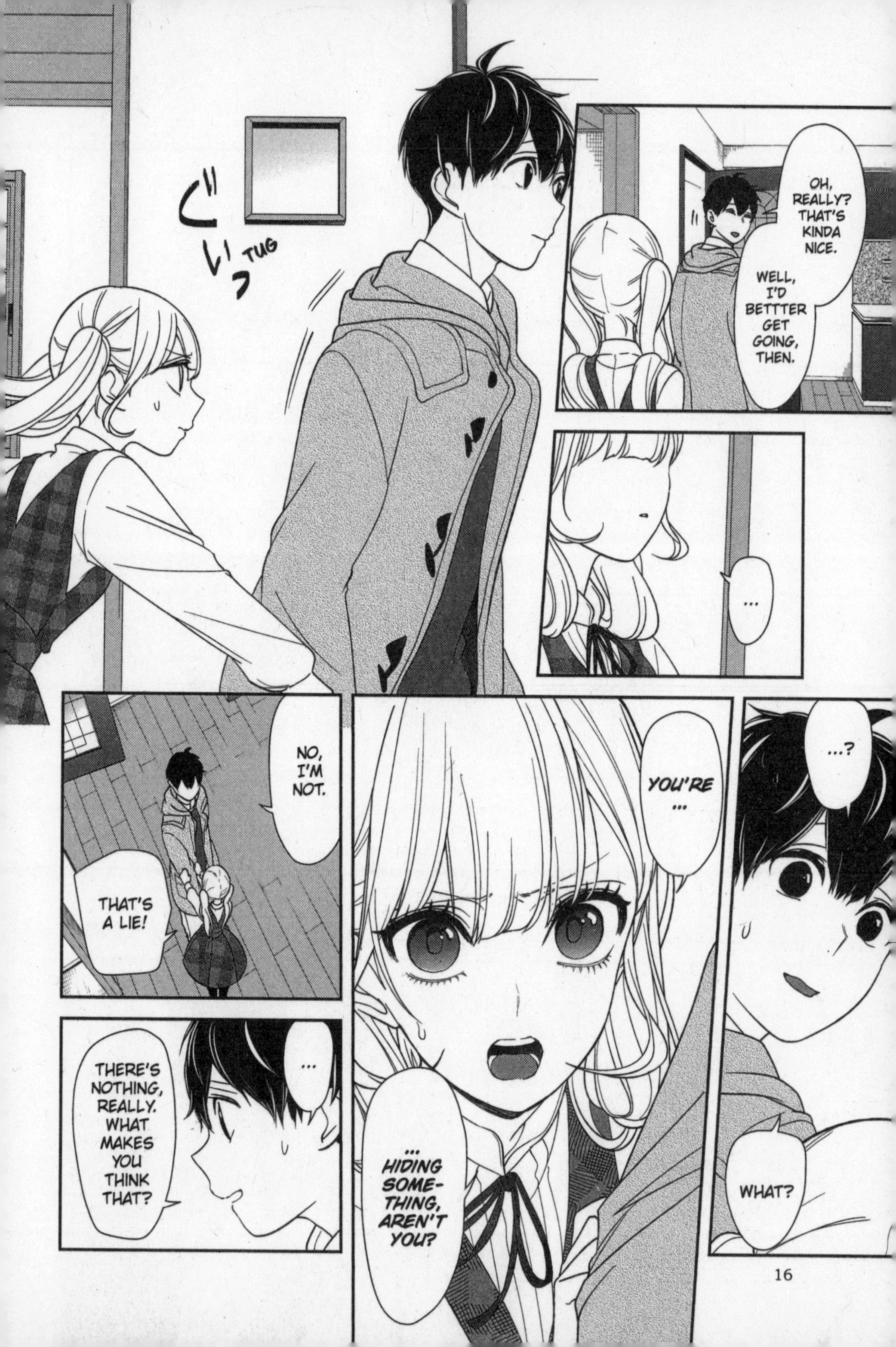
OH, REALLY? THAT'S KINDA NICE.
WELL, I'D BETTTER GET GOING, THEN.
...
ぐいっ
TUG
...?
WHAT?
YOU'RE ...
... HIDING SOME-THING, AREN'T YOU?
NO, I'M NOT.
THAT'S A LIE!
...
THERE'S NOTHING, REALLY. WHAT MAKES YOU THINK THAT?

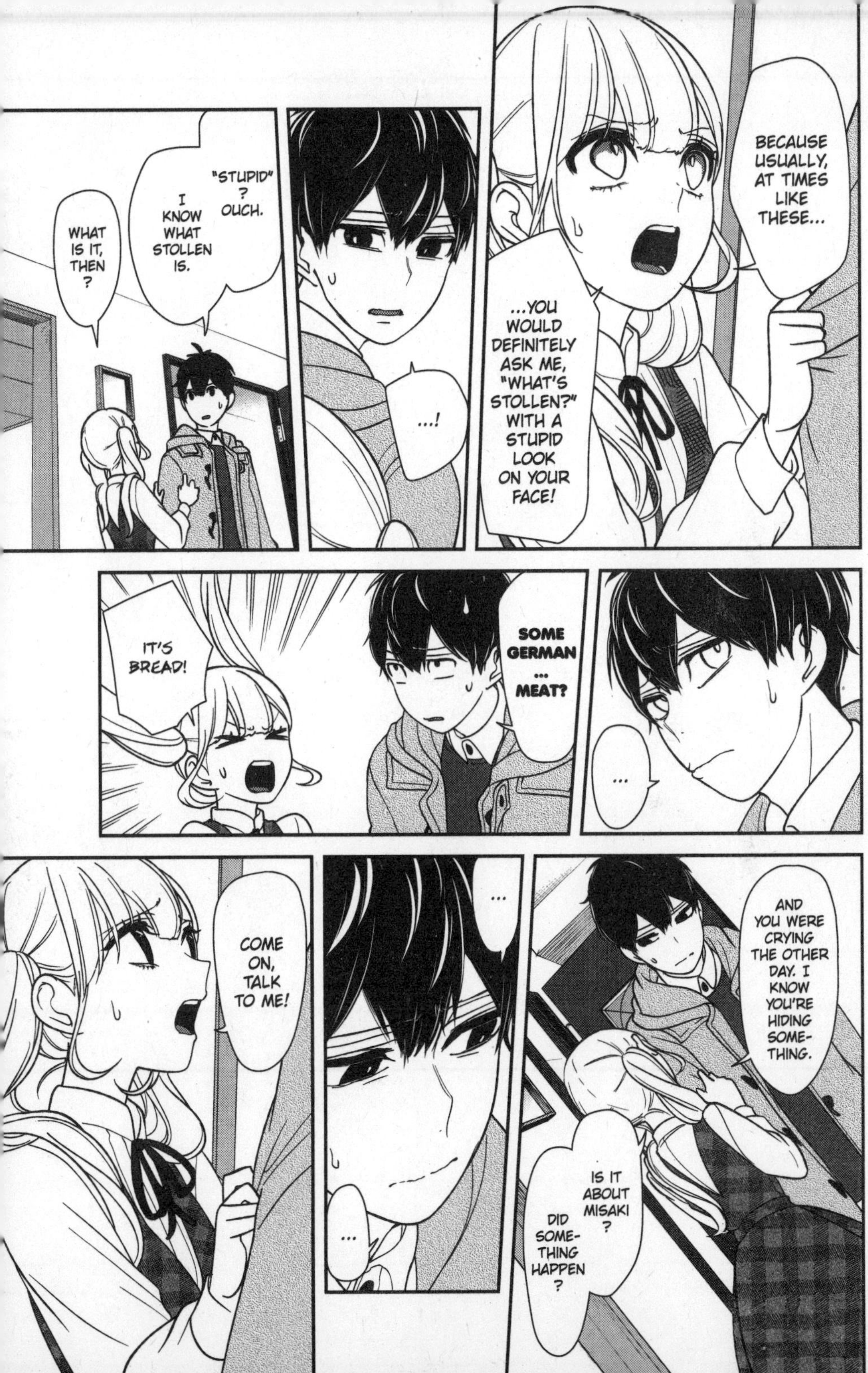
BECAUSE USUALLY, AT TIMES LIKE THESE...
...YOU WOULD DEFINITELY ASK ME, "WHAT'S STOLLEN?" WITH A STUPID LOOK ON YOUR FACE!
...!
"STUPID"? OUCH.
I KNOW WHAT STOLLEN IS.
WHAT IS IT, THEN?
...
SOME GERMAN ... MEAT?
IT'S BREAD!
AND YOU WERE CRYING THE OTHER DAY. I KNOW YOU'RE HIDING SOME-THING.
IS IT ABOUT MISAKI?
DID SOME-THING HAPPEN?
...
...
COME ON, TALK TO ME!

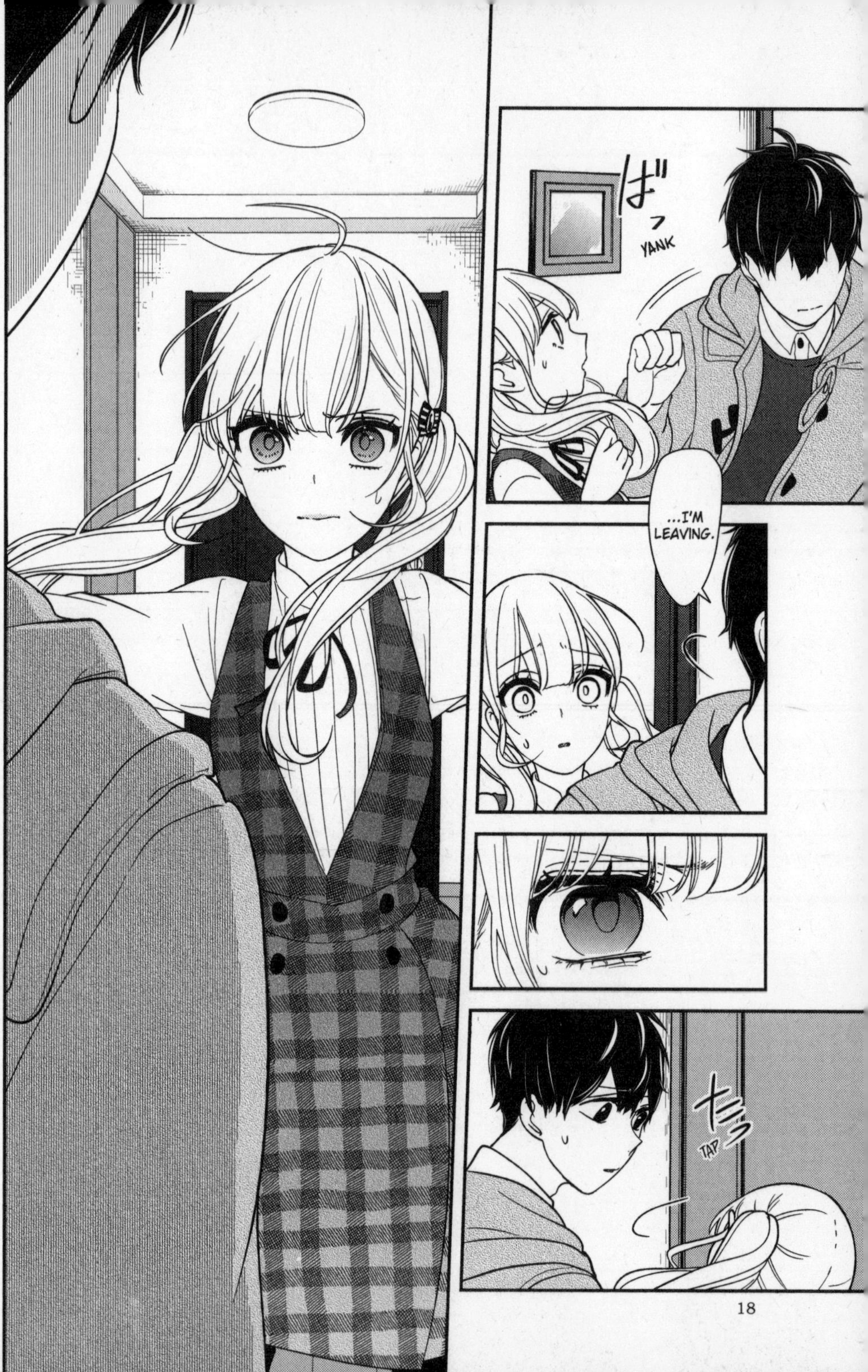
ばっ
YANK
...I'M LEAVING.
たっ
TAP

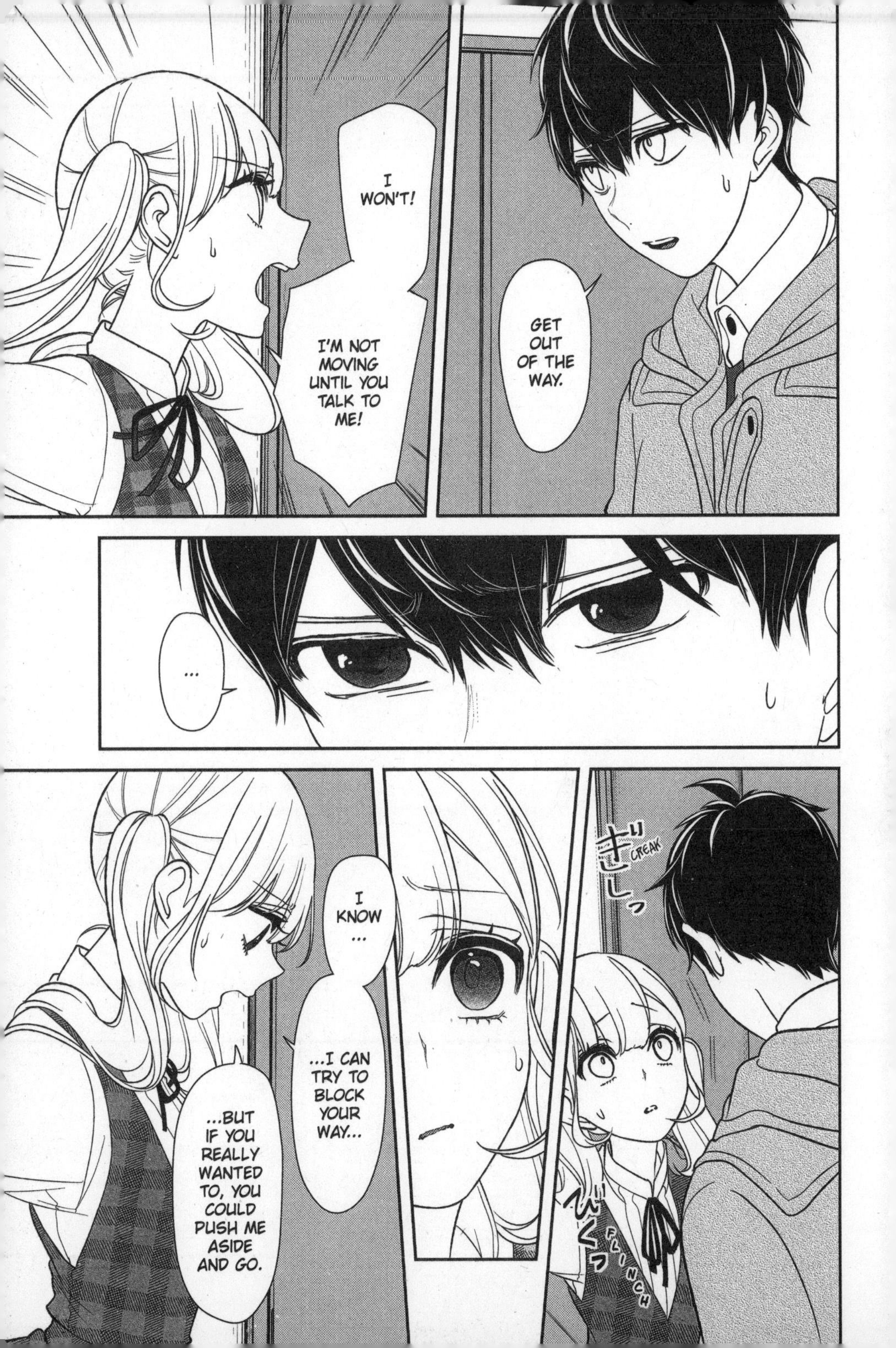
GET OUT OF THE WAY.
I WON'T!
I'M NOT MOVING UNTIL YOU TALK TO ME!
...
CREAK
FLINCH
I KNOW...
...I CAN TRY TO BLOCK YOUR WAY...
...BUT IF YOU REALLY WANTED TO, YOU COULD PUSH ME ASIDE AND GO.

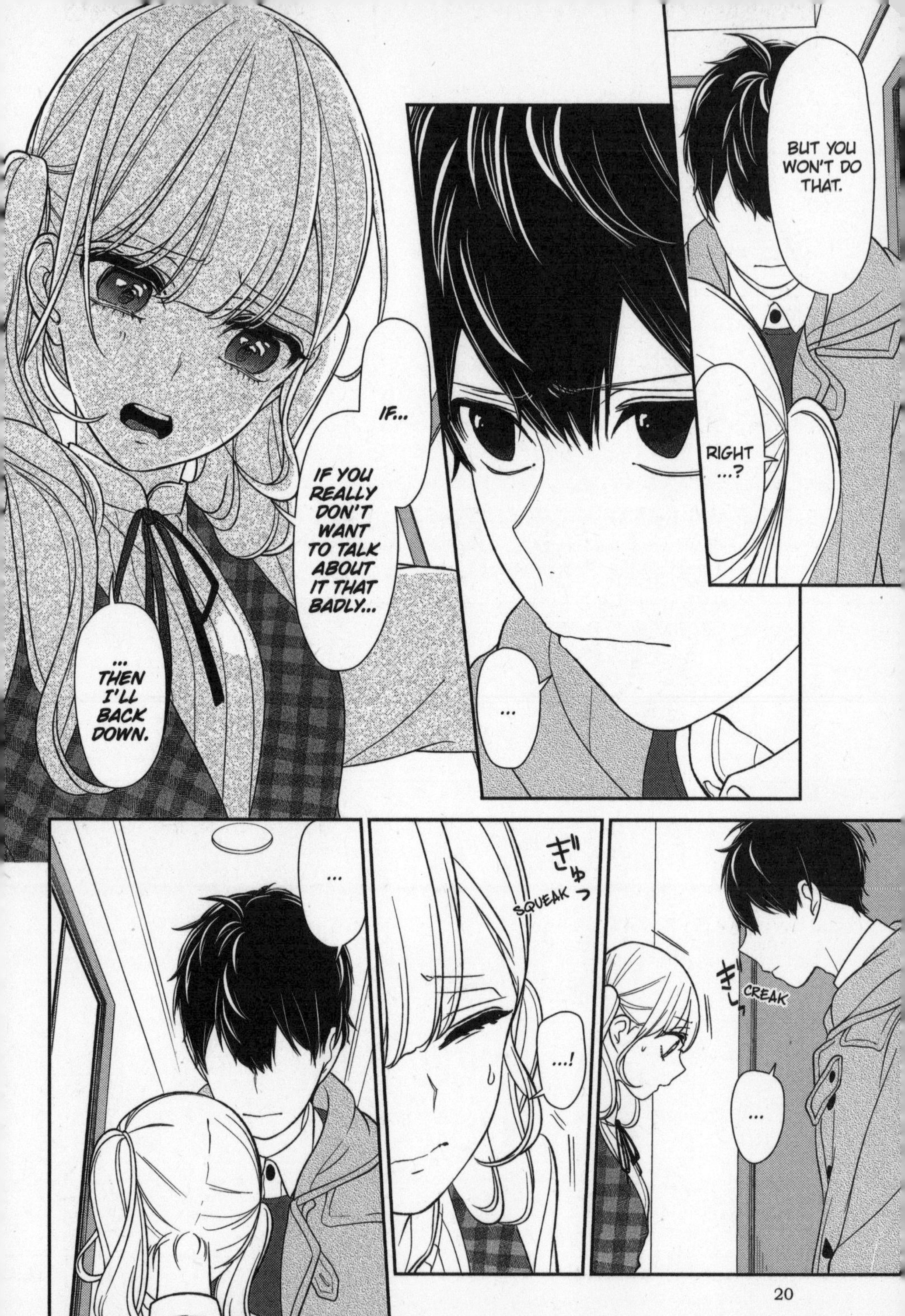
BUT YOU WON'T DO THAT.
RIGHT ...?
...
IF...
IF YOU REALLY DON'T WANT TO TALK ABOUT IT THAT BADLY...
... THEN I'LL BACK DOWN.
ぎしっ
CREAK
...
ぎゅっ
SQUEAK
...!
...

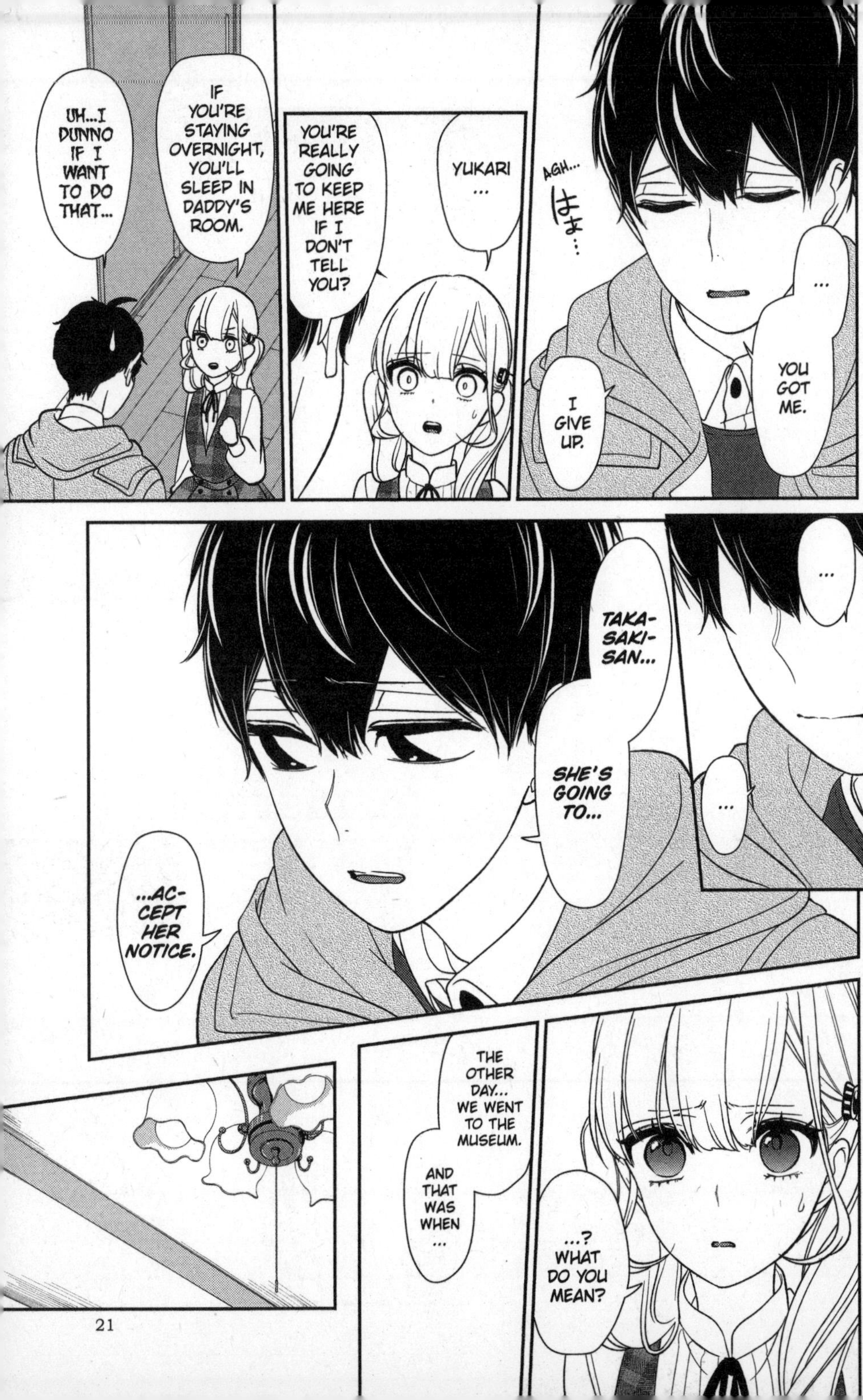
AGH...
はぁ…
...
YOU GOT ME.
I GIVE UP.
YUKARI...
YOU'RE REALLY GOING TO KEEP ME HERE IF I DON'T TELL YOU?
IF YOU'RE STAYING OVERNIGHT, YOU'LL SLEEP IN DADDY'S ROOM.
UH...I DUNNO IF I WANT TO DO THAT...
...
...
TAKA-SAKI-SAN...
SHE'S GOING TO...
...AC-CEPT HER NOTICE.
THE OTHER DAY... WE WENT TO THE MUSEUM.
AND THAT WAS WHEN...
...? WHAT DO YOU MEAN?

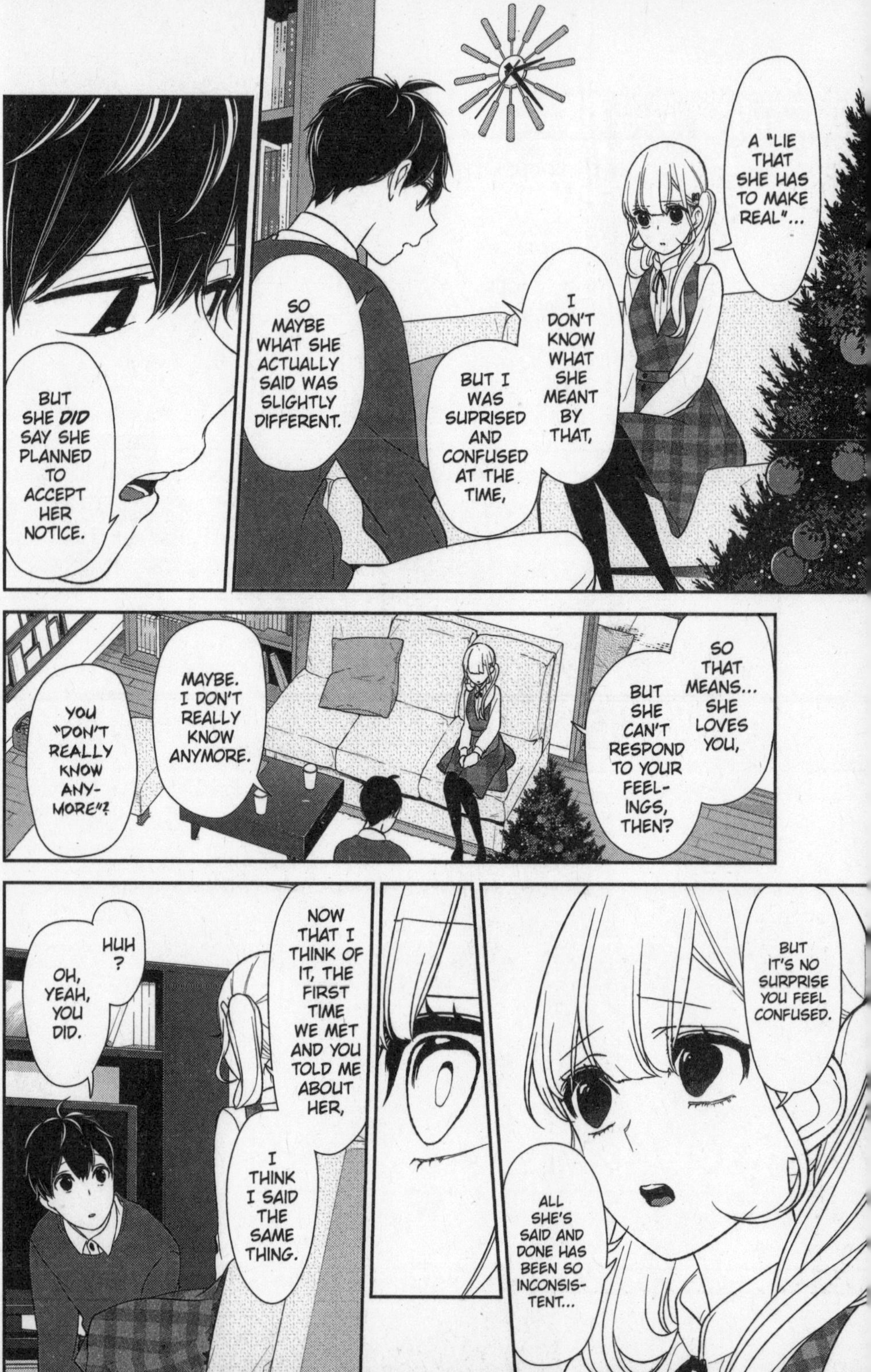
A "LIE THAT SHE HAS TO MAKE REAL"...
I DON'T KNOW WHAT SHE MEANT BY THAT,
BUT I WAS SUPRISED AND CONFUSED AT THE TIME,
SO MAYBE WHAT SHE ACTUALLY SAID WAS SLIGHTLY DIFFERENT.
BUT SHE *DID* SAY SHE PLANNED TO ACCEPT HER NOTICE.
SO THAT MEANS... SHE LOVES YOU,
BUT SHE CAN'T RESPOND TO YOUR FEEL-INGS, THEN?
MAYBE. I DON'T REALLY KNOW ANYMORE.
YOU "DON'T REALLY KNOW ANY-MORE"?
BUT IT'S NO SURPRISE YOU FEEL CONFUSED.
ALL SHE'S SAID AND DONE HAS BEEN SO INCONSIS-TENT...
NOW THAT I THINK OF IT, THE FIRST TIME WE MET AND YOU TOLD ME ABOUT HER,
I THINK I SAID THE SAME THING.
HUH?
OH, YEAH, YOU DID.

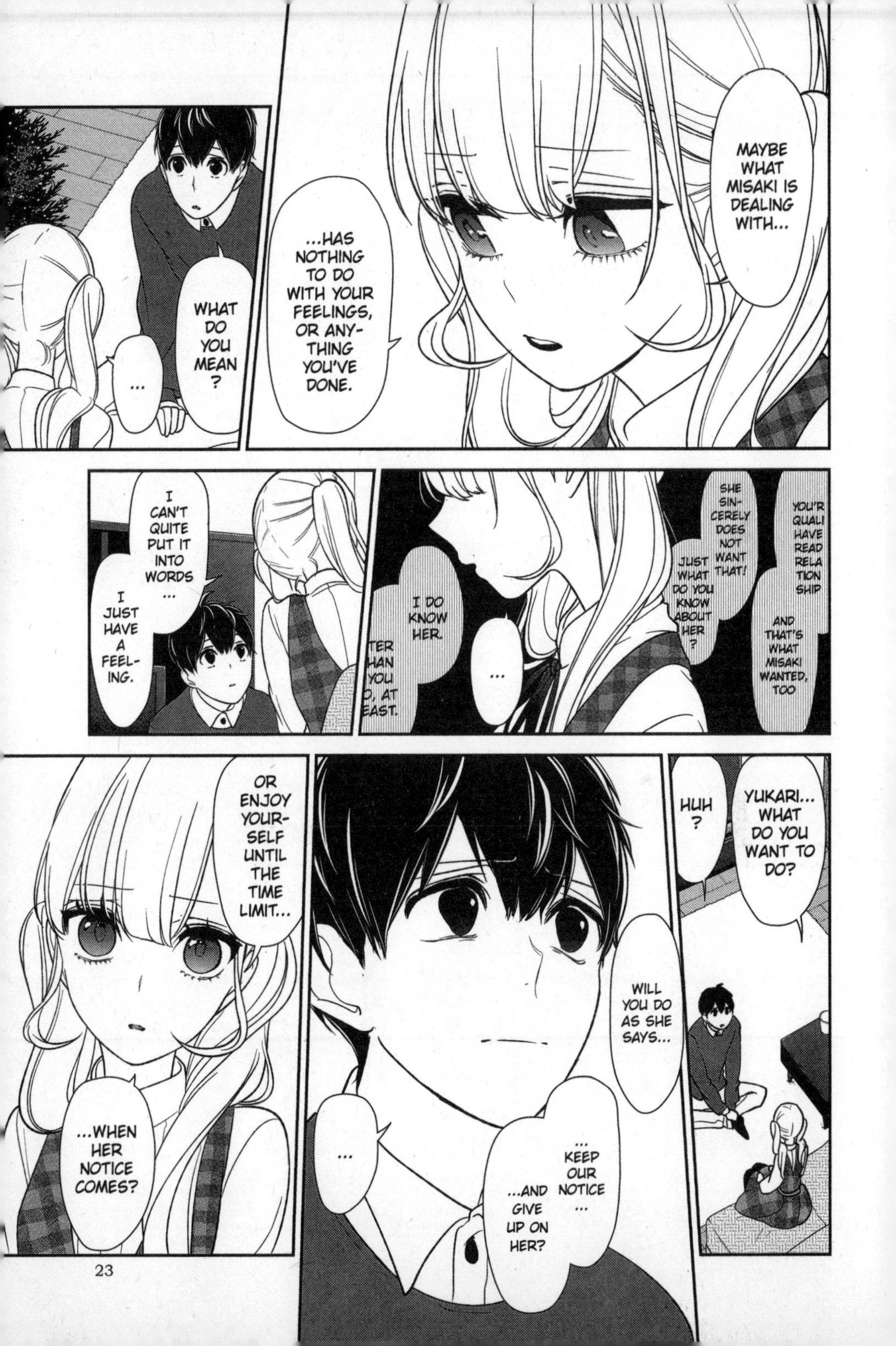

MAYBE WHAT MISAKI IS DEALING WITH...
...HAS NOTHING TO DO WITH YOUR FEELINGS, OR ANY-THING YOU'VE DONE.
WHAT DO YOU MEAN?
...
YOU'R QUALI HAVE READ RELA TION SHIP
AND THAT'S WHAT MISAKI WANTED, TOO
SHE SIN-CERELY DOES NOT WANT THAT!
JUST WHAT DO YOU KNOW ABOUT HER?
...
I DO KNOW HER.
TER HAN YOU O, AT EAST.
I CAN'T QUITE PUT IT INTO WORDS...
I JUST HAVE A FEEL-ING.
YUKARI... WHAT DO YOU WANT TO DO?
HUH?
WILL YOU DO AS SHE SAYS...
...KEEP OUR NOTICE...
...AND GIVE UP ON HER?
...
OR ENJOY YOUR-SELF UNTIL THE TIME LIMIT...
...WHEN HER NOTICE COMES?

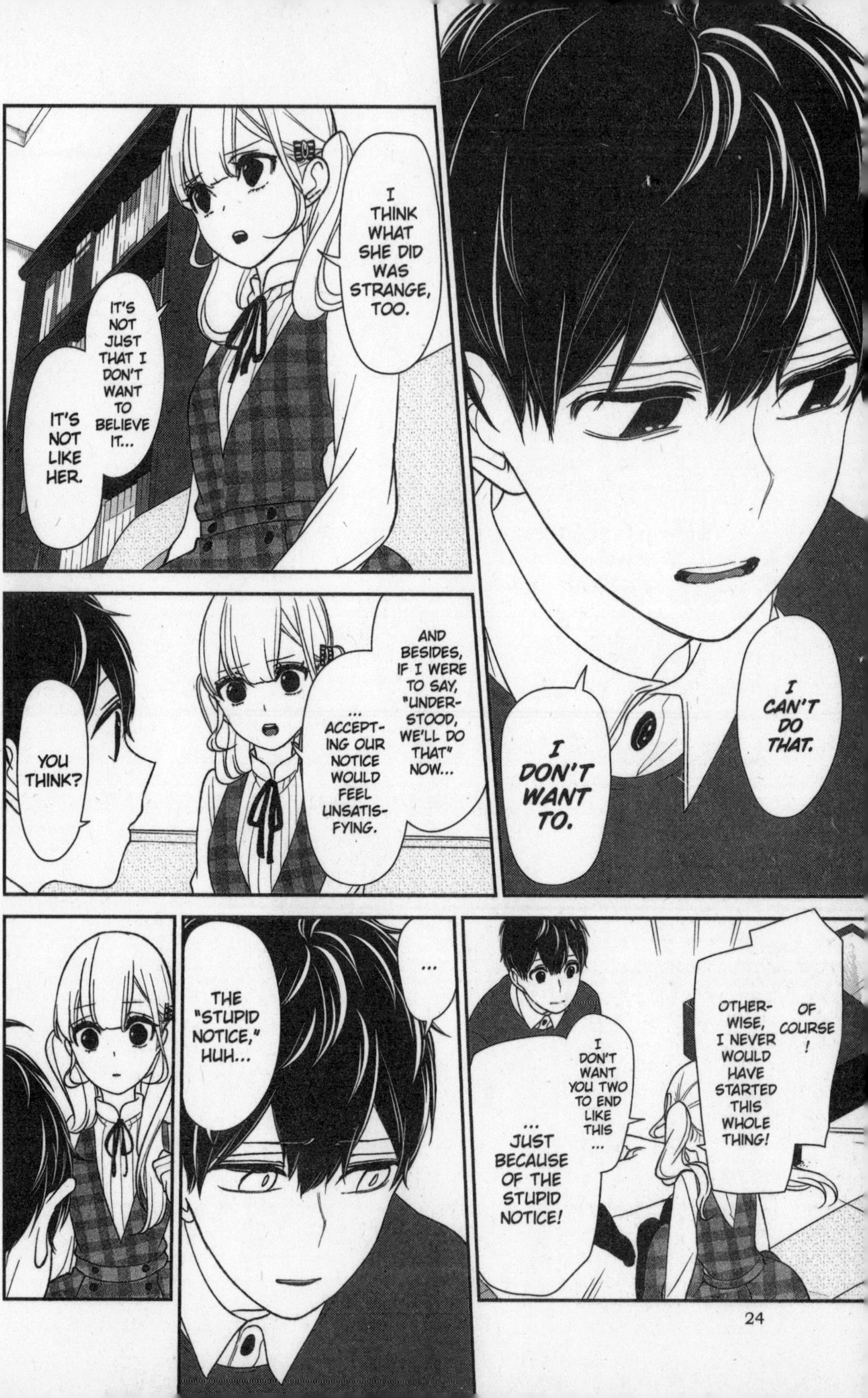
I CAN'T DO THAT.
I DON'T WANT TO.
I THINK WHAT SHE DID WAS STRANGE, TOO.
IT'S NOT JUST THAT I DON'T WANT TO BELIEVE IT...
IT'S NOT LIKE HER.
AND BESIDES, IF I WERE TO SAY, "UNDERSTOOD, WE'LL DO THAT" NOW...
...ACCEPTING OUR NOTICE WOULD FEEL UNSATISFYING.
YOU THINK?
OF COURSE!
OTHERWISE, I NEVER WOULD HAVE STARTED THIS WHOLE THING!
I DON'T WANT YOU TWO TO END LIKE THIS...
...JUST BECAUSE OF THE STUPID NOTICE!
...
THE "STUPID NOTICE," HUH...

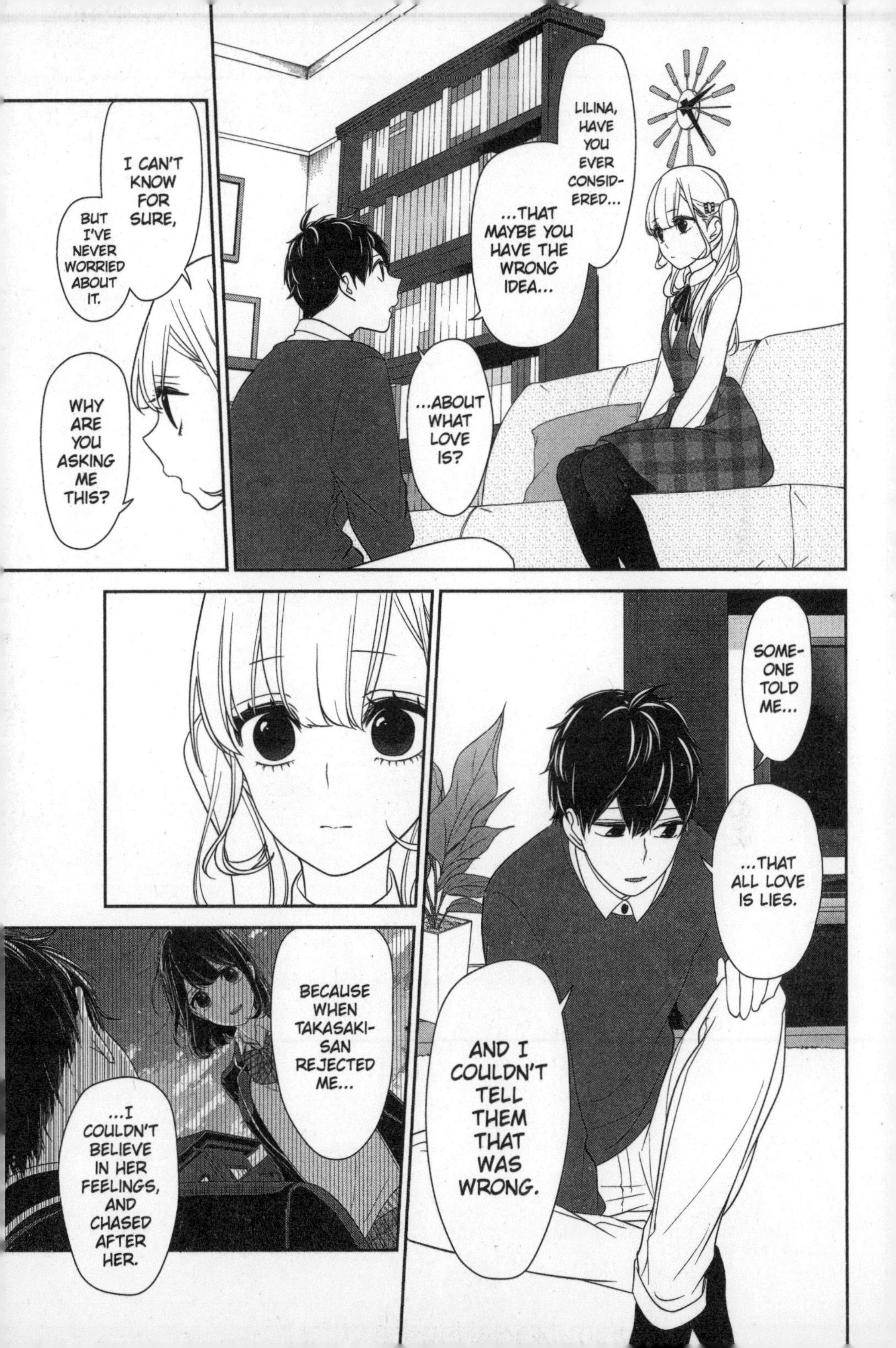
LILINA, HAVE YOU EVER CONSID-ERED...
...THAT MAYBE YOU HAVE THE WRONG IDEA...
...ABOUT WHAT LOVE IS?
I CAN'T KNOW FOR SURE,
BUT I'VE NEVER WORRIED ABOUT IT.
WHY ARE YOU ASKING ME THIS?
SOME-ONE TOLD ME...
...THAT ALL LOVE IS LIES.
AND I COULDN'T TELL THEM THAT WAS WRONG.
BECAUSE WHEN TAKASAKI-SAN REJECTED ME...
...I COULDN'T BELIEVE IN HER FEELINGS, AND CHASED AFTER HER.

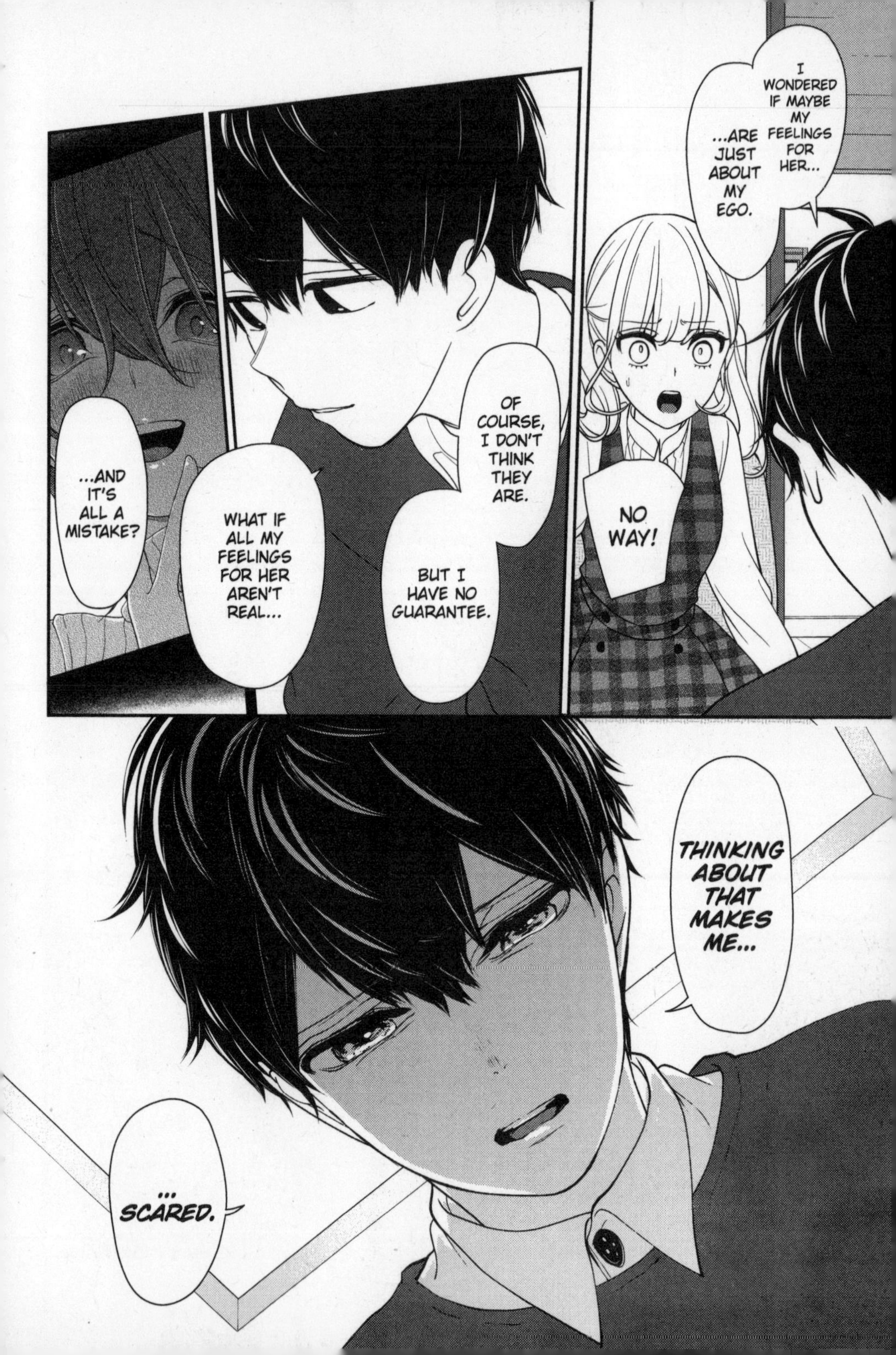
I WONDERED IF MAYBE MY FEELINGS FOR HER...
...ARE JUST ABOUT MY EGO.
NO WAY!
OF COURSE, I DON'T THINK THEY ARE.
BUT I HAVE NO GUARANTEE.
WHAT IF ALL MY FEELINGS FOR HER AREN'T REAL...
...AND IT'S ALL A MISTAKE?
THINKING ABOUT THAT MAKES ME...
...SCARED.

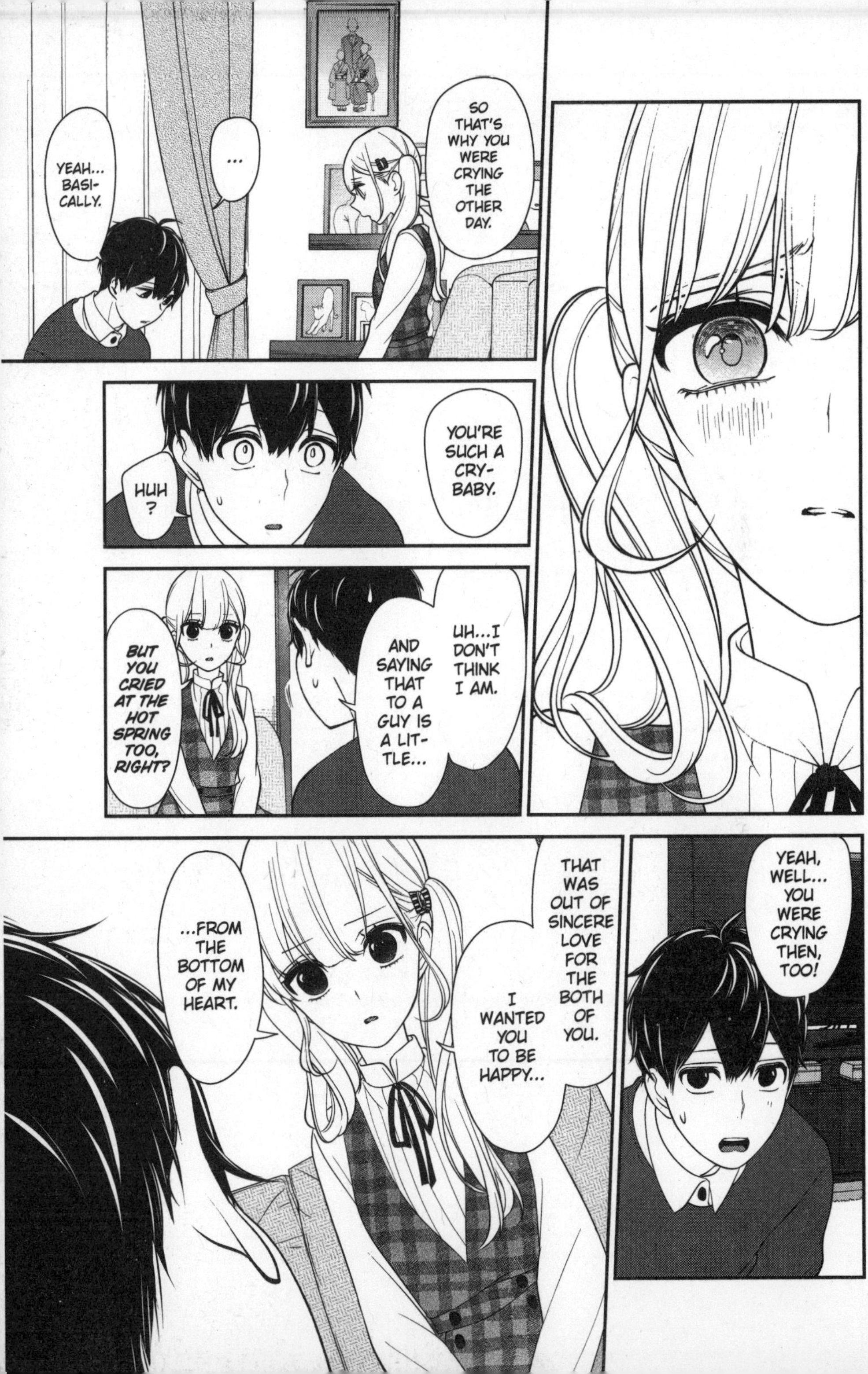
SO THAT'S WHY YOU WERE CRYING THE OTHER DAY.
...
YEAH... BASICALLY.
YOU'RE SUCH A CRYBABY.
HUH?
UH...I DON'T THINK I AM.
AND SAYING THAT TO A GUY IS A LITTLE...
BUT YOU CRIED AT THE HOT SPRING TOO, RIGHT?
YEAH, WELL... YOU WERE CRYING THEN, TOO!
THAT WAS OUT OF SINCERE LOVE FOR THE BOTH OF YOU.
I WANTED YOU TO BE HAPPY...
...FROM THE BOTTOM OF MY HEART.

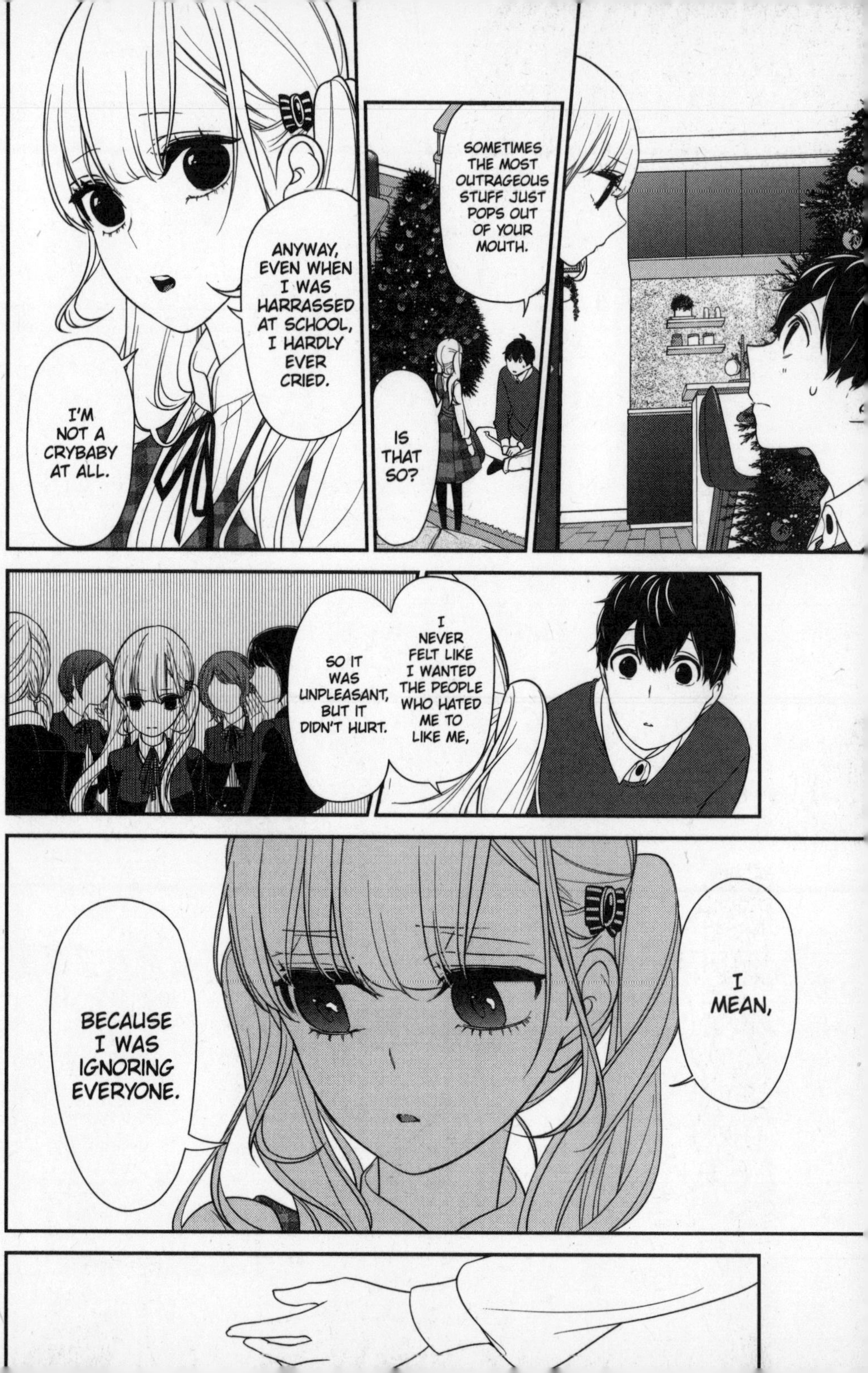
SOMETIMES THE MOST OUTRAGEOUS STUFF JUST POPS OUT OF YOUR MOUTH.
IS THAT SO?
ANYWAY, EVEN WHEN I WAS HARRASSED AT SCHOOL, I HARDLY EVER CRIED.
I'M NOT A CRYBABY AT ALL.
I NEVER FELT LIKE I WANTED THE PEOPLE WHO HATED ME TO LIKE ME,
SO IT WAS UNPLEASANT, BUT IT DIDN'T HURT.
I MEAN,
BECAUSE I WAS IGNORING EVERYONE.

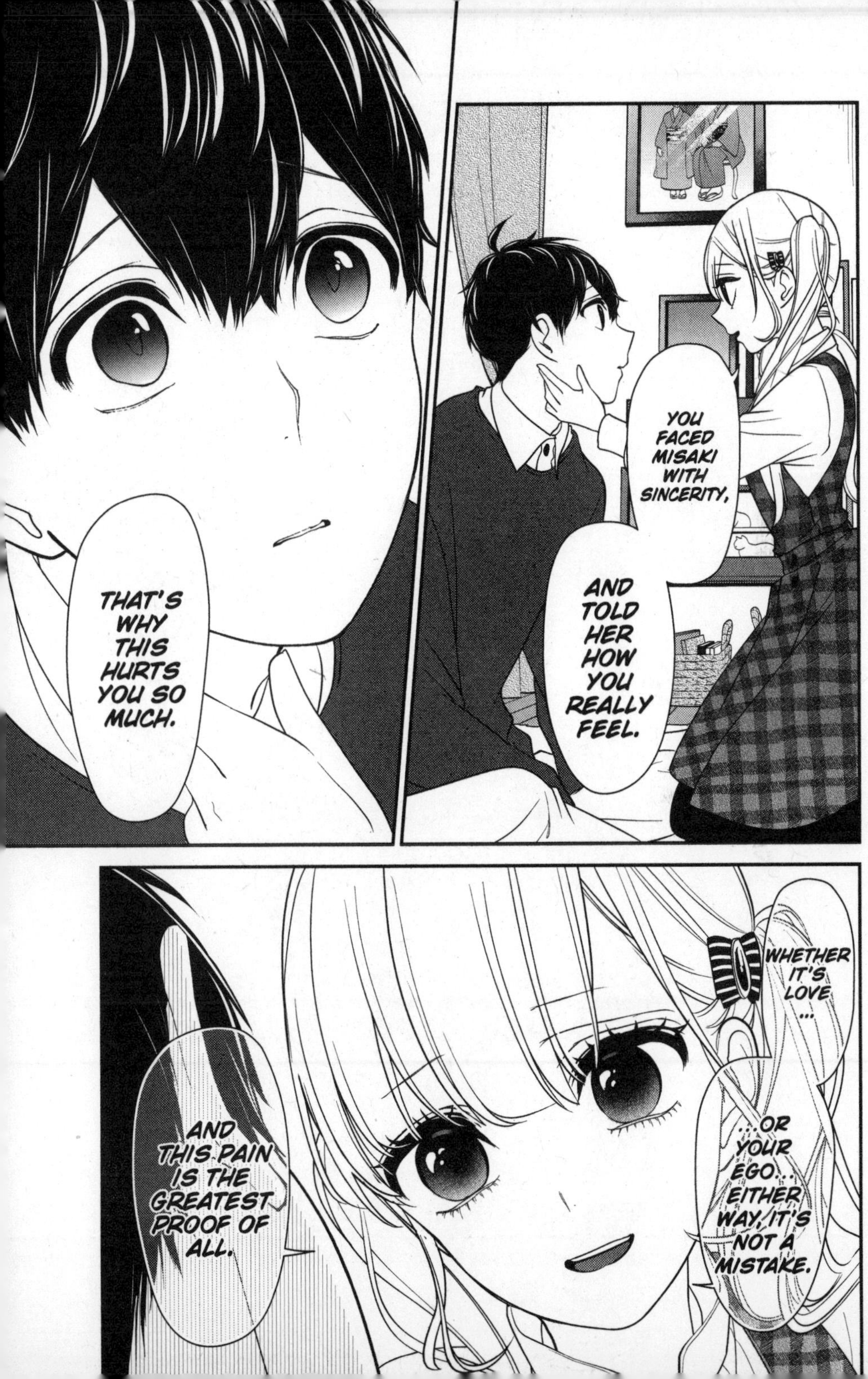
YOU FACED MISAKI WITH SINCERITY,
AND TOLD HER HOW YOU REALLY FEEL.
THAT'S WHY THIS HURTS YOU SO MUCH.
WHETHER IT'S LOVE...
...OR YOUR EGO... EITHER WAY, IT'S NOT A MISTAKE.
AND THIS PAIN IS THE GREATEST PROOF OF ALL.

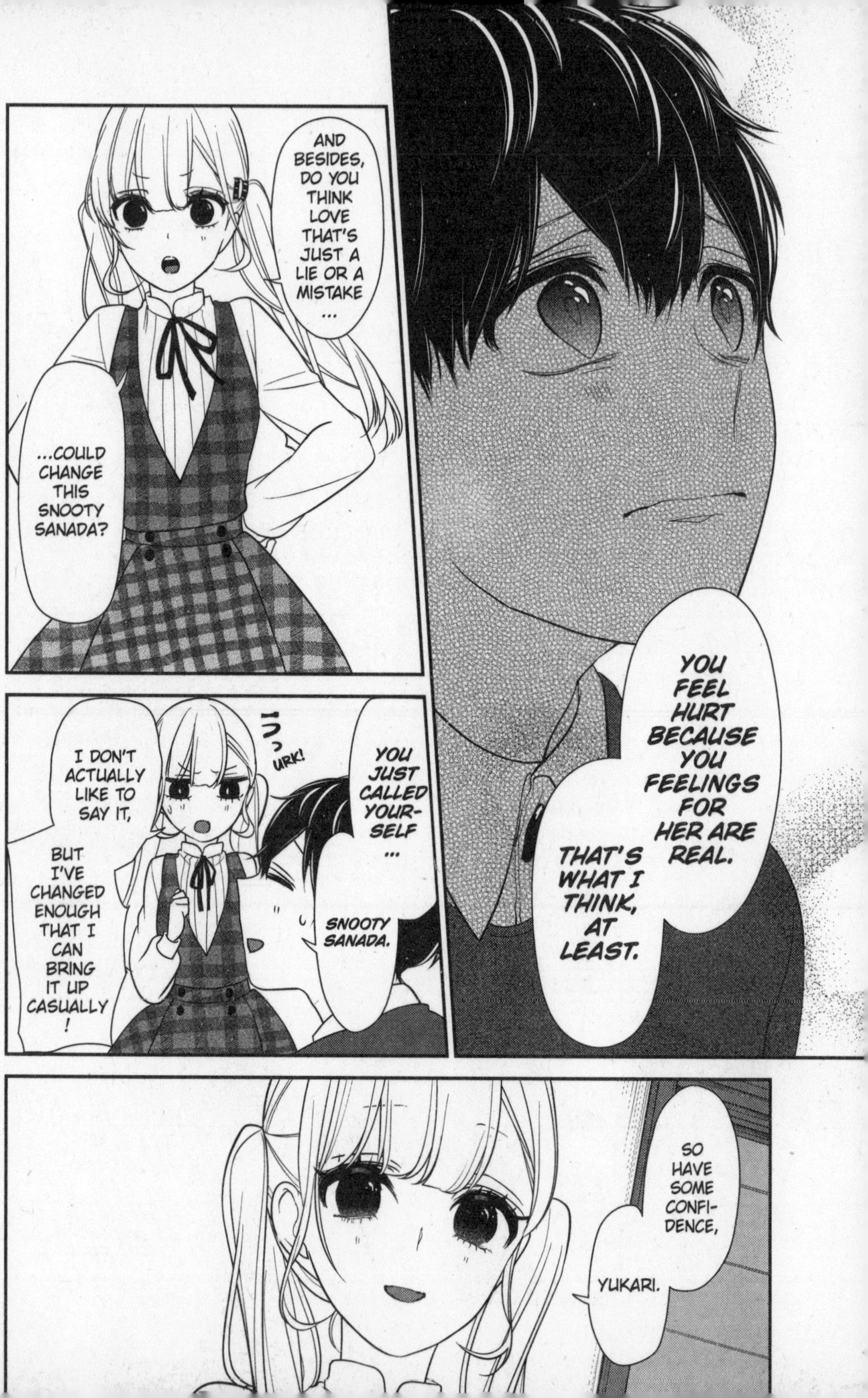
YOU FEEL HURT BECAUSE YOU FEELINGS FOR HER ARE REAL.
THAT'S WHAT I THINK, AT LEAST.
AND BESIDES, DO YOU THINK LOVE THAT'S JUST A LIE OR A MISTAKE ...
...COULD CHANGE THIS SNOOTY SANADA?
YOU JUST CALLED YOURSELF ...
SNOOTY SANADA.
URK!
I DON'T ACTUALLY LIKE TO SAY IT,
BUT I'VE CHANGED ENOUGH THAT I CAN BRING IT UP CASUALLY!
SO HAVE SOME CONFIDENCE,
YUKARI.

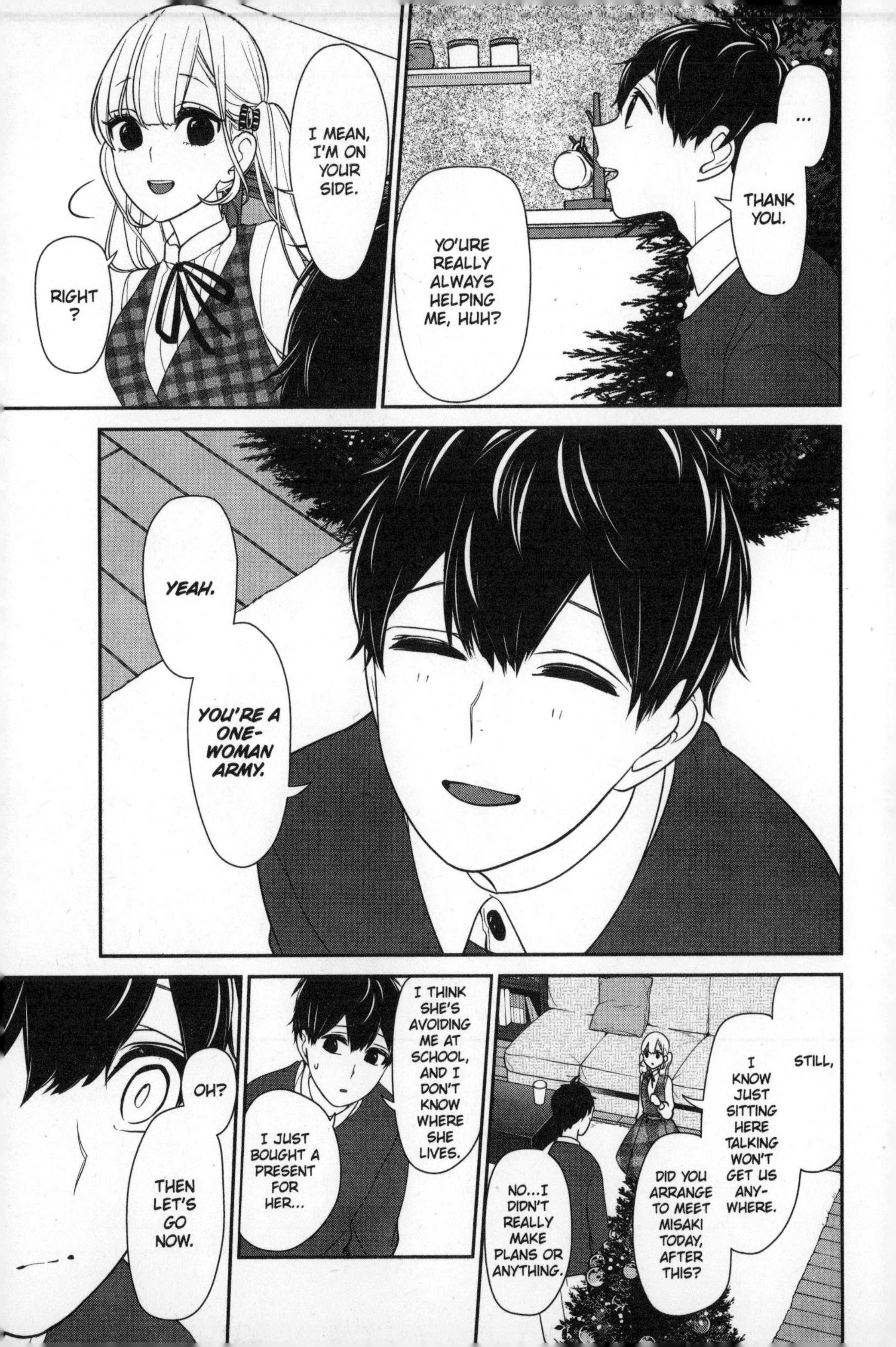
...
THANK YOU.
YOU'RE REALLY ALWAYS HELPING ME, HUH?
I MEAN, I'M ON YOUR SIDE.
RIGHT?
YEAH.
YOU'RE A ONE-WOMAN ARMY.
STILL, I KNOW JUST SITTING HERE TALKING WON'T GET US ANY-WHERE.
DID YOU ARRANGE TO MEET MISAKI TODAY, AFTER THIS?
NO...I DIDN'T REALLY MAKE PLANS OR ANYTHING.
I THINK SHE'S AVOIDING ME AT SCHOOL, AND I DON'T KNOW WHERE SHE LIVES.
I JUST BOUGHT A PRESENT FOR HER...
OH?
THEN LET'S GO NOW.

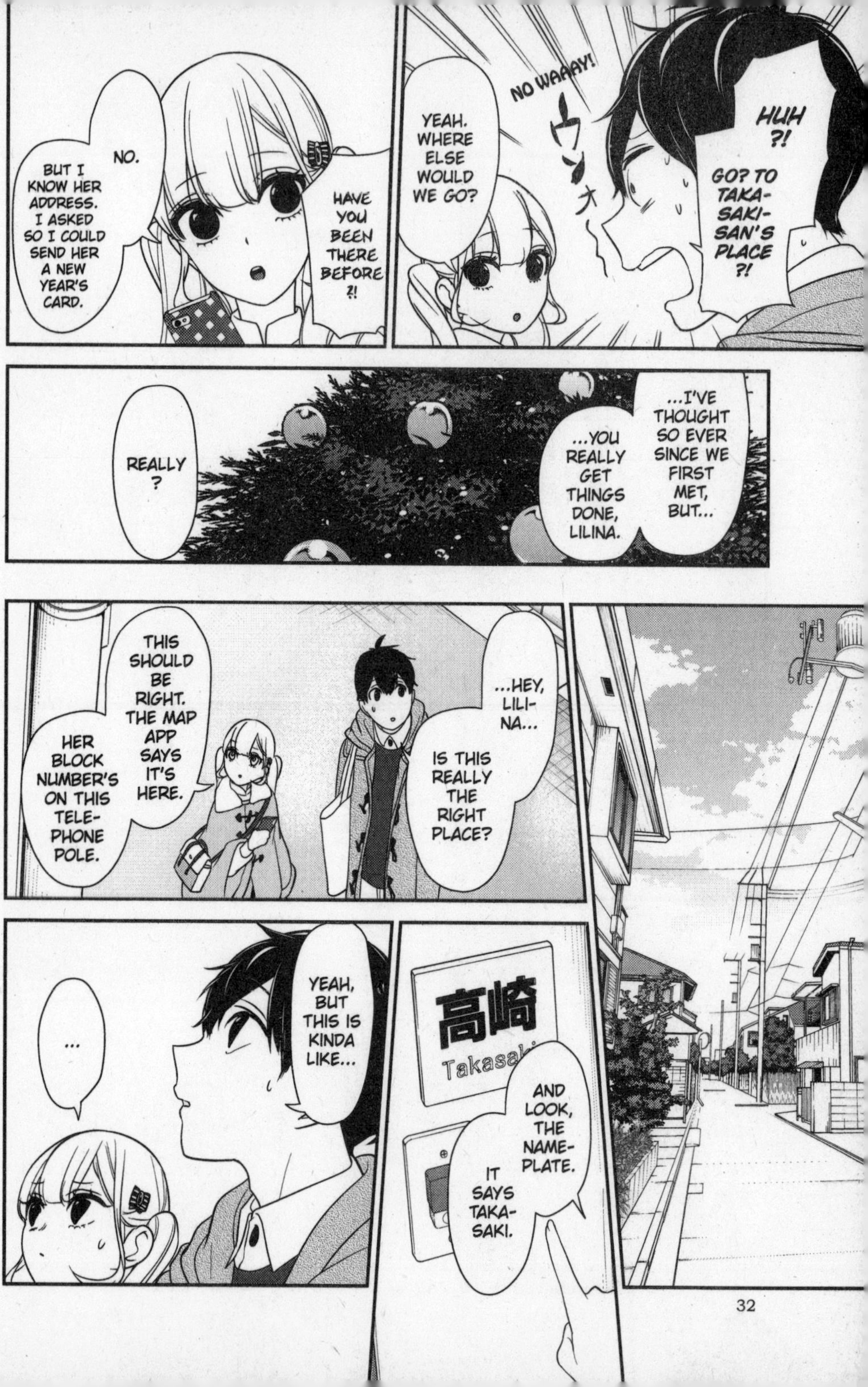
HUH ?!
GO? TO TAKA-SAKI-SAN'S PLACE ?!
NO WAAAY!
YEAH. WHERE ELSE WOULD WE GO?
HAVE YOU BEEN THERE BEFORE ?!
NO.
BUT I KNOW HER ADDRESS. I ASKED SO I COULD SEND HER A NEW YEAR'S CARD.
...I'VE THOUGHT SO EVER SINCE WE FIRST MET, BUT...
...YOU REALLY GET THINGS DONE, LILINA.
REALLY ?
...HEY, LILI-NA...
IS THIS REALLY THE RIGHT PLACE?
THIS SHOULD BE RIGHT. THE MAP APP SAYS IT'S HERE.
HER BLOCK NUMBER'S ON THIS TELE-PHONE POLE.
高崎
AND LOOK, THE NAME-PLATE.
IT SAYS TAKA-SAKI.
YEAH, BUT THIS IS KINDA LIKE...
...

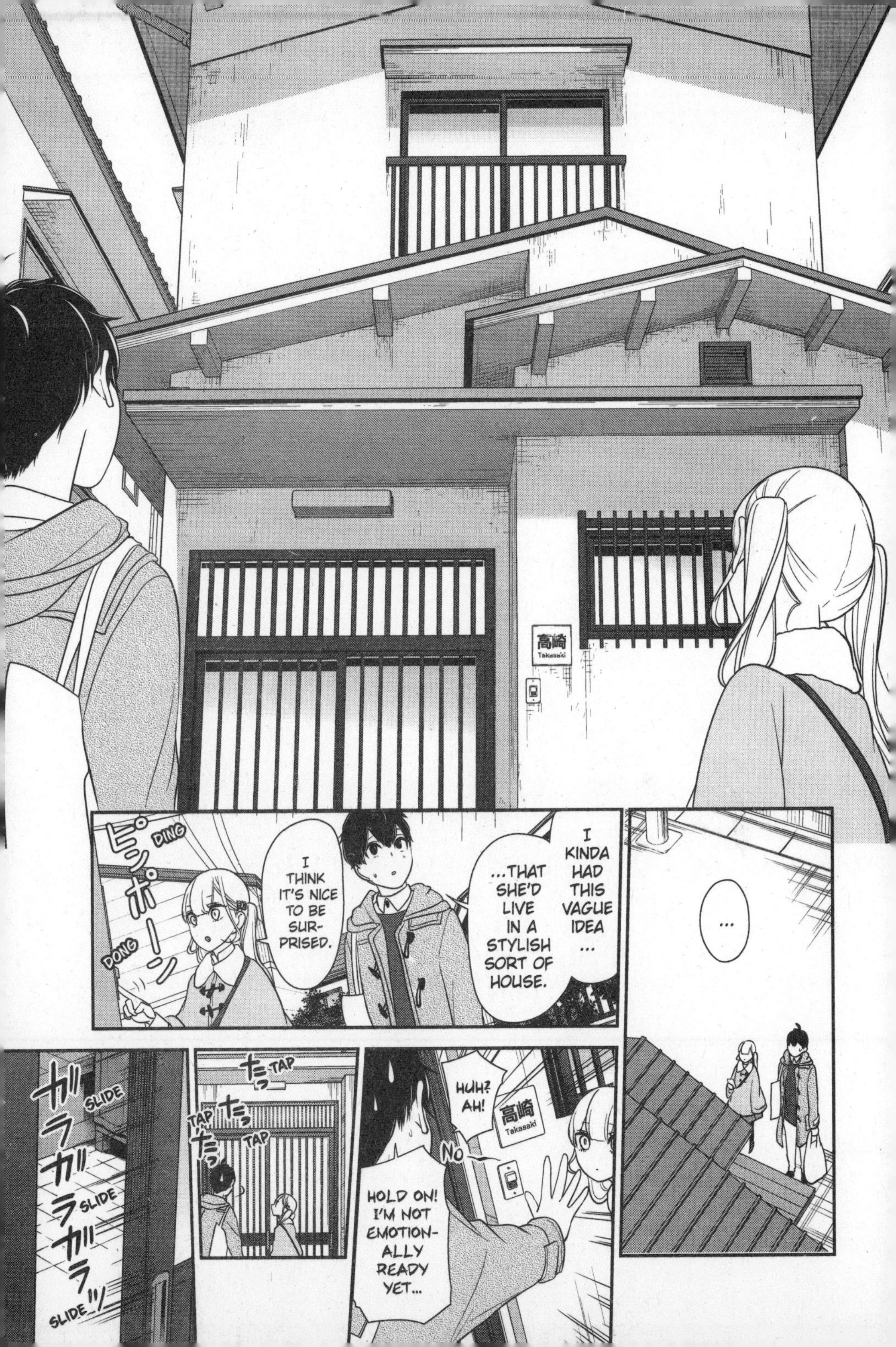
高崎
Takasaki
...
I KINDA HAD THIS VAGUE IDEA ...
...THAT SHE'D LIVE IN A STYLISH SORT OF HOUSE.
I THINK IT'S NICE TO BE SURPRISED.
ピンポーン
DING
DONG
HUH? AH!
高崎
Takasaki
NO—
HOLD ON! I'M NOT EMOTIONALLY READY YET...
TAP
TAP
TAP
SLIDE
SLIDE
SLIDE

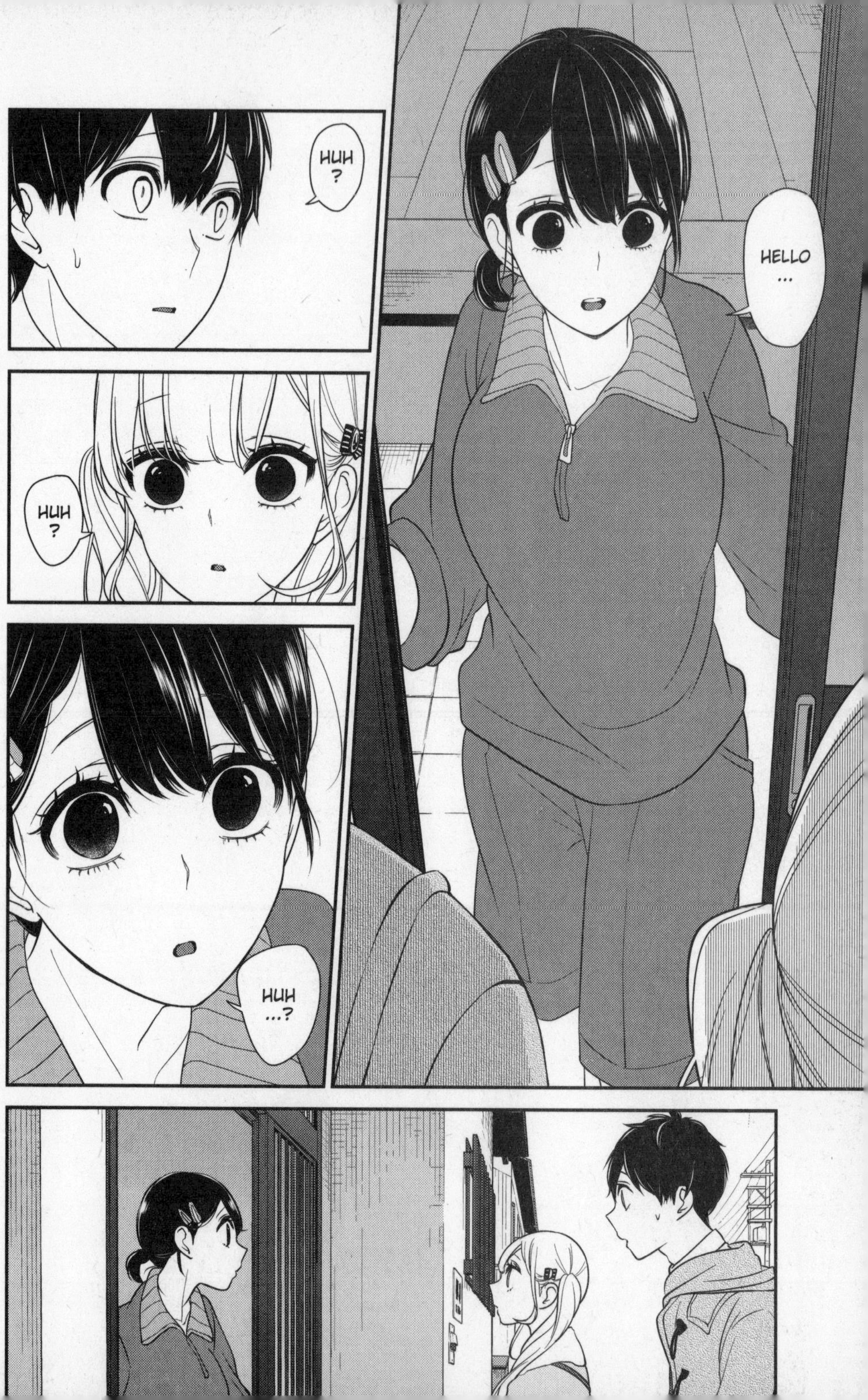
HELLO ...
HUH ?
HUH ?
HUH ...?

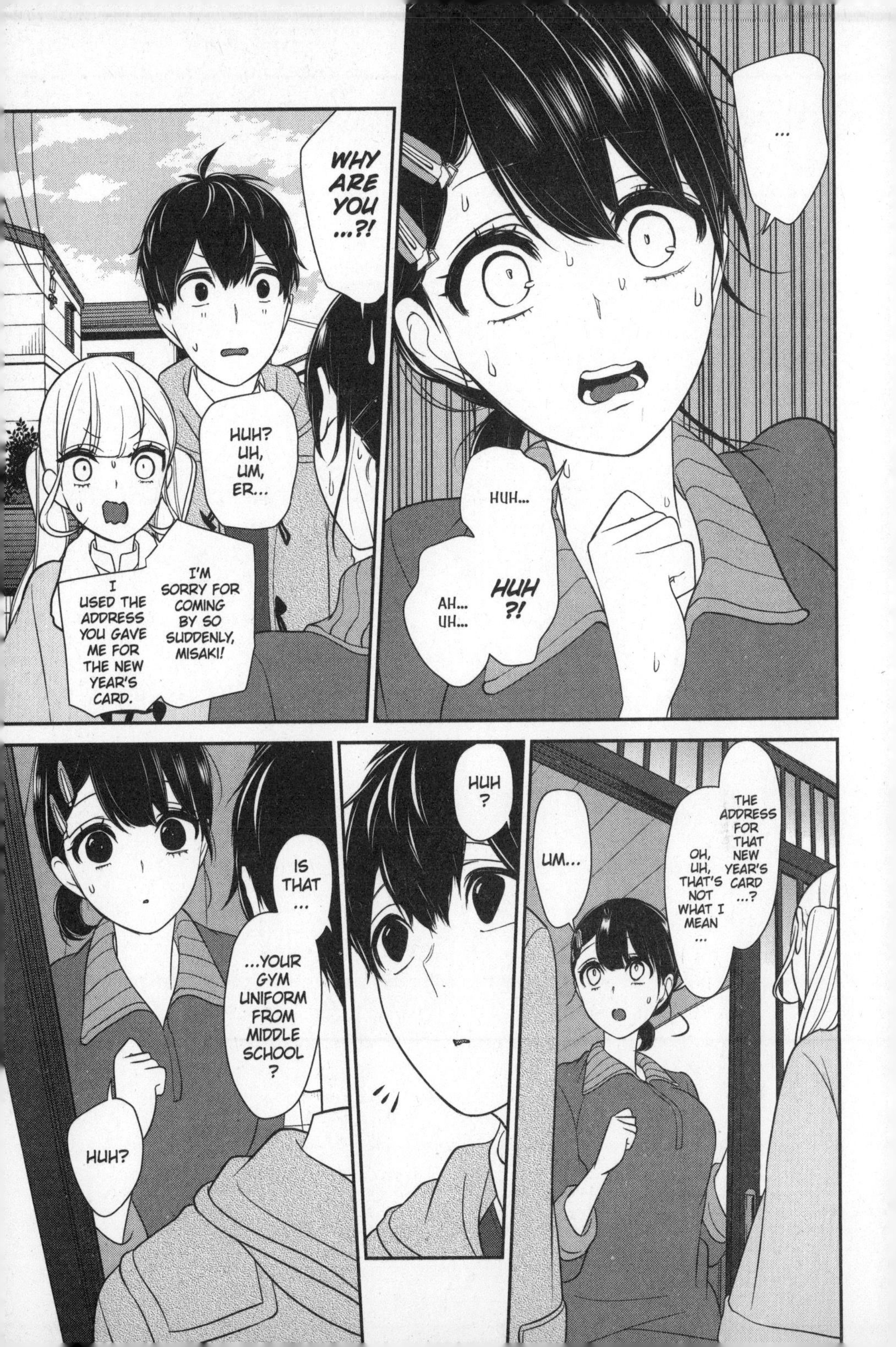
...
HUH...
HUH ?!
AH... UH...
WHY ARE YOU ...?!
HUH? UH, UM, ER...
I'M SORRY FOR COMING BY SO SUDDENLY, MISAKI!
I USED THE ADDRESS YOU GAVE ME FOR THE NEW YEAR'S CARD.
THE ADDRESS FOR THAT NEW YEAR'S CARD ...?
OH, UH, THAT'S NOT WHAT I MEAN ...
UM...
HUH ?
IS THAT ...
...YOUR GYM UNIFORM FROM MIDDLE SCHOOL ?
HUH?

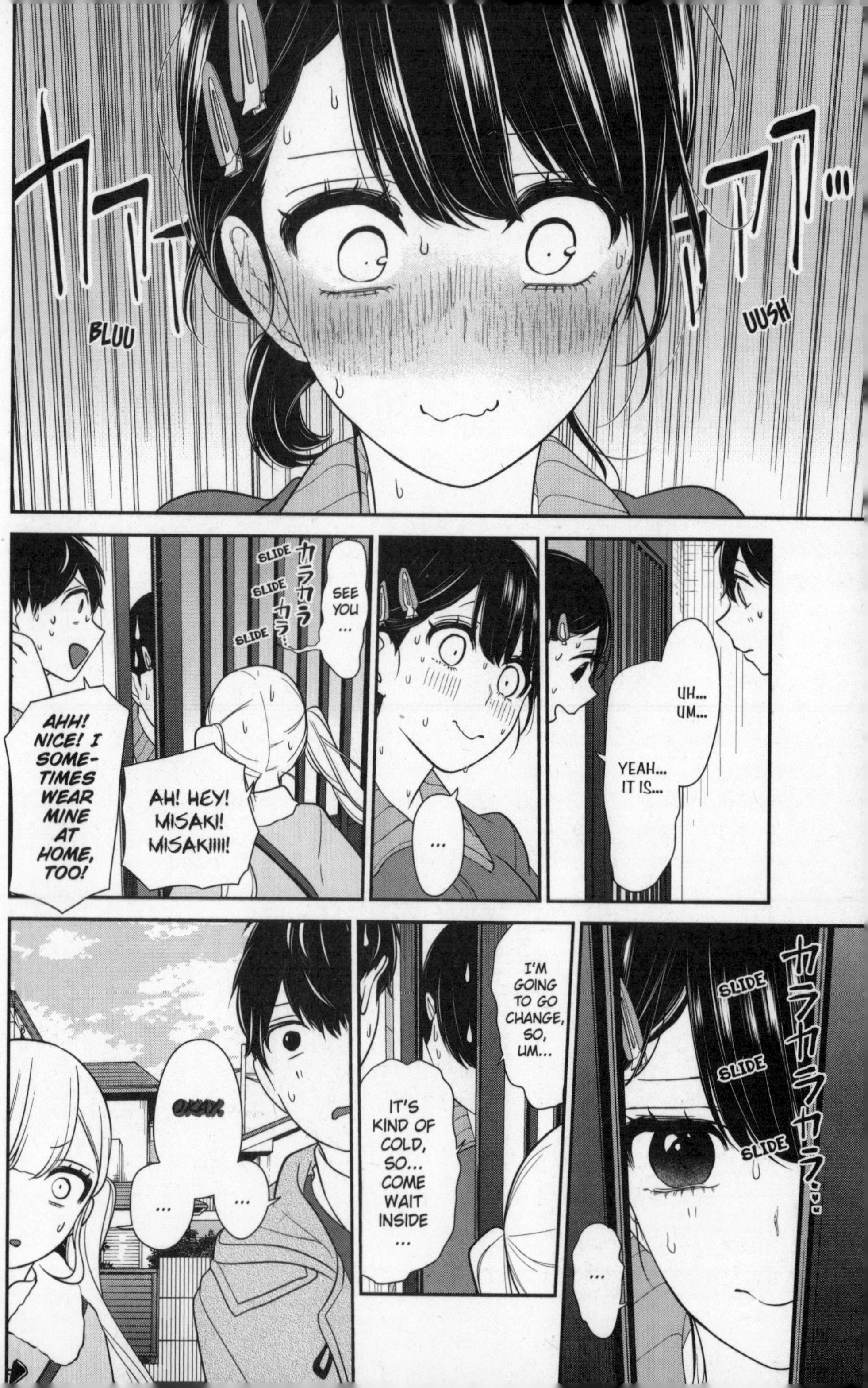
BLUU
UUSH
UH... UM...
YEAH... IT IS...
...
カラカラカラ...
SLIDE
SLIDE
SLIDE
SEE YOU ...
AH! HEY! MISAKI! MISAKIIII!
AHH! NICE! I SOMETIMES WEAR MINE AT HOME, TOO!
カラカラカラ...
SLIDE
SLIDE
SLIDE
...
I'M GOING TO GO CHANGE, SO, UM...
IT'S KIND OF COLD, SO... COME WAIT INSIDE ...
OKAY.
...
...

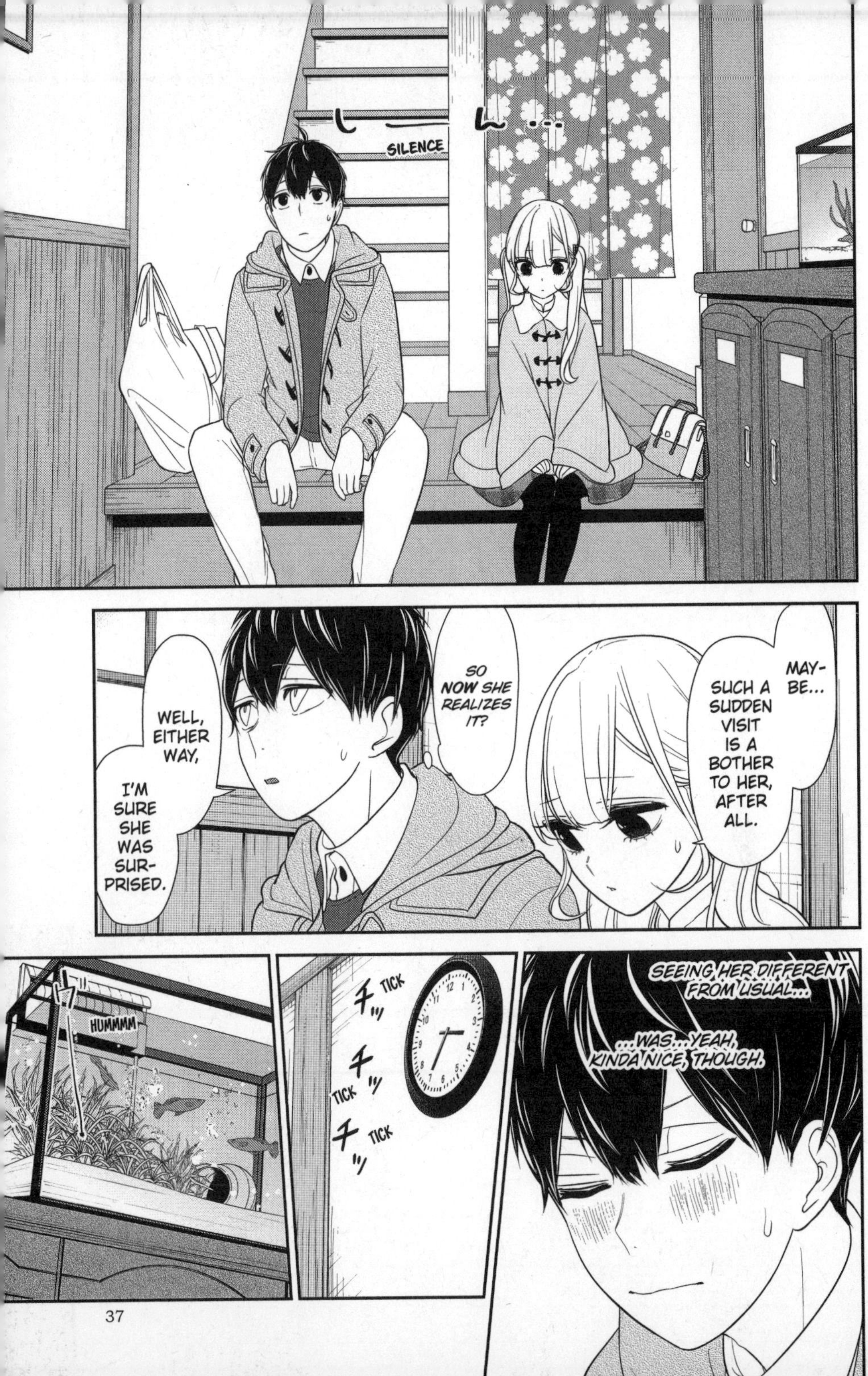
しーん…
SILENCE
MAY-BE... SUCH A SUDDEN VISIT IS A BOTHER TO HER, AFTER ALL.
SO NOW SHE REALIZES IT?
WELL, EITHER WAY,
I'M SURE SHE WAS SUR-PRISED.
SEEING HER DIFFERENT FROM USUAL...
...WAS... YEAH, KINDA NICE, THOUGH.
チッ TICK
チッ TICK
チッ TICK
HUMMMM

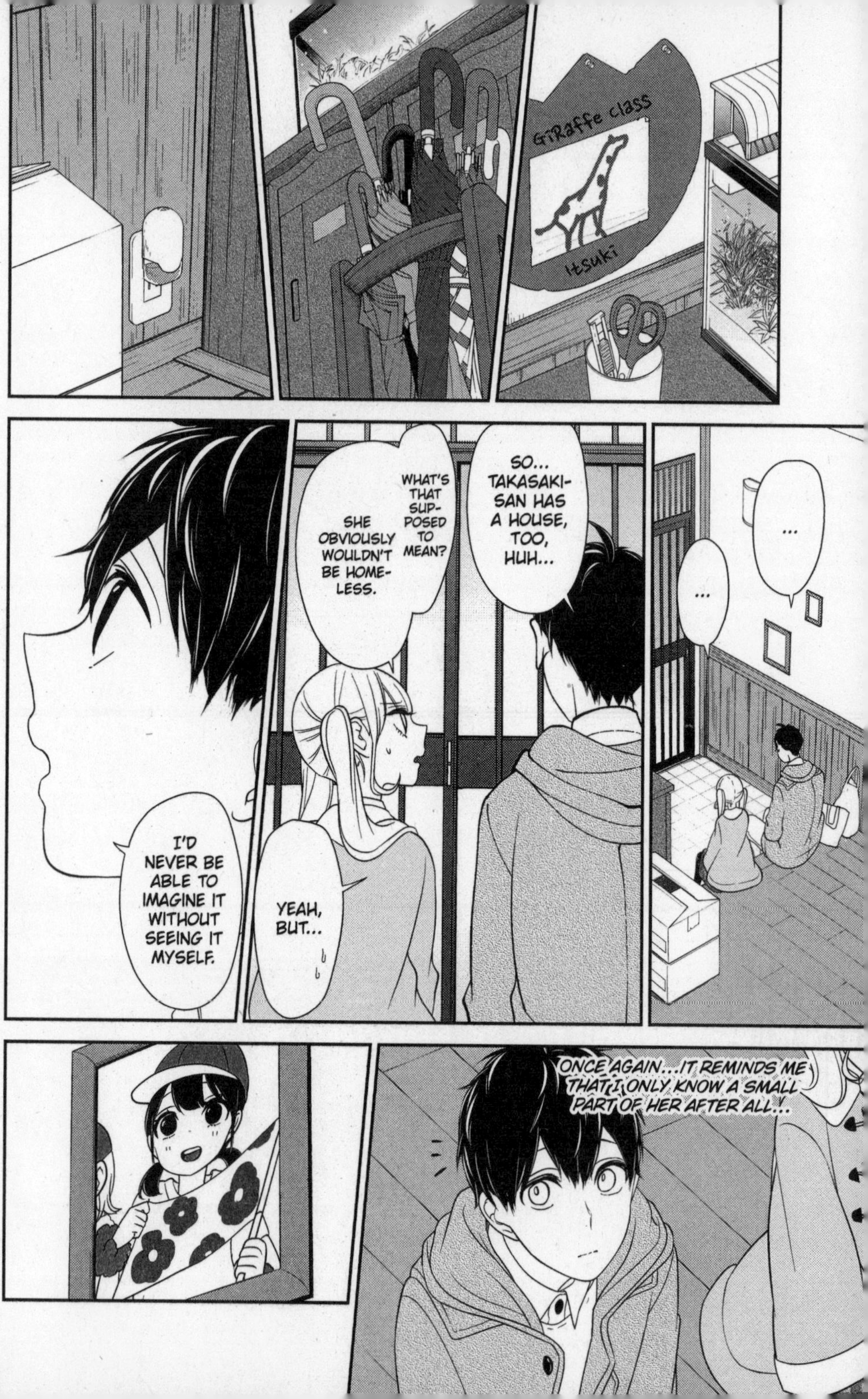
GiRaffe class
itsuki
...
...
SO... TAKASAKI-SAN HAS A HOUSE, TOO, HUH...
WHAT'S THAT SUPPOSED TO MEAN?
SHE OBVIOUSLY WOULDN'T BE HOMELESS.
YEAH, BUT...
I'D NEVER BE ABLE TO IMAGINE IT WITHOUT SEEING IT MYSELF.
ONCE AGAIN... IT REMINDS ME THAT I ONLY KNOW A SMALL PART OF HER AFTER ALL...

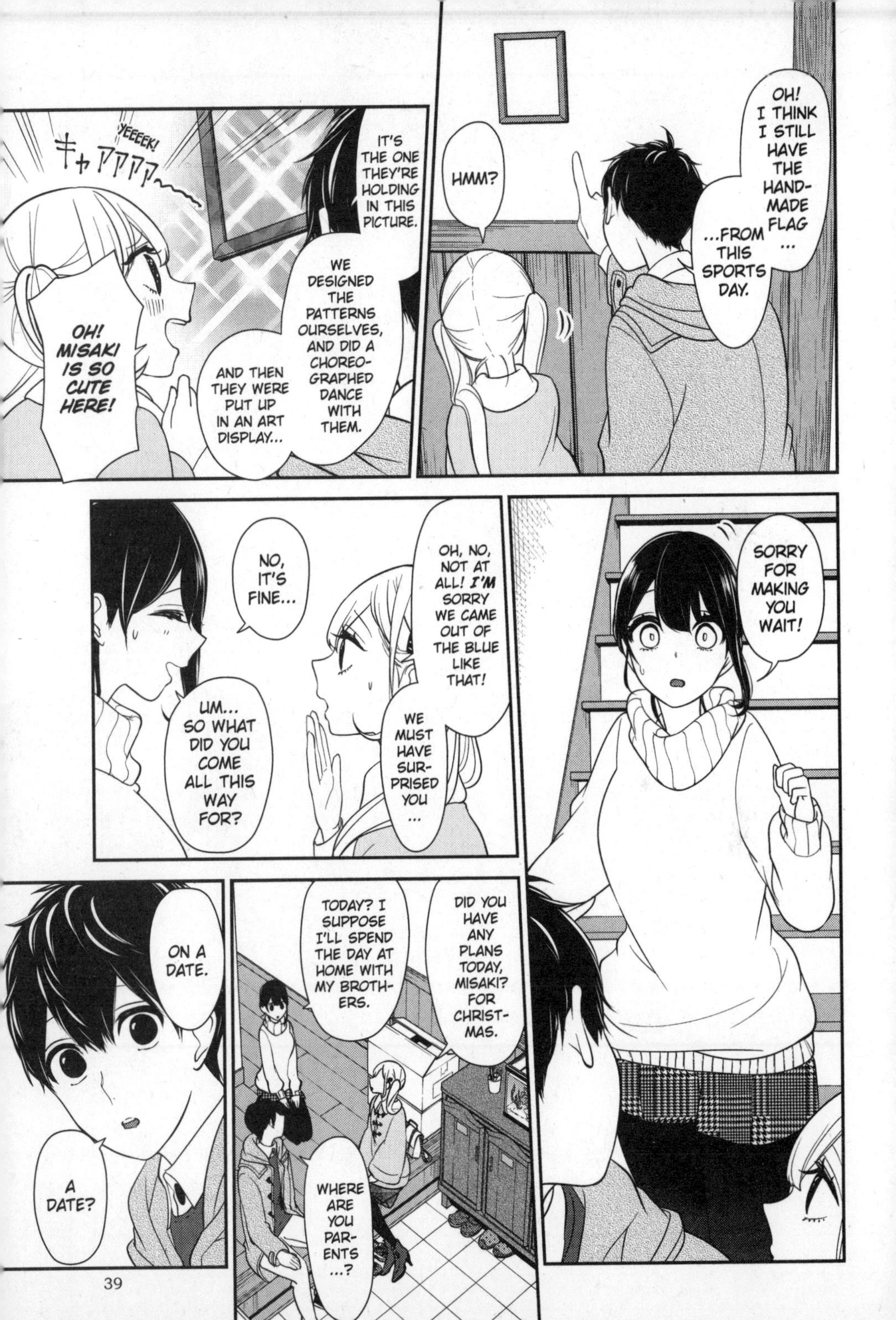
OH! I THINK I STILL HAVE THE HAND-MADE FLAG ...
...FROM THIS SPORTS DAY.
HMM?
YEEEEK!
キャアアアア~
IT'S THE ONE THEY'RE HOLDING IN THIS PICTURE.
WE DESIGNED THE PATTERNS OURSELVES, AND DID A CHOREOGRAPHED DANCE WITH THEM.
AND THEN THEY WERE PUT UP IN AN ART DISPLAY...
OH! MISAKI IS SO CUTE HERE!
SORRY FOR MAKING YOU WAIT!
OH, NO, NOT AT ALL! I'M SORRY WE CAME OUT OF THE BLUE LIKE THAT!
NO, IT'S FINE...
WE MUST HAVE SURPRISED YOU ...
UM... SO WHAT DID YOU COME ALL THIS WAY FOR?
DID YOU HAVE ANY PLANS TODAY, MISAKI? FOR CHRISTMAS.
TODAY? I SUPPOSE I'LL SPEND THE DAY AT HOME WITH MY BROTHERS.
WHERE ARE YOU PARENTS ...?
ON A DATE.
A DATE?

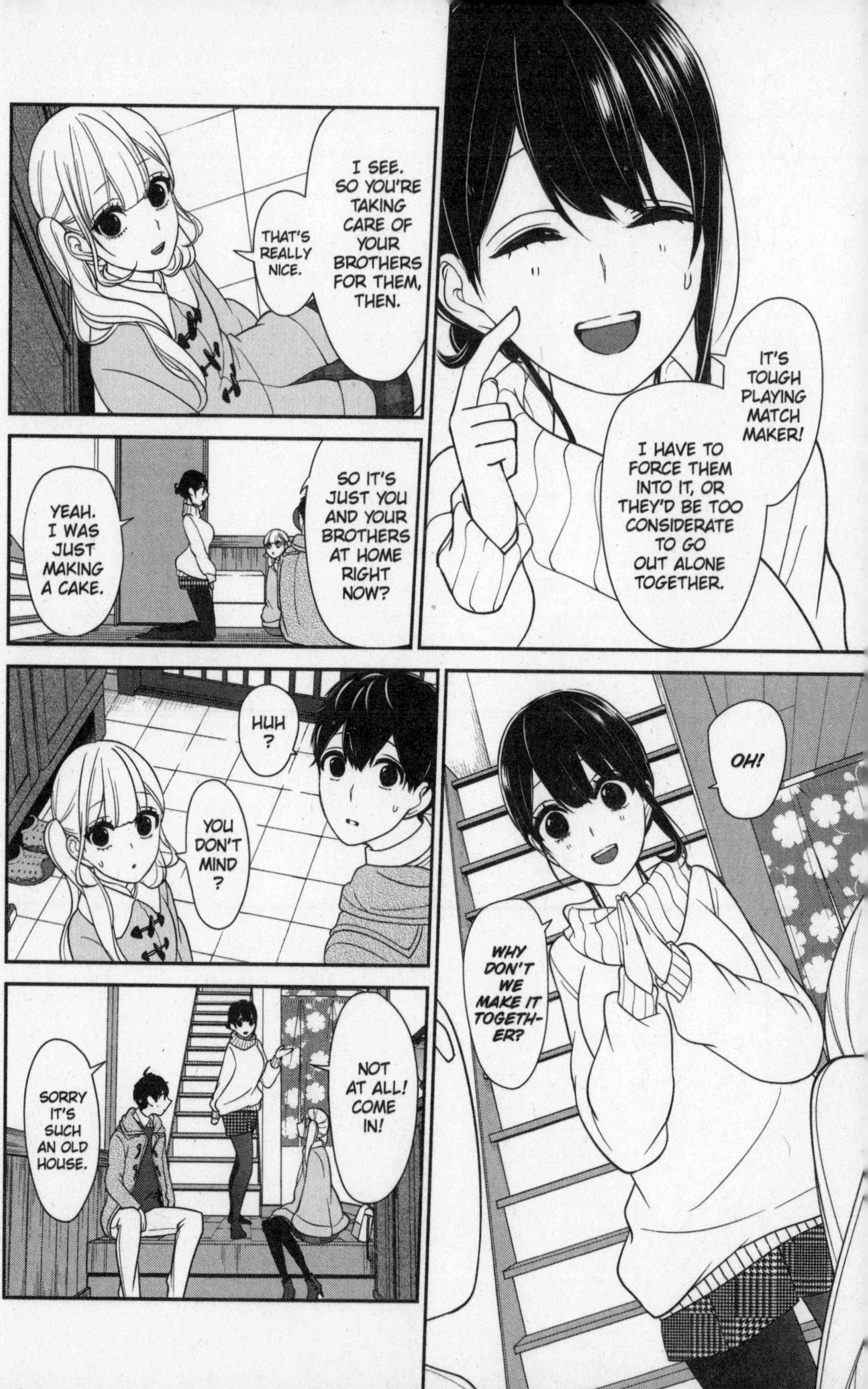
IT'S TOUGH PLAYING MATCH MAKER!
I HAVE TO FORCE THEM INTO IT, OR THEY'D BE TOO CONSIDERATE TO GO OUT ALONE TOGETHER.
I SEE. SO YOU'RE TAKING CARE OF YOUR BROTHERS FOR THEM, THEN.
THAT'S REALLY NICE.
SO IT'S JUST YOU AND YOUR BROTHERS AT HOME RIGHT NOW?
YEAH. I WAS JUST MAKING A CAKE.
OH!
WHY DON'T WE MAKE IT TOGETH-ER?
HUH?
YOU DON'T MIND?
NOT AT ALL! COME IN!
SORRY IT'S SUCH AN OLD HOUSE.

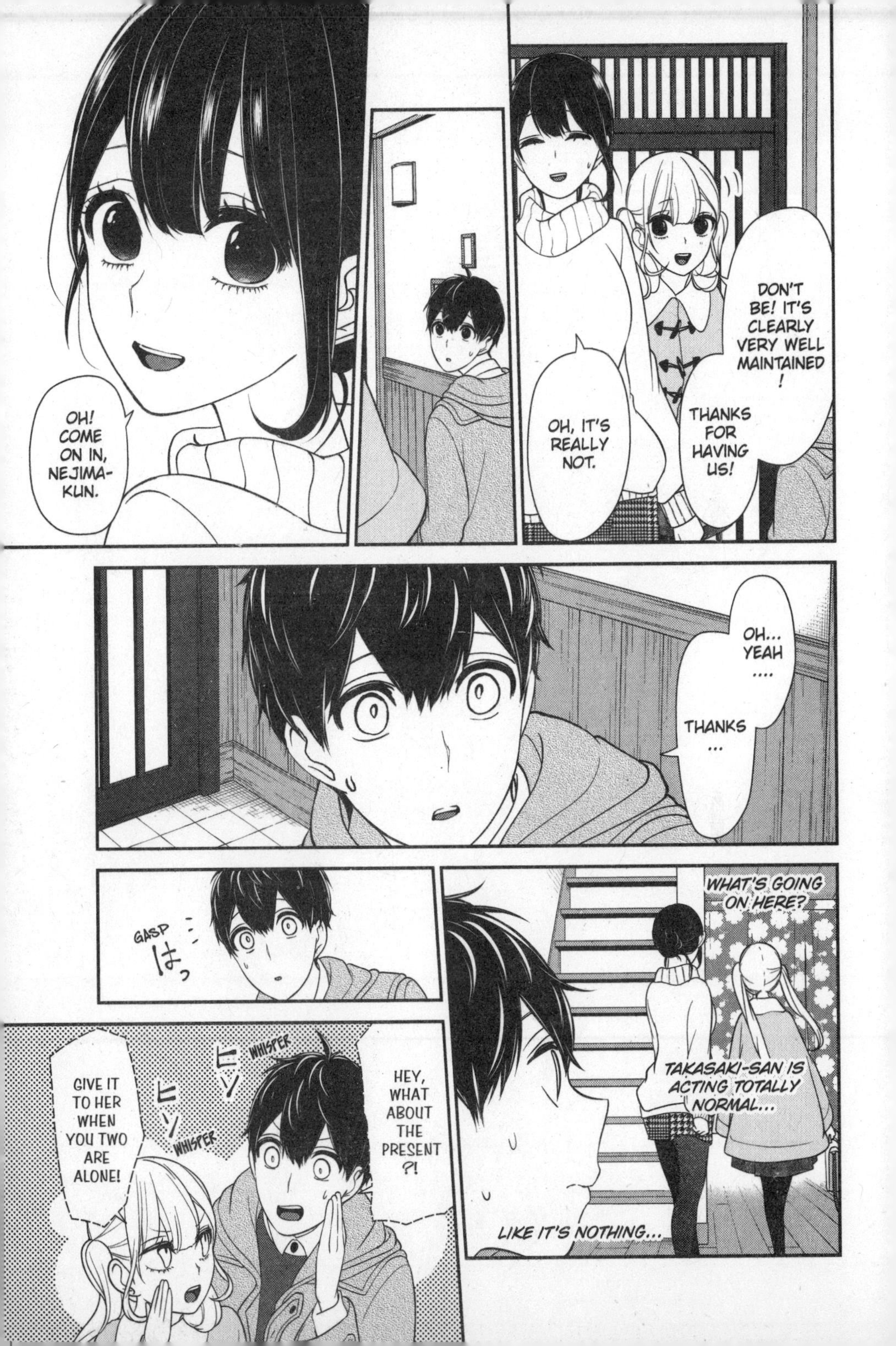
DON'T BE! IT'S CLEARLY VERY WELL MAINTAINED!
THANKS FOR HAVING US!
OH, IT'S REALLY NOT.
OH! COME ON IN, NEJIMA-KUN.
OH... YEAH ....
THANKS ...
WHAT'S GOING ON HERE?
TAKASAKI-SAN IS ACTING TOTALLY NORMAL...
LIKE IT'S NOTHING...
GASP
はっ
HEY, WHAT ABOUT THE PRESENT?!
ヒソ WHISPER
ヒソ WHISPER
GIVE IT TO HER WHEN YOU TWO ARE ALONE!

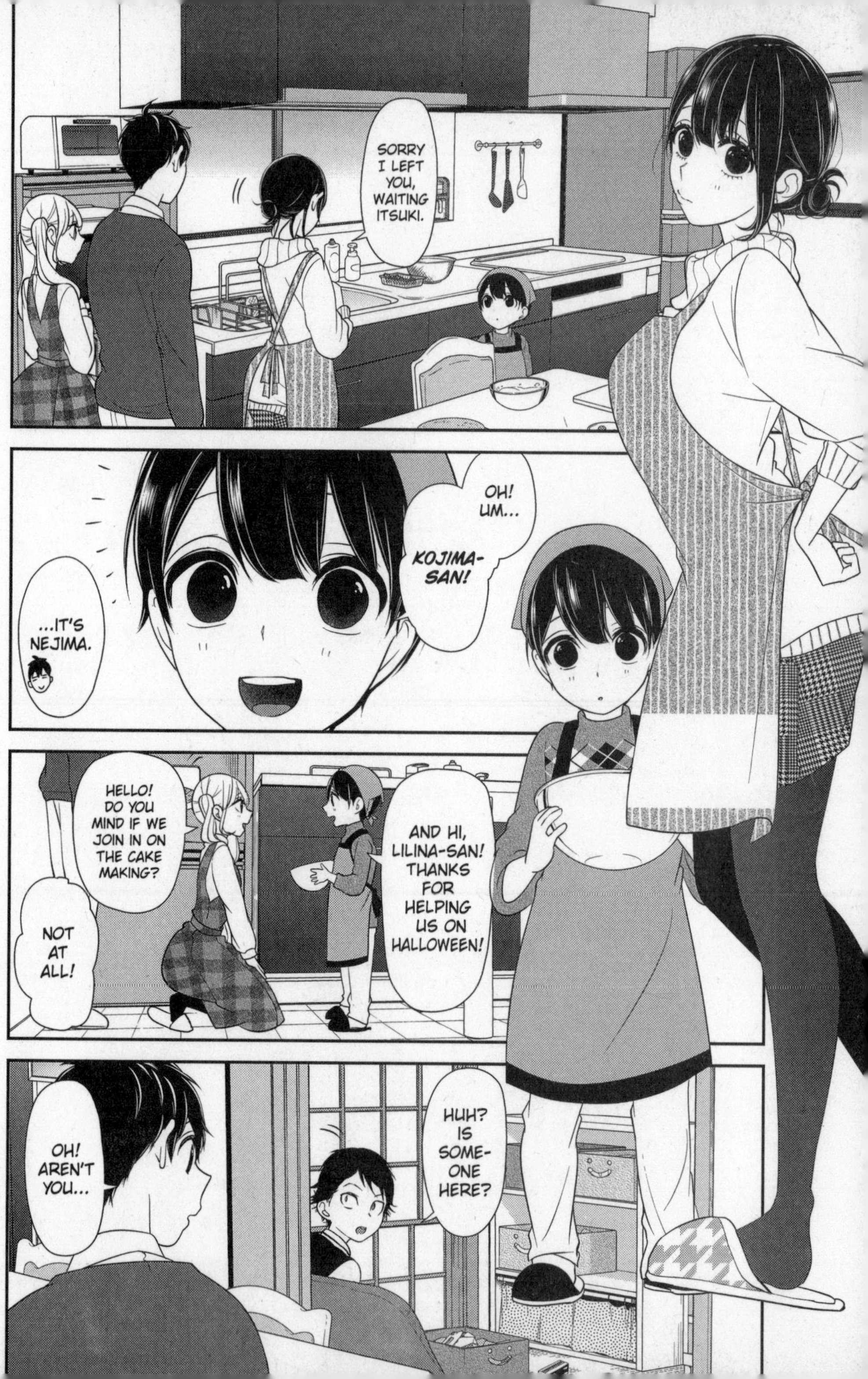
SORRY I LEFT YOU, WAITING ITSUKI.
OH! UM... KOJIMA-SAN!
...IT'S NEJIMA.
AND HI, LILINA-SAN! THANKS FOR HELPING US ON HALLOWEEN!
HELLO! DO YOU MIND IF WE JOIN IN ON THE CAKE MAKING?
NOT AT ALL!
HUH? IS SOME-ONE HERE?
OH! AREN'T YOU...

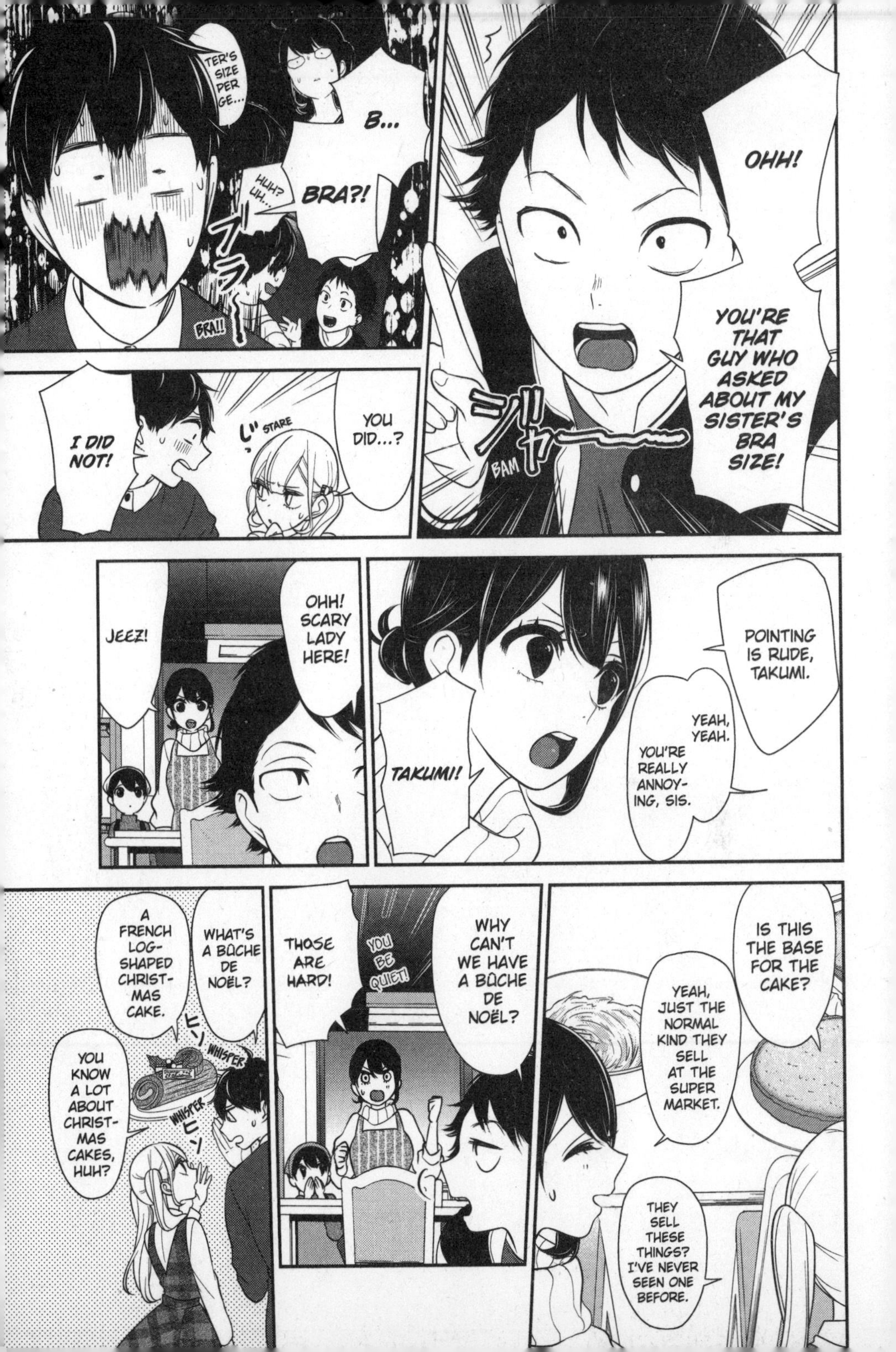
OHH!
YOU'RE THAT GUY WHO ASKED ABOUT MY SISTER'S BRA SIZE!
BAM
B...
BRA?!
TER'S SIZE PER GE...
HUH? UH...
BRA!!
YOU DID...?
STARE
I DID NOT!
POINTING IS RUDE, TAKUMI.
YEAH, YEAH. YOU'RE REALLY ANNOY-ING, SIS.
TAKUMI!
OHH! SCARY LADY HERE!
JEEZ!
IS THIS THE BASE FOR THE CAKE?
YEAH, JUST THE NORMAL KIND THEY SELL AT THE SUPER MARKET.
THEY SELL THESE THINGS? I'VE NEVER SEEN ONE BEFORE.
WHY CAN'T WE HAVE A BÛCHE DE NOËL?
YOU BE QUIET!
THOSE ARE HARD!
WHAT'S A BÛCHE DE NOËL?
A FRENCH LOG-SHAPED CHRIST-MAS CAKE.
WHISPER
YOU KNOW A LOT ABOUT CHRIST-MAS CAKES, HUH?
WHISPER

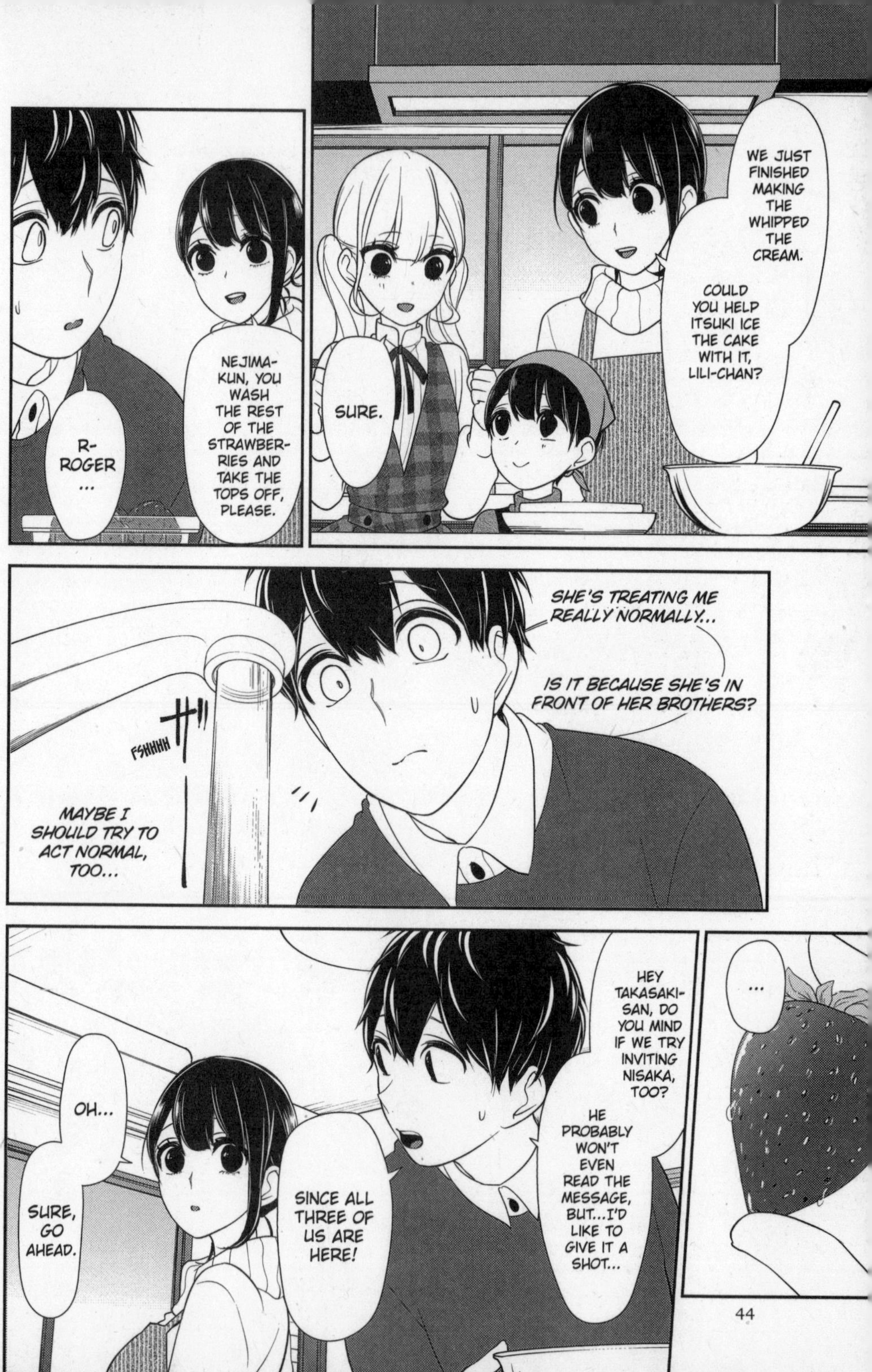
WE JUST FINISHED MAKING THE WHIPPED THE CREAM.
COULD YOU HELP ITSUKI ICE THE CAKE WITH IT, LILI-CHAN?
SURE.
NEJIMA-KUN, YOU WASH THE REST OF THE STRAWBERRIES AND TAKE THE TOPS OFF, PLEASE.
R-ROGER...
SHE'S TREATING ME REALLY NORMALLY...
IS IT BECAUSE SHE'S IN FRONT OF HER BROTHERS?
FSHHHH
MAYBE I SHOULD TRY TO ACT NORMAL, TOO...
...
HEY TAKASAKI-SAN, DO YOU MIND IF WE TRY INVITING NISAKA, TOO?
HE PROBABLY WON'T EVEN READ THE MESSAGE, BUT...I'D LIKE TO GIVE IT A SHOT...
SINCE ALL THREE OF US ARE HERE!
OH...
SURE, GO AHEAD.

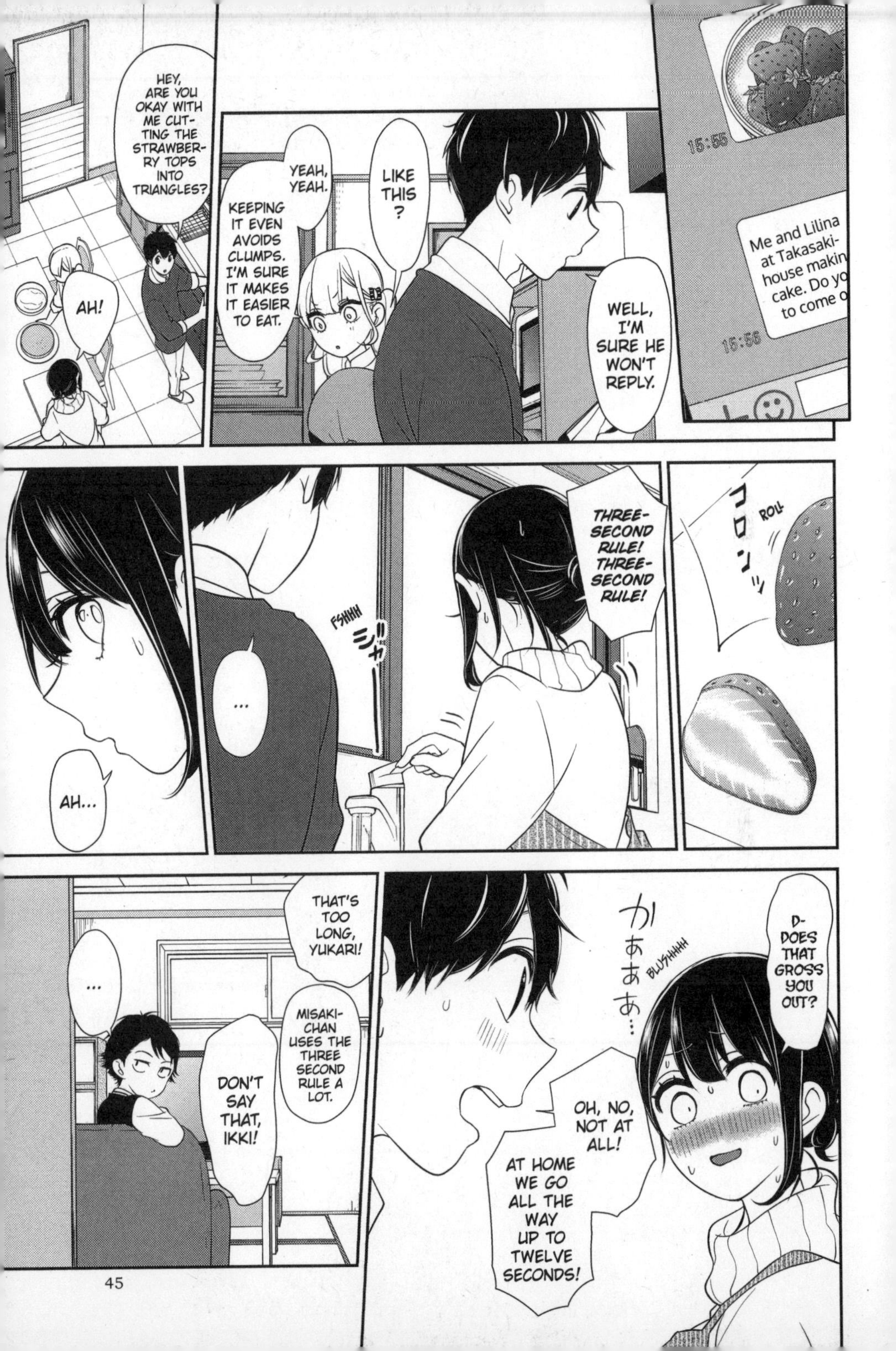
15:55
Me and Lilina at Takasaki- house makin cake. Do yo to come o
15:56
WELL, I'M SURE HE WON'T REPLY.
LIKE THIS?
YEAH, YEAH.
KEEPING IT EVEN AVOIDS CLUMPS. I'M SURE IT MAKES IT EASIER TO EAT.
HEY, ARE YOU OKAY WITH ME CUTTING THE STRAWBERRY TOPS INTO TRIANGLES?
AH!
コロンッ
ROLL
THREE-SECOND RULE! THREE-SECOND RULE!
ジャー
FSHHH
...
AH...
D-DOES THAT GROSS YOU OUT?
かあああ…
BLUSHHHH
OH, NO, NOT AT ALL!
AT HOME WE GO ALL THE WAY UP TO TWELVE SECONDS!
THAT'S TOO LONG, YUKARI!
MISAKI-CHAN USES THE THREE SECOND RULE A LOT.
...
DON'T SAY THAT, IKKI!

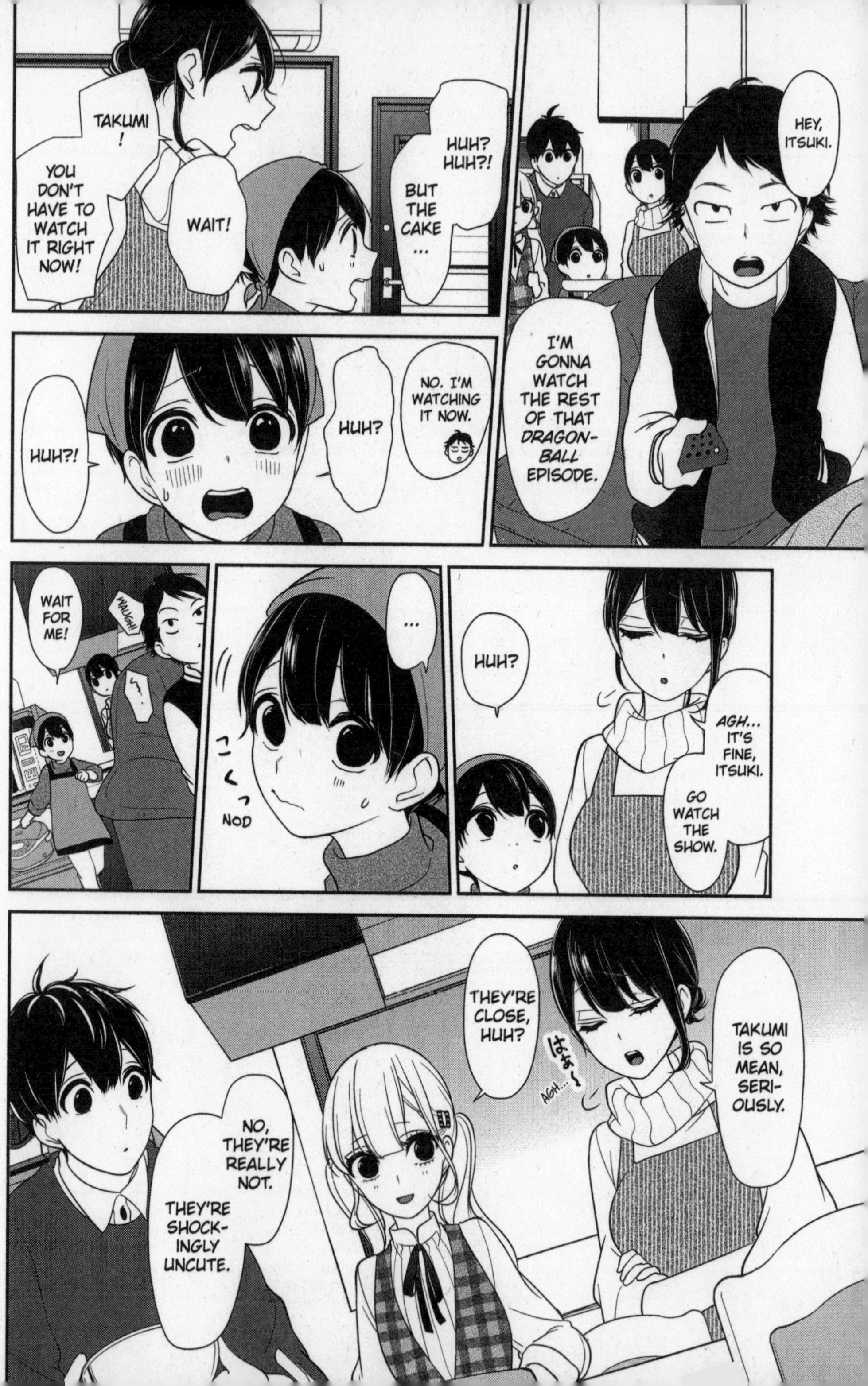
HEY, ITSUKI.
I'M GONNA WATCH THE REST OF THAT DRAGON-BALL EPISODE.
HUH? HUH?! BUT THE CAKE...
TAKUMI!
WAIT!
YOU DON'T HAVE TO WATCH IT RIGHT NOW!
NO. I'M WATCHING IT NOW.
HUH?
HUH?!
HUH?
AGH... IT'S FINE, ITSUKI.
GO WATCH THE SHOW.
...
こくっ
NOD
WAUGH!
WAIT FOR ME!
TAKUMI IS SO MEAN, SERIOUSLY.
はぁ～
AGH...~
THEY'RE CLOSE, HUH?
NO, THEY'RE REALLY NOT.
THEY'RE SHOCKINGLY UNCUTE.

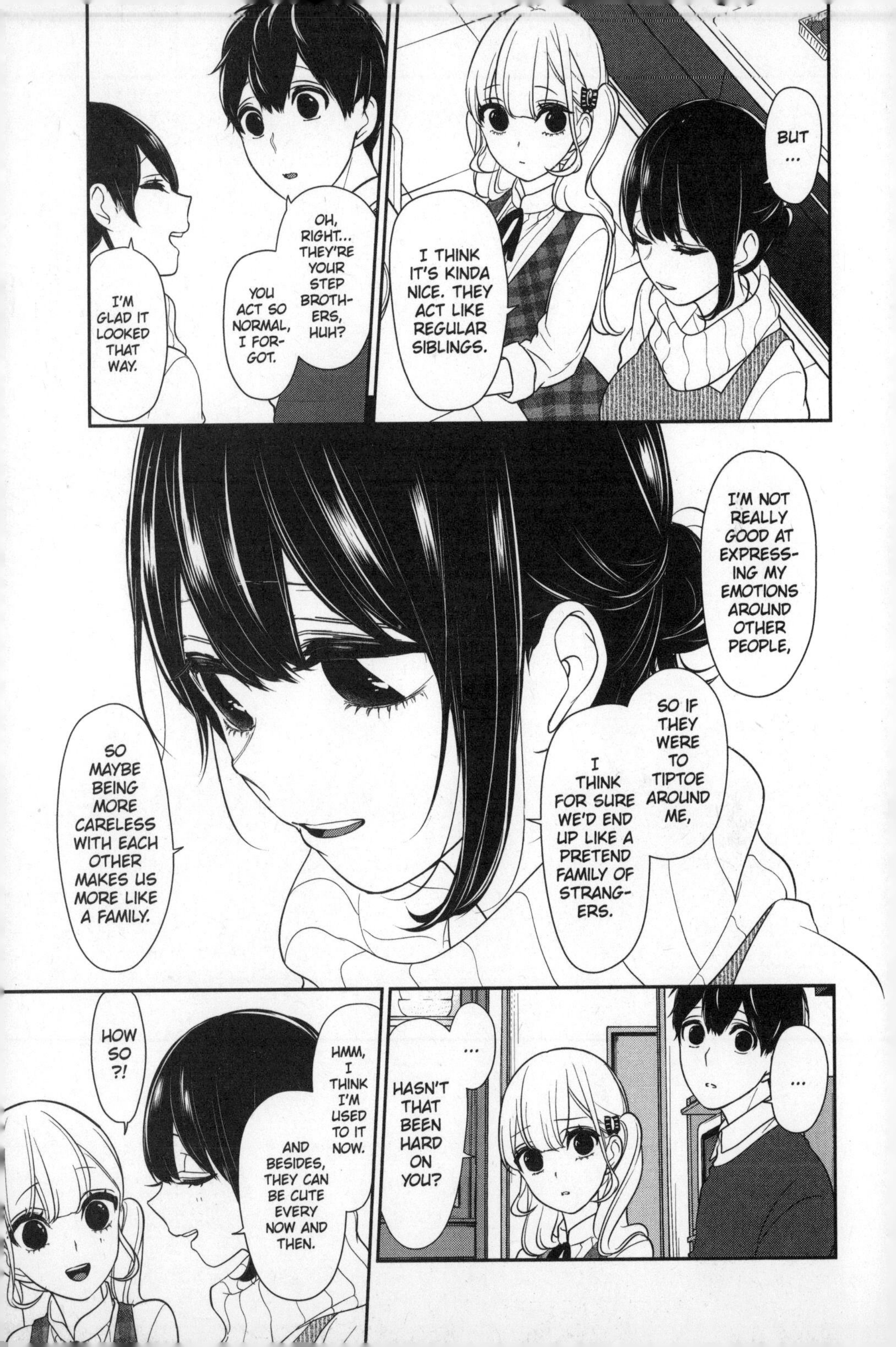
BUT ...
I THINK IT'S KINDA NICE. THEY ACT LIKE REGULAR SIBLINGS.
OH, RIGHT... THEY'RE YOUR STEP BROTH-ERS, HUH?
YOU ACT SO NORMAL, I FOR-GOT.
I'M GLAD IT LOOKED THAT WAY.
I'M NOT REALLY GOOD AT EXPRESS-ING MY EMOTIONS AROUND OTHER PEOPLE,
SO IF THEY WERE TO TIPTOE AROUND ME,
I THINK FOR SURE WE'D END UP LIKE A PRETEND FAMILY OF STRANG-ERS.
SO MAYBE BEING MORE CARELESS WITH EACH OTHER MAKES US MORE LIKE A FAMILY.
...
...
HASN'T THAT BEEN HARD ON YOU?
HMM, I THINK I'M USED TO IT NOW.
AND BESIDES, THEY CAN BE CUTE EVERY NOW AND THEN.
HOW SO ?!

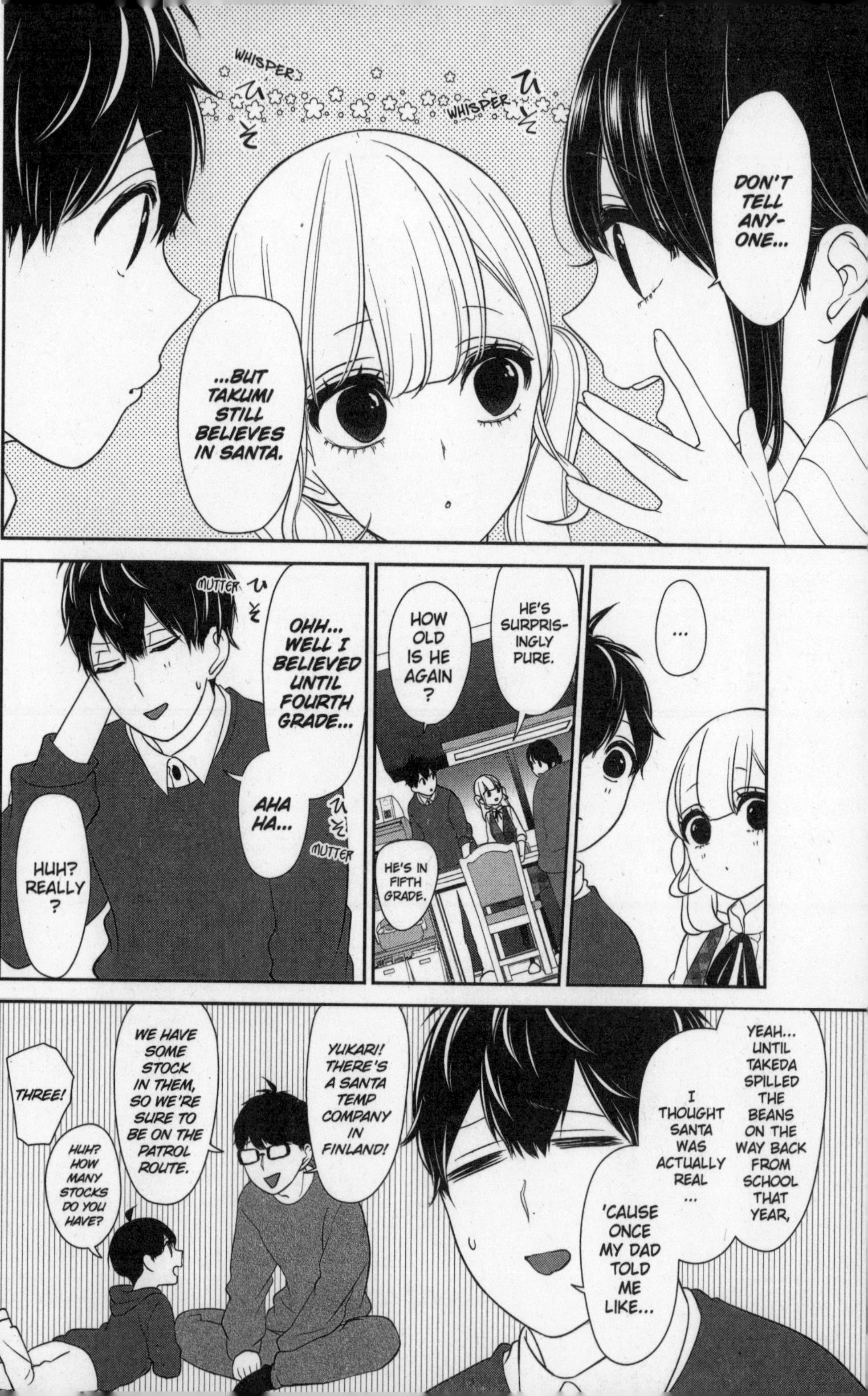
WHISPER
WHISPER
DON'T TELL ANYONE...
...BUT TAKUMI STILL BELIEVES IN SANTA.
...
HE'S SURPRISINGLY PURE.
HOW OLD IS HE AGAIN?
HE'S IN FIFTH GRADE.
MUTTER
OHH... WELL I BELIEVED UNTIL FOURTH GRADE...
AHA HA...
MUTTER
HUH? REALLY?
YEAH... UNTIL TAKEDA SPILLED THE BEANS ON THE WAY BACK FROM SCHOOL THAT YEAR,
I THOUGHT SANTA WAS ACTUALLY REAL...
'CAUSE ONCE MY DAD TOLD ME LIKE...
YUKARI! THERE'S A SANTA TEMP COMPANY IN FINLAND!
WE HAVE SOME STOCK IN THEM, SO WE'RE SURE TO BE ON THE PATROL ROUTE.
HUH? HOW MANY STOCKS DO YOU HAVE?
THREE!

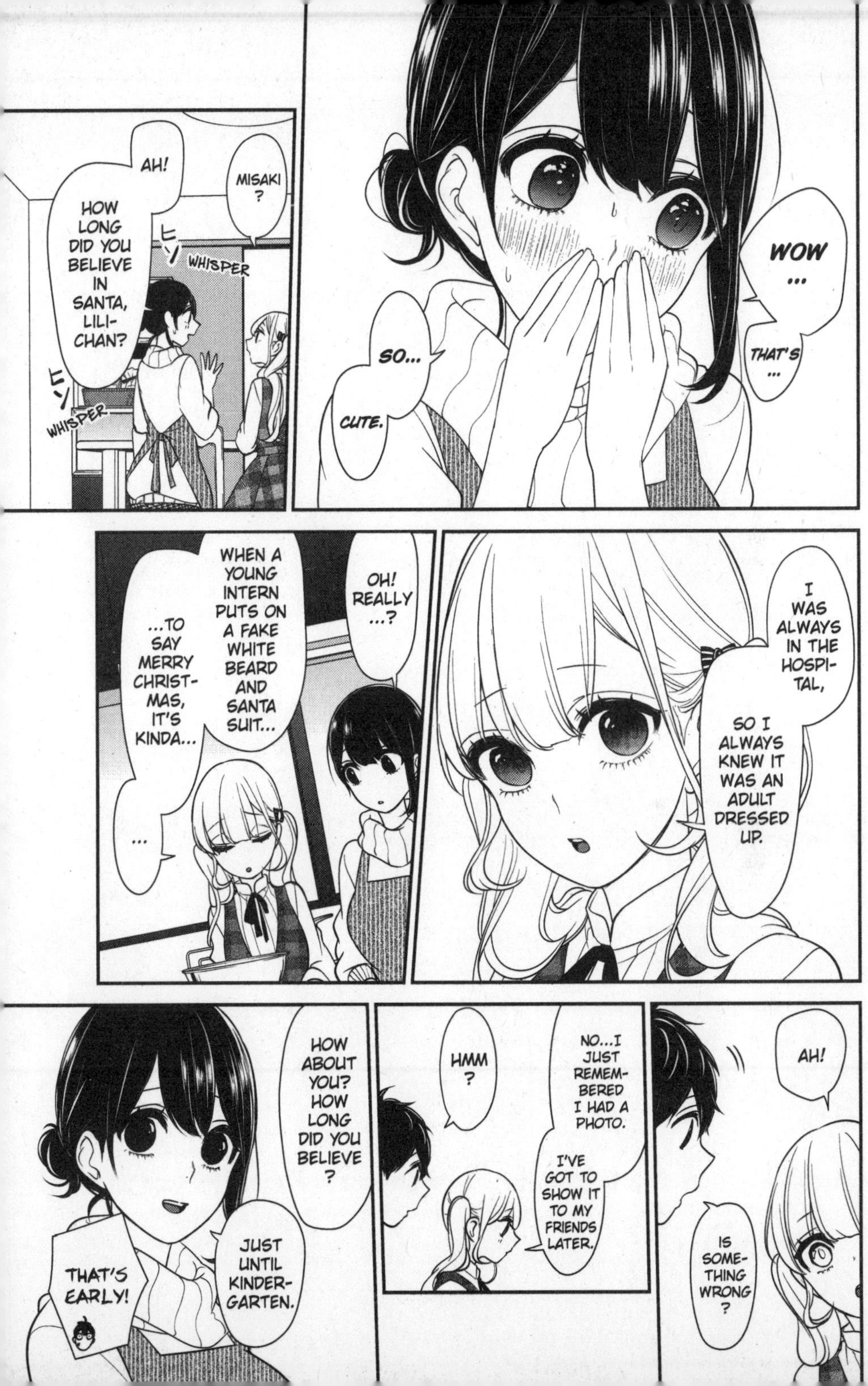
WOW...
THAT'S...
SO...
CUTE.
MISAKI?
AH!
HOW LONG DID YOU BELIEVE IN SANTA, LILI-CHAN?
WHISPER
WHISPER
I WAS ALWAYS IN THE HOSPITAL,
SO I ALWAYS KNEW IT WAS AN ADULT DRESSED UP.
OH! REALLY...?
WHEN A YOUNG INTERN PUTS ON A FAKE WHITE BEARD AND SANTA SUIT...
...TO SAY MERRY CHRIST-MAS, IT'S KINDA...
...
AH!
IS SOME-THING WRONG?
NO...I JUST REMEM-BERED I HAD A PHOTO.
HMM?
I'VE GOT TO SHOW IT TO MY FRIENDS LATER.
HOW ABOUT YOU? HOW LONG DID YOU BELIEVE?
JUST UNTIL KINDER-GARTEN.
THAT'S EARLY!

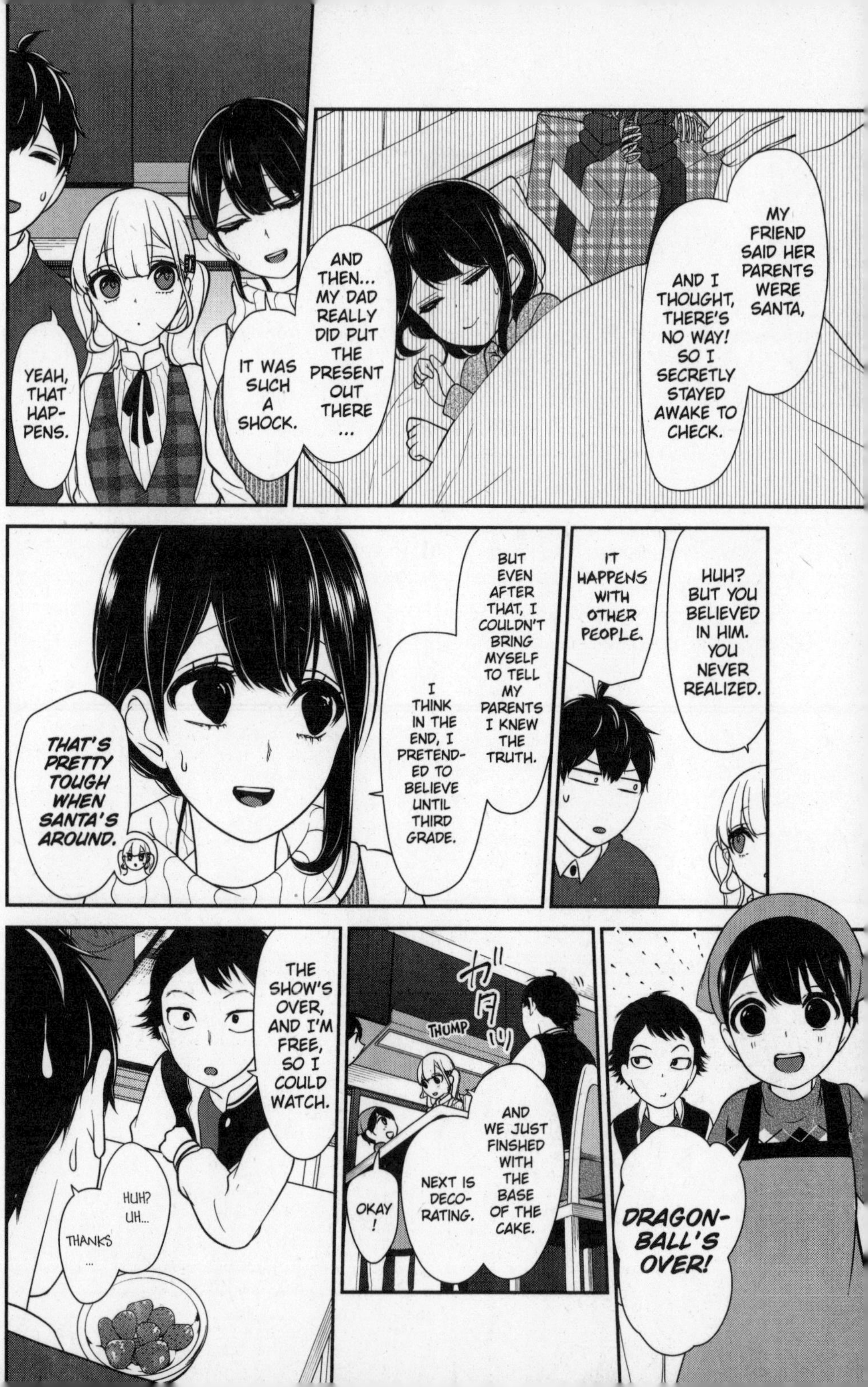
MY FRIEND SAID HER PARENTS WERE SANTA,
AND I THOUGHT, THERE'S NO WAY! SO I SECRETLY STAYED AWAKE TO CHECK.
AND THEN... MY DAD REALLY DID PUT THE PRESENT OUT THERE ...
IT WAS SUCH A SHOCK.
YEAH, THAT HAP-PENS.
HUH? BUT YOU BELIEVED IN HIM. YOU NEVER REALIZED.
IT HAPPENS WITH OTHER PEOPLE.
BUT EVEN AFTER THAT, I COULDN'T BRING MYSELF TO TELL MY PARENTS I KNEW THE TRUTH.
I THINK IN THE END, I PRETEND-ED TO BELIEVE UNTIL THIRD GRADE.
THAT'S PRETTY TOUGH WHEN SANTA'S AROUND.
DRAGON-BALL'S OVER!
ガタッ
THUMP
AND WE JUST FINSHED WITH THE BASE OF THE CAKE.
NEXT IS DECO-RATING.
OKAY!
THE SHOW'S OVER, AND I'M FREE, SO I COULD WATCH.
HUH? UH...
THANKS ...

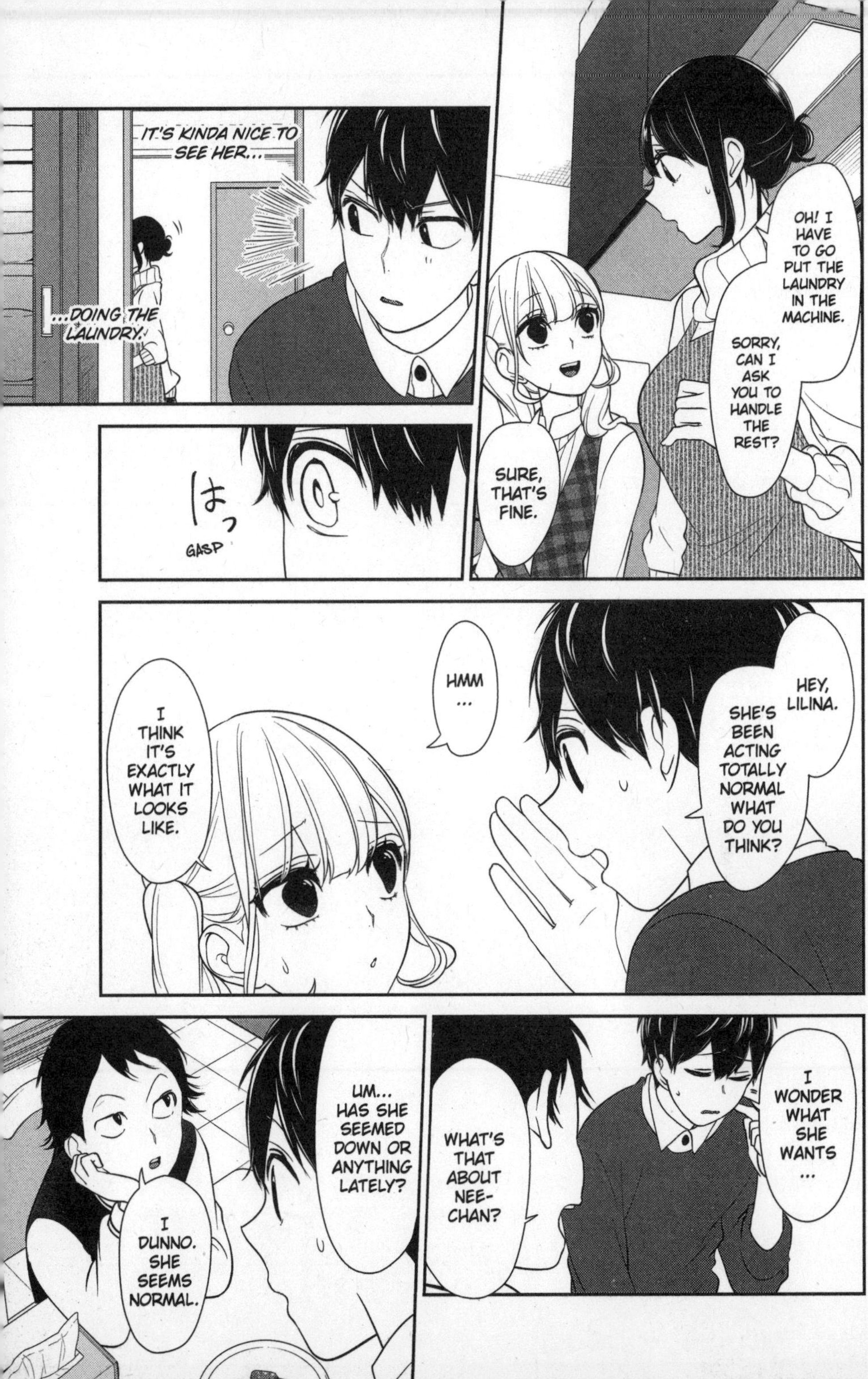
OH! I HAVE TO GO PUT THE LAUNDRY IN THE MACHINE.
SORRY, CAN I ASK YOU TO HANDLE THE REST?
SURE, THAT'S FINE.
IT'S KINDA NICE TO SEE HER...
...DOING THE LAUNDRY.
はっ
GASP
HEY, LILINA.
SHE'S BEEN ACTING TOTALLY NORMAL WHAT DO YOU THINK?
HMM...
I THINK IT'S EXACTLY WHAT IT LOOKS LIKE.
I WONDER WHAT SHE WANTS...
WHAT'S THAT ABOUT NEE-CHAN?
UM... HAS SHE SEEMED DOWN OR ANYTHING LATELY?
I DUNNO. SHE SEEMS NORMAL.

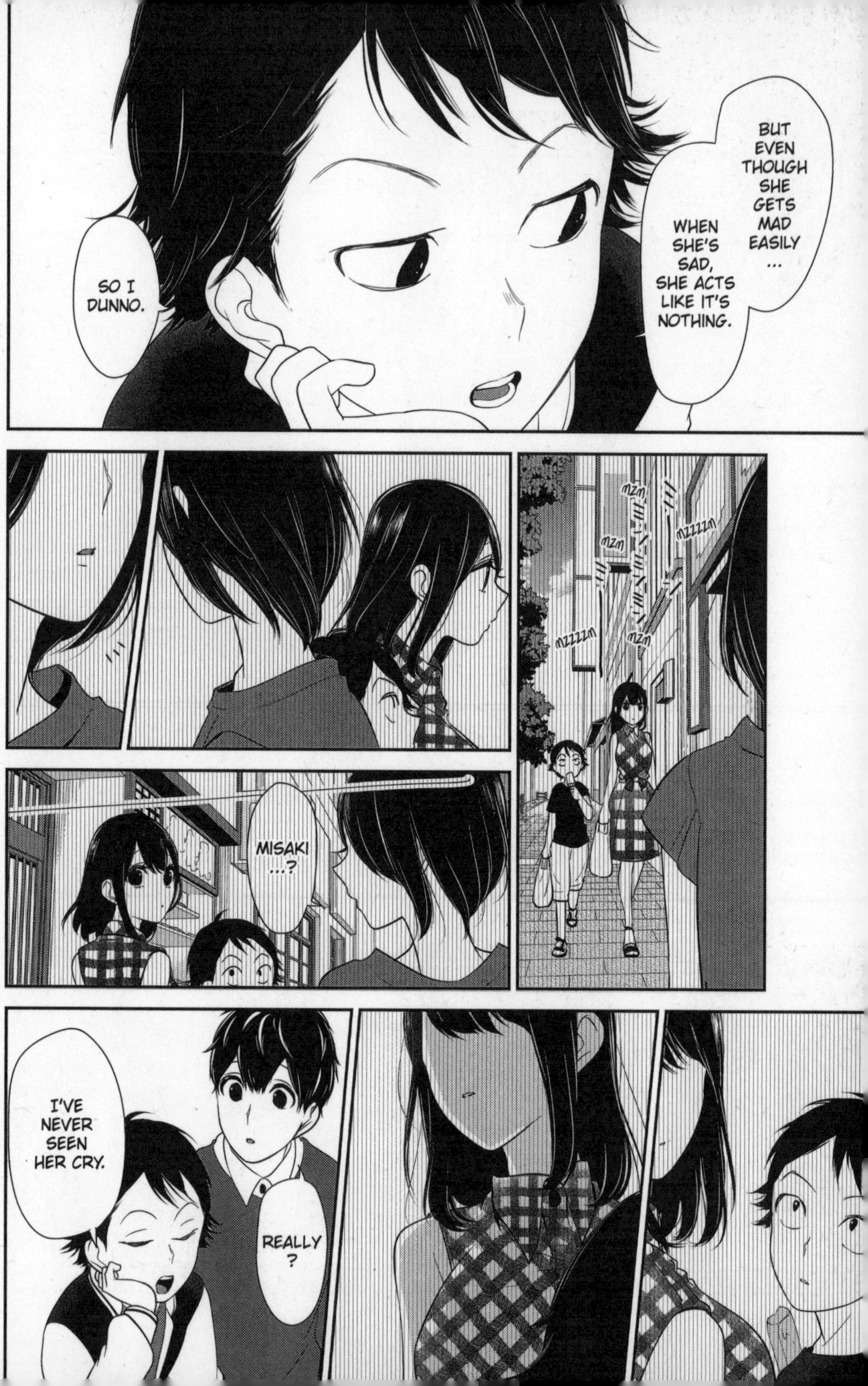
BUT EVEN THOUGH SHE GETS MAD EASILY ...
WHEN SHE'S SAD, SHE ACTS LIKE IT'S NOTHING.
SO I DUNNO.
mzm
mzzzm
mzm
mzzzm
mzm
MISAKI ...?
I'VE NEVER SEEN HER CRY.
REALLY?

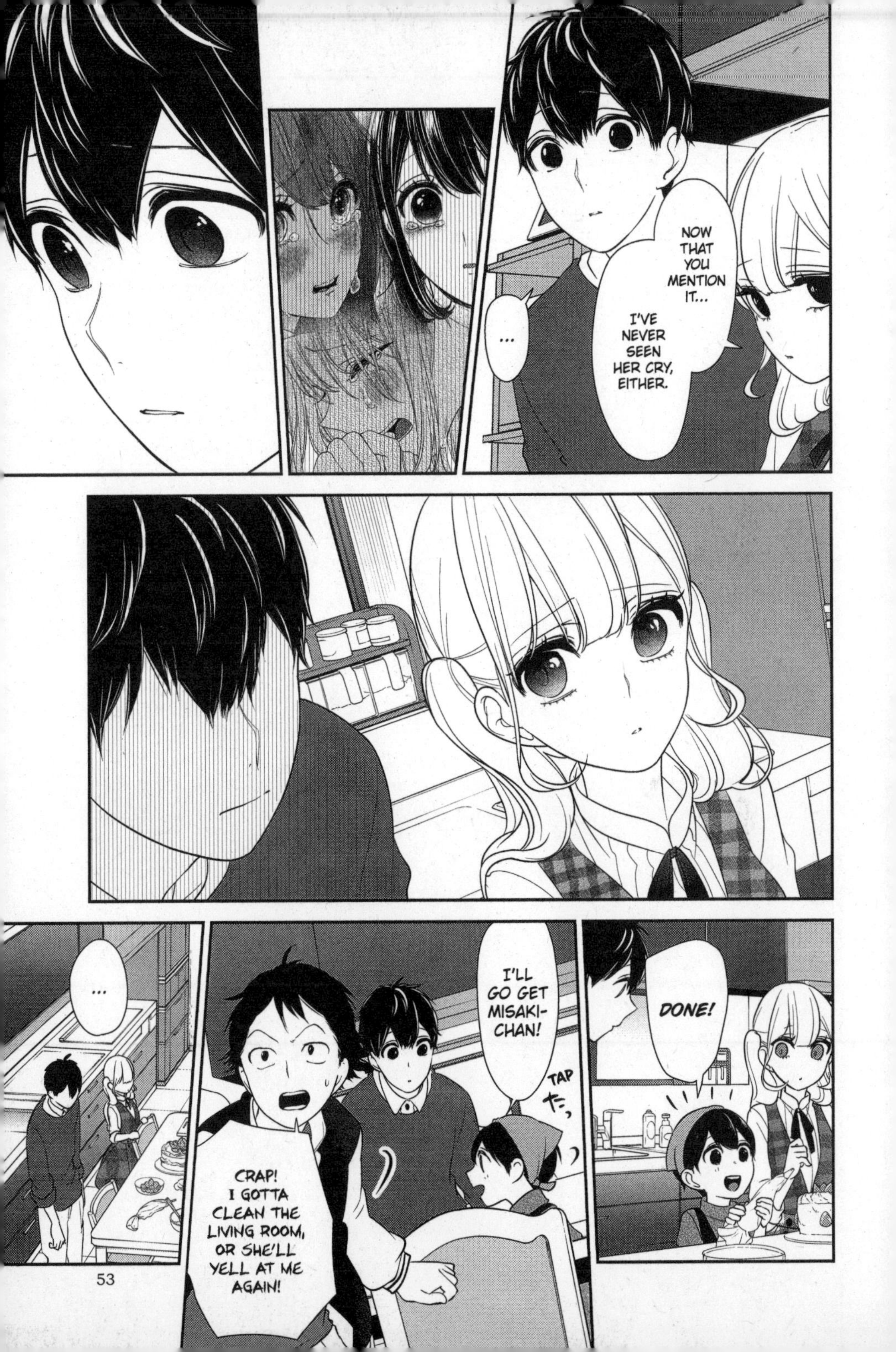
NOW THAT YOU MENTION IT...
I'VE NEVER SEEN HER CRY, EITHER.
...
DONE!
I'LL GO GET MISAKI-CHAN!
TAP
CRAP! I GOTTA CLEAN THE LIVING ROOM, OR SHE'LL YELL AT ME AGAIN!
...

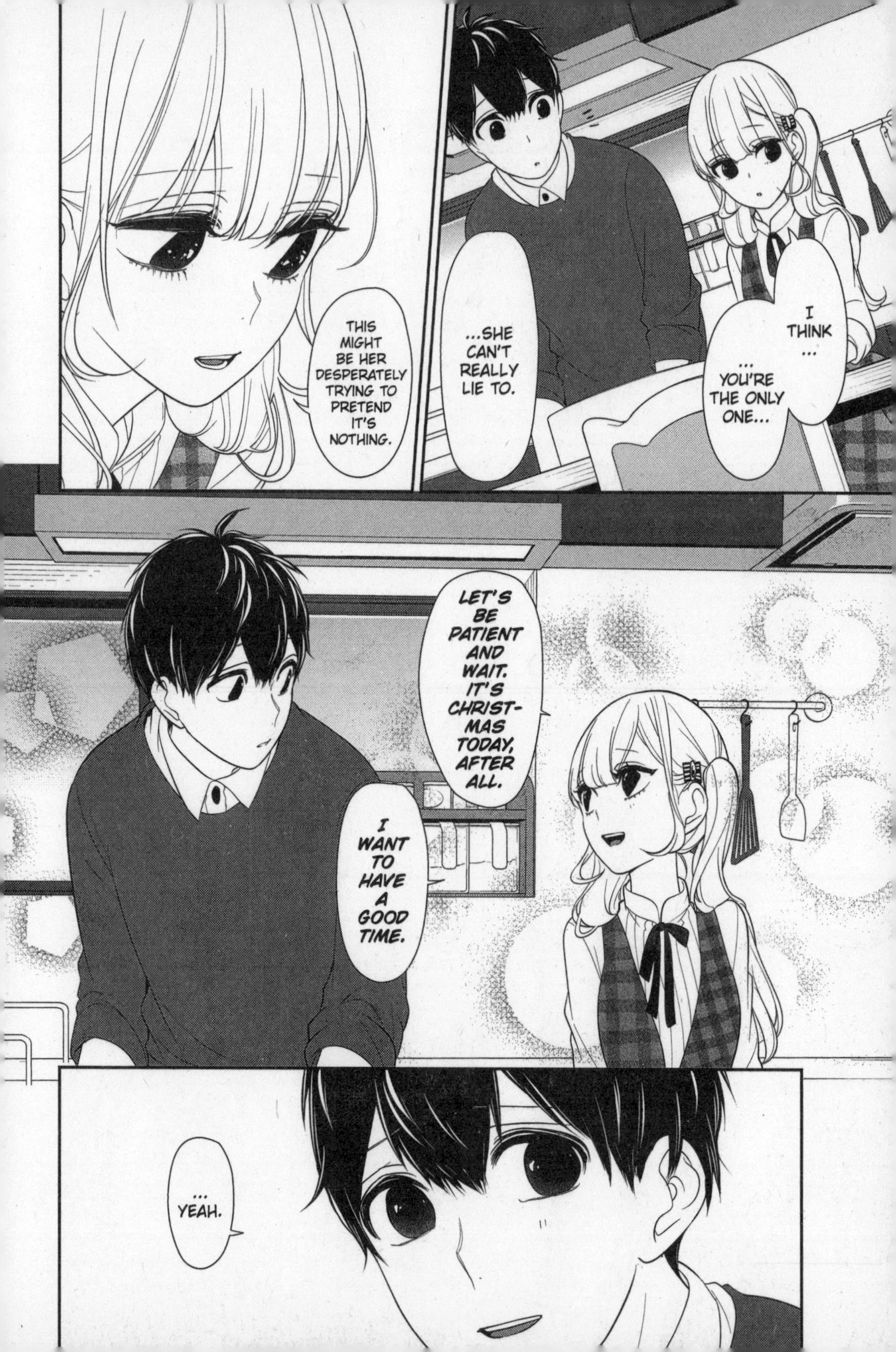
I THINK ... ... YOU'RE THE ONLY ONE...
...SHE CAN'T REALLY LIE TO.
THIS MIGHT BE HER DESPERATELY TRYING TO PRETEND IT'S NOTHING.
LET'S BE PATIENT AND WAIT. IT'S CHRIST-MAS TODAY, AFTER ALL.
I WANT TO HAVE A GOOD TIME.
... YEAH.

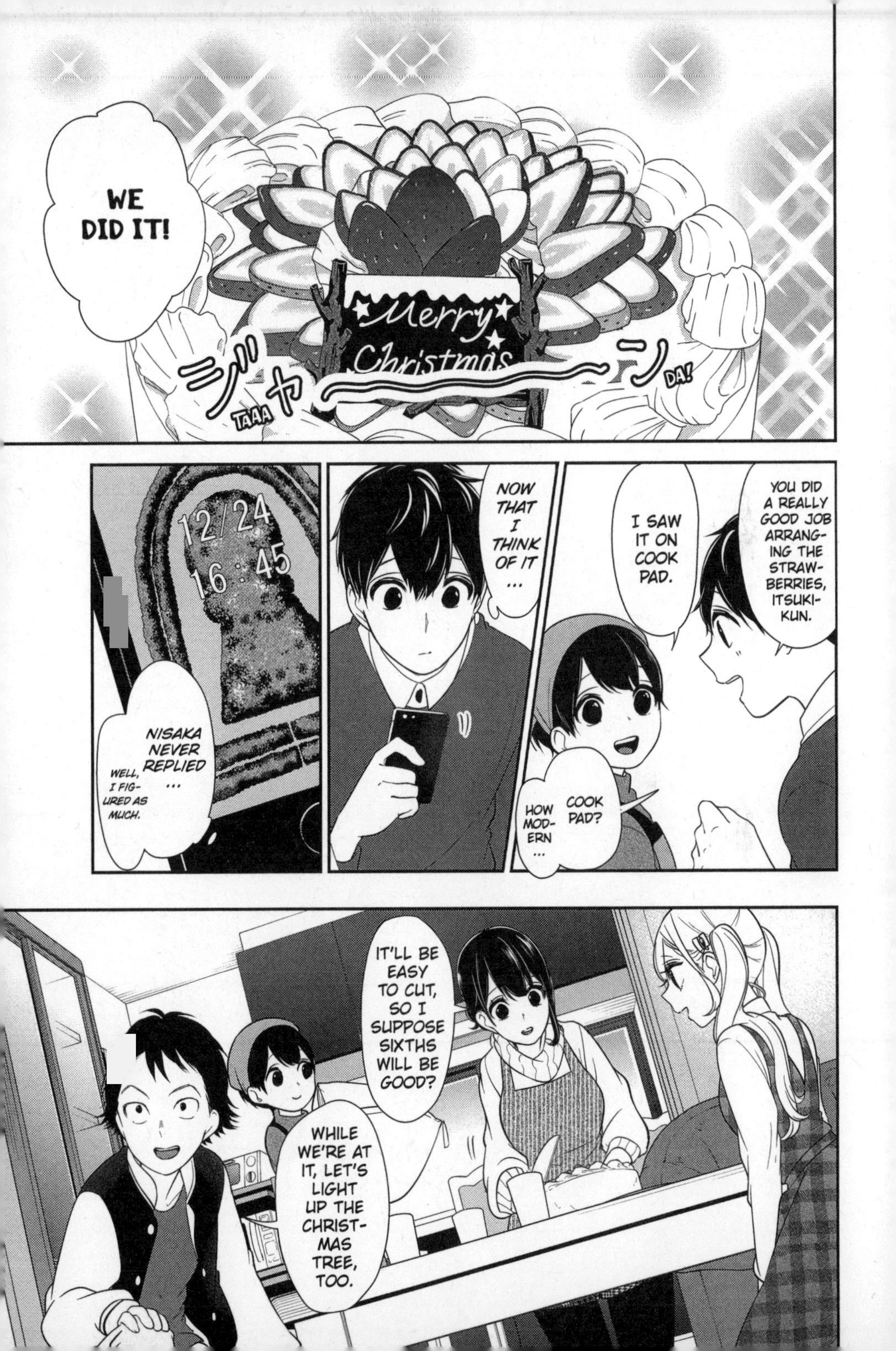
WE DID IT!
Merry Christmas
ジャーン
TAAA
DA!
YOU DID A REALLY GOOD JOB ARRANGING THE STRAWBERRIES, ITSUKI-KUN.
I SAW IT ON COOK PAD.
COOK PAD?
HOW MODERN...
NOW THAT I THINK OF IT...
12/24 16:45
NISAKA NEVER REPLIED...
WELL, I FIGURED AS MUCH.
IT'LL BE EASY TO CUT, SO I SUPPOSE SIXTHS WILL BE GOOD?
WHILE WE'RE AT IT, LET'S LIGHT UP THE CHRISTMAS TREE, TOO.

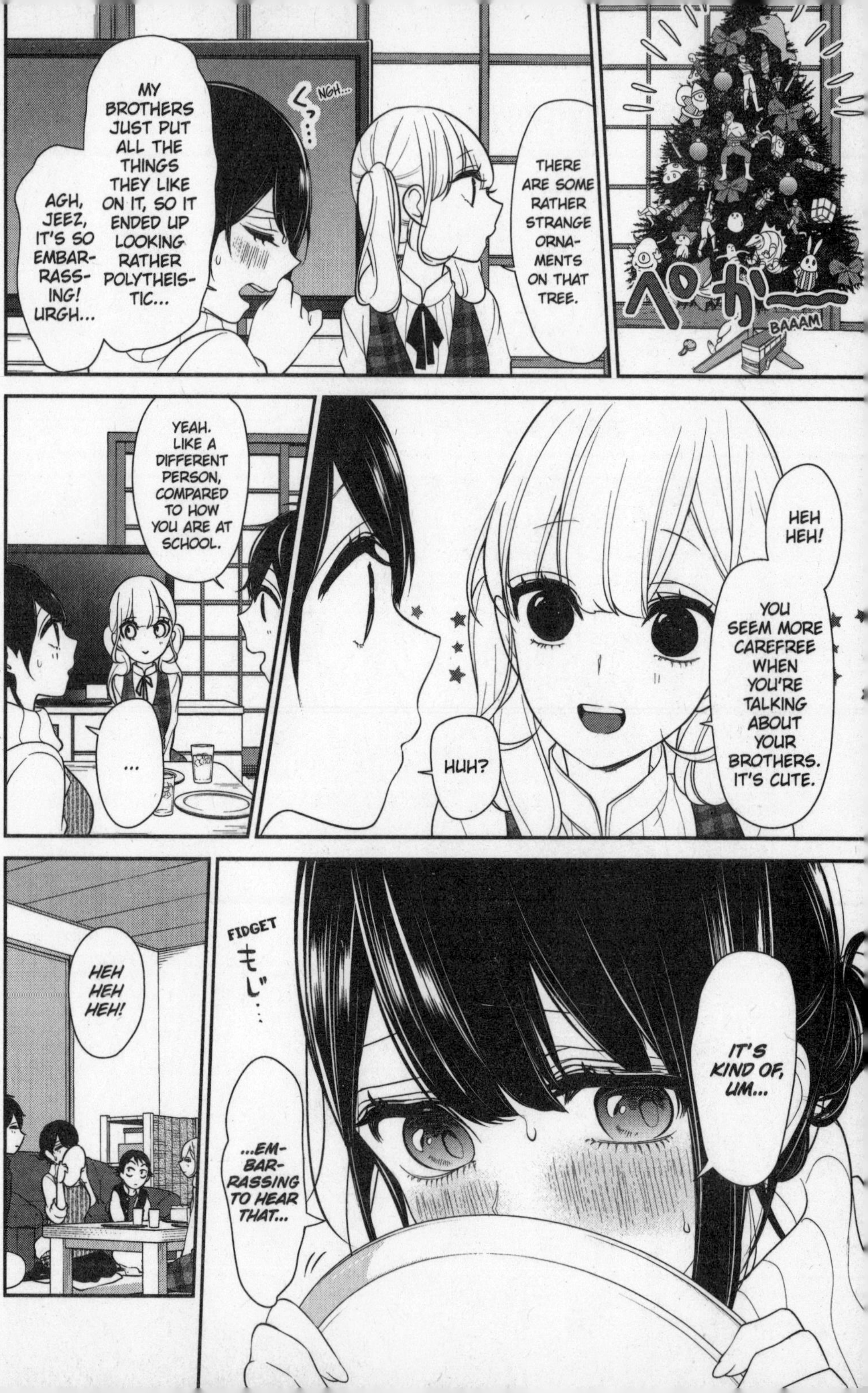
ぺかー
BAAAM
THERE ARE SOME RATHER STRANGE ORNAMENTS ON THAT TREE.
くっ…
NGH...
MY BROTHERS JUST PUT ALL THE THINGS THEY LIKE ON IT, SO IT ENDED UP LOOKING RATHER POLYTHEISTIC...
AGH, JEEZ, IT'S SO EMBARRASSING! URGH...
HEH HEH!
YOU SEEM MORE CAREFREE WHEN YOU'RE TALKING ABOUT YOUR BROTHERS. IT'S CUTE.
HUH?
YEAH. LIKE A DIFFERENT PERSON, COMPARED TO HOW YOU ARE AT SCHOOL.
...
IT'S KIND OF, UM...
...EMBARRASSING TO HEAR THAT...
FIDGET
もじ…
HEH HEH HEH!

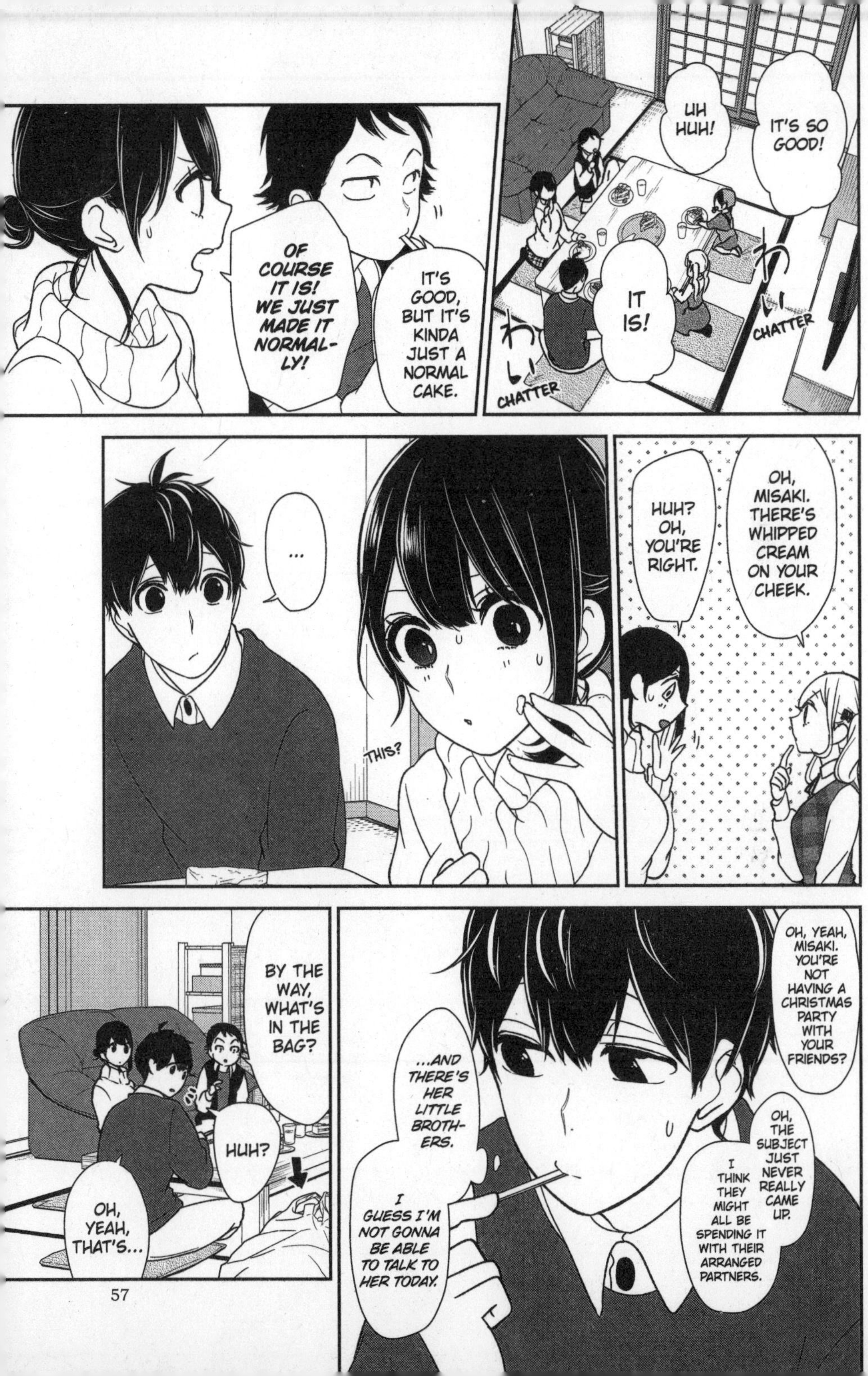
IT'S SO GOOD!
UH HUH!
IT IS!
CHATTER
CHATTER
IT'S GOOD, BUT IT'S KINDA JUST A NORMAL CAKE.
OF COURSE IT IS! WE JUST MADE IT NORMAL-LY!
OH, MISAKI. THERE'S WHIPPED CREAM ON YOUR CHEEK.
HUH? OH, YOU'RE RIGHT.
THIS?
...
OH, YEAH, MISAKI. YOU'RE NOT HAVING A CHRISTMAS PARTY WITH YOUR FRIENDS?
OH, THE SUBJECT JUST NEVER REALLY CAME UP.
I THINK THEY MIGHT ALL BE SPENDING IT WITH THEIR ARRANGED PARTNERS.
...AND THERE'S HER LITTLE BROTH-ERS.
I GUESS I'M NOT GONNA BE ABLE TO TALK TO HER TODAY.
BY THE WAY, WHAT'S IN THE BAG?
HUH?
OH, YEAH, THAT'S...

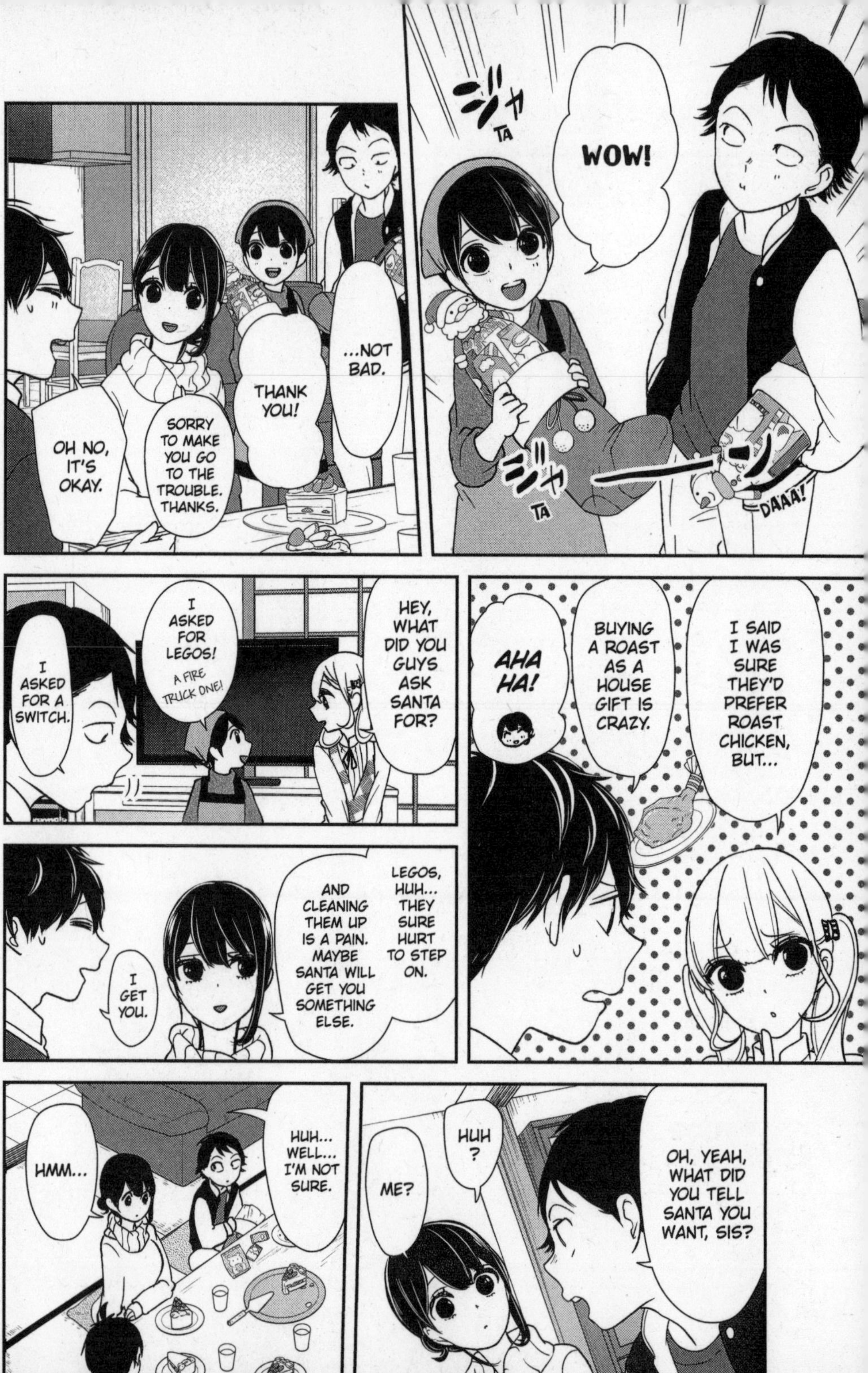
WOW!
TA
TA
DAAA!
...NOT BAD.
THANK YOU!
SORRY TO MAKE YOU GO TO THE TROUBLE. THANKS.
OH NO, IT'S OKAY.
I SAID I WAS SURE THEY'D PREFER ROAST CHICKEN, BUT...
BUYING A ROAST AS A HOUSE GIFT IS CRAZY.
AHA HA!
HEY, WHAT DID YOU GUYS ASK SANTA FOR?
I ASKED FOR LEGOS!
A FIRE TRUCK ONE!
I ASKED FOR A SWITCH.
LEGOS, HUH... THEY SURE HURT TO STEP ON.
AND CLEANING THEM UP IS A PAIN. MAYBE SANTA WILL GET YOU SOMETHING ELSE.
I GET YOU.
OH, YEAH, WHAT DID YOU TELL SANTA YOU WANT, SIS?
HUH?
ME?
HUH... WELL... I'M NOT SURE.
HMM...

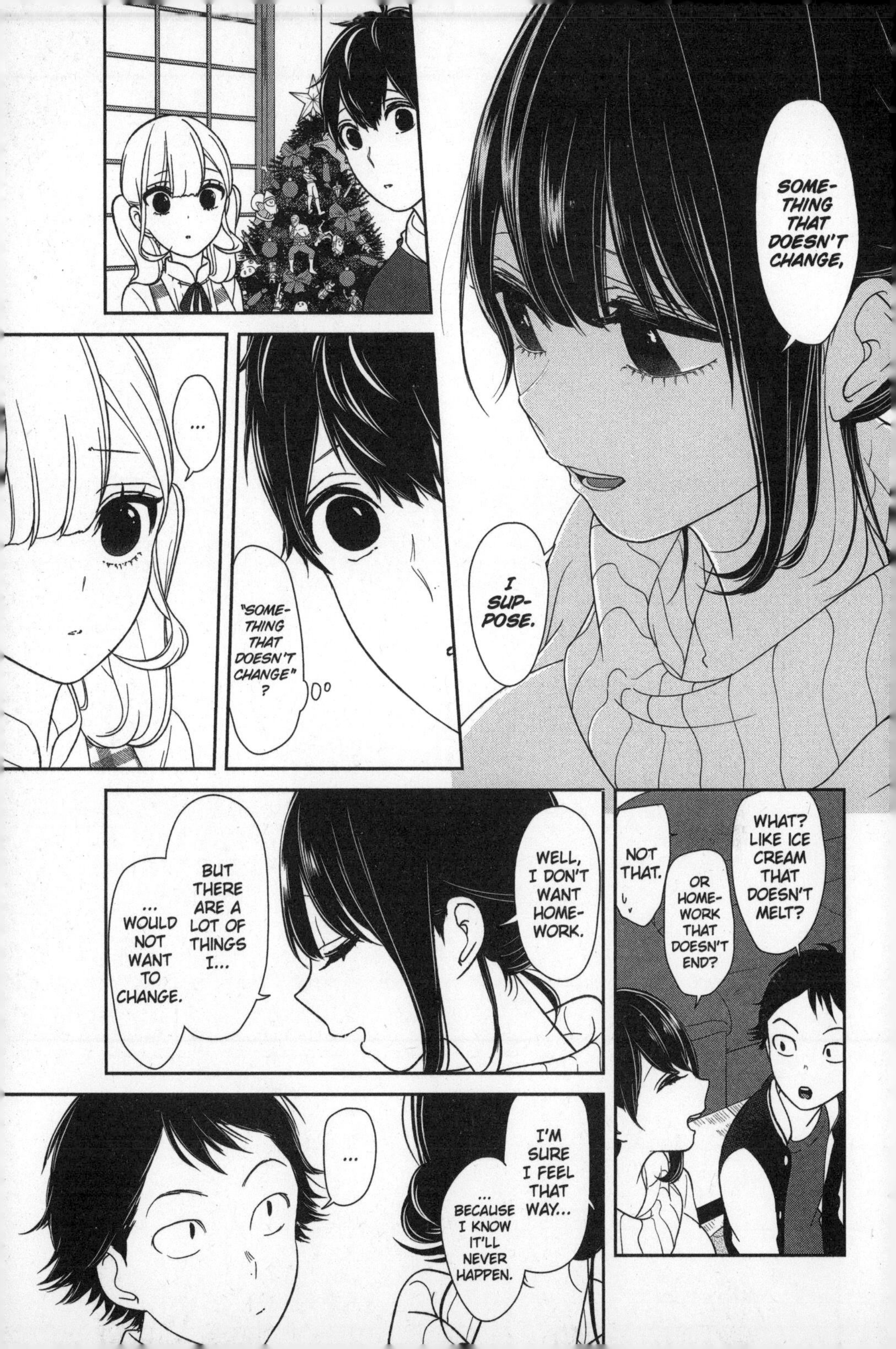
SOME-THING THAT DOESN'T CHANGE,
I SUP-POSE.
"SOME-THING THAT DOESN'T CHANGE"?
...
WHAT? LIKE ICE CREAM THAT DOESN'T MELT?
OR HOME-WORK THAT DOESN'T END?
NOT THAT.
WELL, I DON'T WANT HOME-WORK.
BUT THERE ARE A LOT OF THINGS I...
...WOULD NOT WANT TO CHANGE.
I'M SURE I FEEL THAT WAY...
...BECAUSE I KNOW IT'LL NEVER HAPPEN.
...

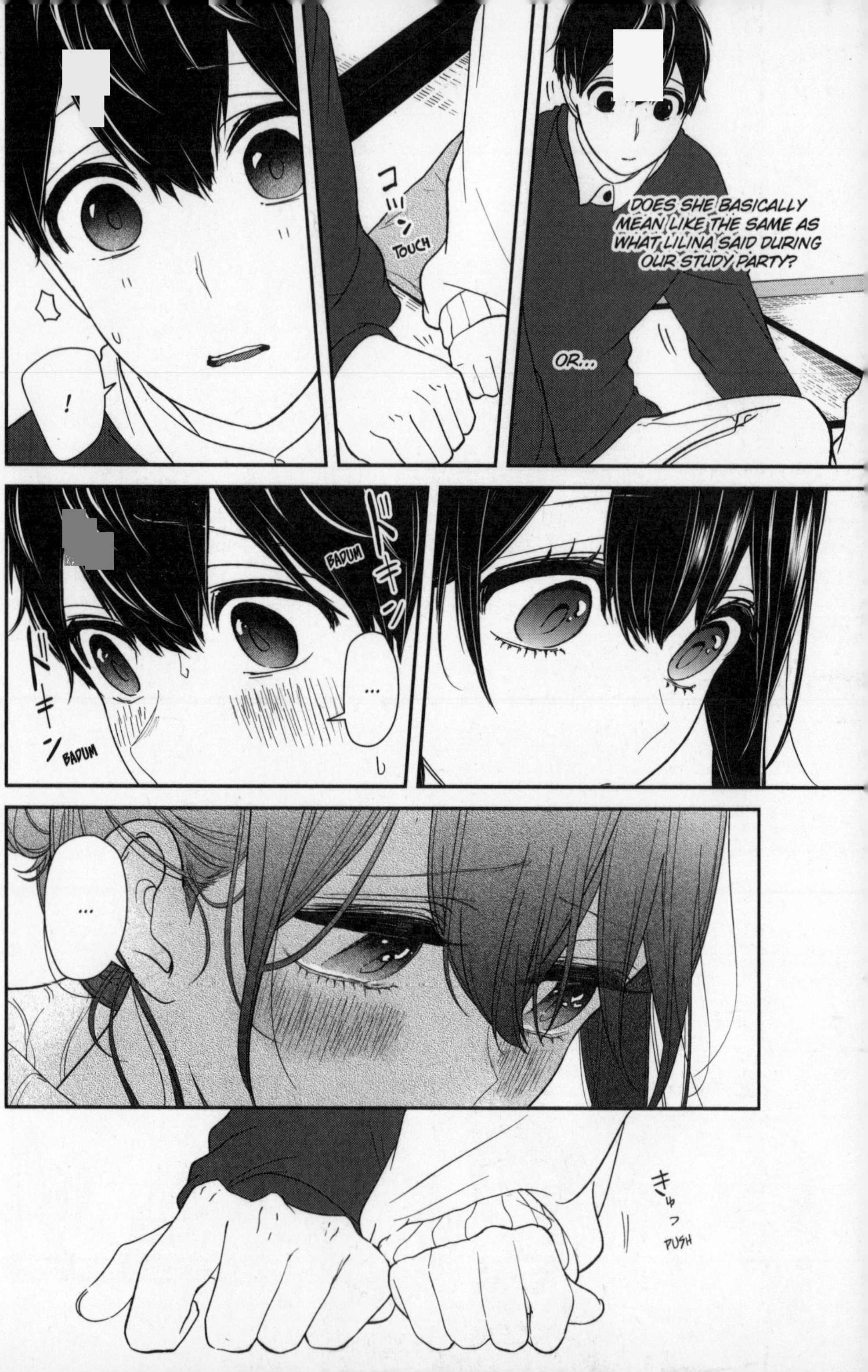
DOES SHE BASICALLY MEAN LIKE THE SAME AS WHAT LILINA SAID DURING OUR STUDY PARTY?
OR...
コツン
TOUCH
!
...
ドキン
BADUM
ドキン
BADUM
...
きゅっ
PUSH

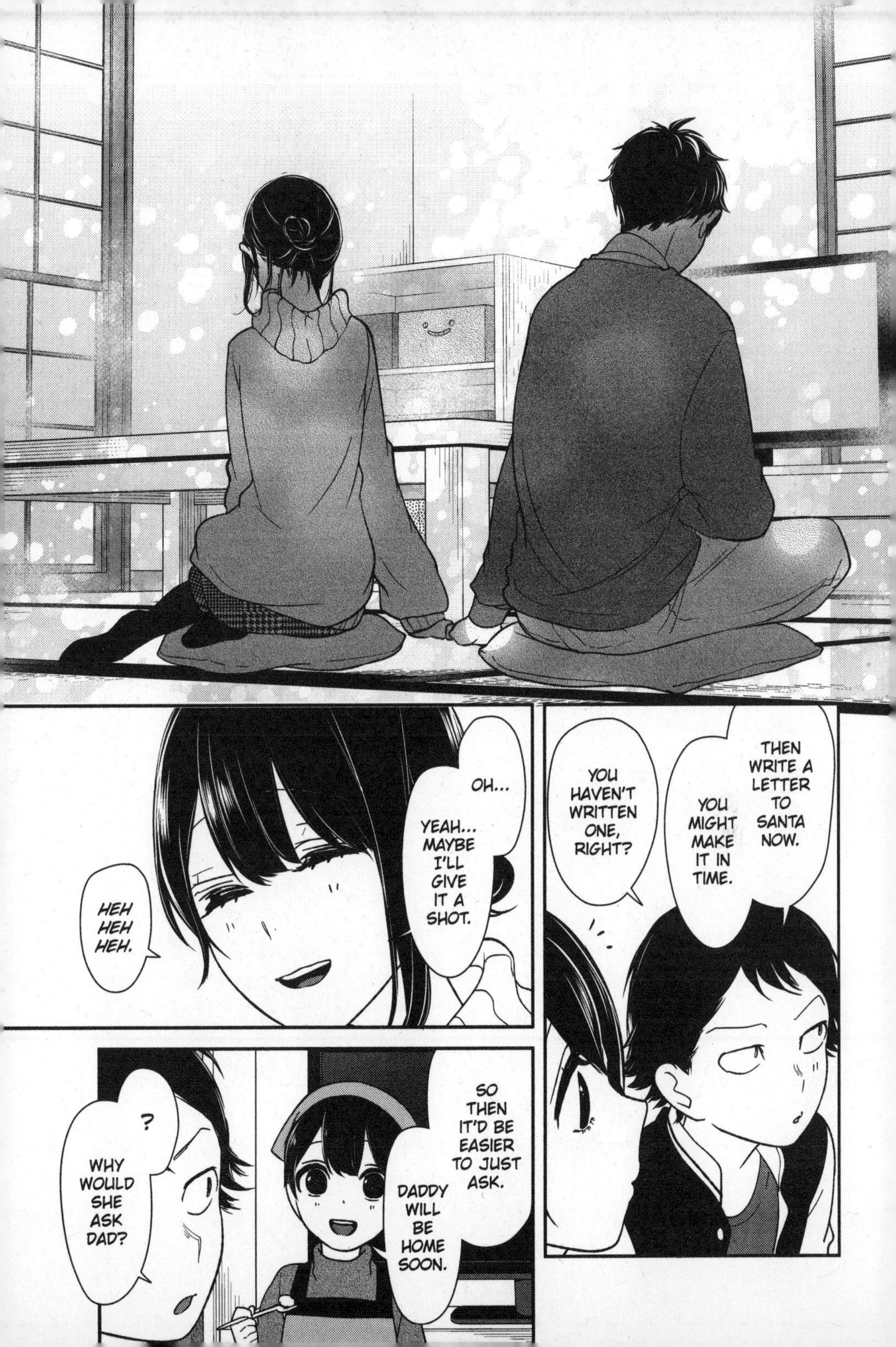
THEN WRITE A LETTER TO SANTA NOW.
YOU MIGHT MAKE IT IN TIME.
YOU HAVEN'T WRITTEN ONE, RIGHT?
OH...
YEAH... MAYBE I'LL GIVE IT A SHOT.
HEH HEH HEH.
SO THEN IT'D BE EASIER TO JUST ASK.
DADDY WILL BE HOME SOON.
?
WHY WOULD SHE ASK DAD?

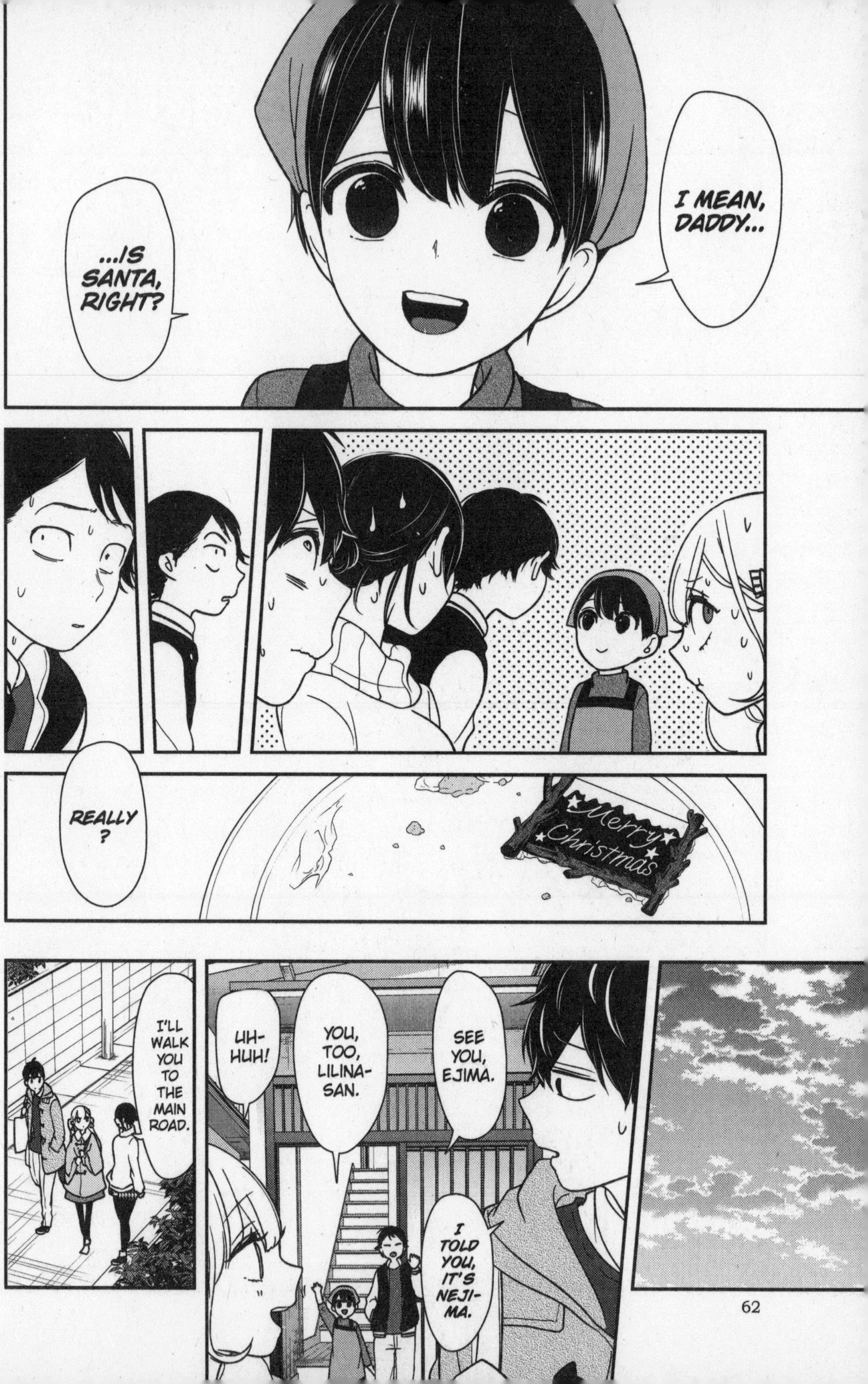
I MEAN, DADDY...
...IS SANTA, RIGHT?
REALLY?
Merry Christmas
SEE YOU, EJIMA.
I TOLD YOU, IT'S NEJIMA.
YOU, TOO, LILINA-SAN.
UH-HUH!
I'LL WALK YOU TO THE MAIN ROAD.

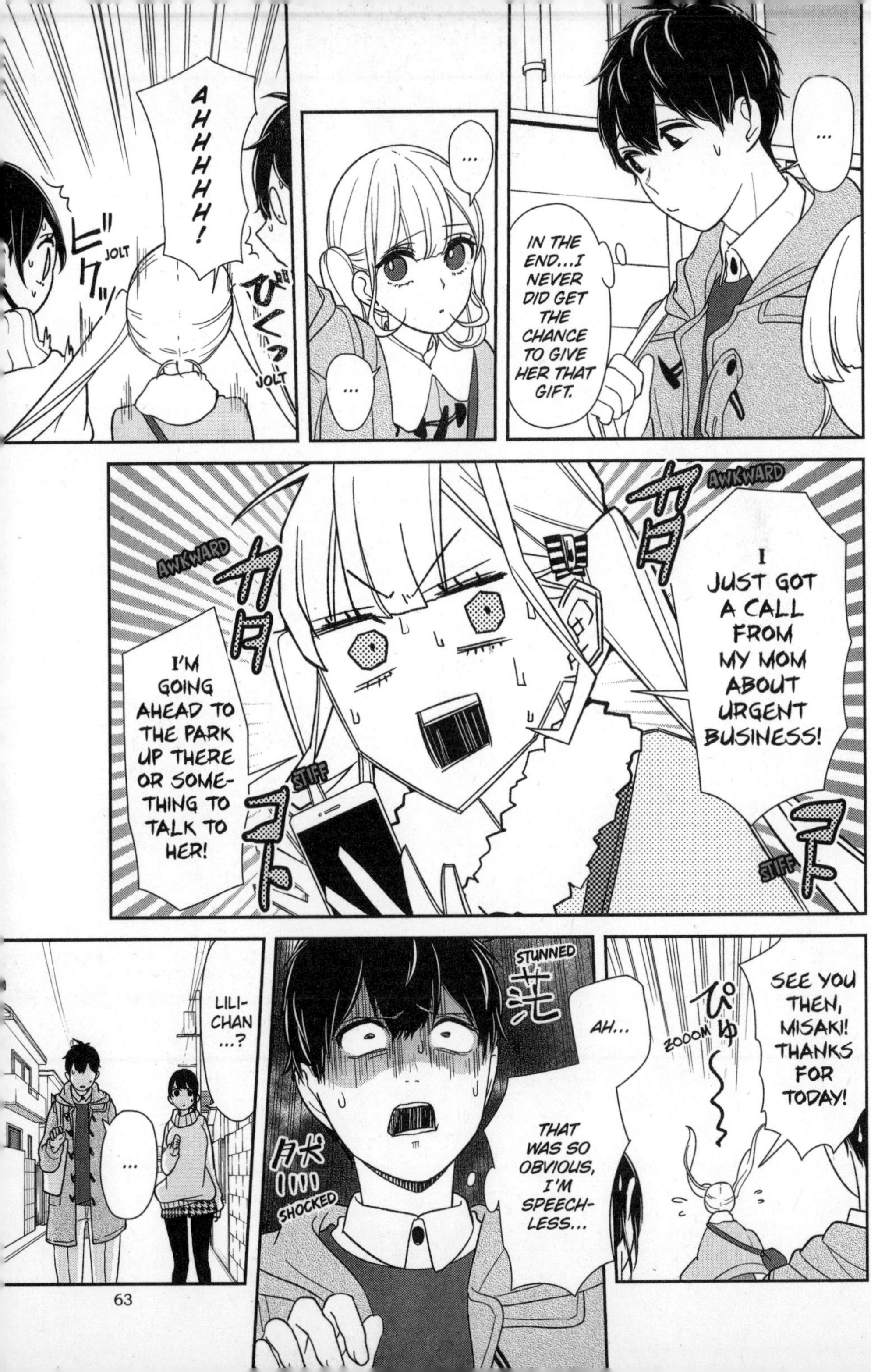
...
IN THE END...I NEVER DID GET THE CHANCE TO GIVE HER THAT GIFT.
...
...
AHHHHHH!
JOLT
JOLT
AWKWARD
I JUST GOT A CALL FROM MY MOM ABOUT URGENT BUSINESS!
STIFF
AWKWARD
I'M GOING AHEAD TO THE PARK UP THERE OR SOMETHING TO TALK TO HER!
STIFF
SEE YOU THEN, MISAKI! THANKS FOR TODAY!
ZOOOM
STUNNED
AH...
THAT WAS SO OBVIOUS, I'M SPEECHLESS...
SHOCKED
LILI-CHAN...?
...

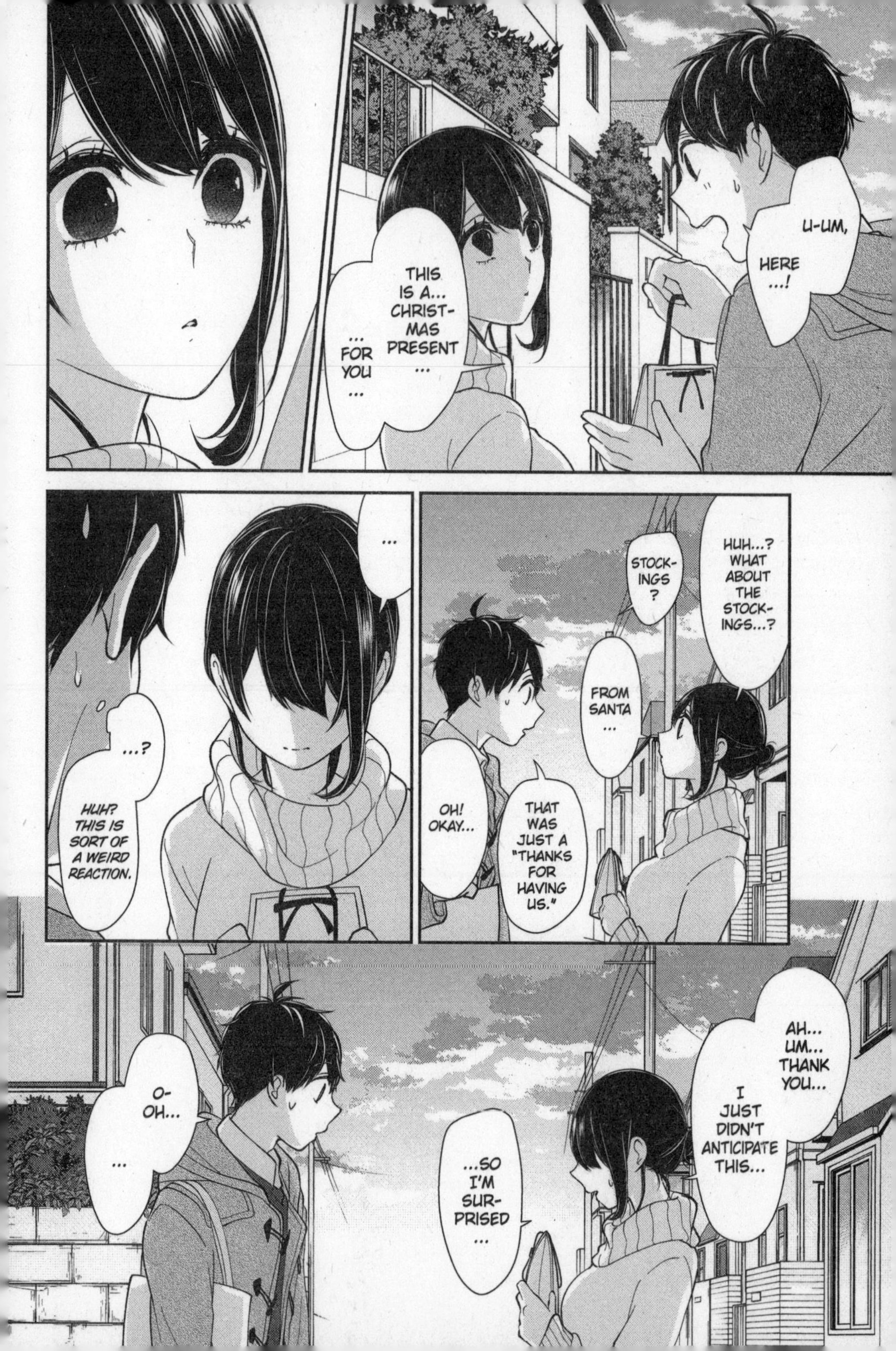
U-UM, HERE ...!
THIS IS A... CHRISTMAS PRESENT ... ... FOR YOU ...
HUH...? WHAT ABOUT THE STOCKINGS...?
STOCKINGS?
FROM SANTA ...
THAT WAS JUST A "THANKS FOR HAVING US."
OH! OKAY...
...
...?
HUH? THIS IS SORT OF A WEIRD REACTION.
AH... UM... THANK YOU... I JUST DIDN'T ANTICIPATE THIS...
...SO I'M SURPRISED ...
O-OH... ...

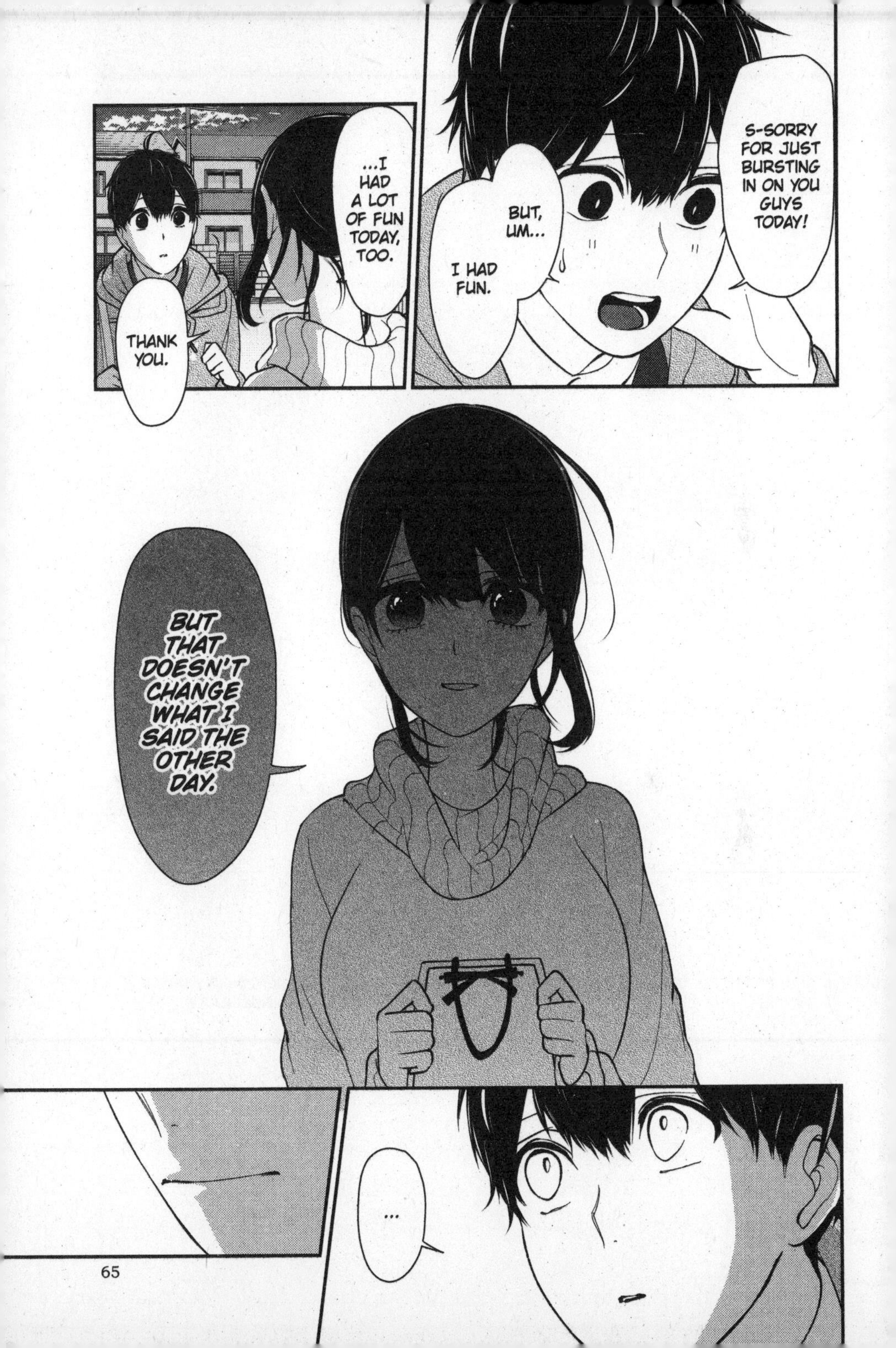
S-SORRY FOR JUST BURSTING IN ON YOU GUYS TODAY!
BUT, UM...
I HAD FUN.
...I HAD A LOT OF FUN TODAY, TOO.
THANK YOU.
BUT THAT DOESN'T CHANGE WHAT I SAID THE OTHER DAY.
...

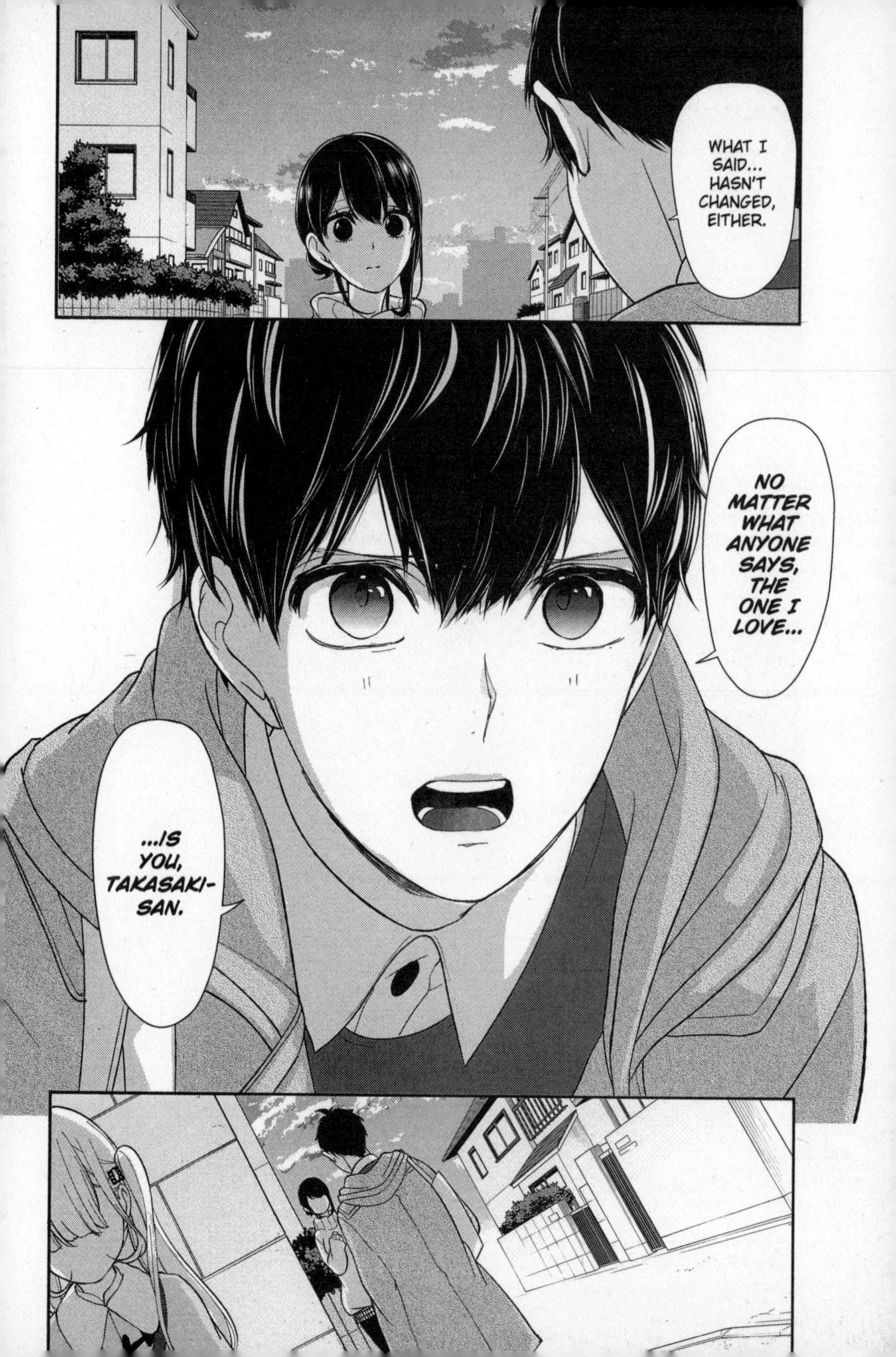
WHAT I SAID... HASN'T CHANGED, EITHER.
NO MATTER WHAT ANYONE SAYS, THE ONE I LOVE...
...IS YOU, TAKASAKI-SAN.

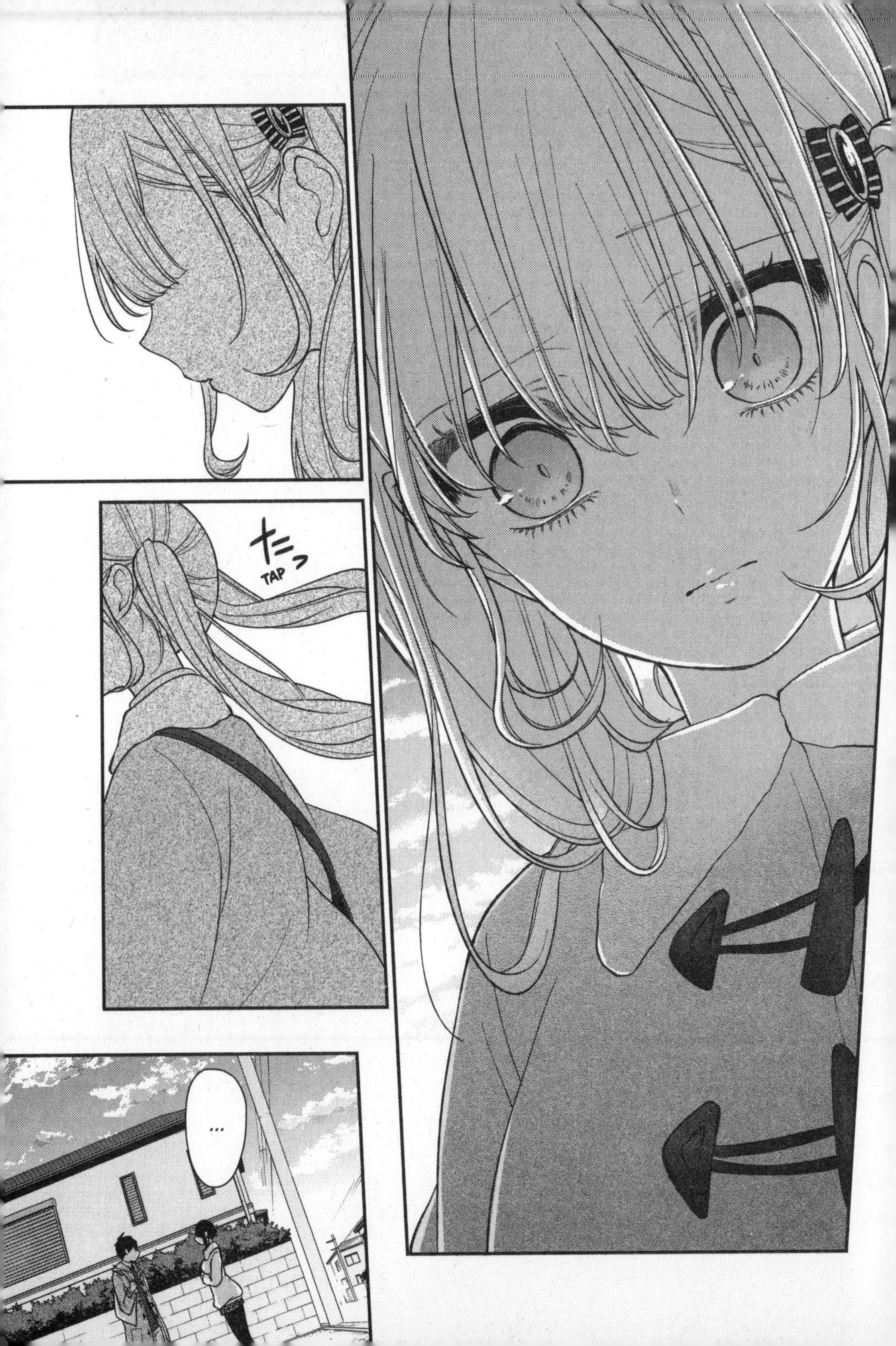
たっ
TAP
...

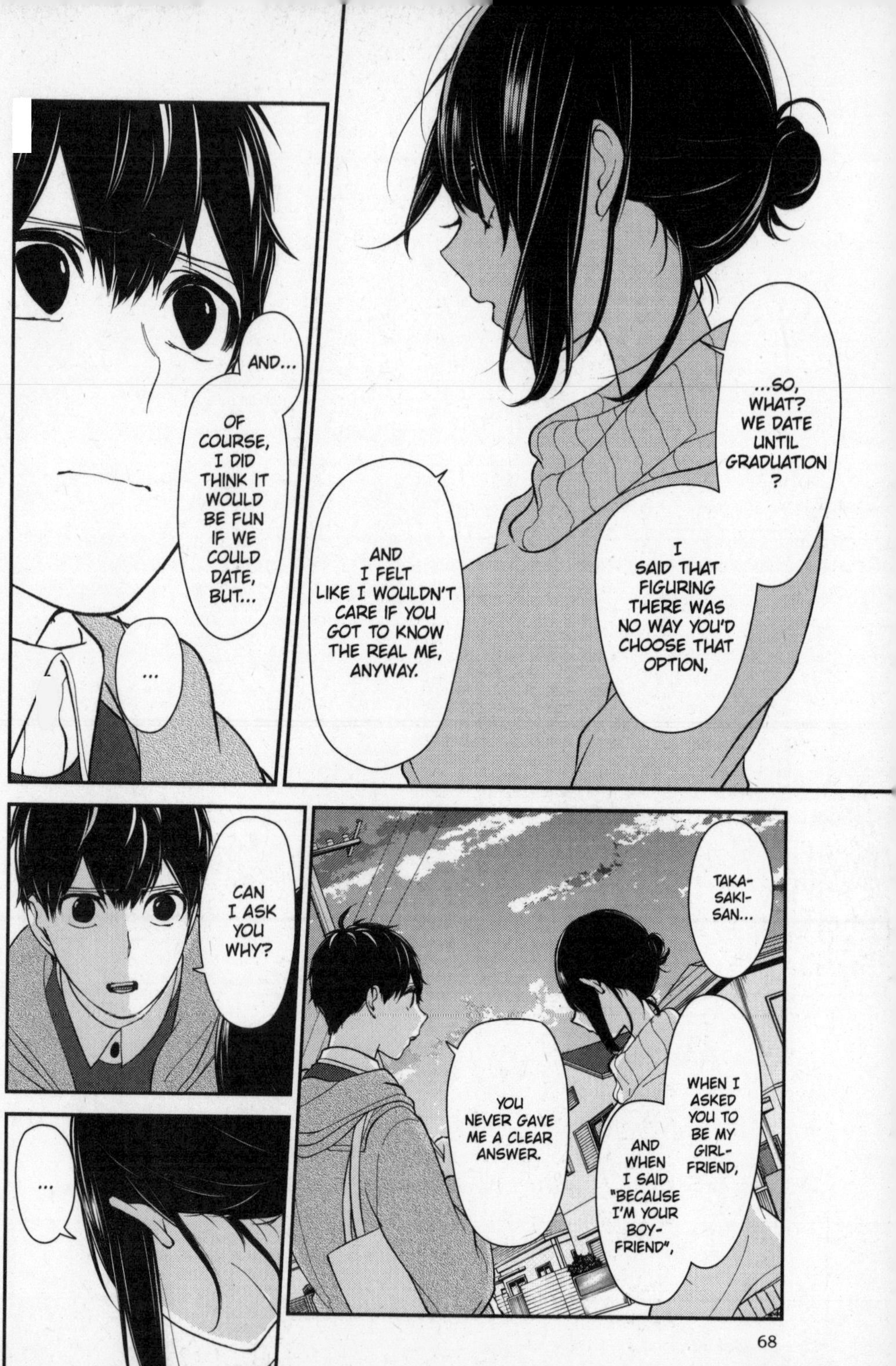
...SO, WHAT? WE DATE UNTIL GRADUATION?
I SAID THAT FIGURING THERE WAS NO WAY YOU'D CHOOSE THAT OPTION,
AND I FELT LIKE I WOULDN'T CARE IF YOU GOT TO KNOW THE REAL ME, ANYWAY.
AND...
OF COURSE, I DID THINK IT WOULD BE FUN IF WE COULD DATE, BUT...
...
TAKA-SAKI-SAN...
WHEN I ASKED YOU TO BE MY GIRL-FRIEND,
AND WHEN I SAID "BECAUSE I'M YOUR BOY-FRIEND",
YOU NEVER GAVE ME A CLEAR ANSWER.
CAN I ASK YOU WHY?
...

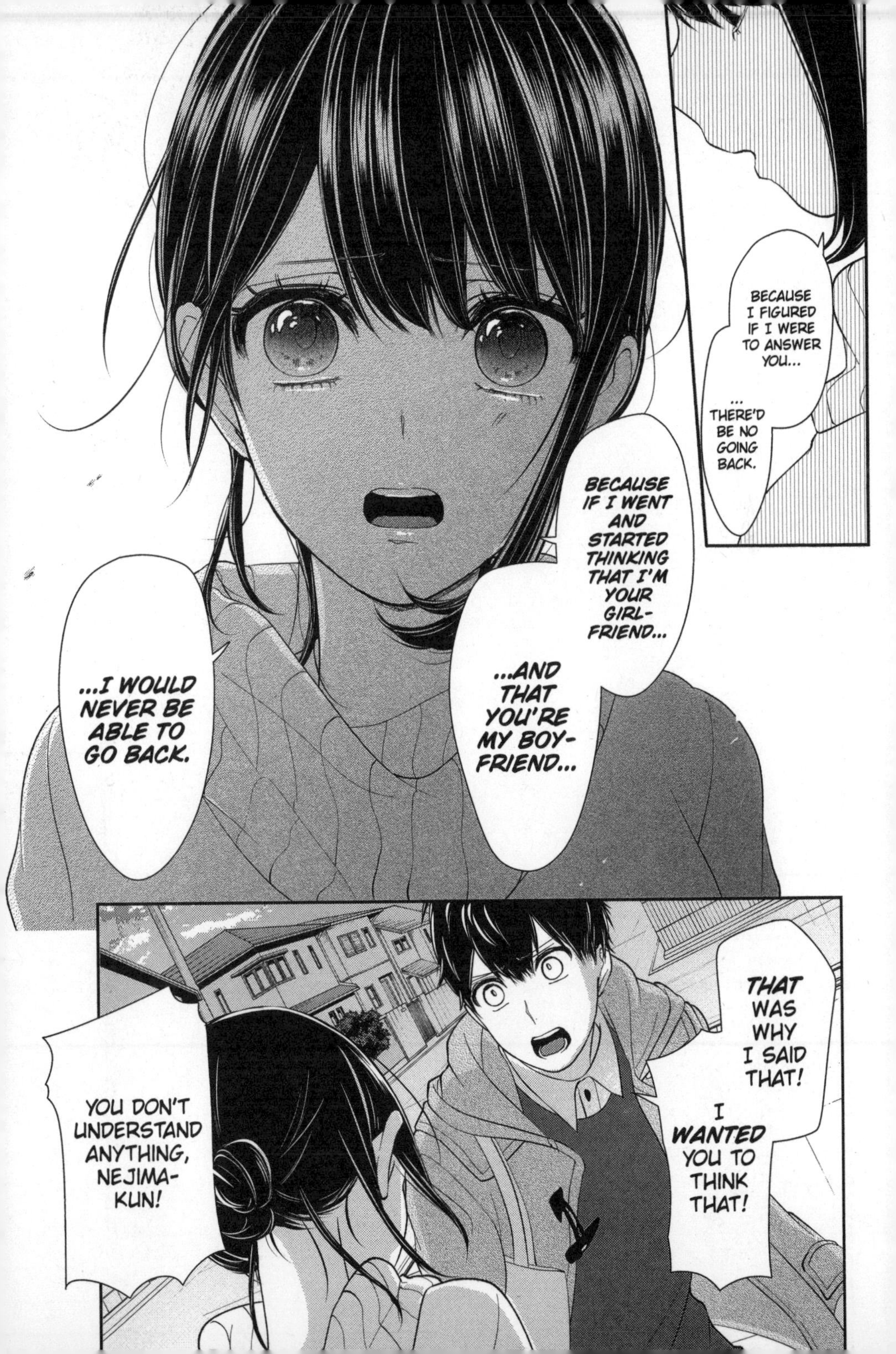
BECAUSE I FIGURED IF I WERE TO ANSWER YOU...
...THERE'D BE NO GOING BACK.
BECAUSE IF I WENT AND STARTED THINKING THAT I'M YOUR GIRLFRIEND...
...AND THAT YOU'RE MY BOYFRIEND...
...I WOULD NEVER BE ABLE TO GO BACK.
THAT WAS WHY I SAID THAT!
I WANTED YOU TO THINK THAT!
YOU DON'T UNDERSTAND ANYTHING, NEJIMA-KUN!

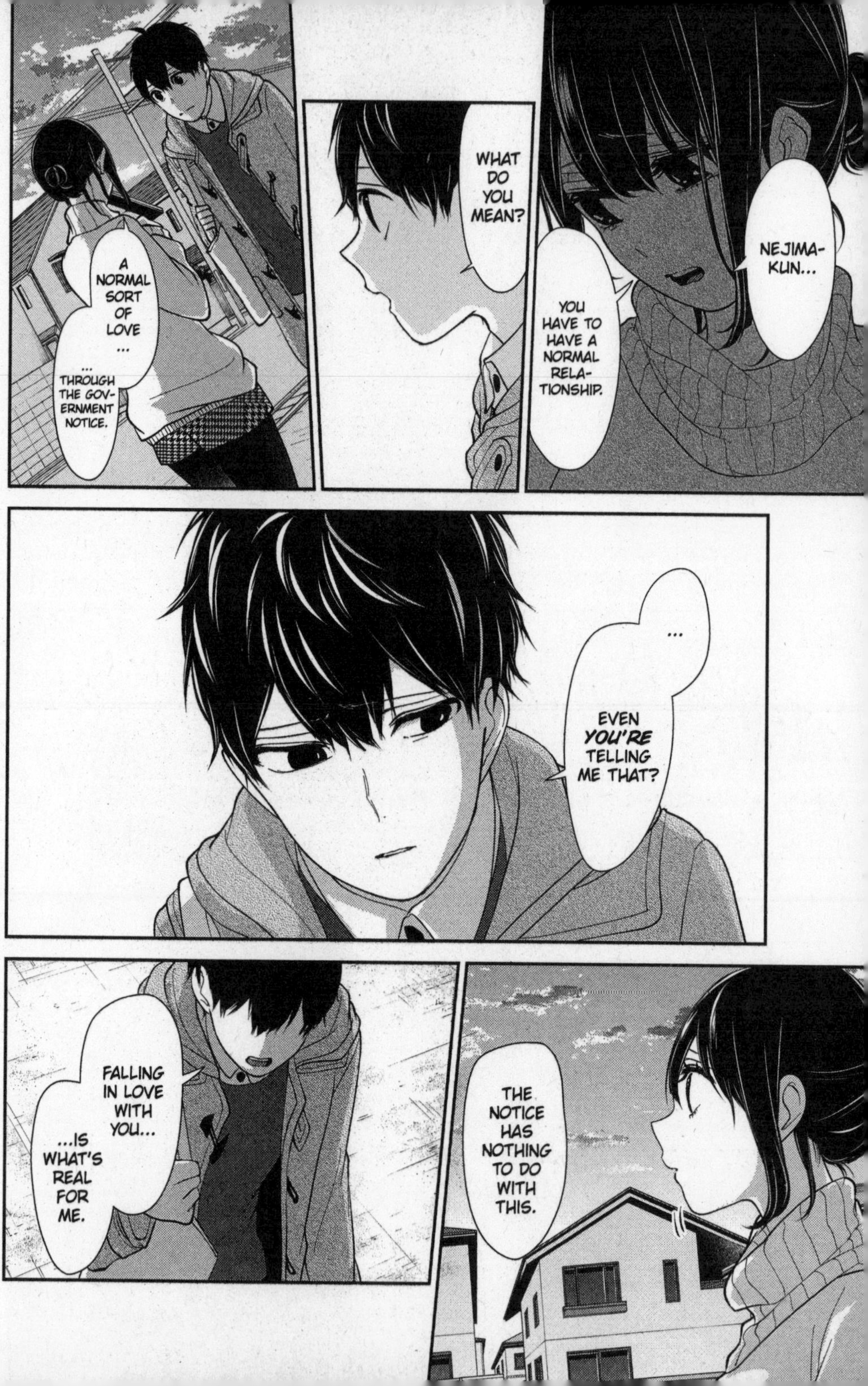
NEJIMA-KUN...
YOU HAVE TO HAVE A NORMAL RELATIONSHIP.
WHAT DO YOU MEAN?
A NORMAL SORT OF LOVE ...
... THROUGH THE GOVERNMENT NOTICE.
...
EVEN *YOU'RE* TELLING ME THAT?
THE NOTICE HAS NOTHING TO DO WITH THIS.
FALLING IN LOVE WITH YOU...
...IS WHAT'S REAL FOR ME.

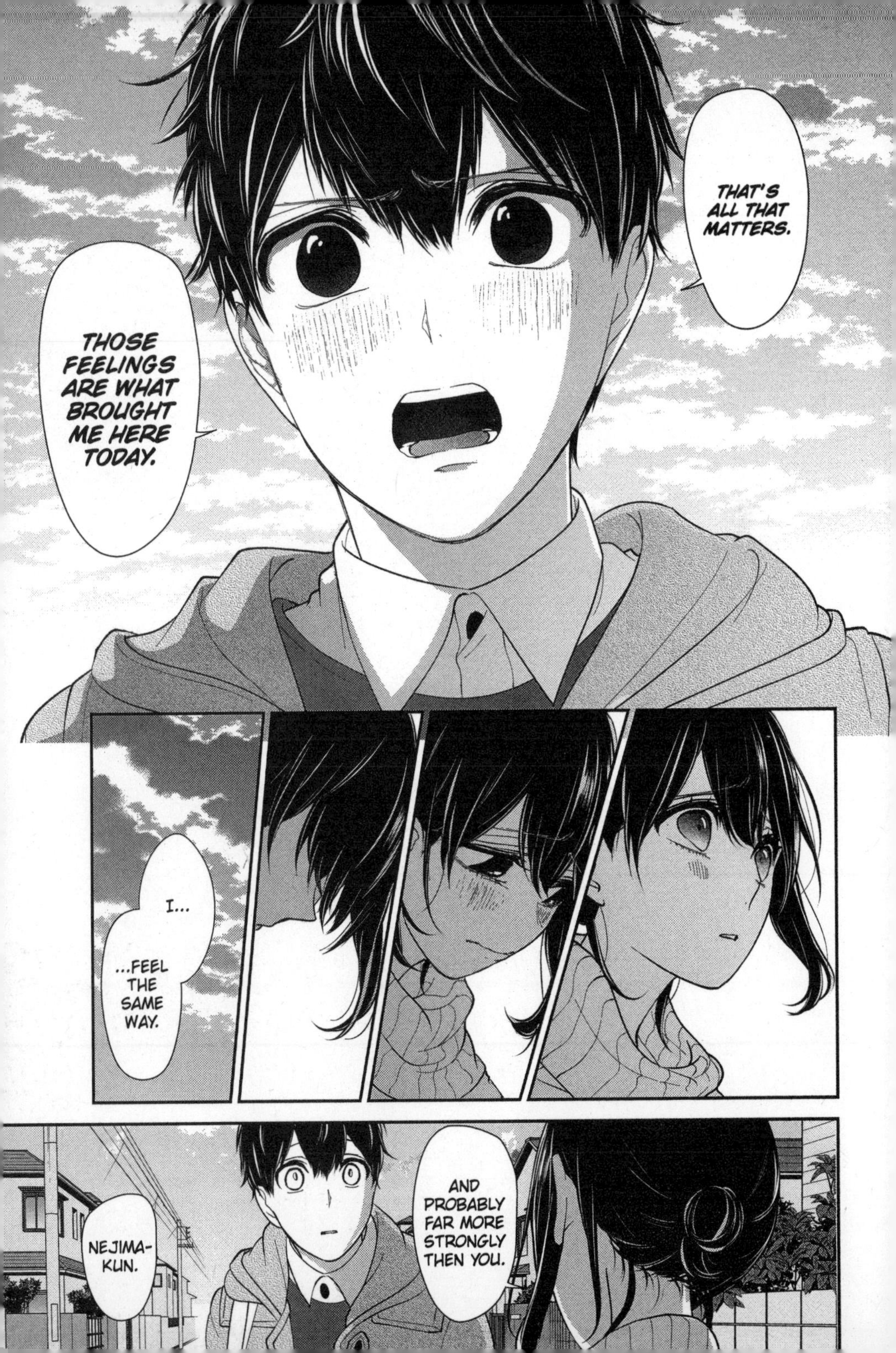
THAT'S ALL THAT MATTERS.
THOSE FEELINGS ARE WHAT BROUGHT ME HERE TODAY.
I...
...FEEL THE SAME WAY.
AND PROBABLY FAR MORE STRONGLY THEN YOU.
NEJIMA-KUN.

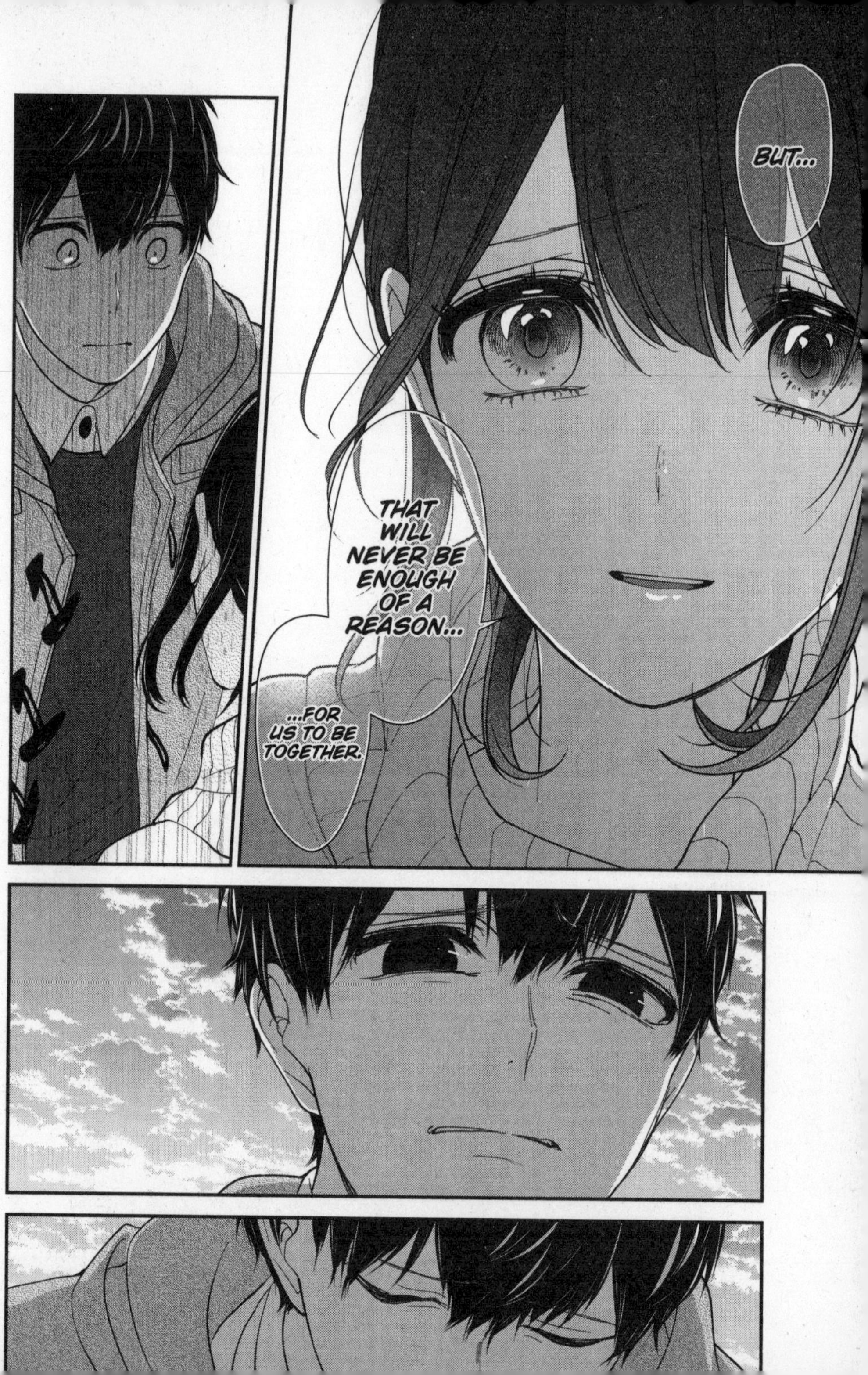
BUT...
THAT WILL NEVER BE ENOUGH OF A REASON...
...FOR US TO BE TOGETHER.

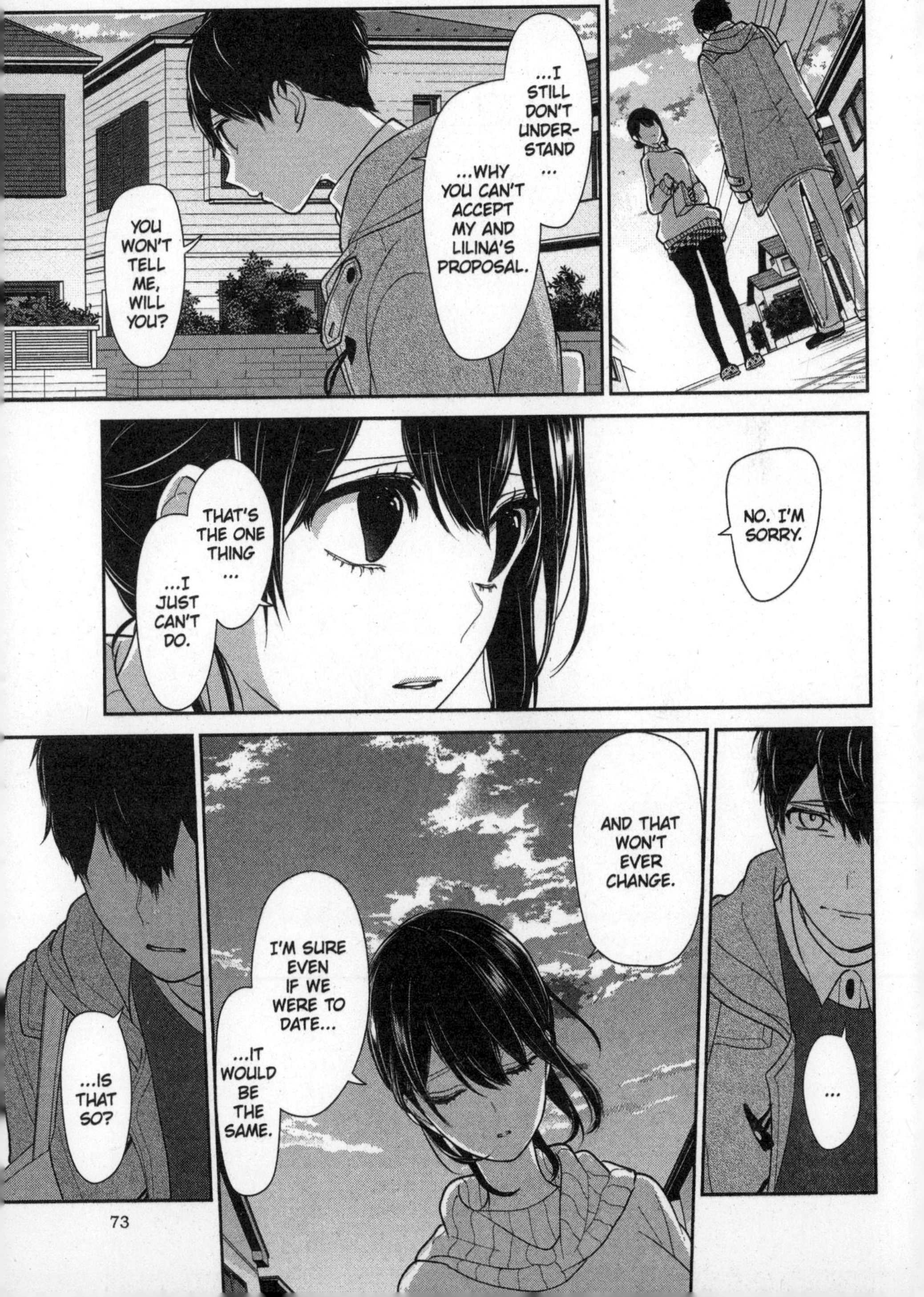
...I STILL DON'T UNDER-STAND ...
...WHY YOU CAN'T ACCEPT MY AND LILINA'S PROPOSAL.
YOU WON'T TELL ME, WILL YOU?
NO. I'M SORRY.
THAT'S THE ONE THING ...
...I JUST CAN'T DO.
...
AND THAT WON'T EVER CHANGE.
I'M SURE EVEN IF WE WERE TO DATE...
...IT WOULD BE THE SAME.
...IS THAT SO?

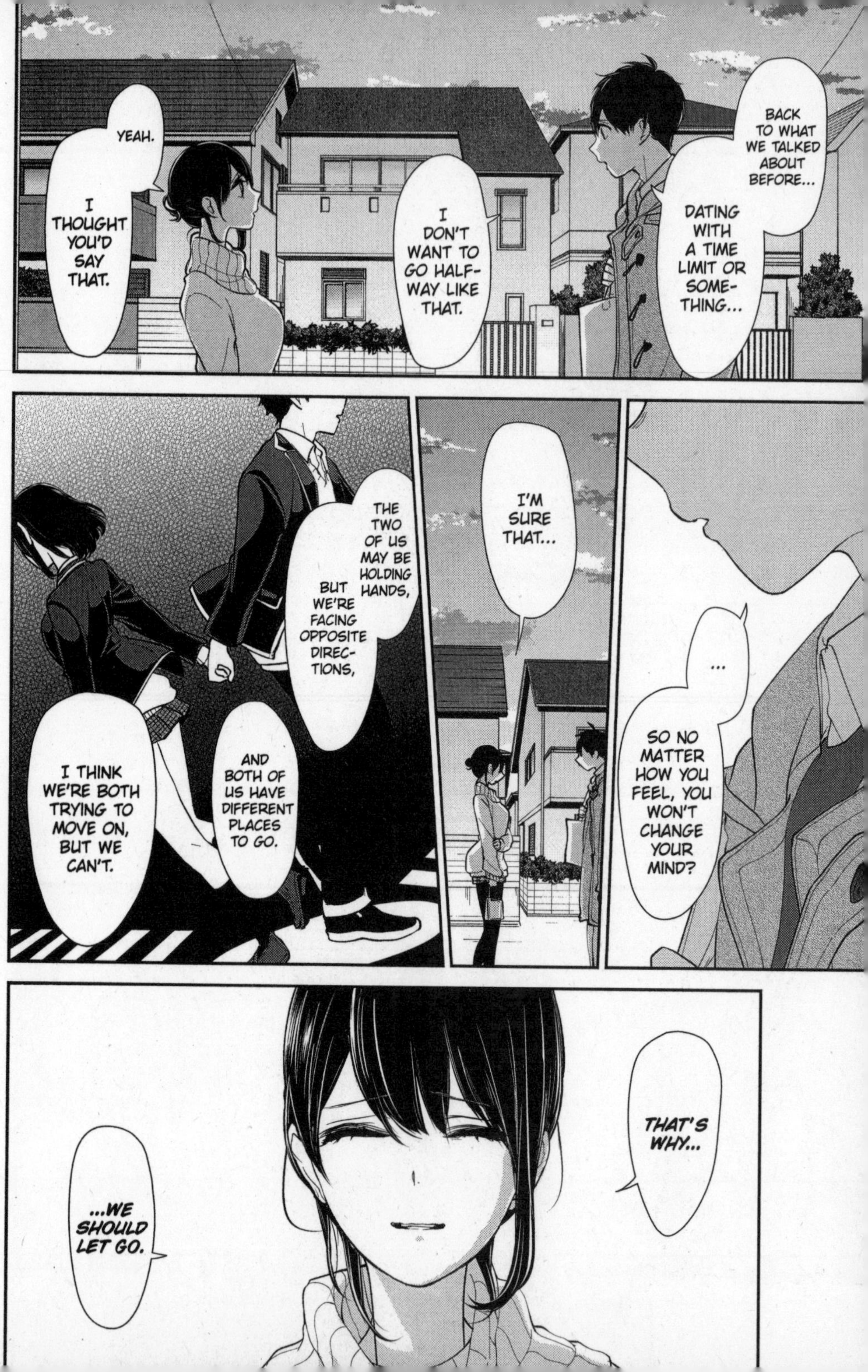
BACK TO WHAT WE TALKED ABOUT BEFORE...
DATING WITH A TIME LIMIT OR SOME-THING...
I DON'T WANT TO GO HALF-WAY LIKE THAT.
YEAH.
I THOUGHT YOU'D SAY THAT.
...
SO NO MATTER HOW YOU FEEL, YOU WON'T CHANGE YOUR MIND?
I'M SURE THAT...
THE TWO OF US MAY BE HOLDING HANDS,
BUT WE'RE FACING OPPOSITE DIREC-TIONS,
AND BOTH OF US HAVE DIFFERENT PLACES TO GO.
I THINK WE'RE BOTH TRYING TO MOVE ON, BUT WE CAN'T.
THAT'S WHY...
...WE SHOULD LET GO.

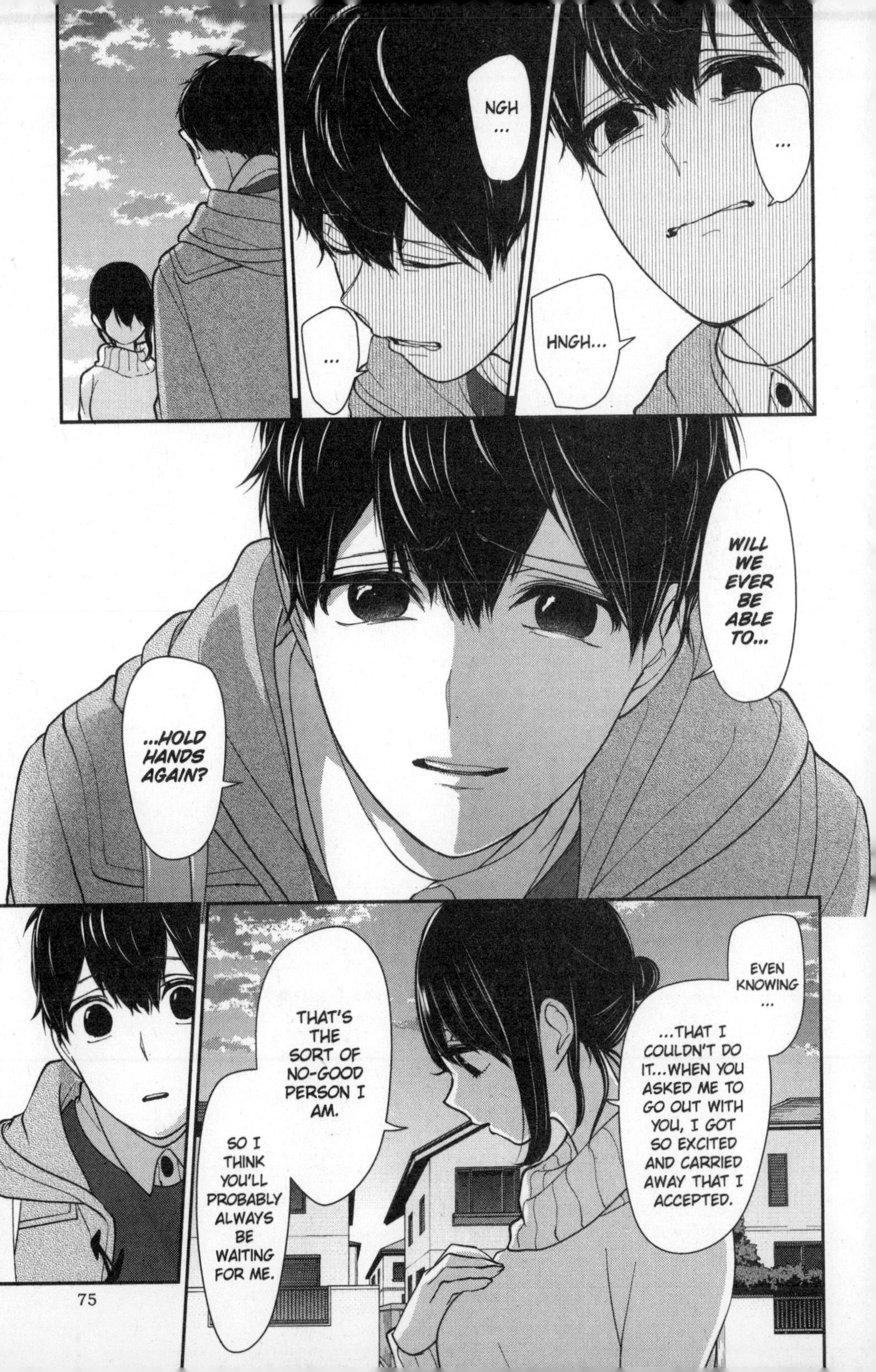
...
HNGH...
NGH...
...
WILL WE EVER BE ABLE TO...
...HOLD HANDS AGAIN?
EVEN KNOWING...
...THAT I COULDN'T DO IT...WHEN YOU ASKED ME TO GO OUT WITH YOU, I GOT SO EXCITED AND CARRIED AWAY THAT I ACCEPTED.
THAT'S THE SORT OF NO-GOOD PERSON I AM.
SO I THINK YOU'LL PROBABLY ALWAYS BE WAITING FOR ME.

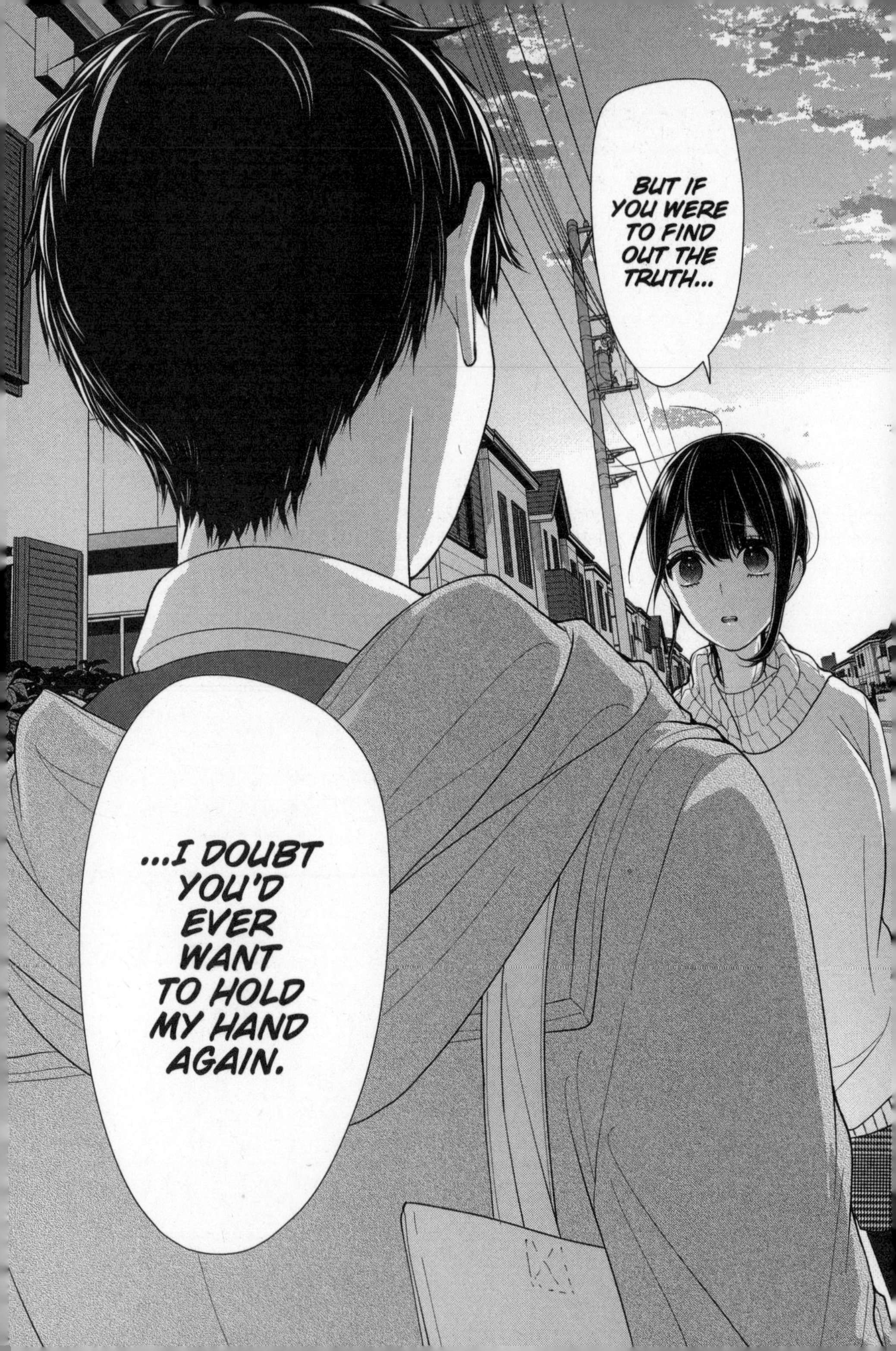
BUT IF YOU WERE TO FIND OUT THE TRUTH...
...I DOUBT YOU'D EVER WANT TO HOLD MY HAND AGAIN.

THAT'S THE SORT OF POSITION I'VE CHOSEN.

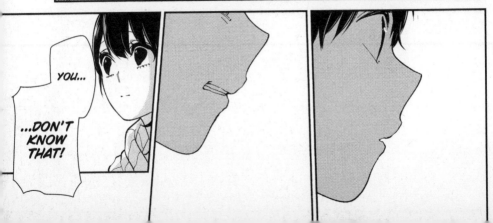

YOU...

...DON'T KNOW THAT!

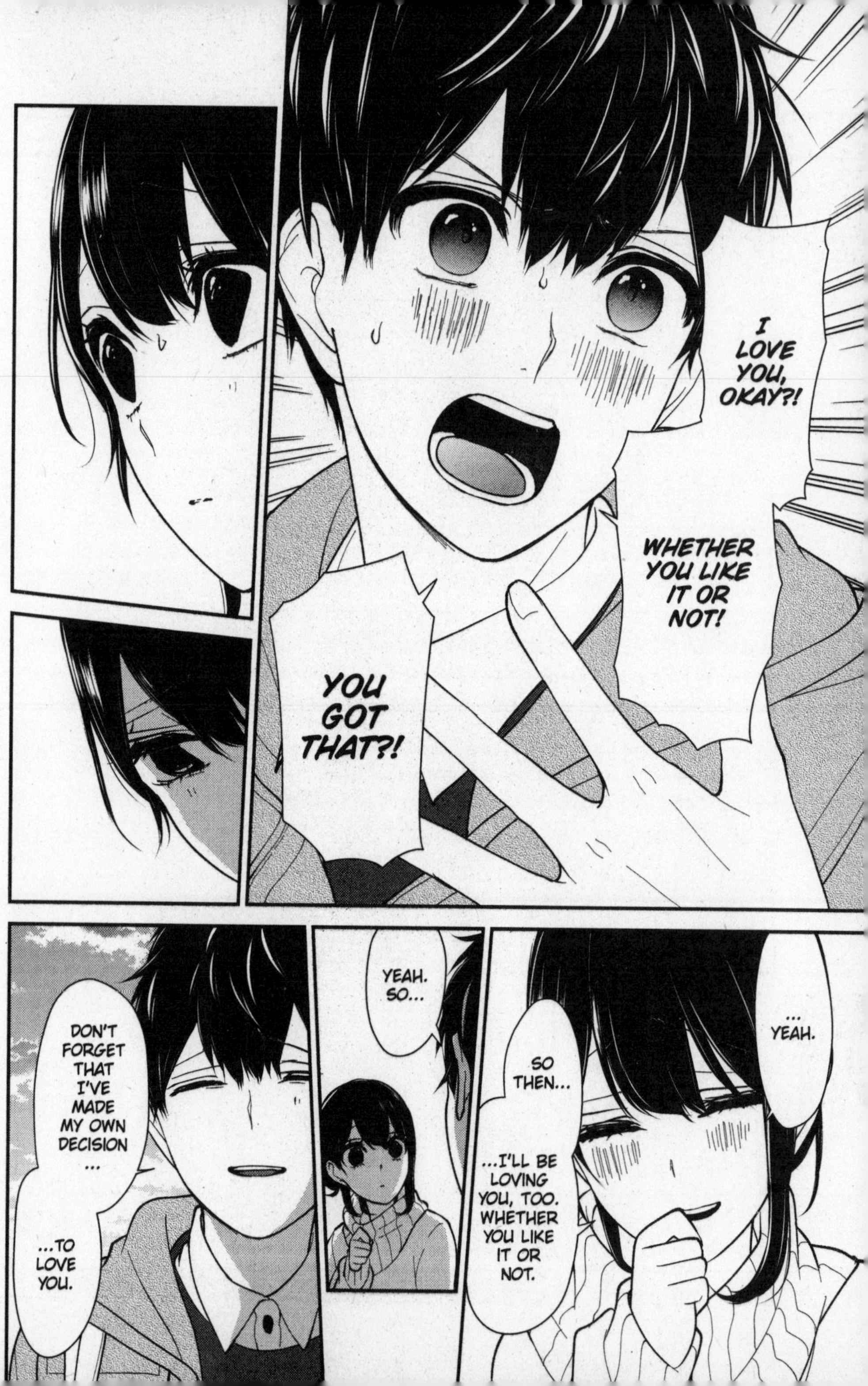
I LOVE YOU, OKAY?!
WHETHER YOU LIKE IT OR NOT!
YOU GOT THAT?!
... YEAH.
SO THEN...
...I'LL BE LOVING YOU, TOO. WHETHER YOU LIKE IT OR NOT.
YEAH. SO...
DON'T FORGET THAT I'VE MADE MY OWN DECISION ...
...TO LOVE YOU.

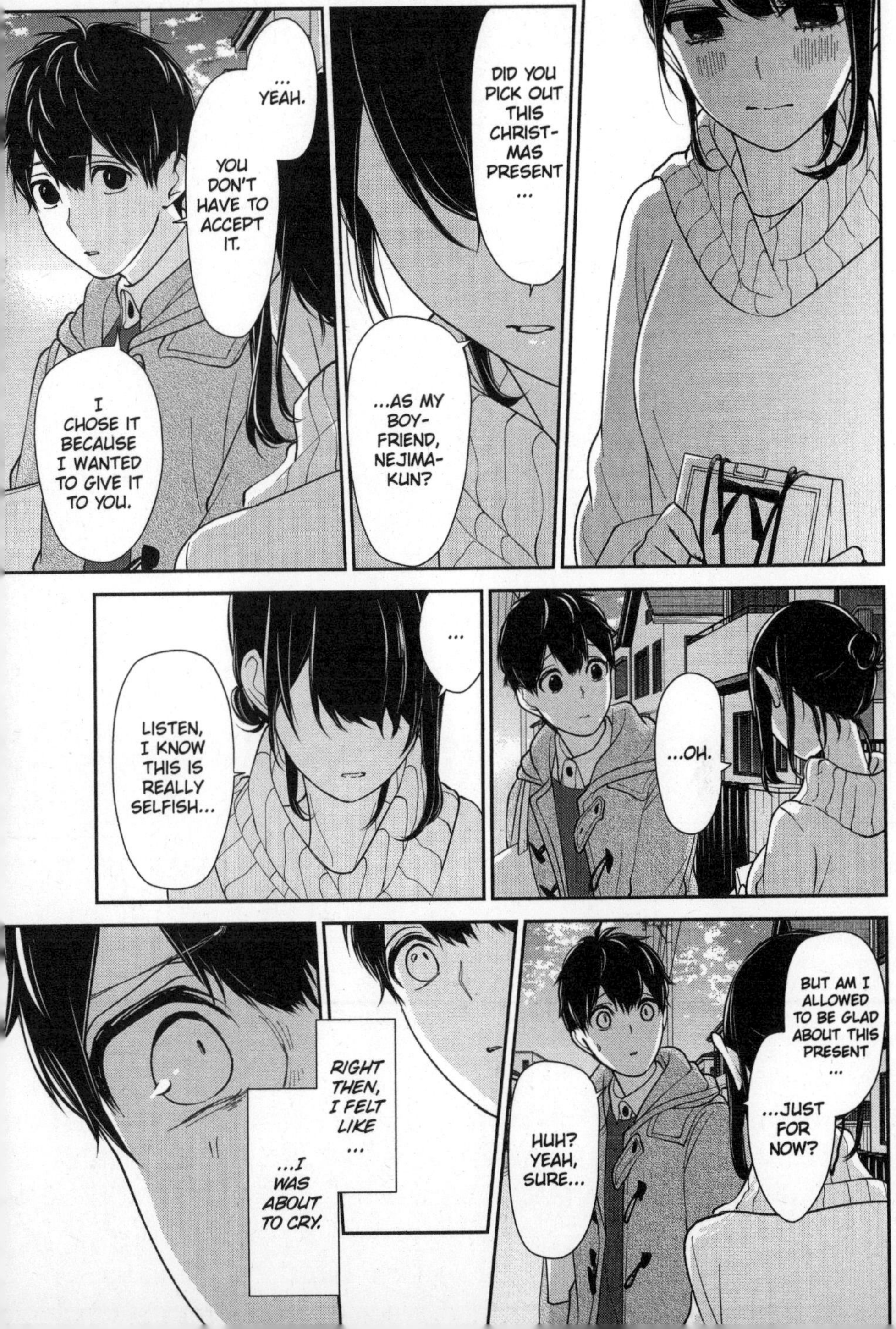
DID YOU PICK OUT THIS CHRISTMAS PRESENT...
...AS MY BOYFRIEND, NEJIMA-KUN?
...YEAH.
YOU DON'T HAVE TO ACCEPT IT.
I CHOSE IT BECAUSE I WANTED TO GIVE IT TO YOU.
...OH.
...
LISTEN, I KNOW THIS IS REALLY SELFISH...
BUT AM I ALLOWED TO BE GLAD ABOUT THIS PRESENT...
...JUST FOR NOW?
HUH? YEAH, SURE...
RIGHT THEN, I FELT LIKE...
...I WAS ABOUT TO CRY.

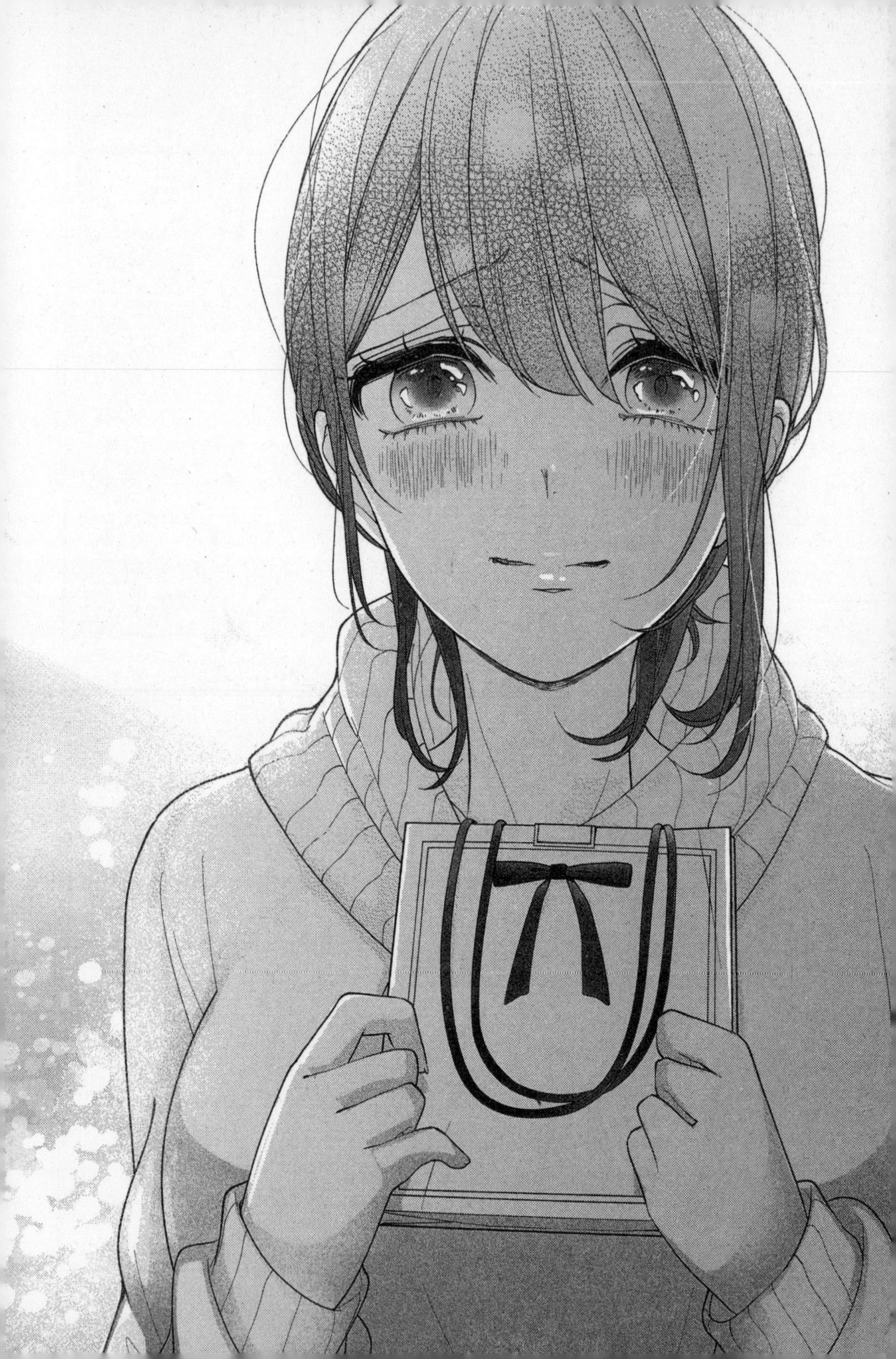

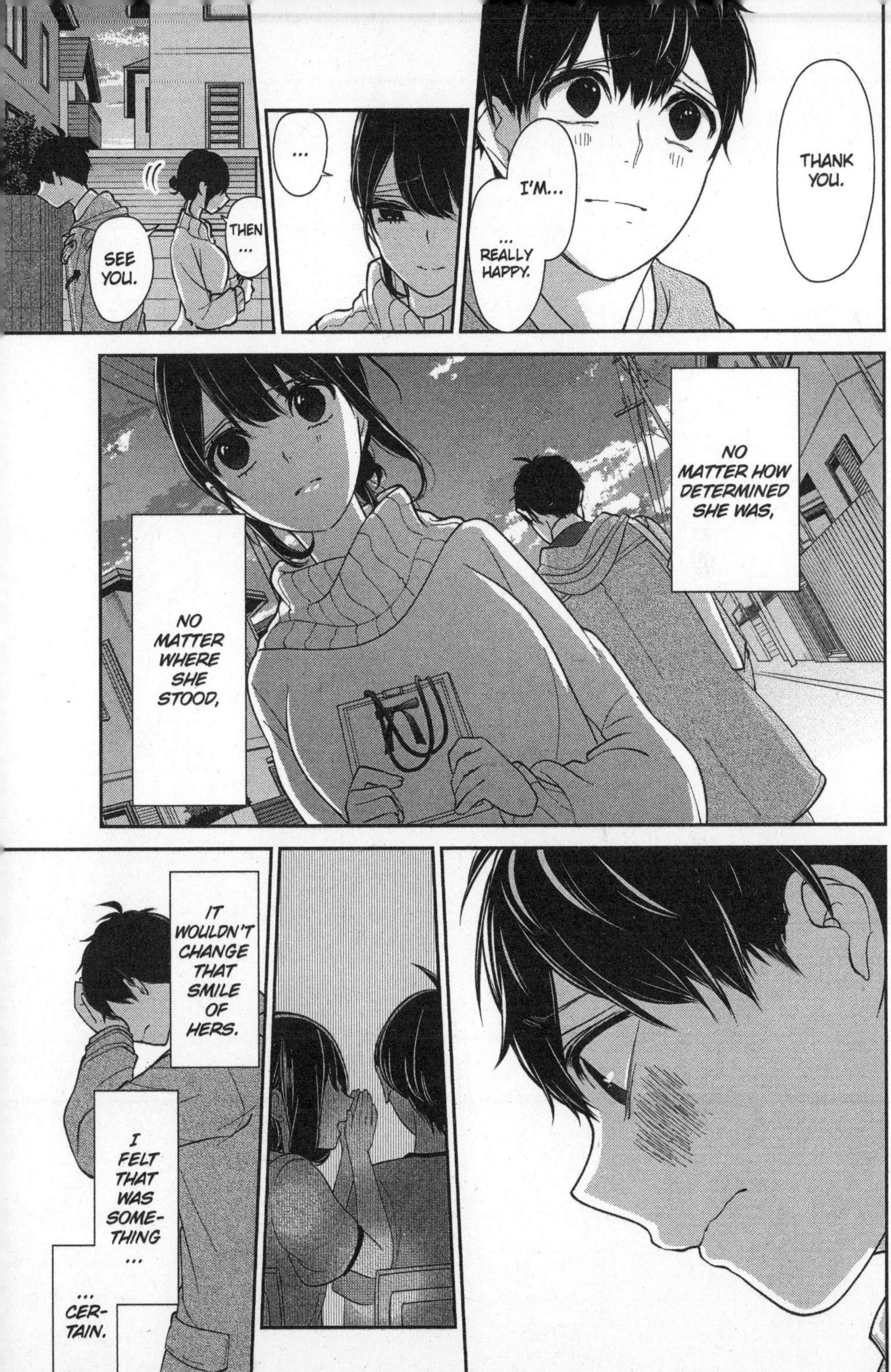
THANK YOU.
I'M...
... REALLY HAPPY.
...
THEN ...
SEE YOU.
NO MATTER HOW DETERMINED SHE WAS,
NO MATTER WHERE SHE STOOD,
IT WOULDN'T CHANGE THAT SMILE OF HERS.
I FELT THAT WAS SOME-THING ...
... CER-TAIN.

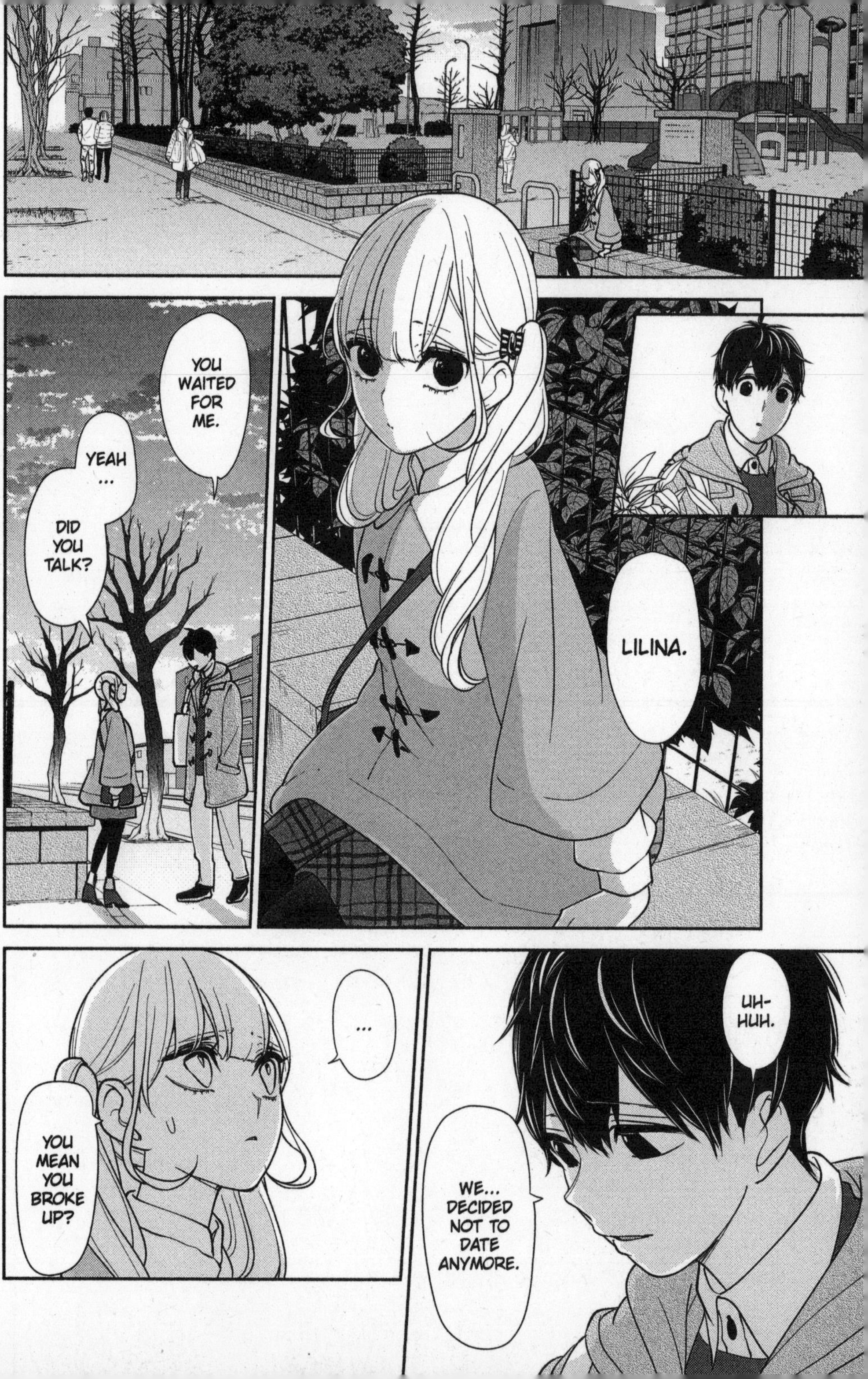
LILINA.
YOU WAITED FOR ME.
YEAH...
DID YOU TALK?
UH-HUH.
WE... DECIDED NOT TO DATE ANYMORE.
...
YOU MEAN YOU BROKE UP?

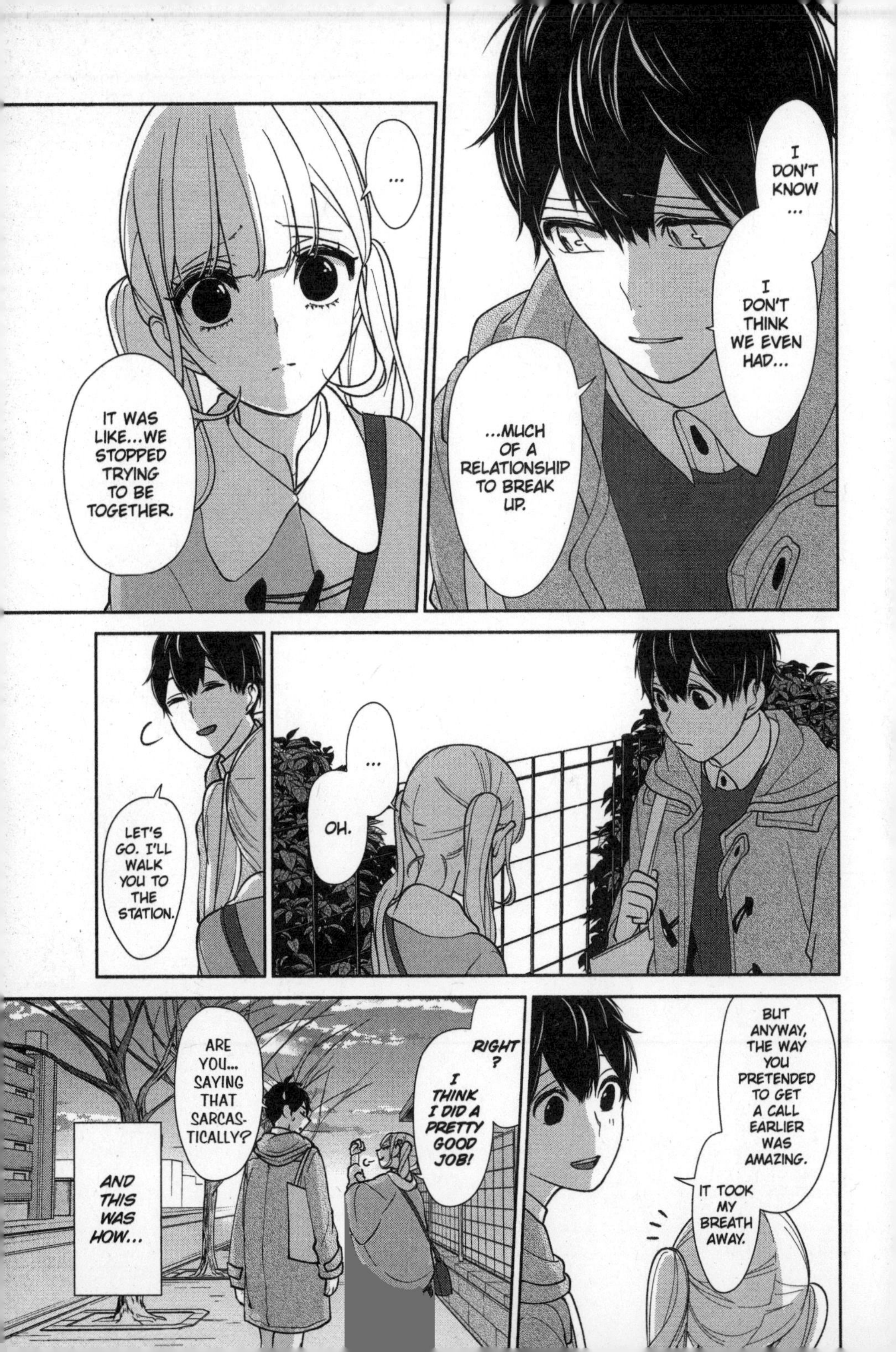
I DON'T KNOW ...
I DON'T THINK WE EVEN HAD...
...MUCH OF A RELATIONSHIP TO BREAK UP.
...
IT WAS LIKE...WE STOPPED TRYING TO BE TOGETHER.
...
OH.
LET'S GO. I'LL WALK YOU TO THE STATION.
BUT ANYWAY, THE WAY YOU PRETENDED TO GET A CALL EARLIER WAS AMAZING.
IT TOOK MY BREATH AWAY.
RIGHT?
I THINK I DID A PRETTY GOOD JOB!
ARE YOU... SAYING THAT SARCASTICALLY?
AND THIS WAS HOW...

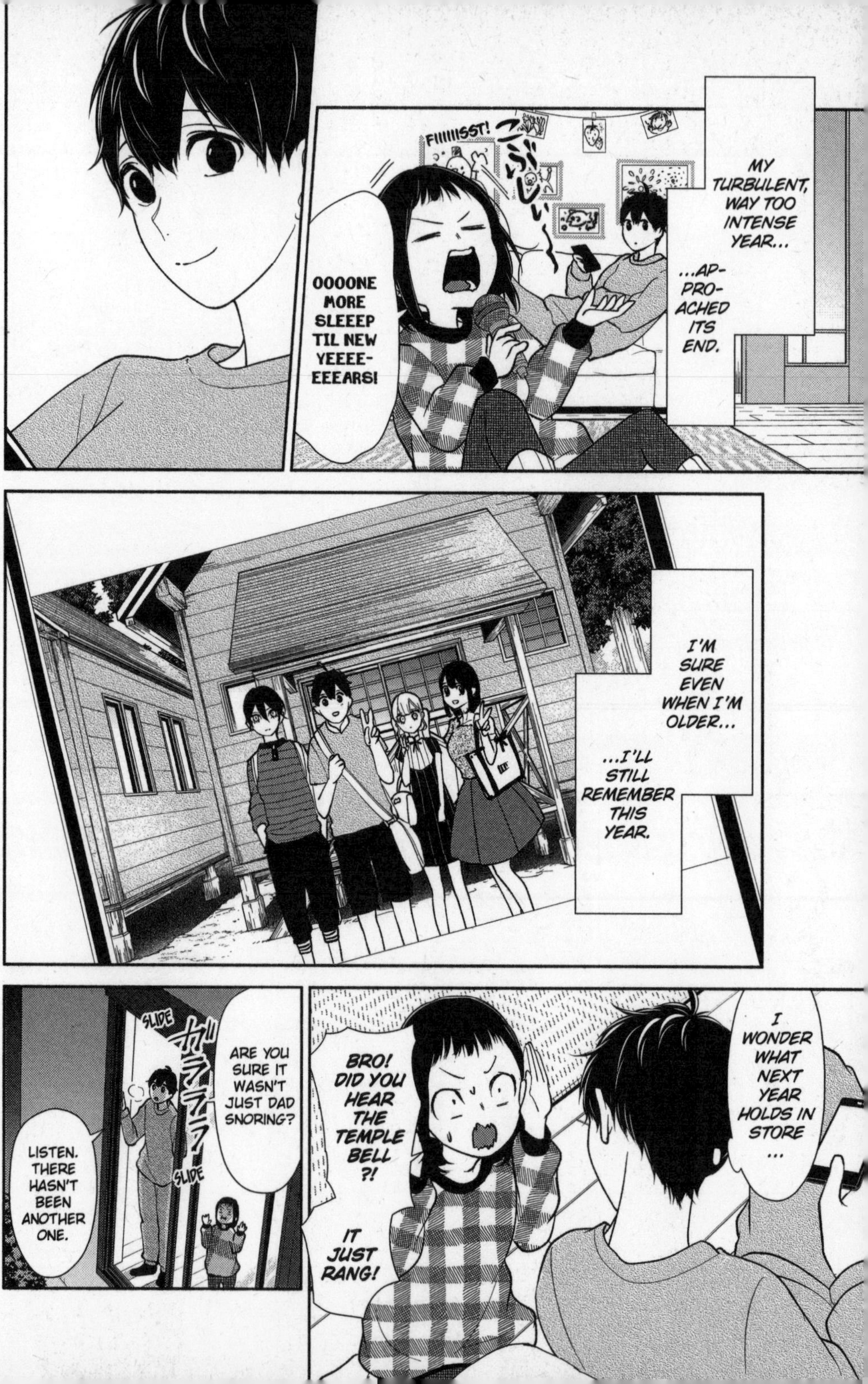
MY TURBULENT, WAY TOO INTENSE YEAR...
...AP-PRO-ACHED ITS END.
FIIIIIISST!
OOOONE MORE SLEEEP TIL NEW YEEEE-EEEARS!
I'M SURE EVEN WHEN I'M OLDER...
...I'LL STILL REMEMBER THIS YEAR.
I WONDER WHAT NEXT YEAR HOLDS IN STORE ...
BRO! DID YOU HEAR THE TEMPLE BELL ?!
IT JUST RANG!
ARE YOU SURE IT WASN'T JUST DAD SNORING?
SLIDE
SLIDE
LISTEN. THERE HASN'T BEEN ANOTHER ONE.

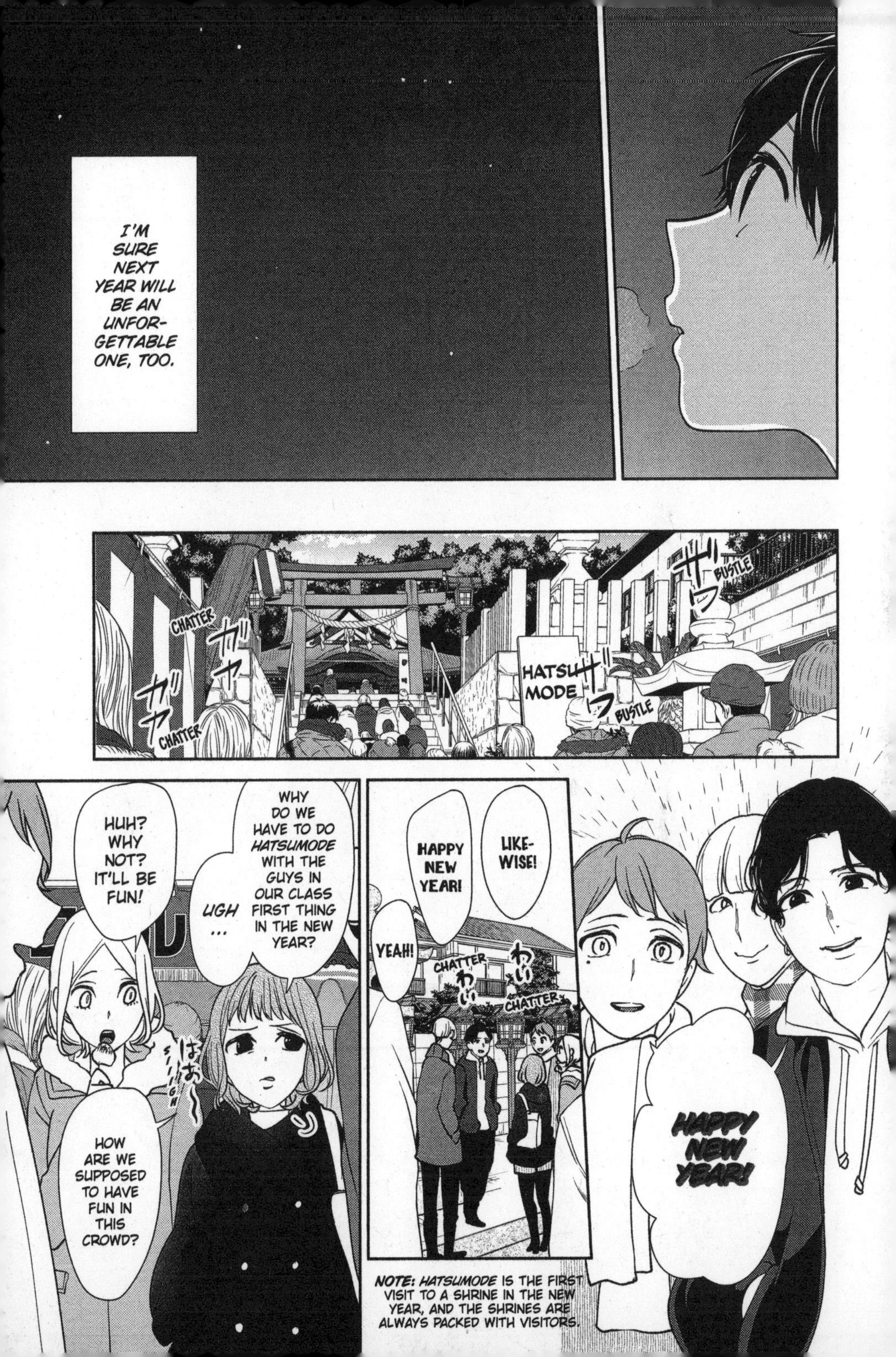

I'M SURE NEXT YEAR WILL BE AN UNFORGETTABLE ONE, TOO.
ザワ BUSTLE
ザワ BUSTLE
HATSUMODE
ガヤ CHATTER
ガヤ CHATTER
HAPPY NEW YEAR!
LIKE-WISE!
HAPPY NEW YEAR!
YEAH!
わい CHATTER
わい CHATTER
NOTE: HATSUMODE IS THE FIRST VISIT TO A SHRINE IN THE NEW YEAR, AND THE SHRINES ARE ALWAYS PACKED WITH VISITORS.
WHY DO WE HAVE TO DO HATSUMODE WITH THE GUYS IN OUR CLASS FIRST THING IN THE NEW YEAR?
UGH...
HUH? WHY NOT? IT'LL BE FUN!
はぁ〜 S-SIGH
HOW ARE WE SUPPOSED TO HAVE FUN IN THIS CROWD?

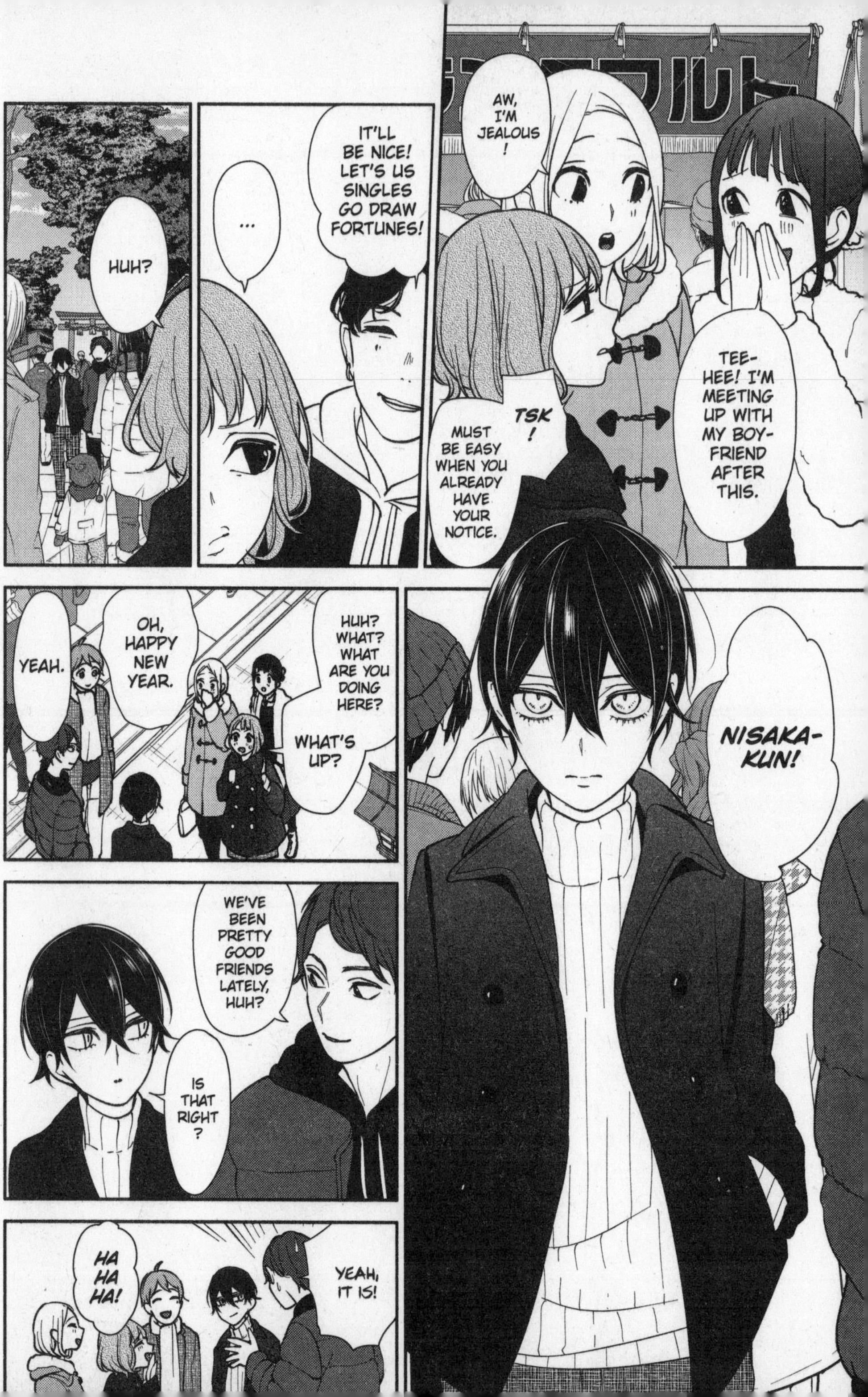
TEE-HEE! I'M MEETING UP WITH MY BOY-FRIEND AFTER THIS.
AW, I'M JEALOUS!
TSK!
MUST BE EASY WHEN YOU ALREADY HAVE YOUR NOTICE.
IT'LL BE NICE! LET'S US SINGLES GO DRAW FORTUNES!
...
HUH?
NISAKA-KUN!
HUH? WHAT? WHAT ARE YOU DOING HERE?
WHAT'S UP?
OH, HAPPY NEW YEAR.
YEAH.
WE'VE BEEN PRETTY GOOD FRIENDS LATELY, HUH?
IS THAT RIGHT?
YEAH, IT IS!
HA HA HA!

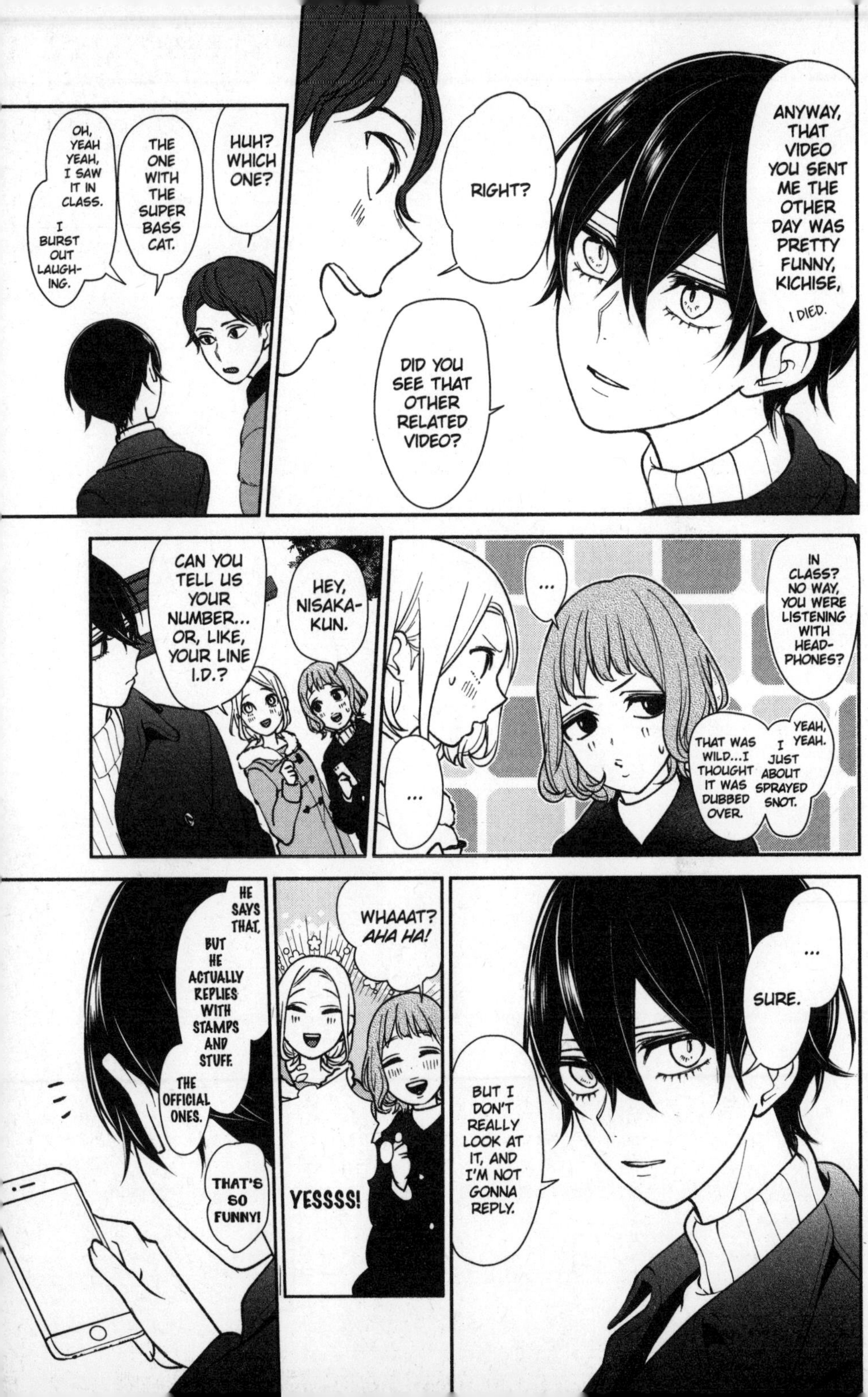
ANYWAY, THAT VIDEO YOU SENT ME THE OTHER DAY WAS PRETTY FUNNY, KICHISE,
I DIED.
RIGHT?
DID YOU SEE THAT OTHER RELATED VIDEO?
HUH? WHICH ONE?
THE ONE WITH THE SUPER BASS CAT.
OH, YEAH YEAH, I SAW IT IN CLASS.
I BURST OUT LAUGHING.
IN CLASS? NO WAY, YOU WERE LISTENING WITH HEADPHONES?
YEAH, YEAH. I JUST ABOUT SPRAYED SNOT.
THAT WAS WILD...I THOUGHT IT WAS DUBBED OVER.
...
...
HEY, NISAKA-KUN.
CAN YOU TELL US YOUR NUMBER... OR, LIKE, YOUR LINE I.D.?
...
SURE.
BUT I DON'T REALLY LOOK AT IT, AND I'M NOT GONNA REPLY.
WHAAAT? *AHA HA!*
YESSSS!
HE SAYS THAT, BUT HE ACTUALLY REPLIES WITH STAMPS AND STUFF.
THE OFFICIAL ONES.
THAT'S SO FUNNY!

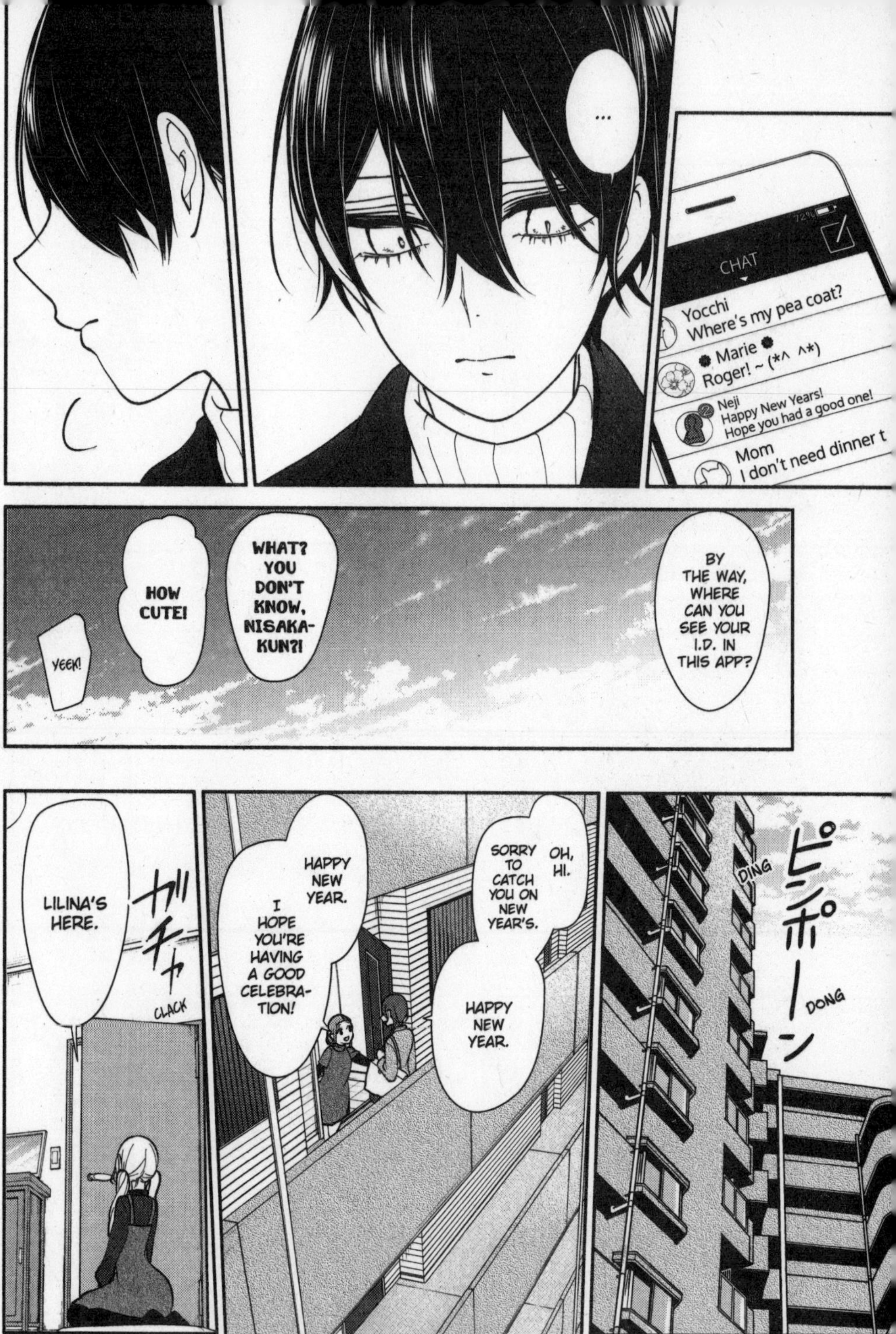
CHAT
Yocchi
Where's my pea coat?
Marie
Roger! ~ (*^ ^*)
Neji
Happy New Years!
Hope you had a good one!
Mom
I don't need dinner t
...
BY THE WAY, WHERE CAN YOU SEE YOUR I.D. IN THIS APP?
WHAT? YOU DON'T KNOW, NISAKA-KUN?!
HOW CUTE!
YEEK!
ピンポーン
DING
DONG
OH, HI.
SORRY TO CATCH YOU ON NEW YEAR'S.
HAPPY NEW YEAR.
I HOPE YOU'RE HAVING A GOOD CELEBRATION!
HAPPY NEW YEAR.
ガチャ
CLACK
LILINA'S HERE.

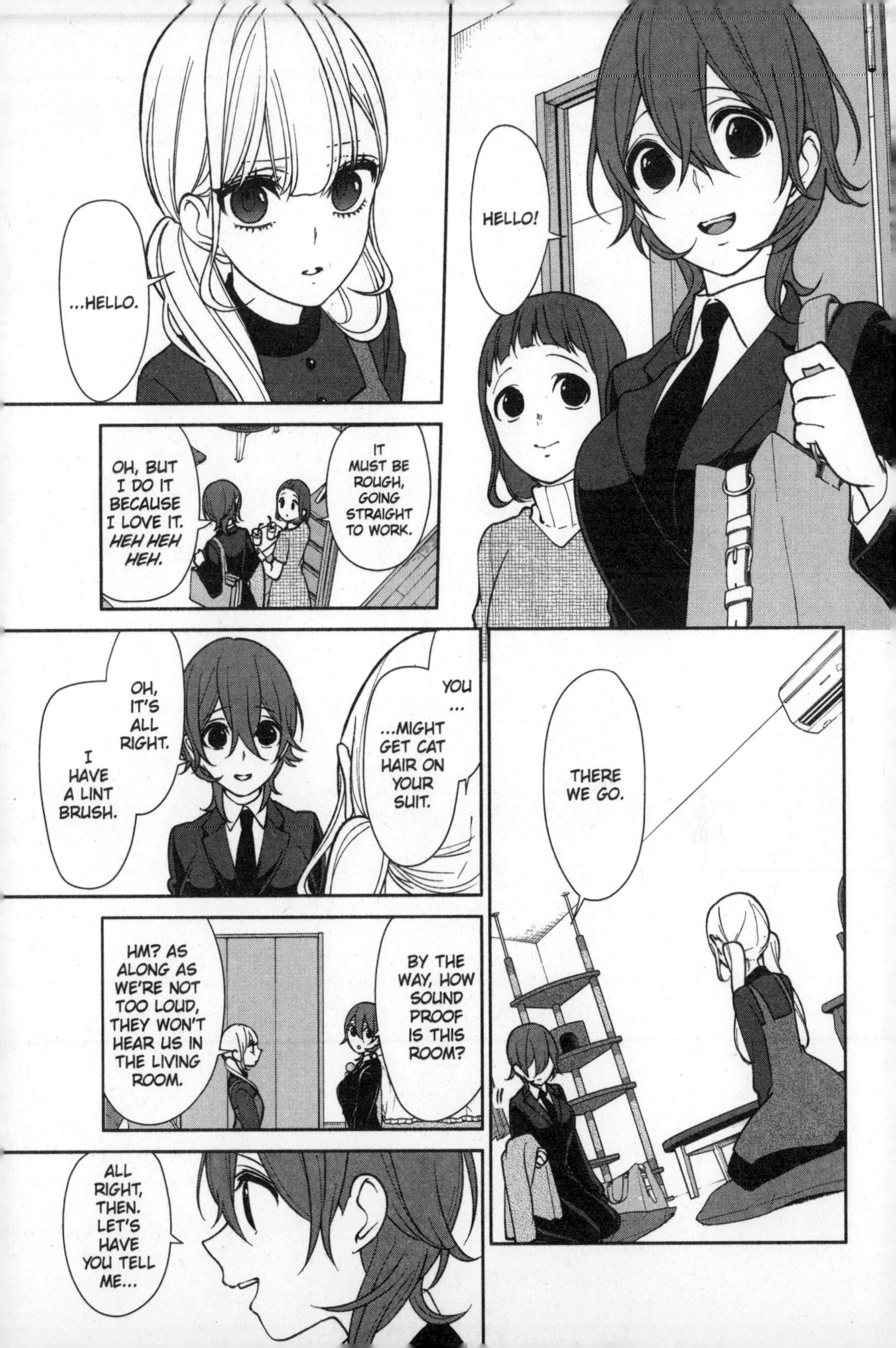
HELLO!
...HELLO.
IT MUST BE ROUGH, GOING STRAIGHT TO WORK.
OH, BUT I DO IT BECAUSE I LOVE IT. *HEH HEH HEH.*
THERE WE GO.
YOU ...
...MIGHT GET CAT HAIR ON YOUR SUIT.
OH, IT'S ALL RIGHT.
I HAVE A LINT BRUSH.
BY THE WAY, HOW SOUND PROOF IS THIS ROOM?
HM? AS ALONG AS WE'RE NOT TOO LOUD, THEY WON'T HEAR US IN THE LIVING ROOM.
ALL RIGHT, THEN. LET'S HAVE YOU TELL ME...

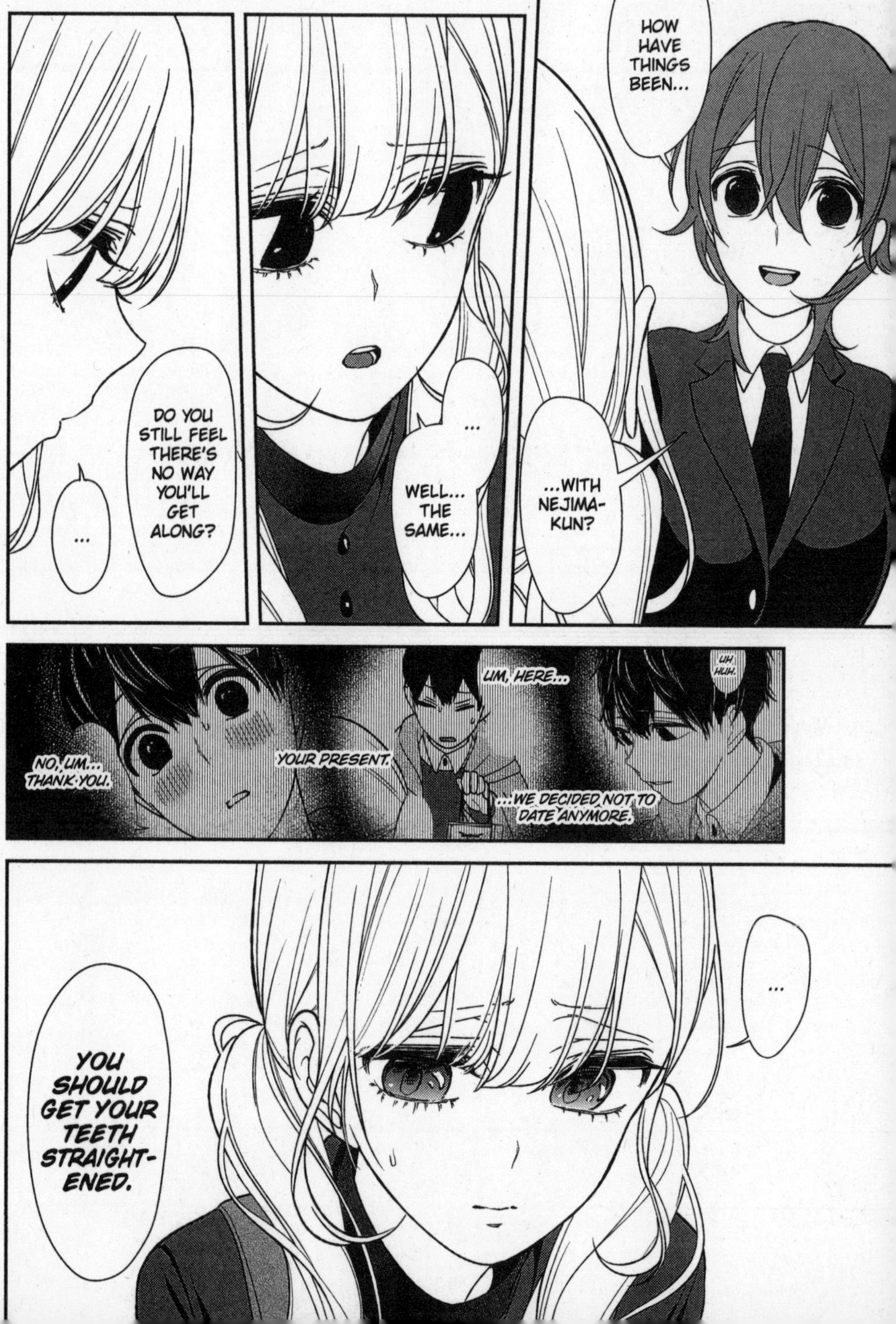
HOW HAVE THINGS BEEN...
...WITH NEJIMA-KUN?
...
WELL... THE SAME...
DO YOU STILL FEEL THERE'S NO WAY YOU'LL GET ALONG?
...
UH HUH.
...WE DECIDED NOT TO DATE ANYMORE.
UM, HERE...
YOUR PRESENT.
NO, UM... THANK YOU.
...
YOU SHOULD GET YOUR TEETH STRAIGHT-ENED.

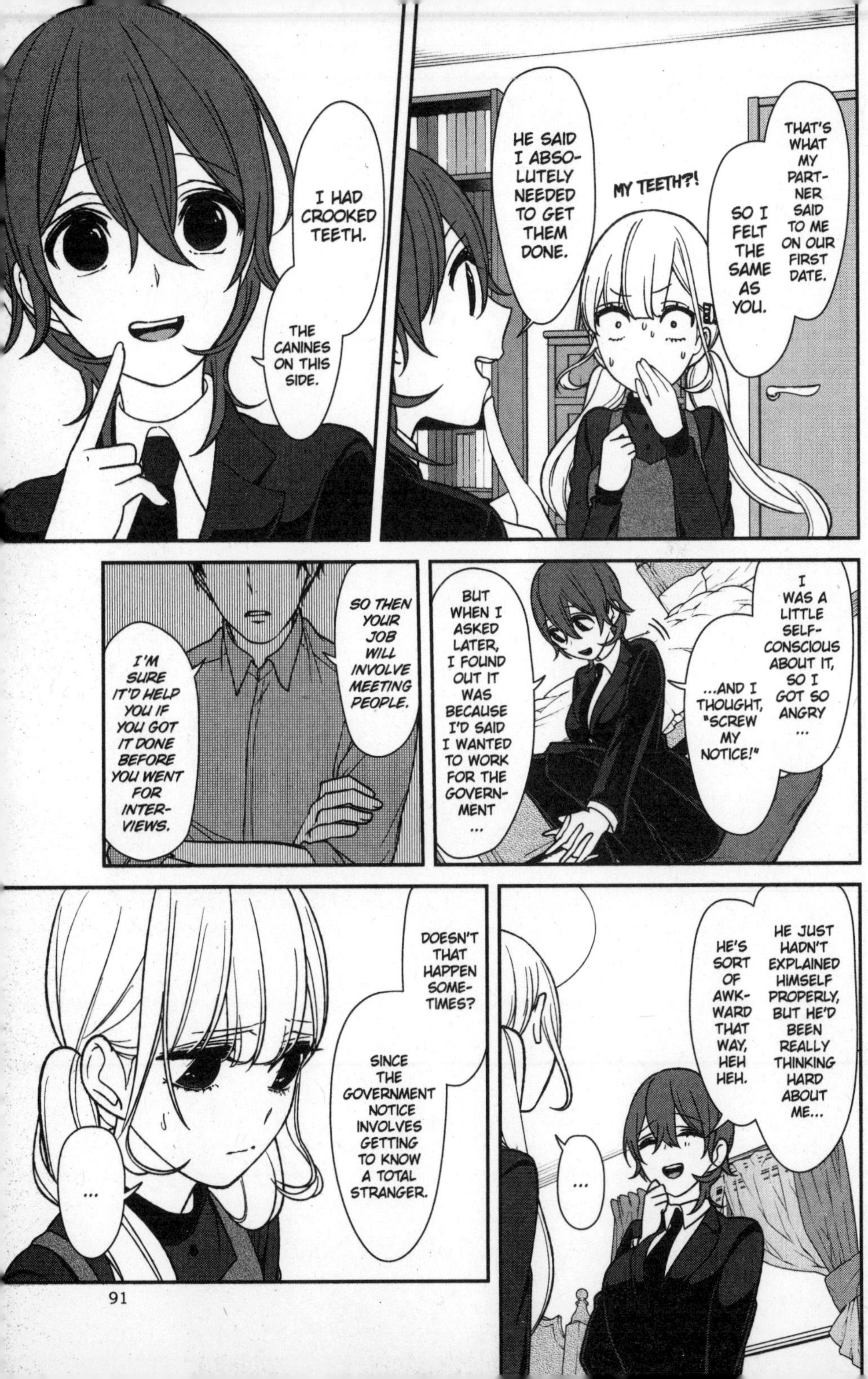
THAT'S WHAT MY PARTNER SAID TO ME ON OUR FIRST DATE.
SO I FELT THE SAME AS YOU.
MY TEETH?!
HE SAID I ABSOLUTELY NEEDED TO GET THEM DONE.
I HAD CROOKED TEETH.
THE CANINES ON THIS SIDE.
I WAS A LITTLE SELF-CONSCIOUS ABOUT IT, SO I GOT SO ANGRY...
...AND I THOUGHT, "SCREW MY NOTICE!"
BUT WHEN I ASKED LATER, I FOUND OUT IT WAS BECAUSE I'D SAID I WANTED TO WORK FOR THE GOVERNMENT...
SO THEN YOUR JOB WILL INVOLVE MEETING PEOPLE.
I'M SURE IT'D HELP YOU IF YOU GOT IT DONE BEFORE YOU WENT FOR INTERVIEWS.
HE JUST HADN'T EXPLAINED HIMSELF PROPERLY, BUT HE'D BEEN REALLY THINKING HARD ABOUT ME...
HE'S SORT OF AWKWARD THAT WAY, HEH HEH.
...
DOESN'T THAT HAPPEN SOMETIMES?
SINCE THE GOVERNMENT NOTICE INVOLVES GETTING TO KNOW A TOTAL STRANGER.
...

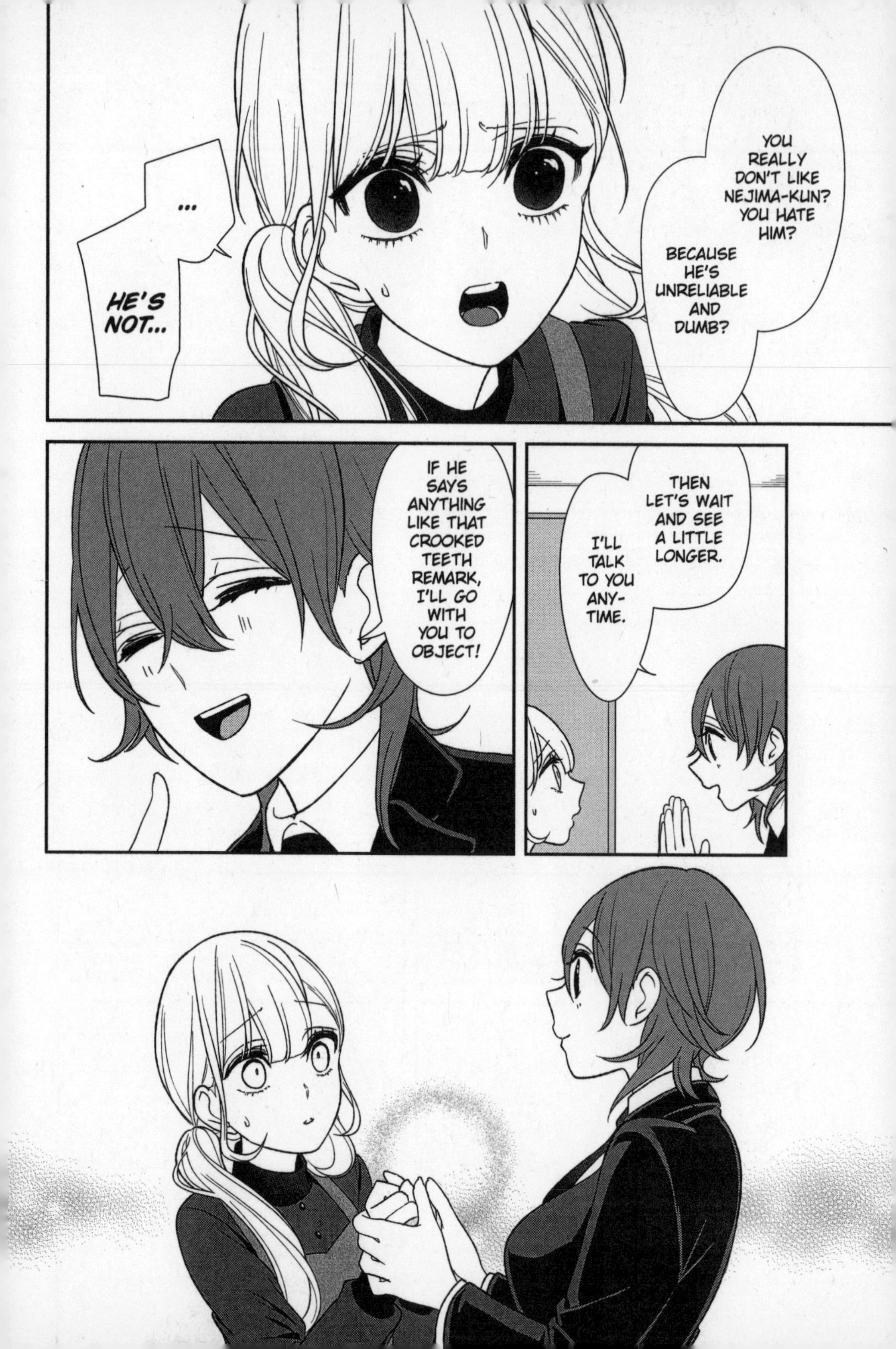
YOU REALLY DON'T LIKE NEJIMA-KUN? YOU HATE HIM?
BECAUSE HE'S UNRELIABLE AND DUMB?
...
HE'S NOT...
THEN LET'S WAIT AND SEE A LITTLE LONGER.
I'LL TALK TO YOU ANY-TIME.
IF HE SAYS ANYTHING LIKE THAT CROOKED TEETH REMARK, I'LL GO WITH YOU TO OBJECT!

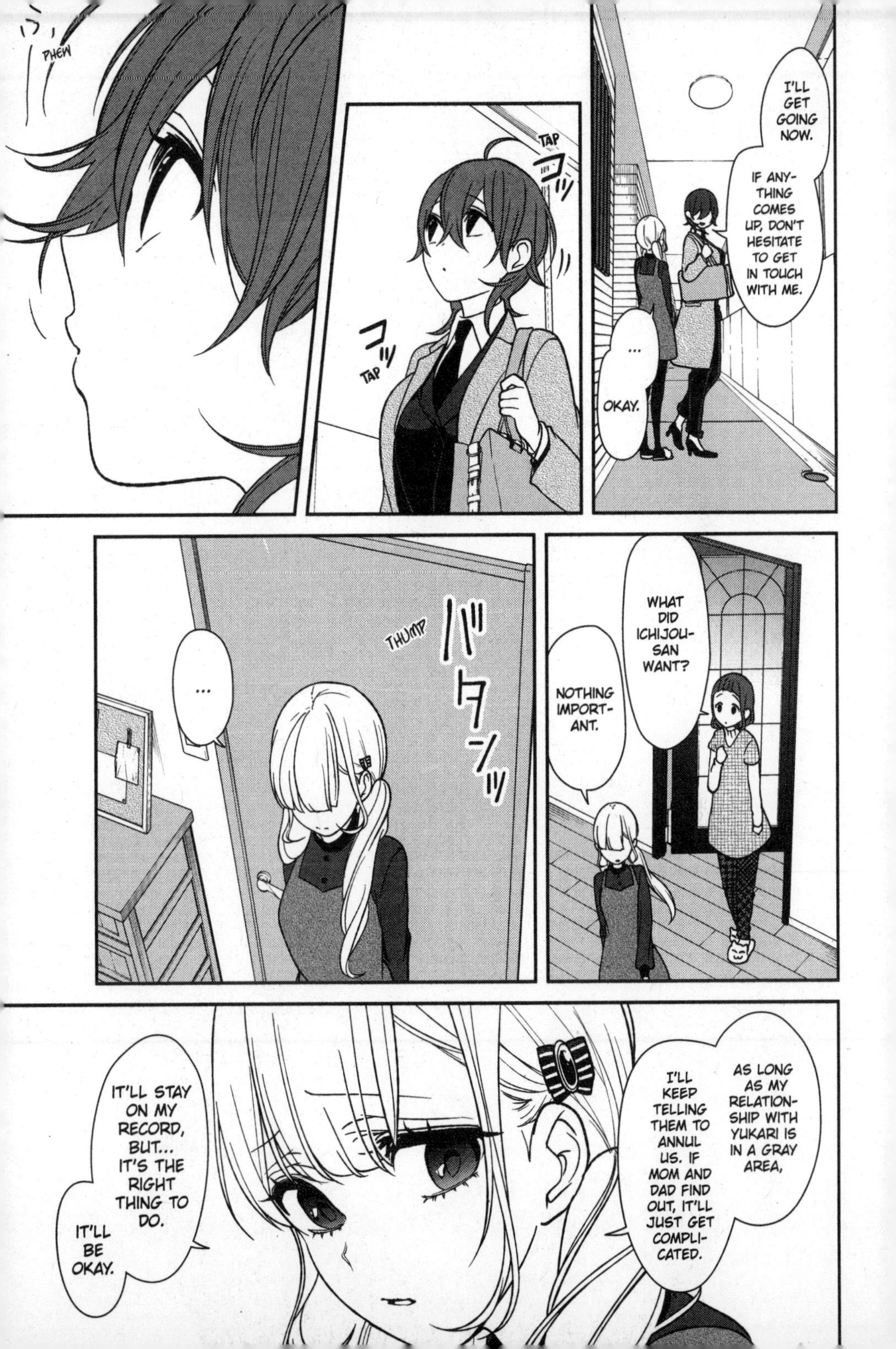

I'LL GET GOING NOW.
IF ANYTHING COMES UP, DON'T HESITATE TO GET IN TOUCH WITH ME.
...
OKAY.
コツ TAP
コツ TAP
ふぅ PHEW
WHAT DID ICHIJOU-SAN WANT?
NOTHING IMPORTANT.
バタンッ THUMP
...
AS LONG AS MY RELATIONSHIP WITH YUKARI IS IN A GRAY AREA,
I'LL KEEP TELLING THEM TO ANNUL US. IF MOM AND DAD FIND OUT, IT'LL JUST GET COMPLICATED.
IT'LL STAY ON MY RECORD, BUT... IT'S THE RIGHT THING TO DO.
IT'LL BE OKAY.

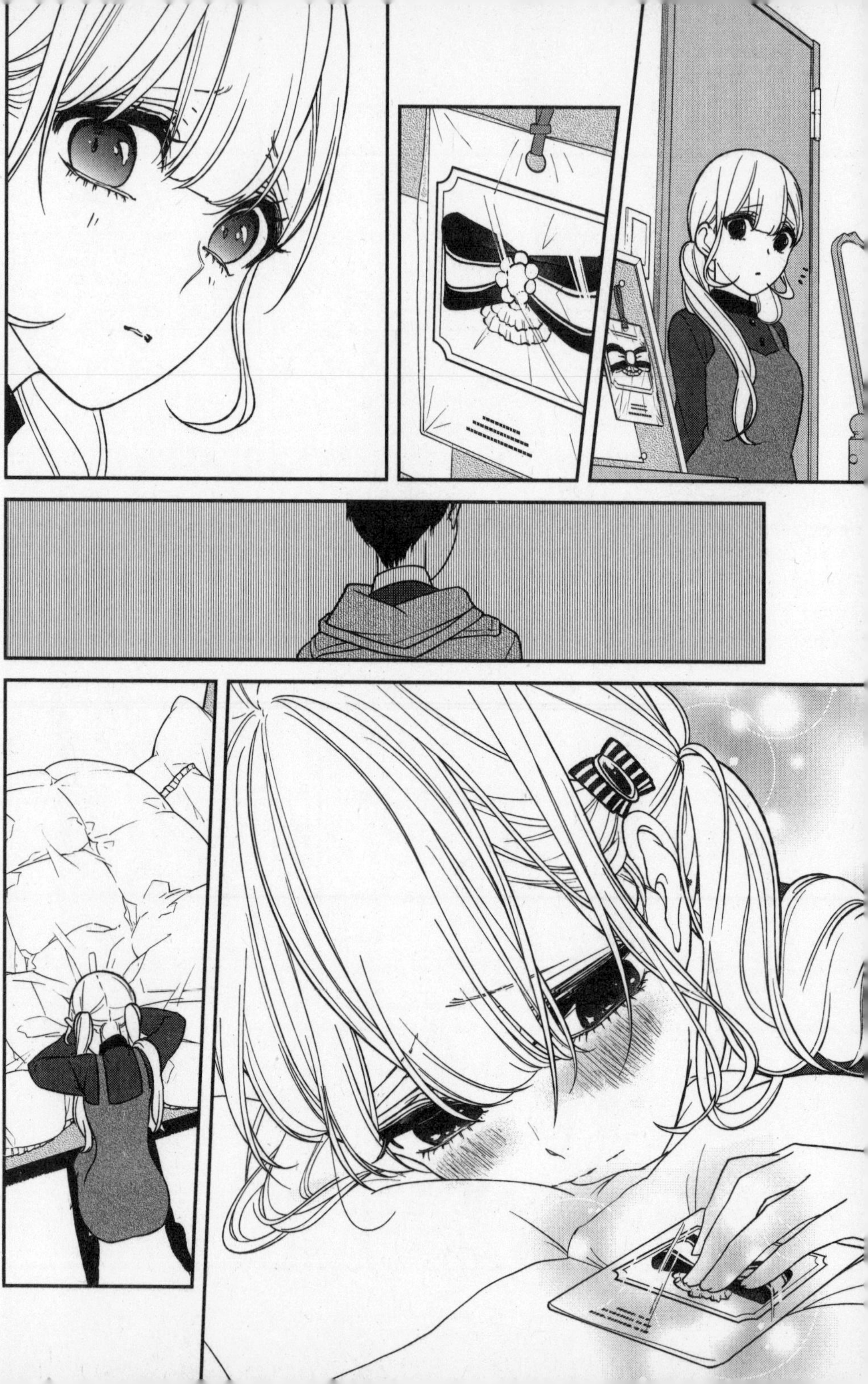

Love & Lies

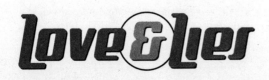

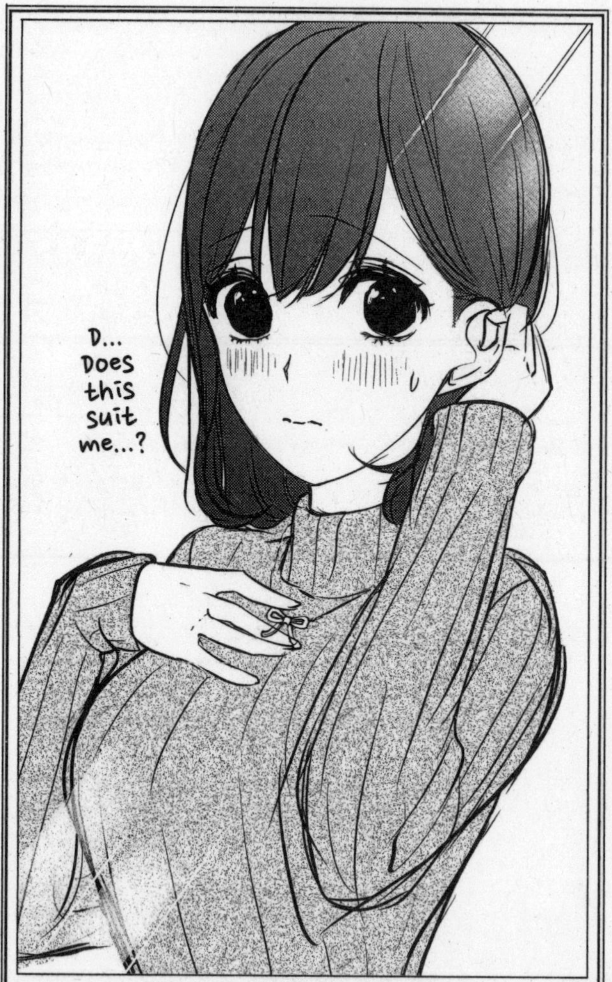
D... Does this suit me...?

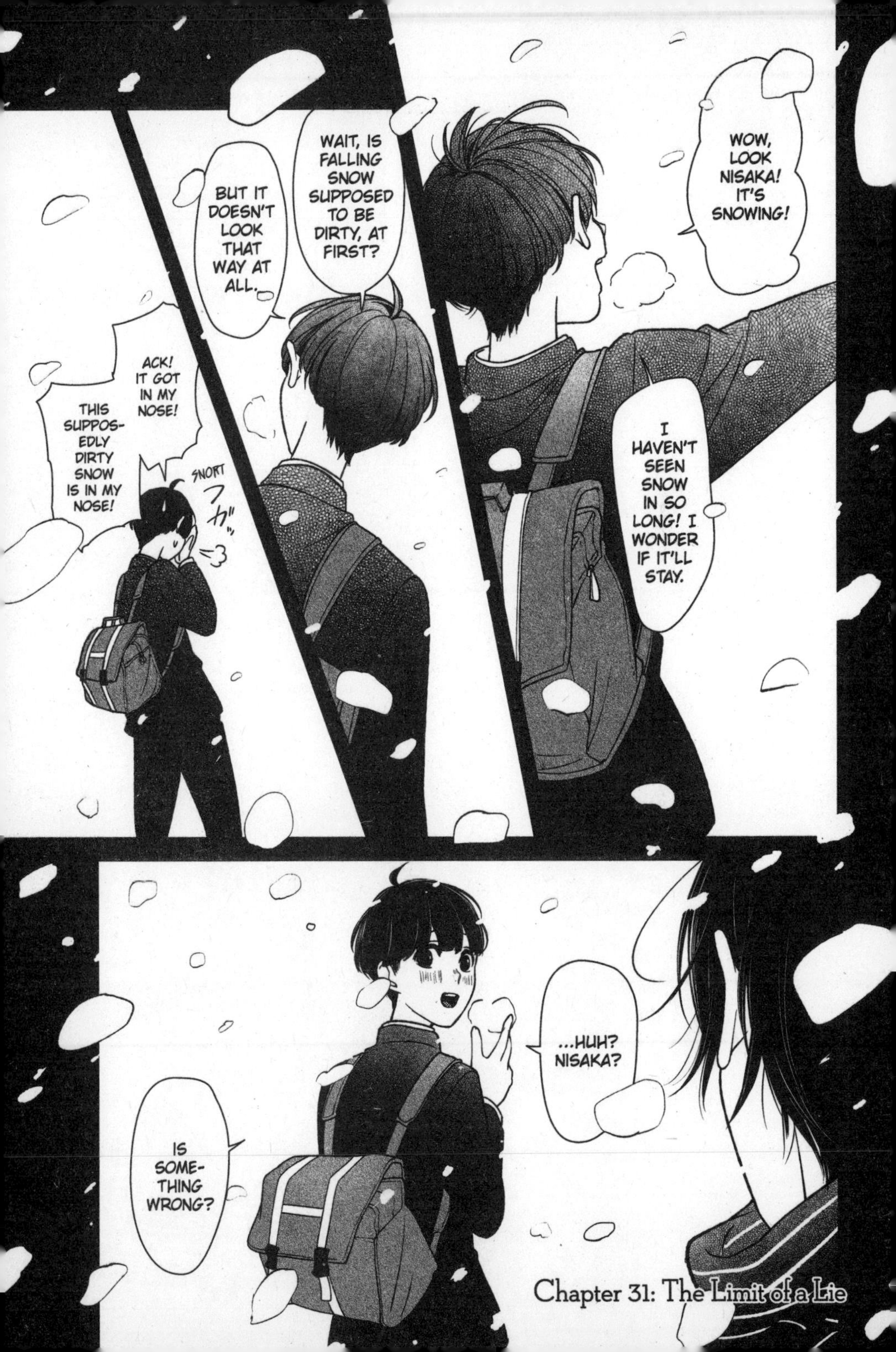
WOW, LOOK NISAKA! IT'S SNOWING!
I HAVEN'T SEEN SNOW IN SO LONG! I WONDER IF IT'LL STAY.
WAIT, IS FALLING SNOW SUPPOSED TO BE DIRTY, AT FIRST?
BUT IT DOESN'T LOOK THAT WAY AT ALL.
ACK! IT GOT IN MY NOSE!
THIS SUPPOSEDLY DIRTY SNOW IS IN MY NOSE!
SNORT
...HUH? NISAKA?
IS SOMETHING WRONG?

Chapter 31: The Limit of a Lie

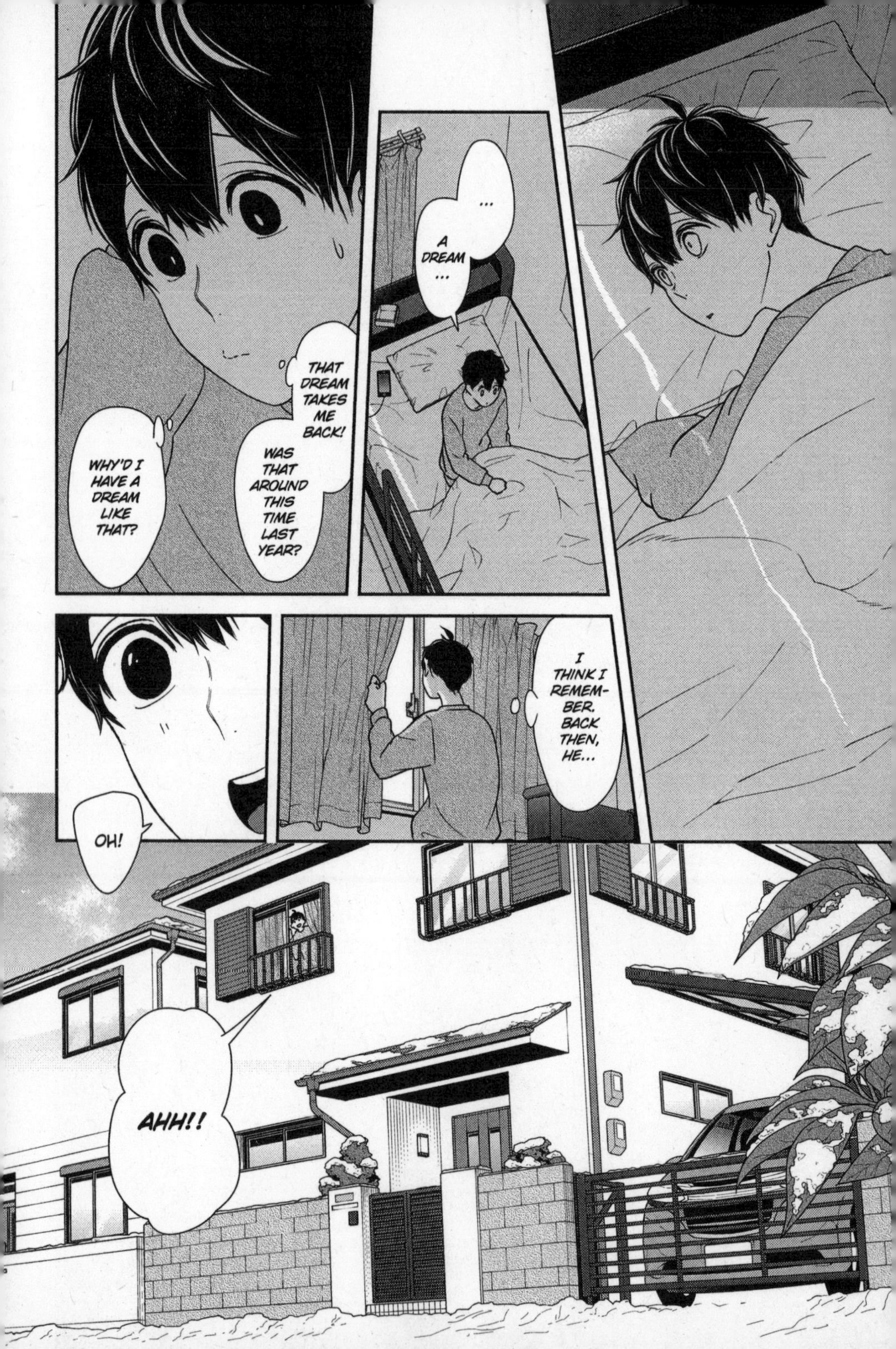
...
A DREAM...
THAT DREAM TAKES ME BACK!
WAS THAT AROUND THIS TIME LAST YEAR?
WHY'D I HAVE A DREAM LIKE THAT?
I THINK I REMEMBER. BACK THEN, HE...
OH!
AHH!!

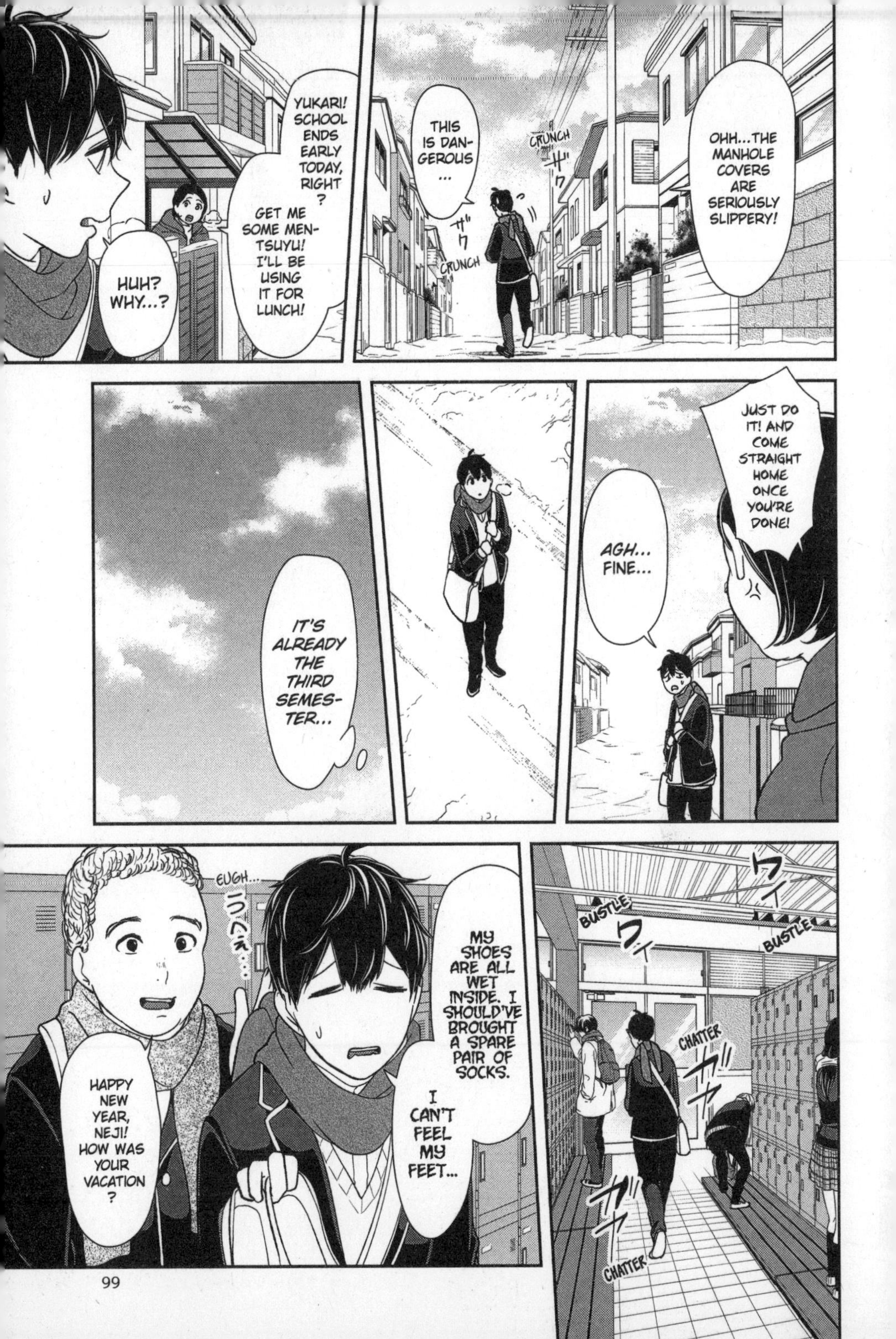
OHH...THE MANHOLE COVERS ARE SERIOUSLY SLIPPERY!
CRUNCH
ザク
THIS IS DANGEROUS...
ザク
CRUNCH
YUKARI! SCHOOL ENDS EARLY TODAY, RIGHT? GET ME SOME MEN-TSUYU! I'LL BE USING IT FOR LUNCH!
HUH? WHY...?
JUST DO IT! AND COME STRAIGHT HOME ONCE YOU'RE DONE!
AGH... FINE...
IT'S ALREADY THE THIRD SEMESTER...
ワイ
BUSTLE
ワイ
BUSTLE
CHATTER
ガヤ
ガヤ
CHATTER
MY SHOES ARE ALL WET INSIDE. I SHOULD'VE BROUGHT A SPARE PAIR OF SOCKS.
I CAN'T FEEL MY FEET...
EUGH...
うへぇ…
HAPPY NEW YEAR, NEJI! HOW WAS YOUR VACATION?

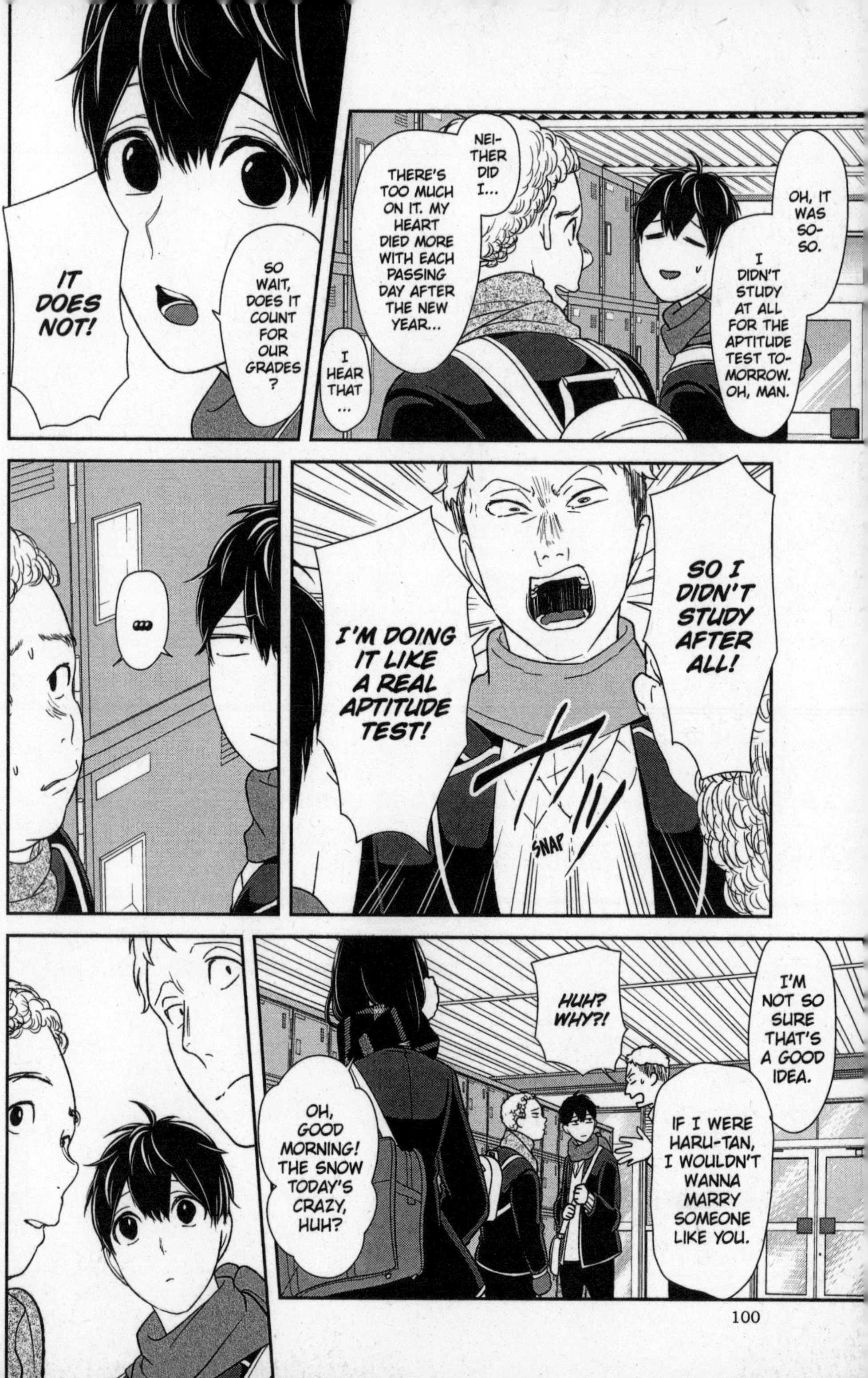
OH, IT WAS SO-SO.
I DIDN'T STUDY AT ALL FOR THE APTITUDE TEST TOMORROW. OH, MAN.
NEITHER DID I...
THERE'S TOO MUCH ON IT. MY HEART DIED MORE WITH EACH PASSING DAY AFTER THE NEW YEAR...
I HEAR THAT...
SO WAIT, DOES IT COUNT FOR OUR GRADES?
IT DOES NOT!
SO I DIDN'T STUDY AFTER ALL!
I'M DOING IT LIKE A REAL APTITUDE TEST!
SNAP
...
I'M NOT SO SURE THAT'S A GOOD IDEA.
IF I WERE HARU-TAN, I WOULDN'T WANNA MARRY SOMEONE LIKE YOU.
HUH? WHY?!
OH, GOOD MORNING! THE SNOW TODAY'S CRAZY, HUH?

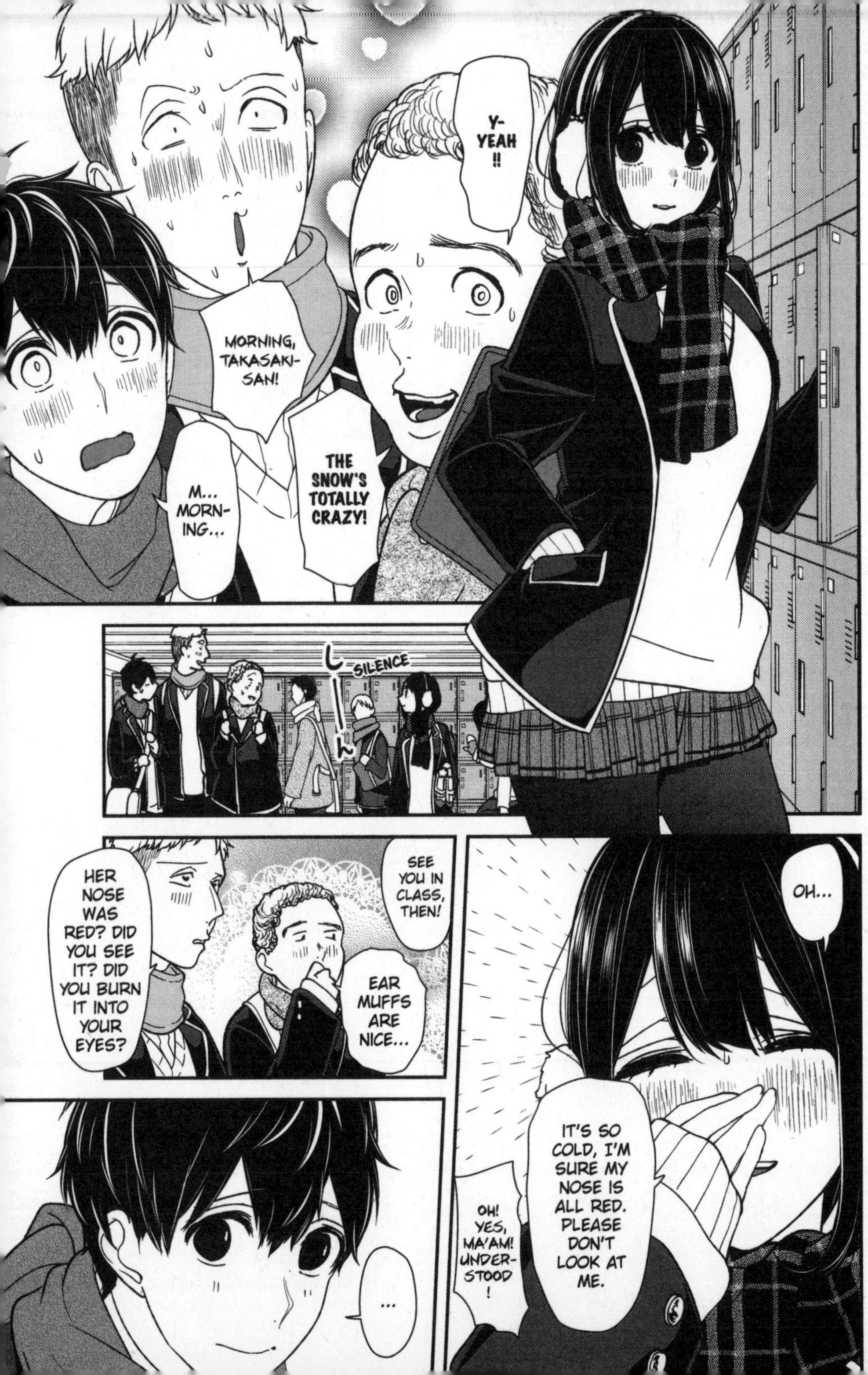
Y-YEAH!!
MORNING, TAKASAKI-SAN!
THE SNOW'S TOTALLY CRAZY!
M... MORNING...
しーん SILENCE
OH...
IT'S SO COLD, I'M SURE MY NOSE IS ALL RED. PLEASE DON'T LOOK AT ME.
OH! YES, MA'AM! UNDERSTOOD!
SEE YOU IN CLASS, THEN!
EAR MUFFS ARE NICE...
HER NOSE WAS RED? DID YOU SEE IT? DID YOU BURN IT INTO YOUR EYES?
...

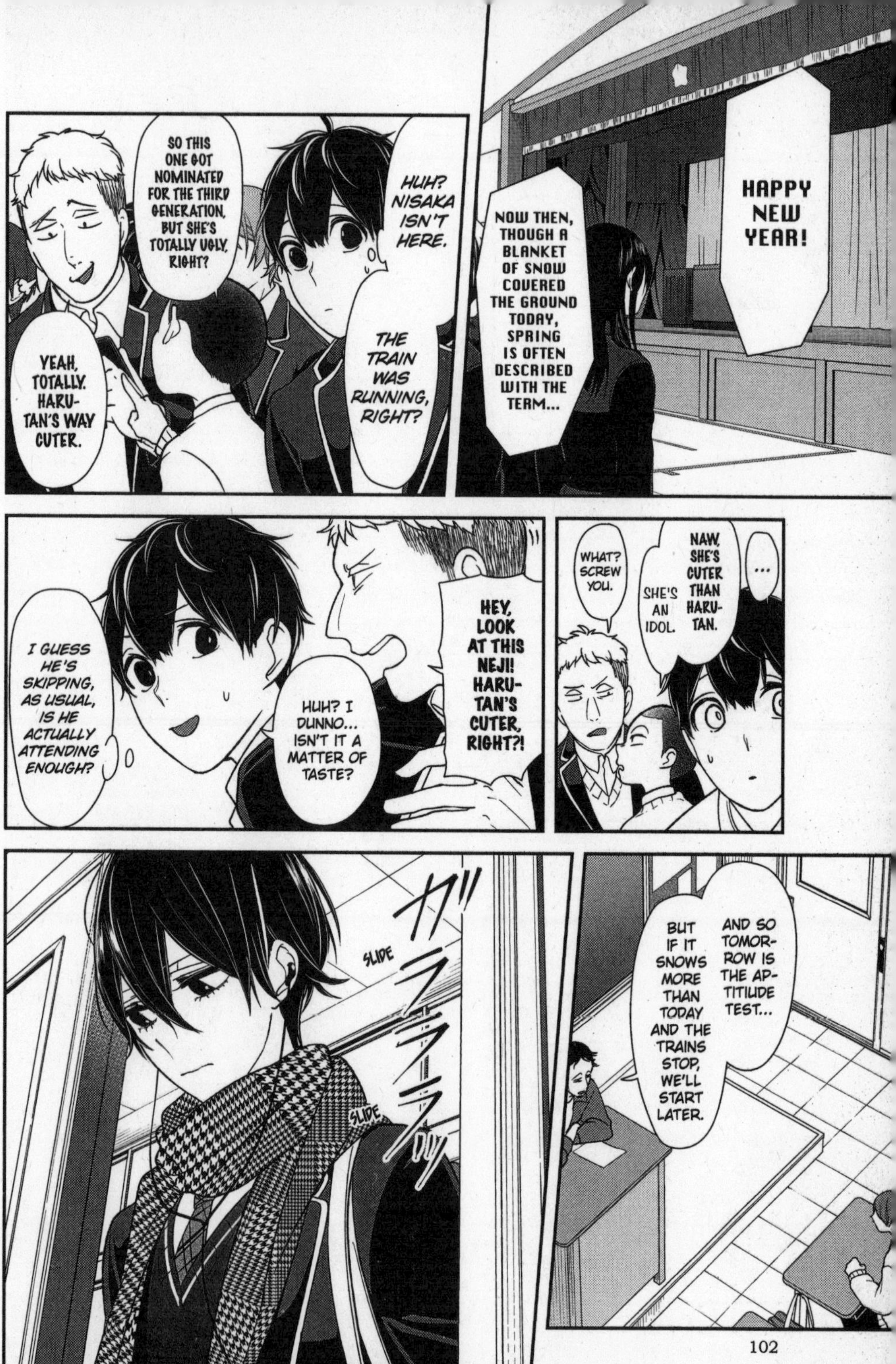

HAPPY NEW YEAR!
NOW THEN, THOUGH A BLANKET OF SNOW COVERED THE GROUND TODAY, SPRING IS OFTEN DESCRIBED WITH THE TERM...
HUH? NISAKA ISN'T HERE.
THE TRAIN WAS RUNNING, RIGHT?
SO THIS ONE GOT NOMINATED FOR THE THIRD GENERATION, BUT SHE'S TOTALLY UGLY, RIGHT?
YEAH, TOTALLY. HARU-TAN'S WAY CUTER.
...
NAW, SHE'S CUTER THAN HARU-TAN.
SHE'S AN IDOL.
WHAT? SCREW YOU.
HEY, LOOK AT THIS NEJI! HARU-TAN'S CUTER, RIGHT?!
HUH? I DUNNO... ISN'T IT A MATTER OF TASTE?
I GUESS HE'S SKIPPING, AS USUAL. IS HE ACTUALLY ATTENDING ENOUGH?
AND SO TOMORROW IS THE APTITUDE TEST...
BUT IF IT SNOWS MORE THAN TODAY AND THE TRAINS STOP, WE'LL START LATER.
SLIDE
SLIDE

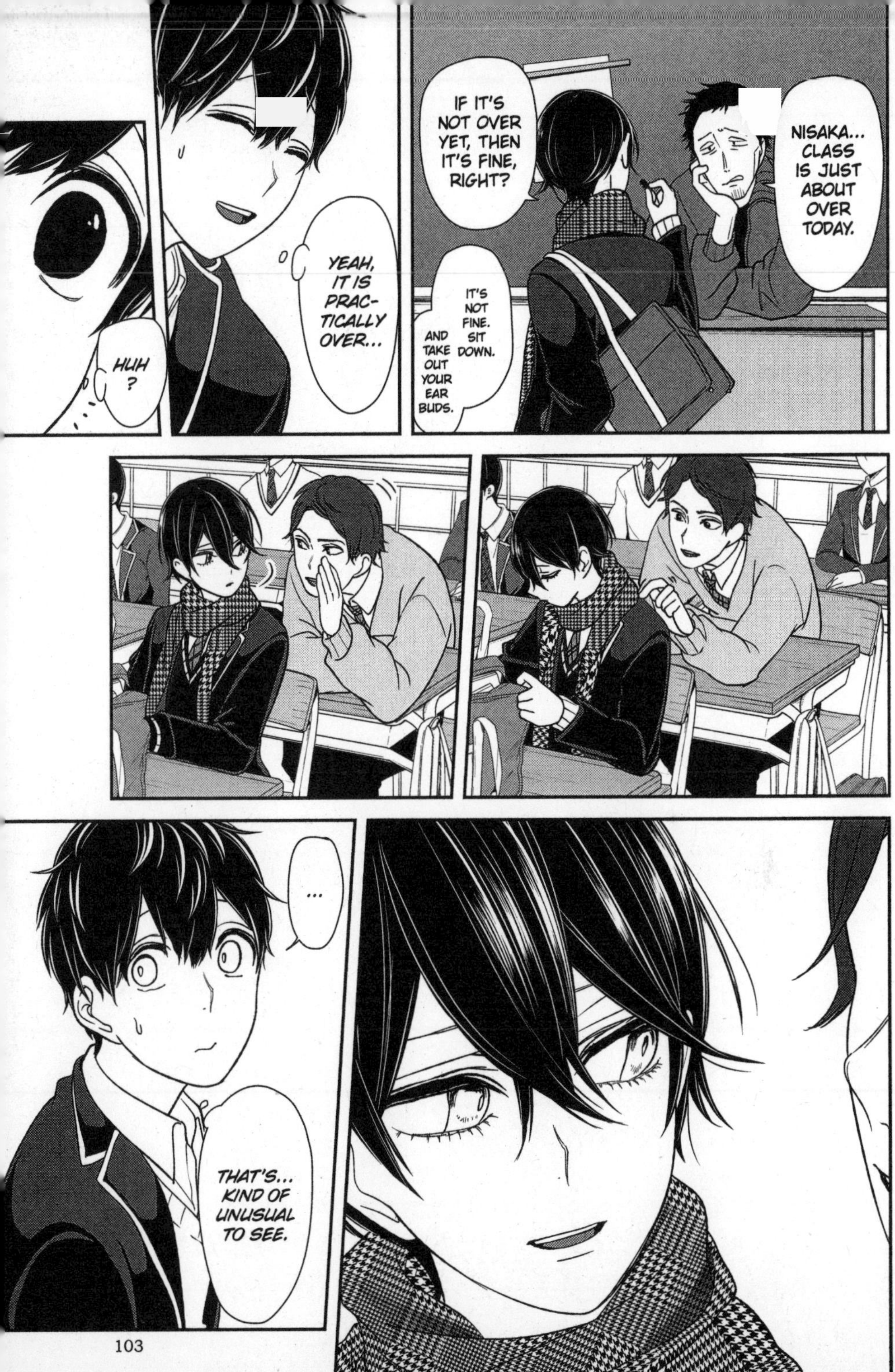

NISAKA... CLASS IS JUST ABOUT OVER TODAY.
IF IT'S NOT OVER YET, THEN IT'S FINE, RIGHT?
IT'S NOT FINE. SIT DOWN.
AND TAKE OUT YOUR EAR BUDS.
YEAH, IT IS PRAC-TICALLY OVER...
HUH?
...
THAT'S... KIND OF UNUSUAL TO SEE.

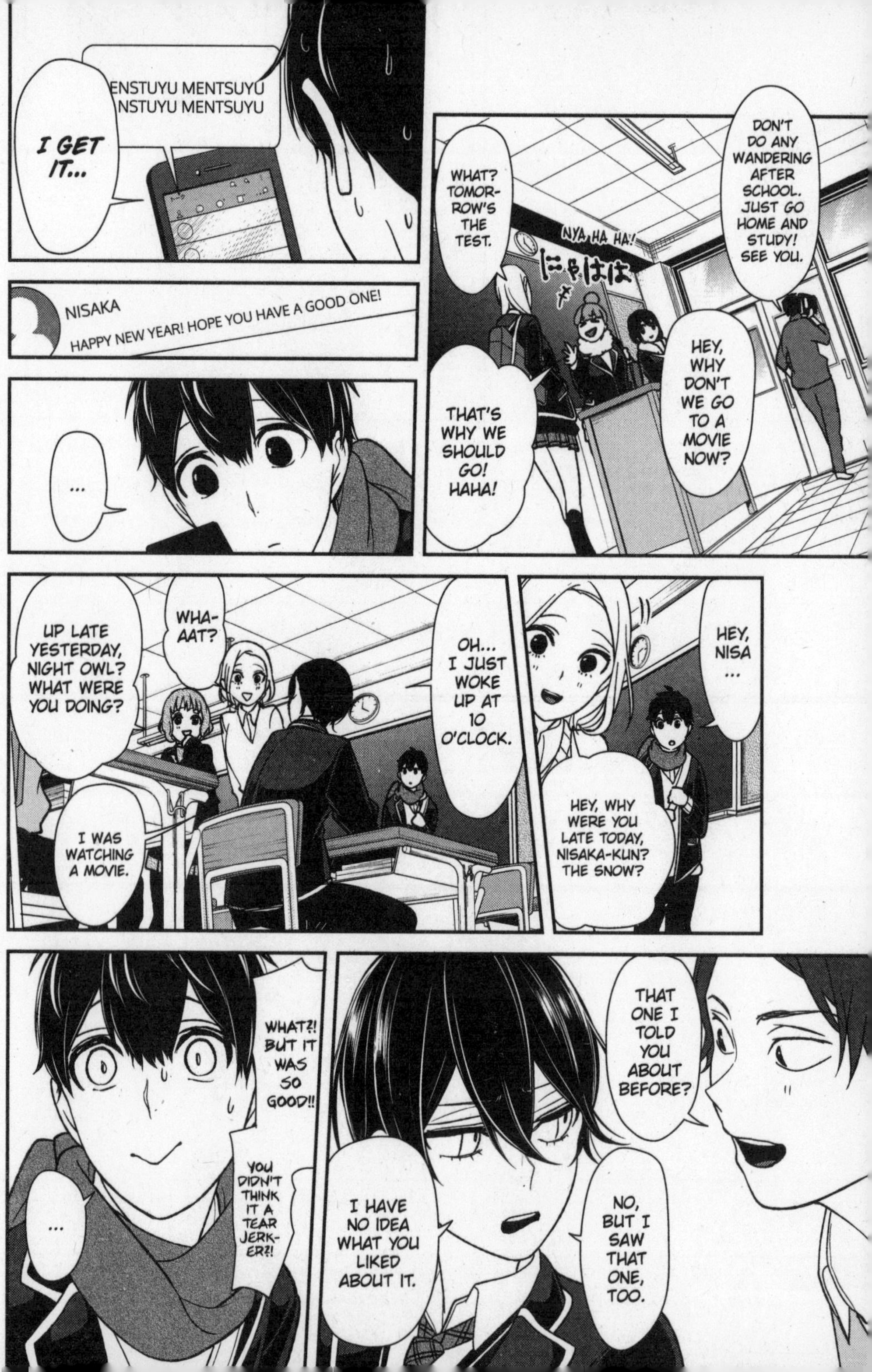
DON'T DO ANY WANDERING AFTER SCHOOL. JUST GO HOME AND STUDY! SEE YOU.
WHAT? TOMORROW'S THE TEST.
NYA HA HA!
にゃはは
HEY, WHY DON'T WE GO TO A MOVIE NOW?
THAT'S WHY WE SHOULD GO! HAHA!
ENSTUYU MENTSUYU
NSTUYU MENTSUYU
I GET IT...
NISAKA
HAPPY NEW YEAR! HOPE YOU HAVE A GOOD ONE!
...
HEY, NISA...
HEY, WHY WERE YOU LATE TODAY, NISAKA-KUN? THE SNOW?
OH... I JUST WOKE UP AT 10 O'CLOCK.
WHA-AAT?
UP LATE YESTERDAY, NIGHT OWL? WHAT WERE YOU DOING?
I WAS WATCHING A MOVIE.
THAT ONE I TOLD YOU ABOUT BEFORE?
NO, BUT I SAW THAT ONE, TOO.
I HAVE NO IDEA WHAT YOU LIKED ABOUT IT.
WHAT?! BUT IT WAS SO GOOD!!
YOU DIDN'T THINK IT A TEAR JERKER?!
...

OH, UH-HUH.

SEE YOU TOMORROW, NISAKA!

LET'S GO, NEJI.

OH, YEAH...

YEEP! THEY WERE KINDA SCARY...

MEN-TSUYU, MEN-TSUYU...

YEEP!

STARE

OKAY, PUT DOWN YOUR PENS AND PASS YOUR PAPERS UP FROM THE BACK.

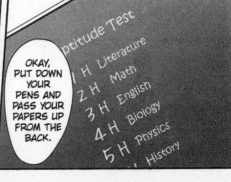

Aptitude Test

1 H Literature

2 H Math

3 H English

4 H Biology

5 H Physics

History

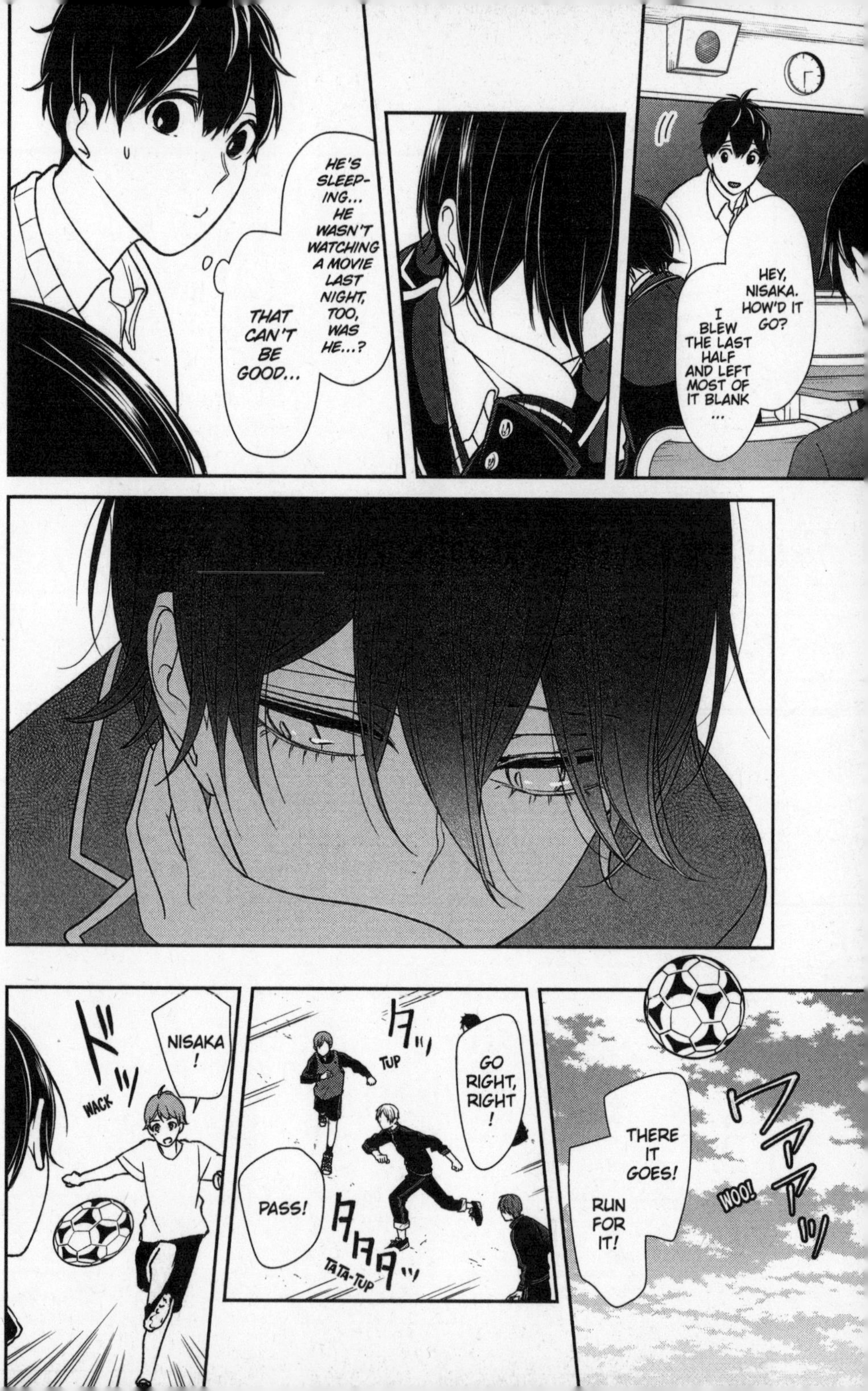
HEY, NISAKA. HOW'D IT GO?
I BLEW THE LAST HALF AND LEFT MOST OF IT BLANK...
HE'S SLEEPING... HE WASN'T WATCHING A MOVIE LAST NIGHT, TOO, WAS HE...?
THAT CAN'T BE GOOD...
WOO!
THERE IT GOES!
RUN FOR IT!
TUP
GO RIGHT, RIGHT!
PASS!
TATA-TUP
NISAKA!
WACK

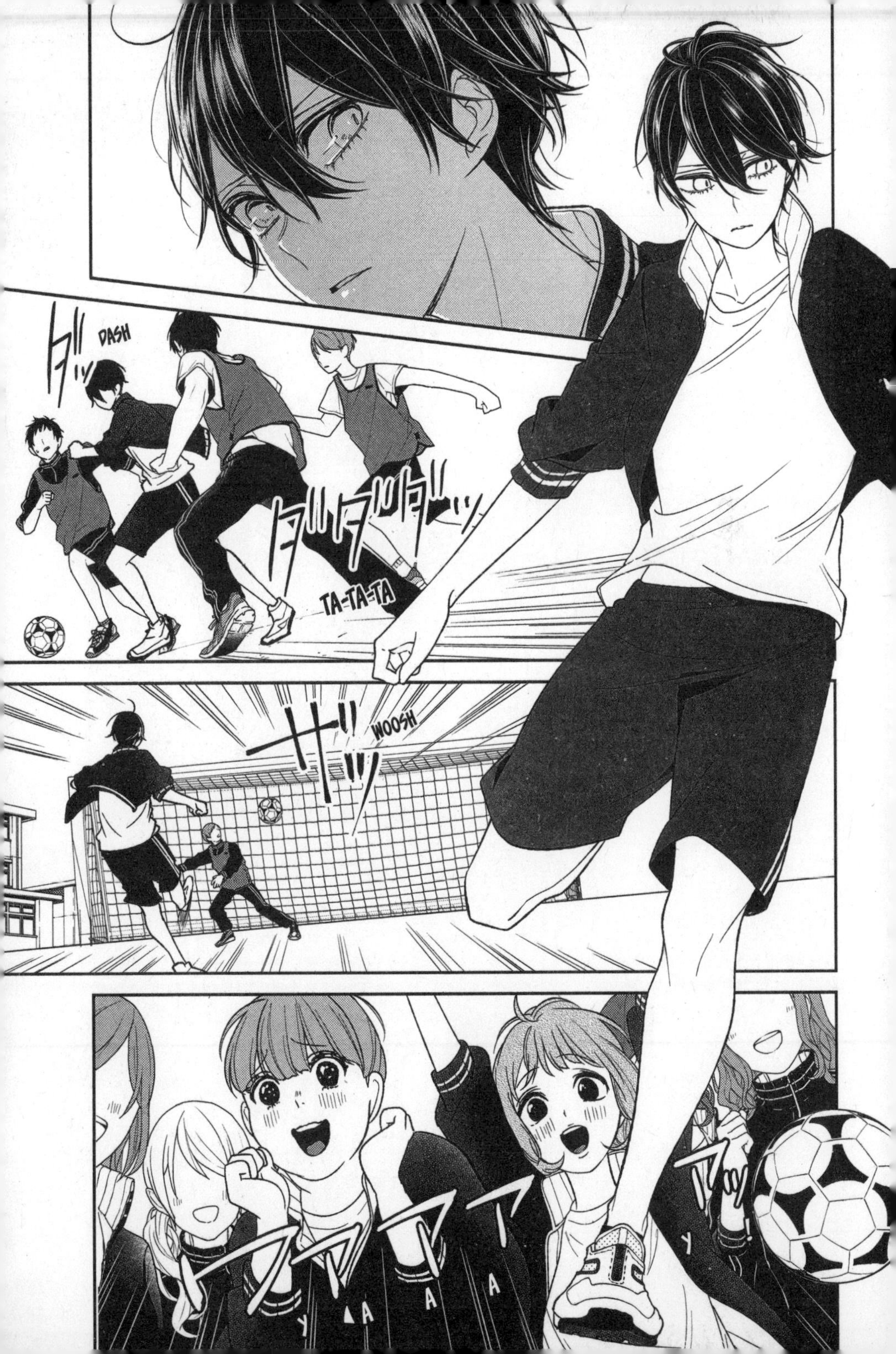
DASH
TA-TA-TA
WOOSH

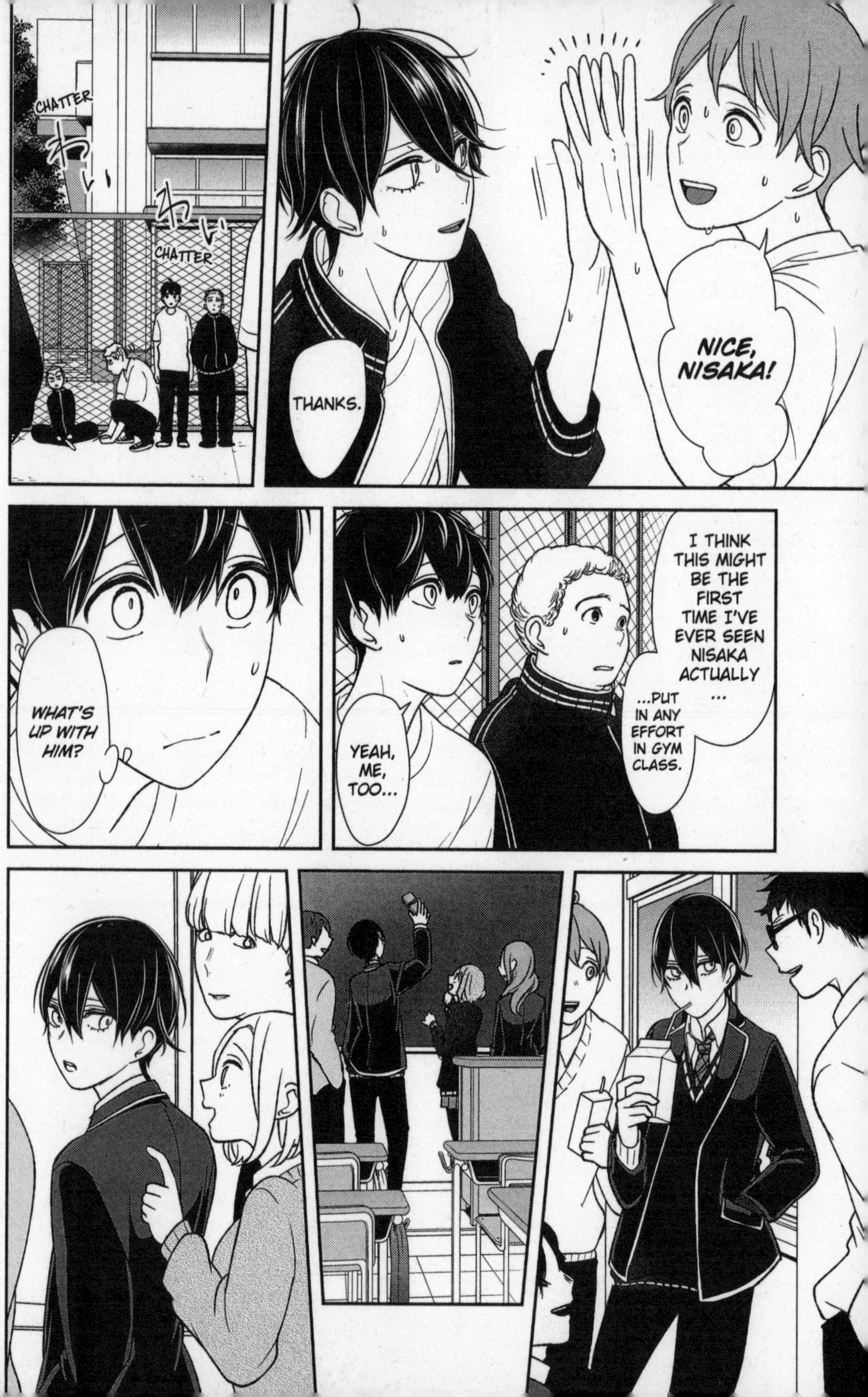
NICE, NISAKA!
THANKS.
CHATTER
わい
CHATTER
わい
I THINK THIS MIGHT BE THE FIRST TIME I'VE EVER SEEN NISAKA ACTUALLY ...
...PUT IN ANY EFFORT IN GYM CLASS.
YEAH, ME, TOO...
WHAT'S UP WITH HIM?

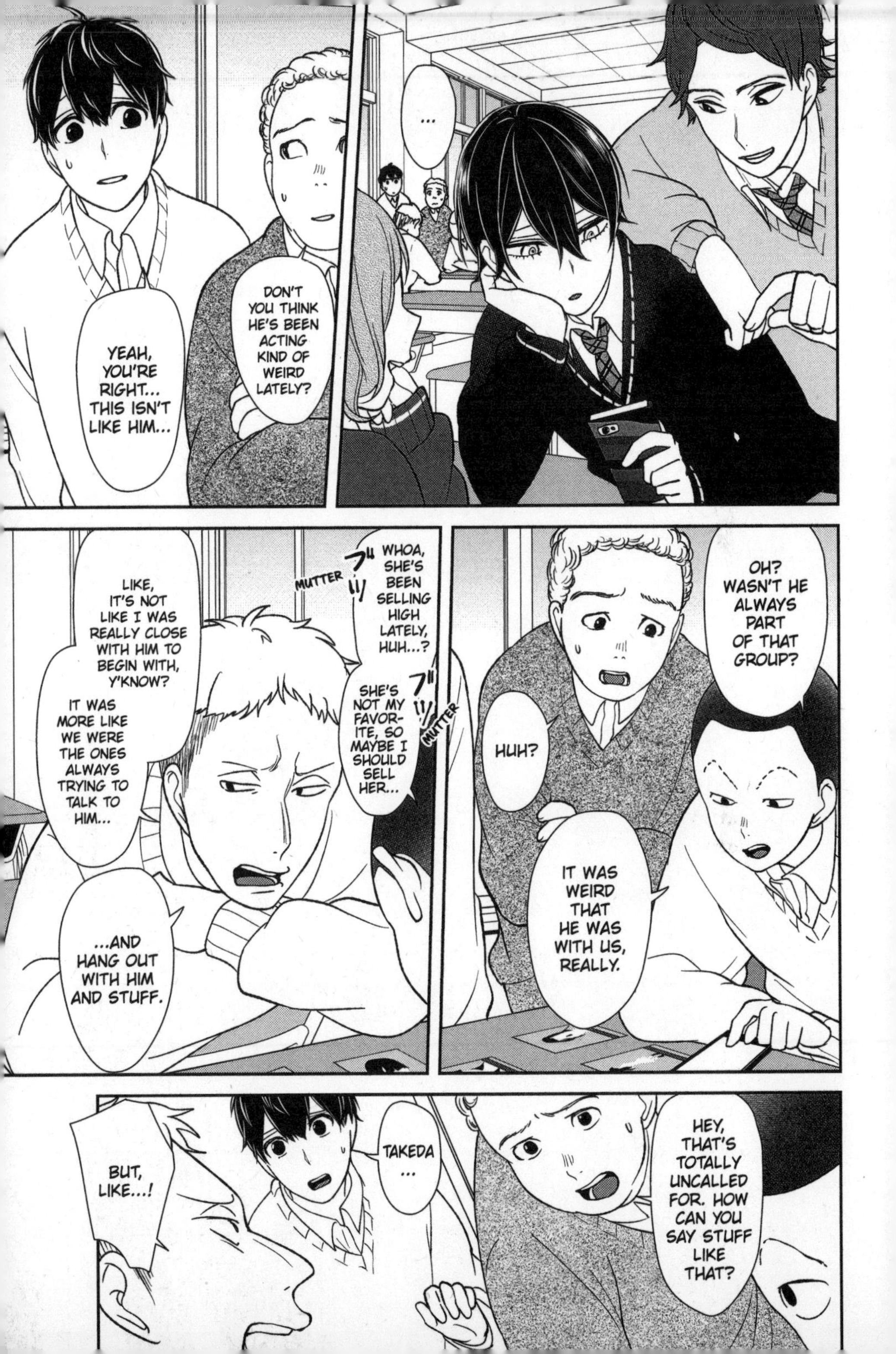
...
DON'T YOU THINK HE'S BEEN ACTING KIND OF WEIRD LATELY?
YEAH, YOU'RE RIGHT... THIS ISN'T LIKE HIM...
OH? WASN'T HE ALWAYS PART OF THAT GROUP?
HUH?
IT WAS WEIRD THAT HE WAS WITH US, REALLY.
WHOA, SHE'S BEEN SELLING HIGH LATELY, HUH...?
MUTTER
SHE'S NOT MY FAVOR-ITE, SO MAYBE I SHOULD SELL HER...
MUTTER
LIKE, IT'S NOT LIKE I WAS REALLY CLOSE WITH HIM TO BEGIN WITH, Y'KNOW?
IT WAS MORE LIKE WE WERE THE ONES ALWAYS TRYING TO TALK TO HIM...
...AND HANG OUT WITH HIM AND STUFF.
HEY, THAT'S TOTALLY UNCALLED FOR. HOW CAN YOU SAY STUFF LIKE THAT?
TAKEDA...
BUT, LIKE...!

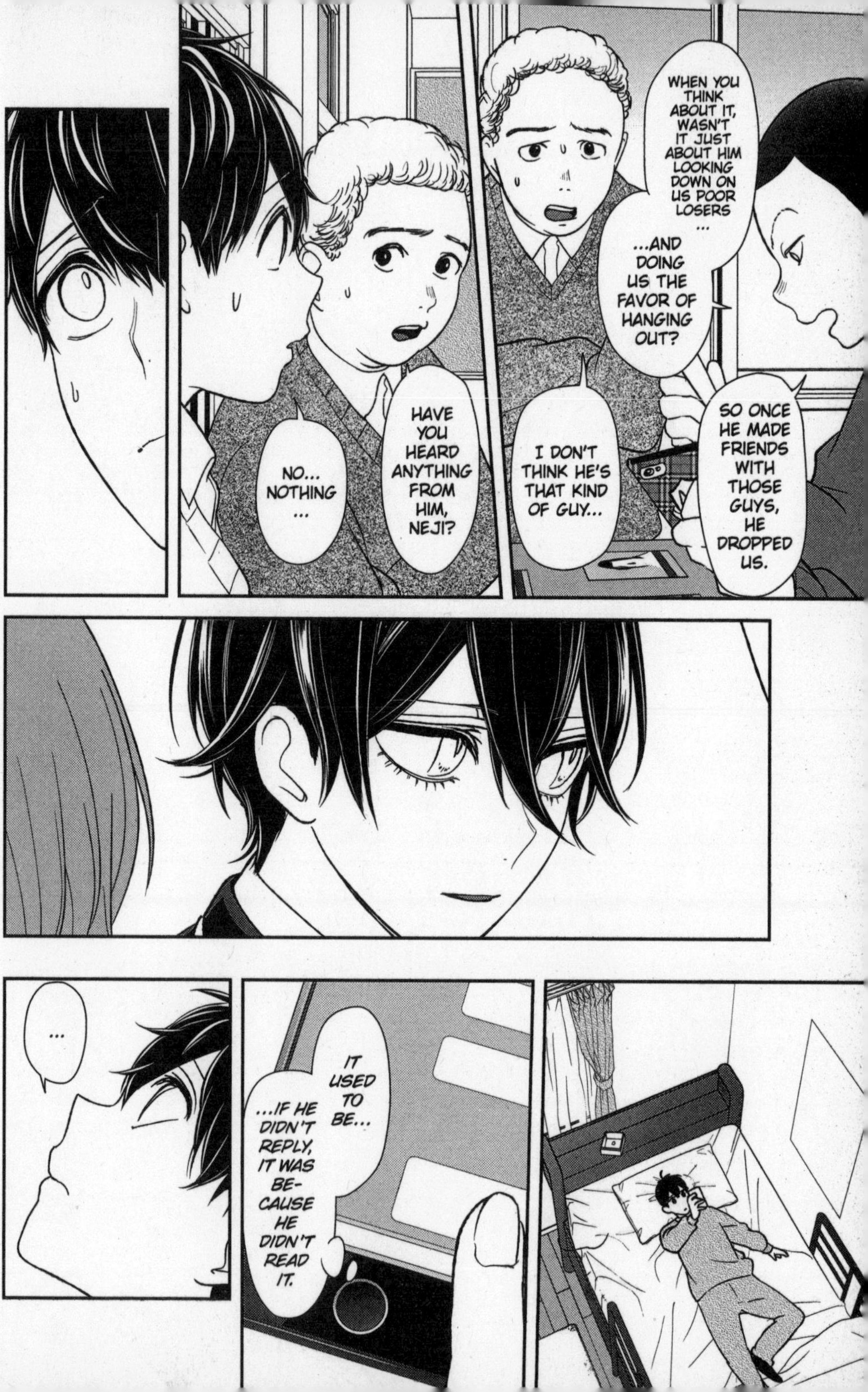
WHEN YOU THINK ABOUT IT, WASN'T IT JUST ABOUT HIM LOOKING DOWN ON US POOR LOSERS ...
...AND DOING US THE FAVOR OF HANGING OUT?
SO ONCE HE MADE FRIENDS WITH THOSE GUYS, HE DROPPED US.
I DON'T THINK HE'S THAT KIND OF GUY...
HAVE YOU HEARD ANYTHING FROM HIM, NEJI?
NO... NOTHING ...
IT USED TO BE...
...IF HE DIDN'T REPLY, IT WAS BE-CAUSE HE DIDN'T READ IT.
...

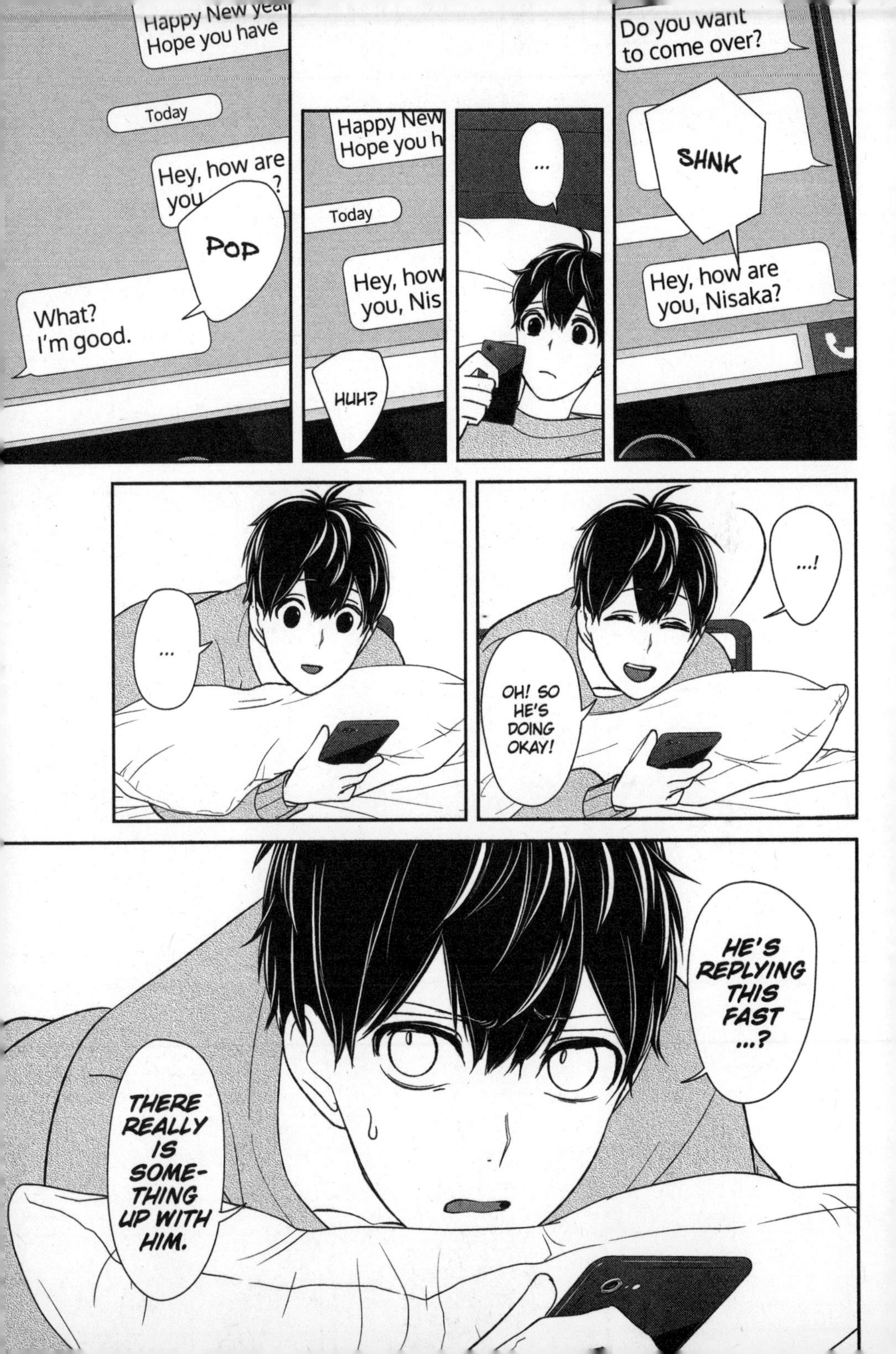
Do you want to come over?
SHNK
Hey, how are you, Nisaka?
...
Happy New
Hope you h
Today
Hey, how
you, Nis
HUH?
Happy New year
Hope you have
Today
Hey, how are you ?
POP
What? I'm good.
...!
OH! SO HE'S DOING OKAY!
...
HE'S REPLYING THIS FAST ...?
THERE REALLY IS SOME-THING UP WITH HIM.

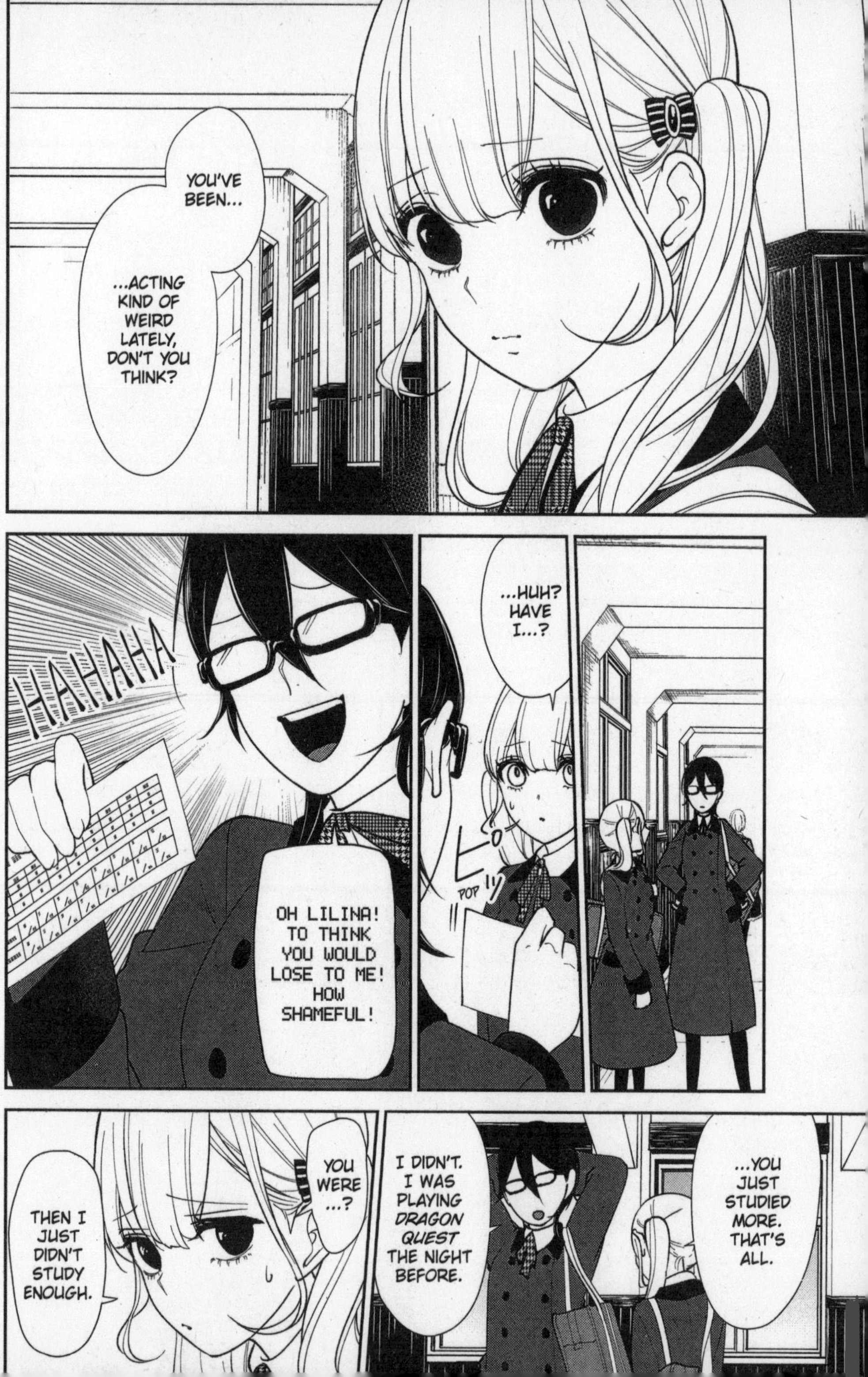

YOU'VE BEEN...
...ACTING KIND OF WEIRD LATELY, DON'T YOU THINK?
...HUH? HAVE I...?
POP
HAHAHA
OH LILINA! TO THINK YOU WOULD LOSE TO ME! HOW SHAMEFUL!
...YOU JUST STUDIED MORE. THAT'S ALL.
I DIDN'T. I WAS PLAYING *DRAGON QUEST* THE NIGHT BEFORE.
YOU WERE ...?
THEN I JUST DIDN'T STUDY ENOUGH.

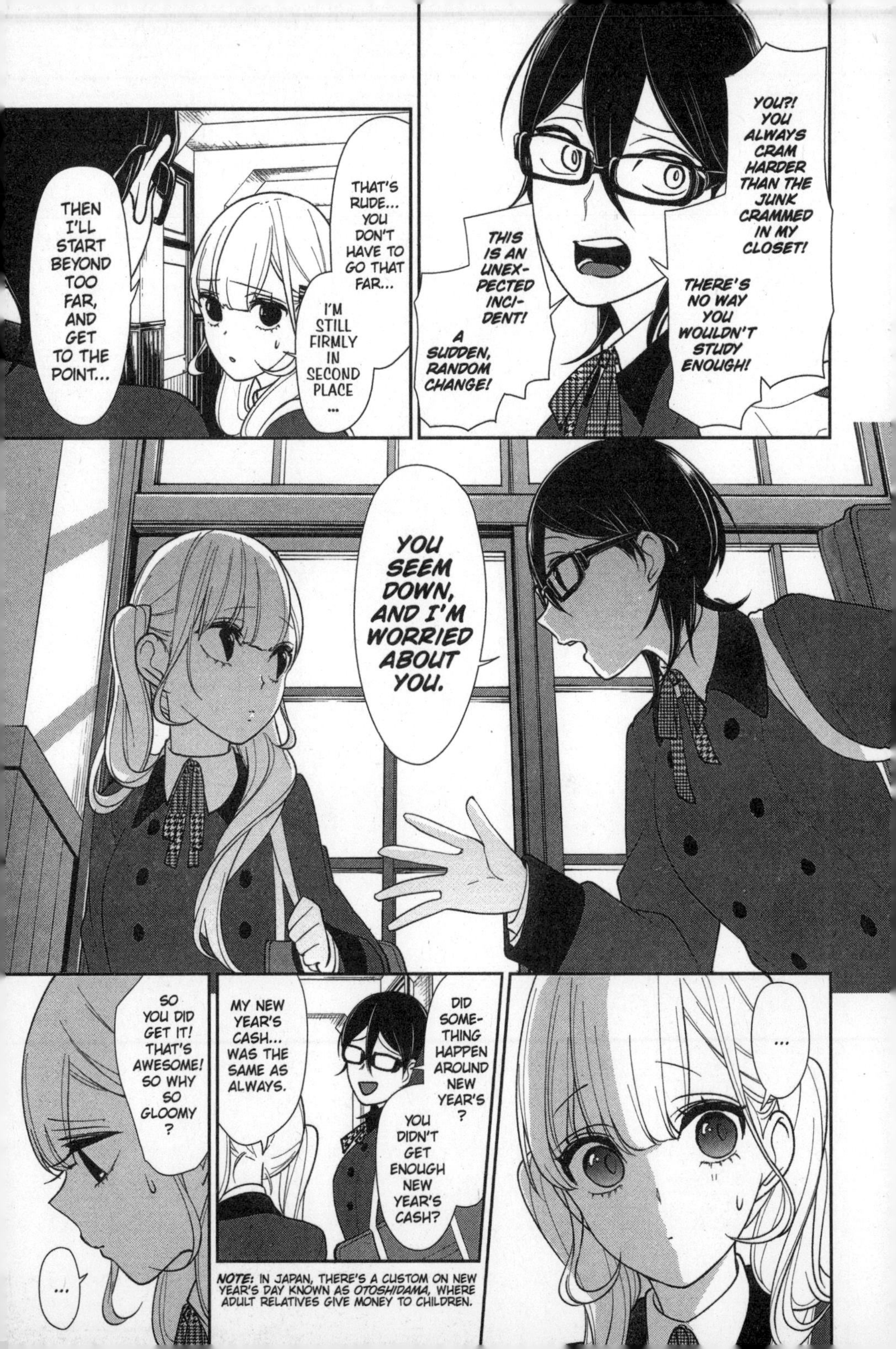
YOU?! YOU ALWAYS CRAM HARDER THAN THE JUNK CRAMMED IN MY CLOSET!
THIS IS AN UNEX-PECTED INCI-DENT!
THERE'S NO WAY YOU WOULDN'T STUDY ENOUGH!
A SUDDEN, RANDOM CHANGE!
THAT'S RUDE... YOU DON'T HAVE TO GO THAT FAR...
I'M STILL FIRMLY IN SECOND PLACE ...
THEN I'LL START BEYOND TOO FAR, AND GET TO THE POINT...
YOU SEEM DOWN, AND I'M WORRIED ABOUT YOU.
...
DID SOME-THING HAPPEN AROUND NEW YEAR'S ?
YOU DIDN'T GET ENOUGH NEW YEAR'S CASH?
MY NEW YEAR'S CASH... WAS THE SAME AS ALWAYS.
NOTE: IN JAPAN, THERE'S A CUSTOM ON NEW YEAR'S DAY KNOWN AS OTOSHIDAMA, WHERE ADULT RELATIVES GIVE MONEY TO CHILDREN.
SO YOU DID GET IT! THAT'S AWESOME! SO WHY SO GLOOMY ?
...

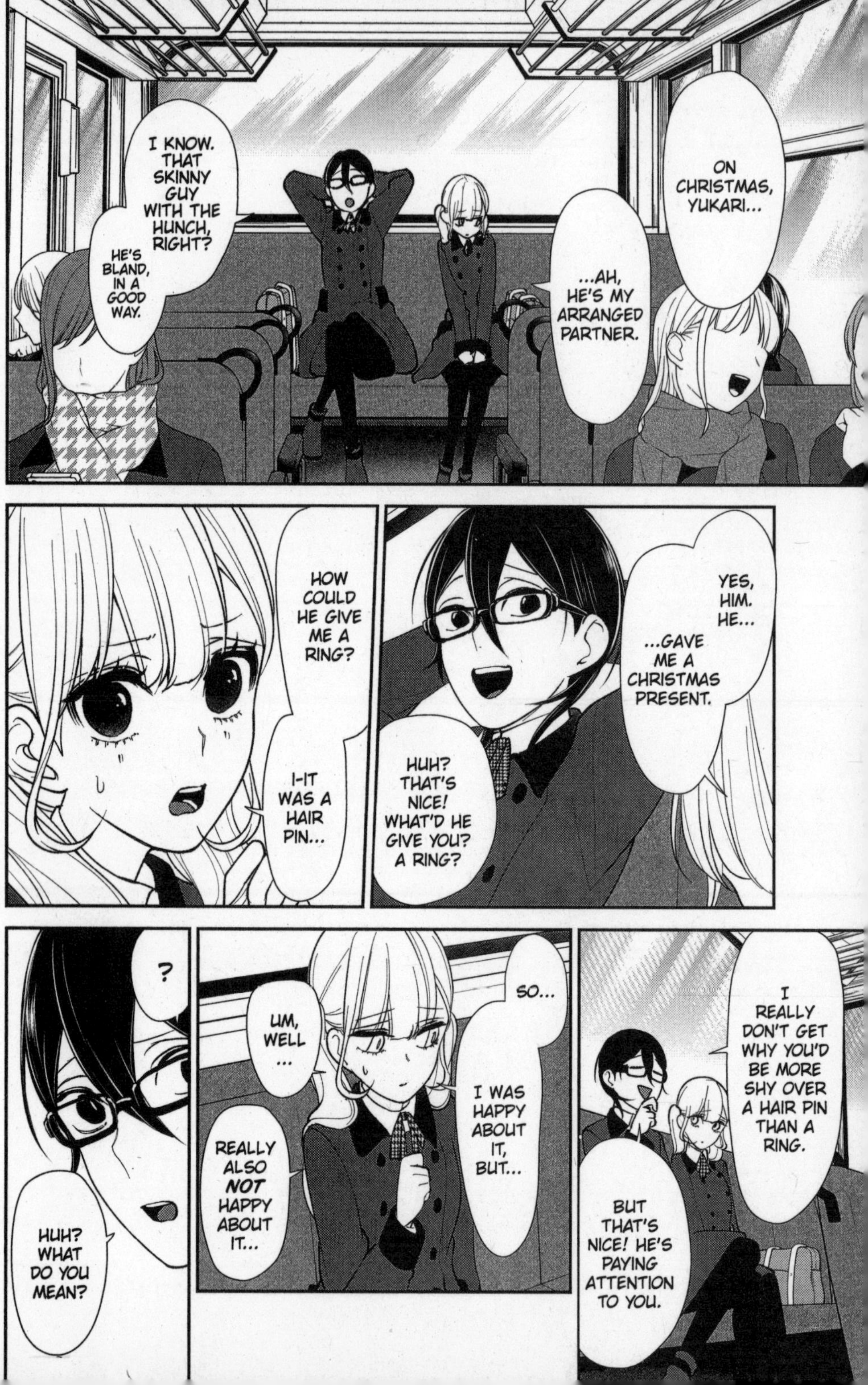
ON CHRISTMAS, YUKARI...
...AH, HE'S MY ARRANGED PARTNER.
I KNOW. THAT SKINNY GUY WITH THE HUNCH, RIGHT?
HE'S BLAND, IN A GOOD WAY.
YES, HIM. HE...
...GAVE ME A CHRISTMAS PRESENT.
HUH? THAT'S NICE! WHAT'D HE GIVE YOU? A RING?
HOW COULD HE GIVE ME A RING?
I-IT WAS A HAIR PIN...
I REALLY DON'T GET WHY YOU'D BE MORE SHY OVER A HAIR PIN THAN A RING.
BUT THAT'S NICE! HE'S PAYING ATTENTION TO YOU.
SO...
I WAS HAPPY ABOUT IT, BUT...
UM, WELL ...
REALLY ALSO ***NOT*** HAPPY ABOUT IT...
?
HUH? WHAT DO YOU MEAN?

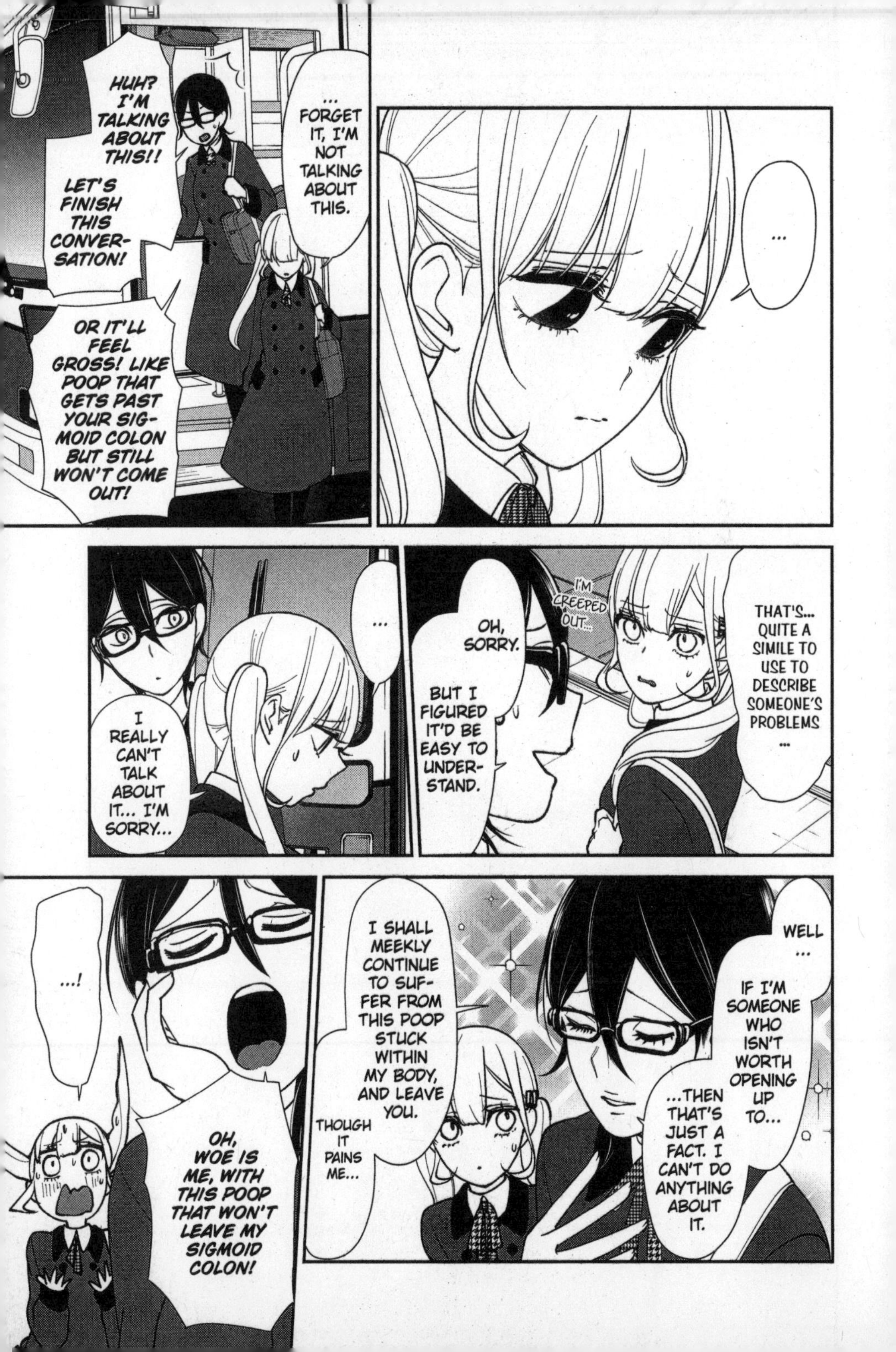
...
... FORGET IT, I'M NOT TALKING ABOUT THIS.
HUH? I'M TALKING ABOUT THIS!! LET'S FINISH THIS CONVERSATION!
OR IT'LL FEEL GROSS! LIKE POOP THAT GETS PAST YOUR SIGMOID COLON BUT STILL WON'T COME OUT!
THAT'S... QUITE A SIMILE TO USE TO DESCRIBE SOMEONE'S PROBLEMS ...
I'M CREEPED OUT...
OH, SORRY.
BUT I FIGURED IT'D BE EASY TO UNDERSTAND.
...
I REALLY CAN'T TALK ABOUT IT... I'M SORRY...
WELL ...
IF I'M SOMEONE WHO ISN'T WORTH OPENING UP TO...
...THEN THAT'S JUST A FACT. I CAN'T DO ANYTHING ABOUT IT.
I SHALL MEEKLY CONTINUE TO SUFFER FROM THIS POOP STUCK WITHIN MY BODY, AND LEAVE YOU.
THOUGH IT PAINS ME...
...!
OH, WOE IS ME, WITH THIS POOP THAT WON'T LEAVE MY SIGMOID COLON!

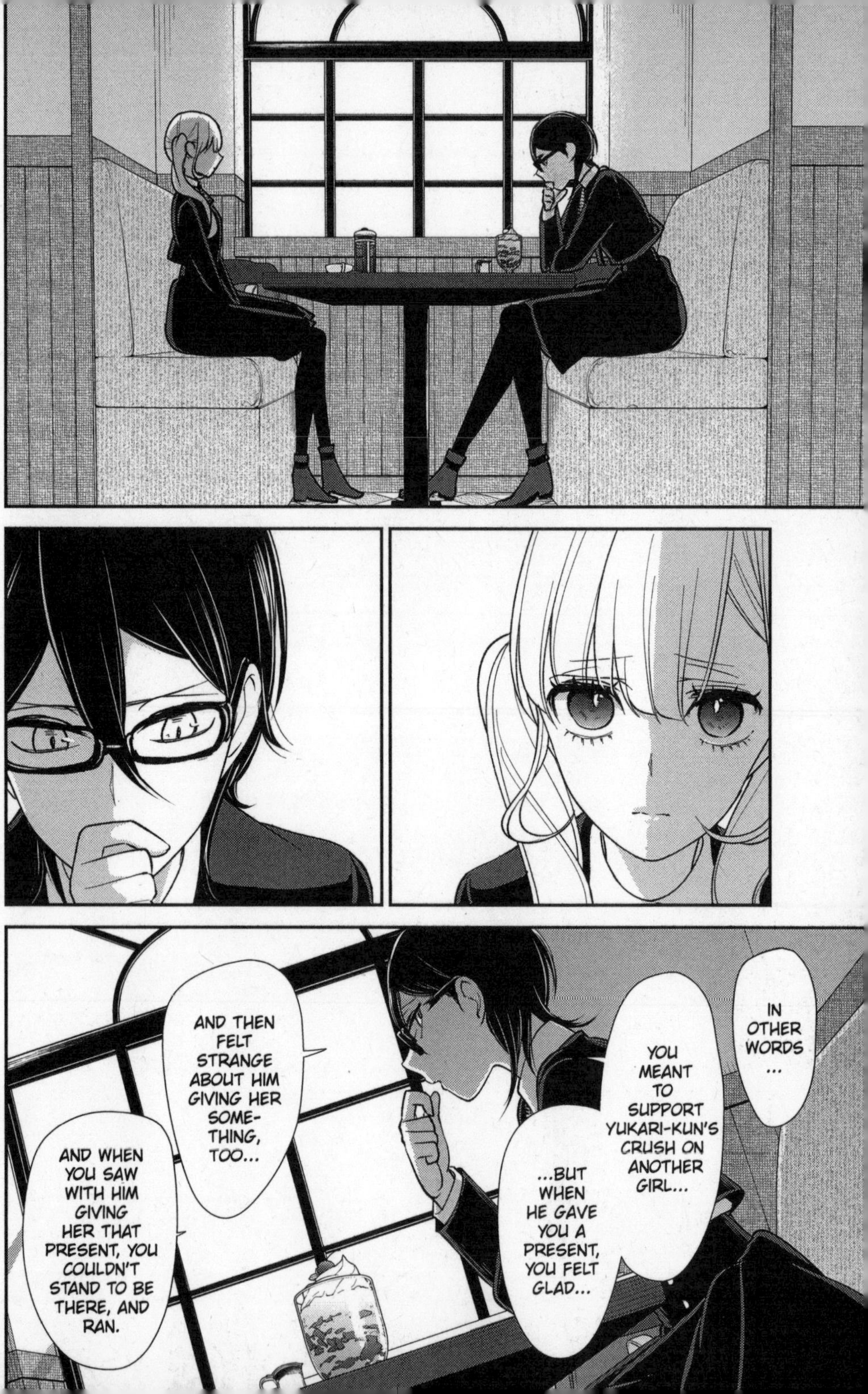
IN OTHER WORDS...
YOU MEANT TO SUPPORT YUKARI-KUN'S CRUSH ON ANOTHER GIRL...
...BUT WHEN HE GAVE YOU A PRESENT, YOU FELT GLAD...
AND THEN FELT STRANGE ABOUT HIM GIVING HER SOME-THING, TOO...
AND WHEN YOU SAW WITH HIM GIVING HER THAT PRESENT, YOU COULDN'T STAND TO BE THERE, AND RAN.

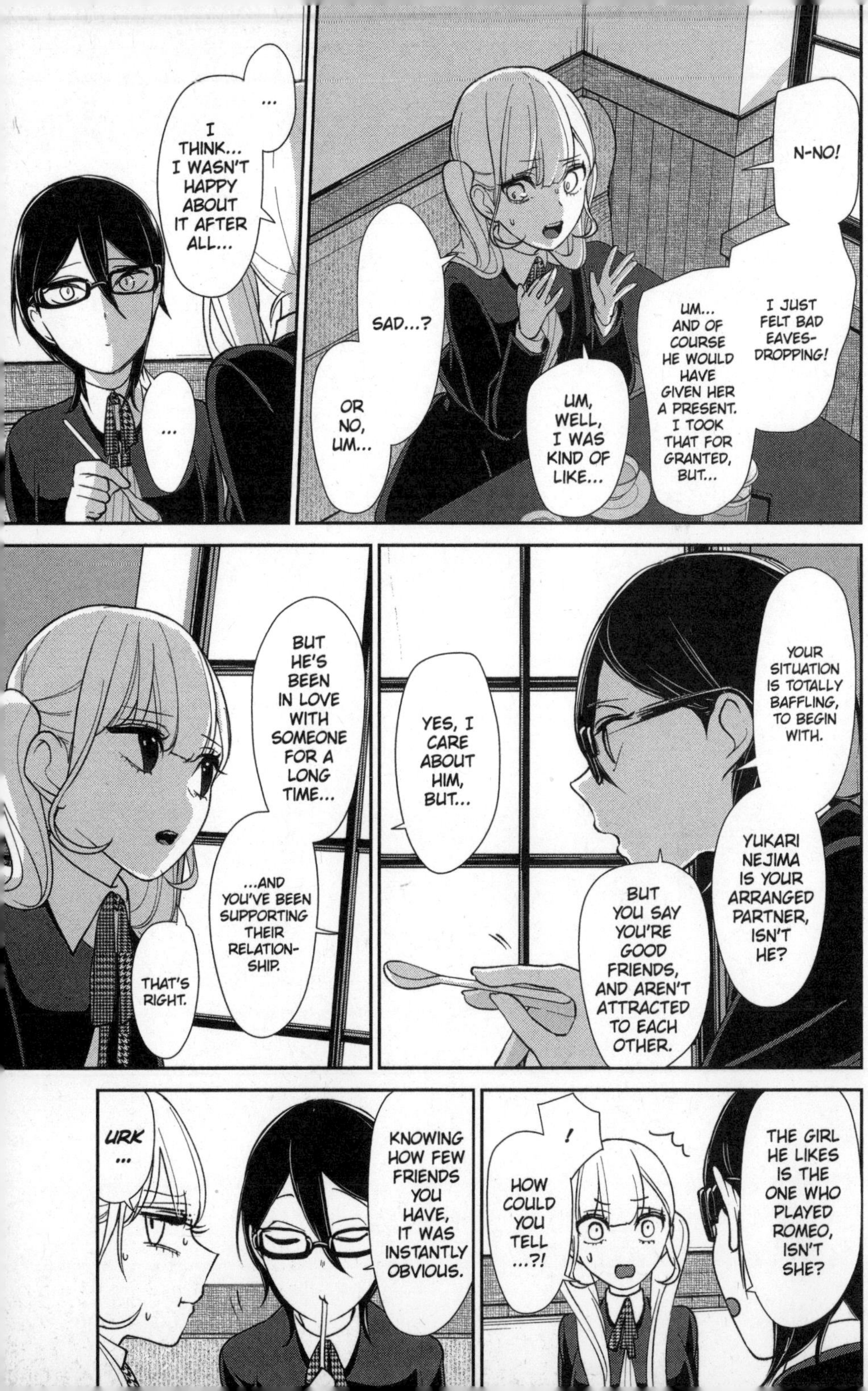
N-NO!
I JUST FELT BAD EAVES-DROPPING!
UM... AND OF COURSE HE WOULD HAVE GIVEN HER A PRESENT. I TOOK THAT FOR GRANTED, BUT...
UM, WELL, I WAS KIND OF LIKE...
SAD...?
OR NO, UM...
...
I THINK... I WASN'T HAPPY ABOUT IT AFTER ALL...
...
YOUR SITUATION IS TOTALLY BAFFLING, TO BEGIN WITH.
YUKARI NEJIMA IS YOUR ARRANGED PARTNER, ISN'T HE?
BUT YOU SAY YOU'RE GOOD FRIENDS, AND AREN'T ATTRACTED TO EACH OTHER.
YES, I CARE ABOUT HIM, BUT...
BUT HE'S BEEN IN LOVE WITH SOMEONE FOR A LONG TIME...
...AND YOU'VE BEEN SUPPORTING THEIR RELATION-SHIP.
THAT'S RIGHT.
THE GIRL HE LIKES IS THE ONE WHO PLAYED ROMEO, ISN'T SHE?
!
HOW COULD YOU TELL ...?!
KNOWING HOW FEW FRIENDS YOU HAVE, IT WAS INSTANTLY OBVIOUS.
URK ...

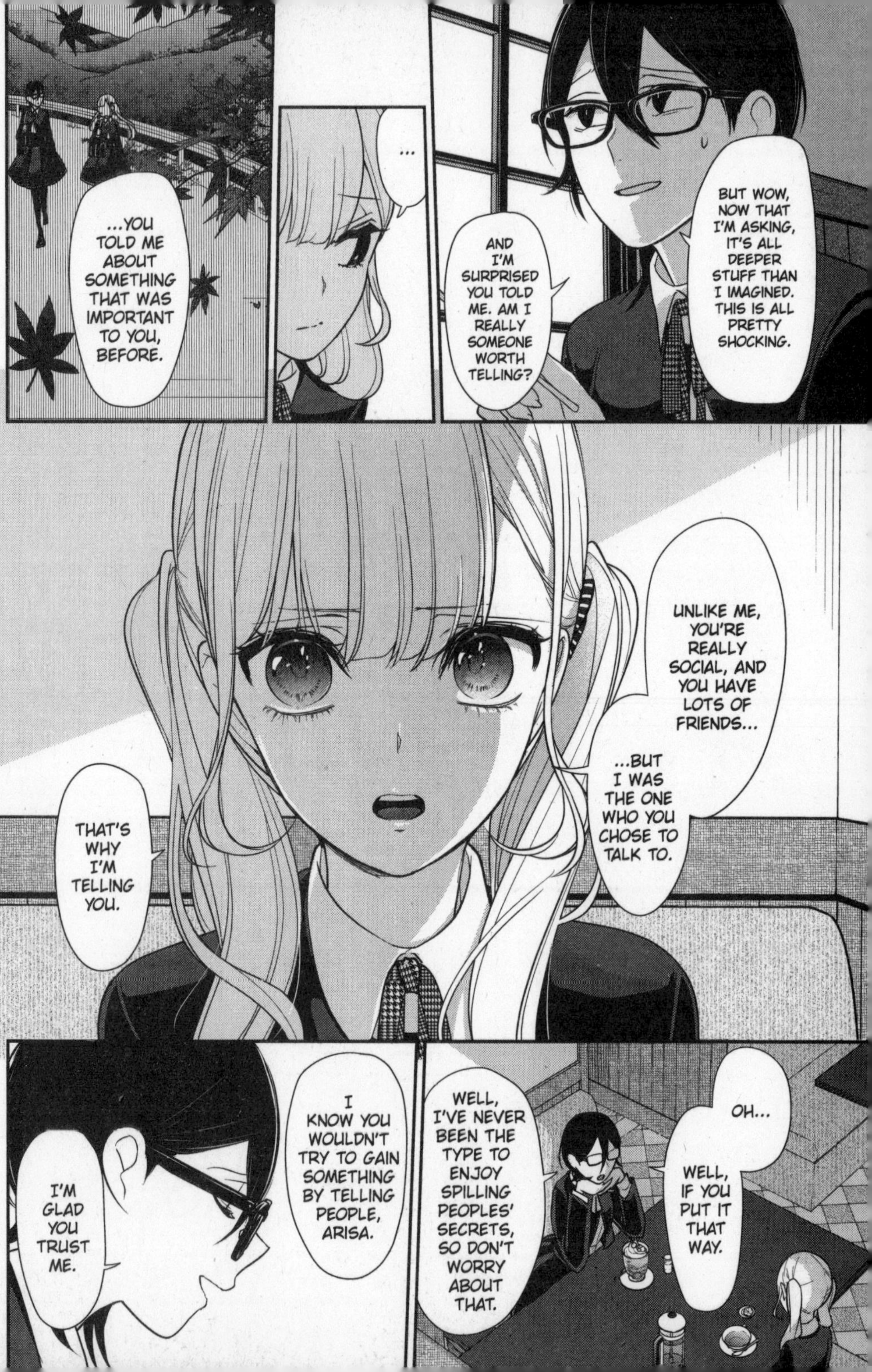
BUT WOW, NOW THAT I'M ASKING, IT'S ALL DEEPER STUFF THAN I IMAGINED. THIS IS ALL PRETTY SHOCKING.
AND I'M SURPRISED YOU TOLD ME. AM I REALLY SOMEONE WORTH TELLING?
...
...YOU TOLD ME ABOUT SOMETHING THAT WAS IMPORTANT TO YOU, BEFORE.
UNLIKE ME, YOU'RE REALLY SOCIAL, AND YOU HAVE LOTS OF FRIENDS...
...BUT I WAS THE ONE WHO YOU CHOSE TO TALK TO.
THAT'S WHY I'M TELLING YOU.
OH...
WELL, IF YOU PUT IT THAT WAY.
WELL, I'VE NEVER BEEN THE TYPE TO ENJOY SPILLING PEOPLES' SECRETS, SO DON'T WORRY ABOUT THAT.
I KNOW YOU WOULDN'T TRY TO GAIN SOMETHING BY TELLING PEOPLE, ARISA.
I'M GLAD YOU TRUST ME.

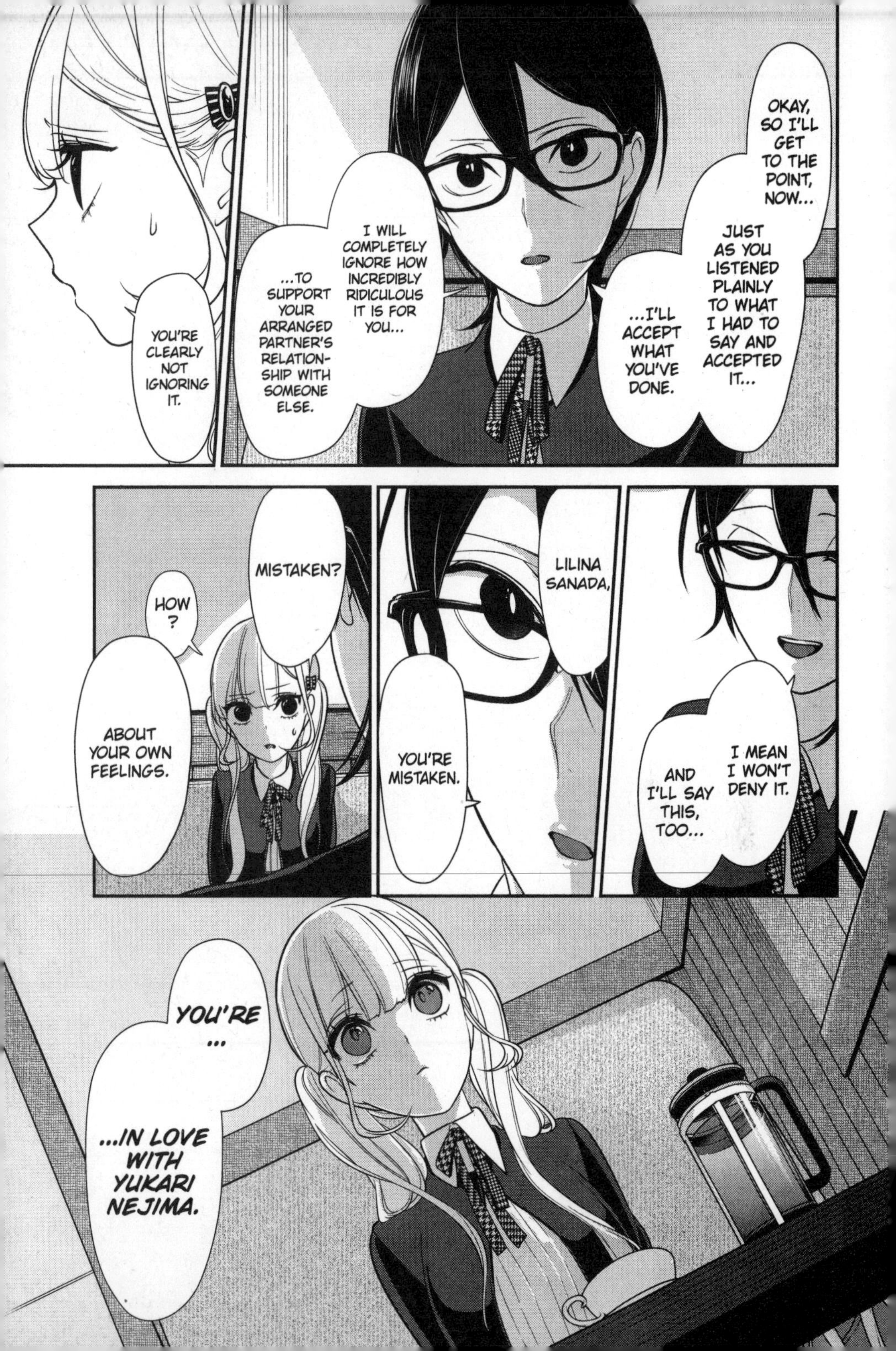
OKAY, SO I'LL GET TO THE POINT, NOW...
JUST AS YOU LISTENED PLAINLY TO WHAT I HAD TO SAY AND ACCEPTED IT...
...I'LL ACCEPT WHAT YOU'VE DONE.
I WILL COMPLETELY IGNORE HOW INCREDIBLY RIDICULOUS IT IS FOR YOU...
...TO SUPPORT YOUR ARRANGED PARTNER'S RELATION-SHIP WITH SOMEONE ELSE.
YOU'RE CLEARLY NOT IGNORING IT.
I MEAN I WON'T DENY IT.
AND I'LL SAY THIS, TOO...
LILINA SANADA,
YOU'RE MISTAKEN.
MISTAKEN?
HOW?
ABOUT YOUR OWN FEELINGS.
YOU'RE ...
...IN LOVE WITH YUKARI NEJIMA.

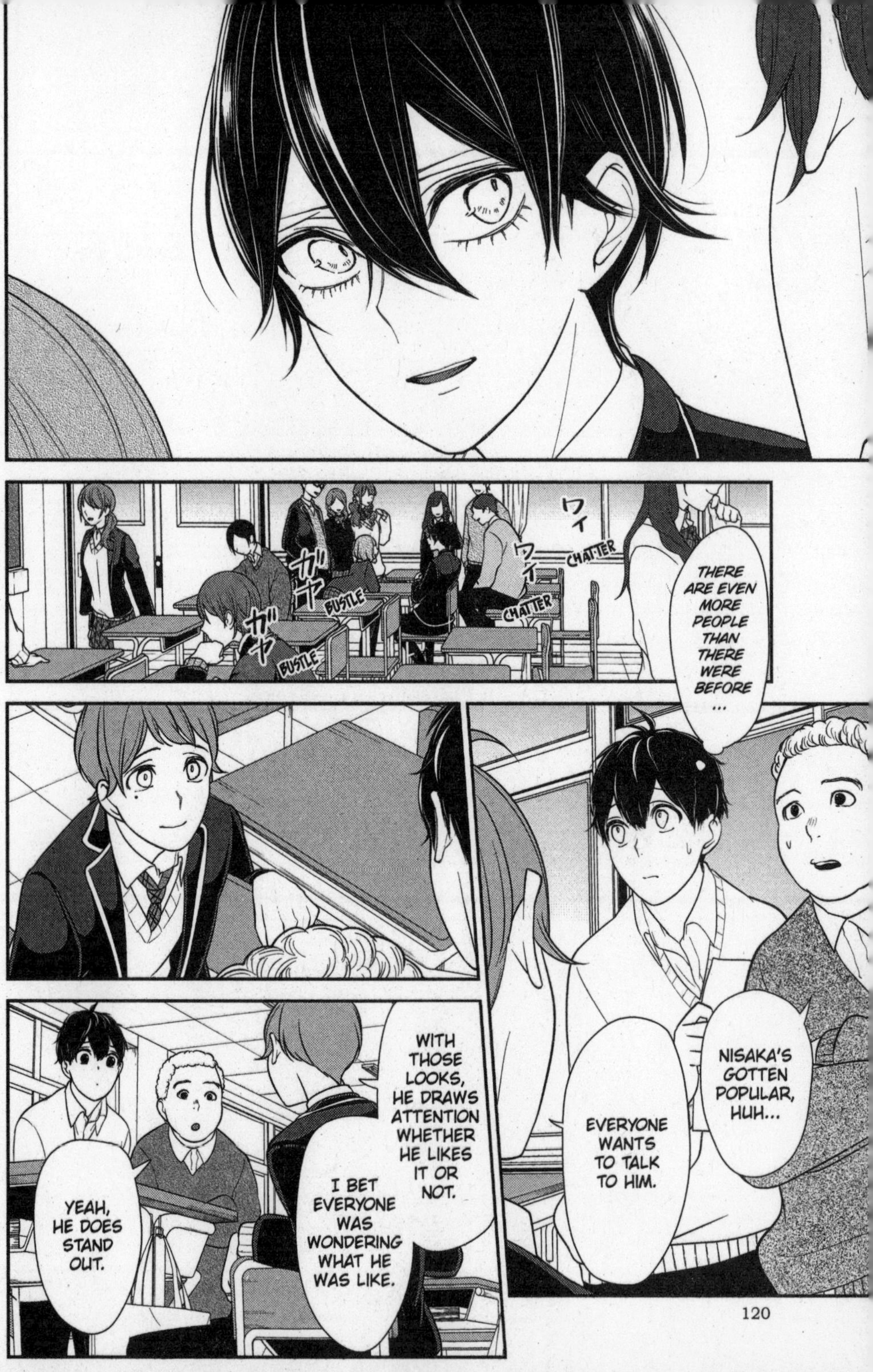
THERE ARE EVEN MORE PEOPLE THAN THERE WERE BEFORE...
ワイ ワイ
CHATTER
CHATTER
ガヤ
BUSTLE
ガヤ
BUSTLE
NISAKA'S GOTTEN POPULAR, HUH...
EVERYONE WANTS TO TALK TO HIM.
WITH THOSE LOOKS, HE DRAWS ATTENTION WHETHER HE LIKES IT OR NOT.
I BET EVERYONE WAS WONDERING WHAT HE WAS LIKE.
YEAH, HE DOES STAND OUT.

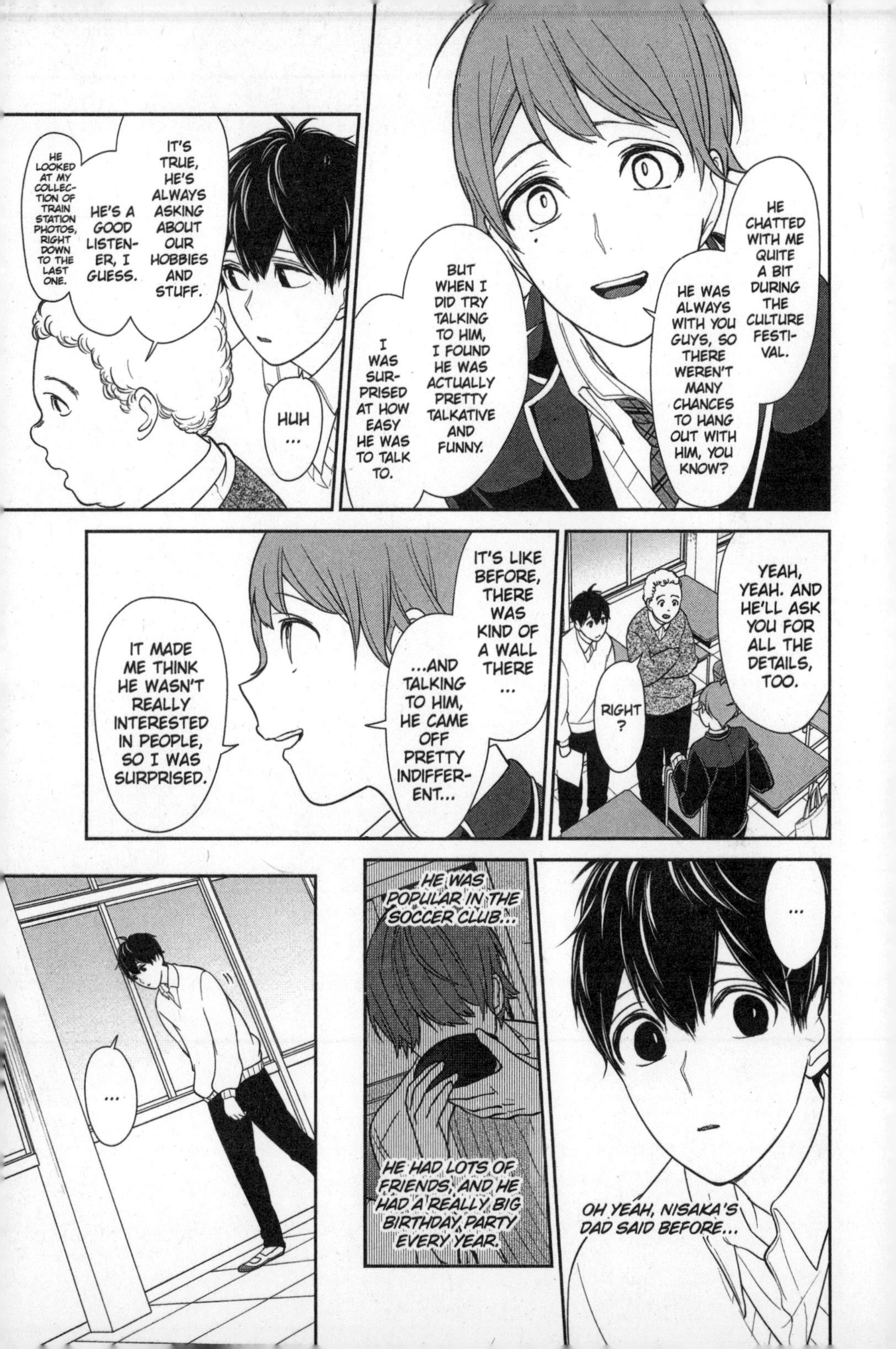
HE CHATTED WITH ME QUITE A BIT DURING THE CULTURE FESTI-VAL.
HE WAS ALWAYS WITH YOU GUYS, SO THERE WEREN'T MANY CHANCES TO HANG OUT WITH HIM, YOU KNOW?
BUT WHEN I DID TRY TALKING TO HIM, I FOUND HE WAS ACTUALLY PRETTY TALKATIVE AND FUNNY.
I WAS SUR-PRISED AT HOW EASY HE WAS TO TALK TO.
IT'S TRUE, HE'S ALWAYS ASKING ABOUT OUR HOBBIES AND STUFF.
HE'S A GOOD LISTEN-ER, I GUESS.
HE LOOKED AT MY COLLEC-TION OF TRAIN STATION PHOTOS, RIGHT DOWN TO THE LAST ONE.
HUH ...
YEAH, YEAH. AND HE'LL ASK YOU FOR ALL THE DETAILS, TOO.
RIGHT ?
IT'S LIKE BEFORE, THERE WAS KIND OF A WALL THERE ...
...AND TALKING TO HIM, HE CAME OFF PRETTY INDIFFER-ENT...
IT MADE ME THINK HE WASN'T REALLY INTERESTED IN PEOPLE, SO I WAS SURPRISED.
...
OH YEAH, NISAKA'S DAD SAID BEFORE...
HE WAS POPULAR IN THE SOCCER CLUB...
HE HAD LOTS OF FRIENDS, AND HE HAD A REALLY BIG BIRTHDAY PARTY EVERY YEAR.
...

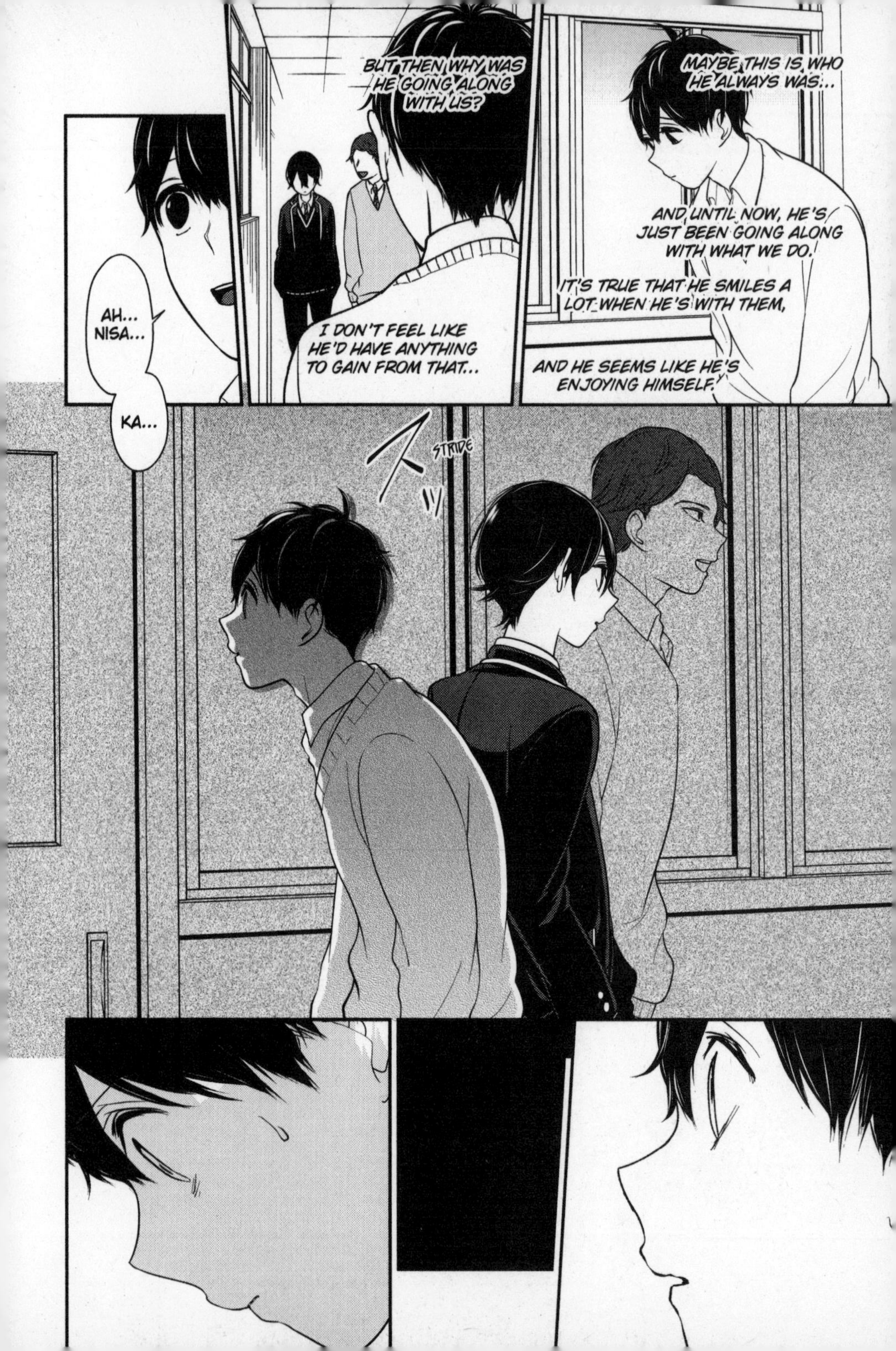
MAYBE THIS IS WHO HE ALWAYS WAS...
AND UNTIL NOW, HE'S JUST BEEN GOING ALONG WITH WHAT WE DO.
IT'S TRUE THAT HE SMILES A LOT WHEN HE'S WITH THEM,
AND HE SEEMS LIKE HE'S ENJOYING HIMSELF.
BUT THEN WHY WAS HE GOING ALONG WITH US?
I DON'T FEEL LIKE HE'D HAVE ANYTHING TO GAIN FROM THAT...
AH... NISA...
KA...
STRIDE

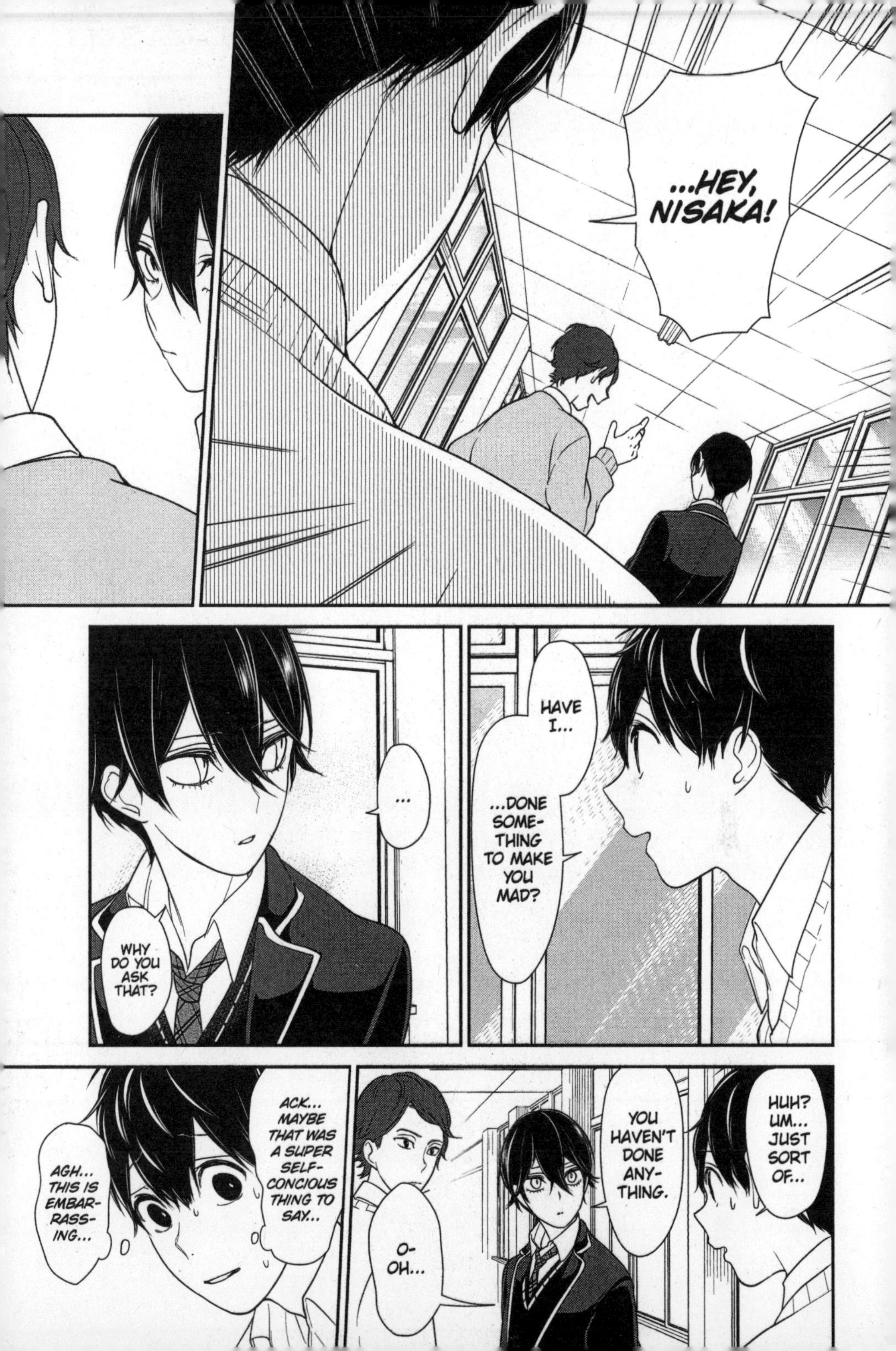
...HEY, NISAKA!
HAVE I...
...DONE SOMETHING TO MAKE YOU MAD?
...
WHY DO YOU ASK THAT?
HUH? UM... JUST SORT OF...
YOU HAVEN'T DONE ANYTHING.
O-OH...
ACK... MAYBE THAT WAS A SUPER SELF-CONCIOUS THING TO SAY...
AGH... THIS IS EMBARRASSING...

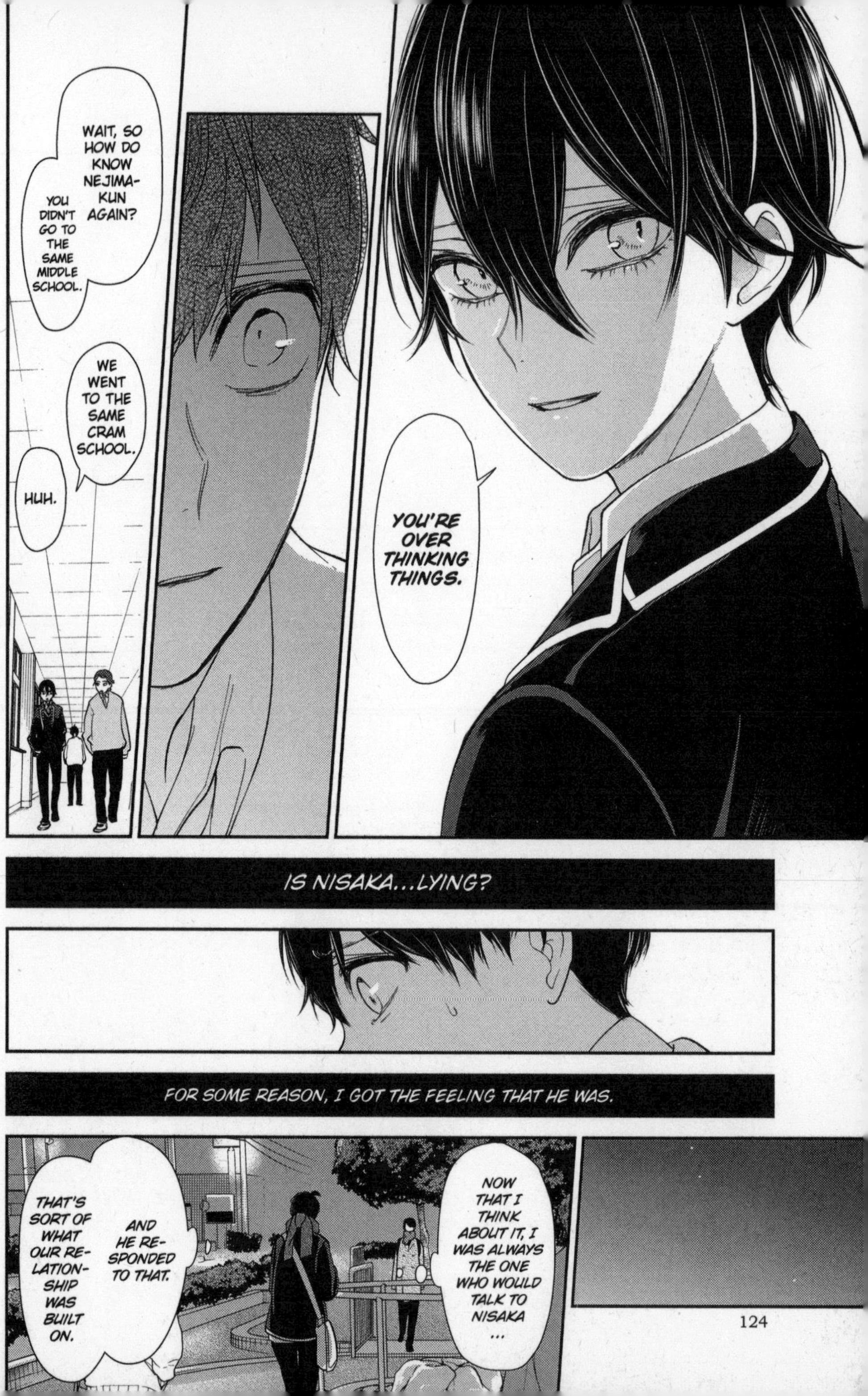
YOU'RE OVER THINKING THINGS.
WAIT, SO HOW DO KNOW NEJIMA-KUN AGAIN?
YOU DIDN'T GO TO THE SAME MIDDLE SCHOOL.
WE WENT TO THE SAME CRAM SCHOOL.
HUH.
IS NISAKA...LYING?
FOR SOME REASON, I GOT THE FEELING THAT HE WAS.
NOW THAT I THINK ABOUT IT, I WAS ALWAYS THE ONE WHO WOULD TALK TO NISAKA ...
AND HE RE-SPONDED TO THAT.
THAT'S SORT OF WHAT OUR RE-LATION-SHIP WAS BUILT ON.

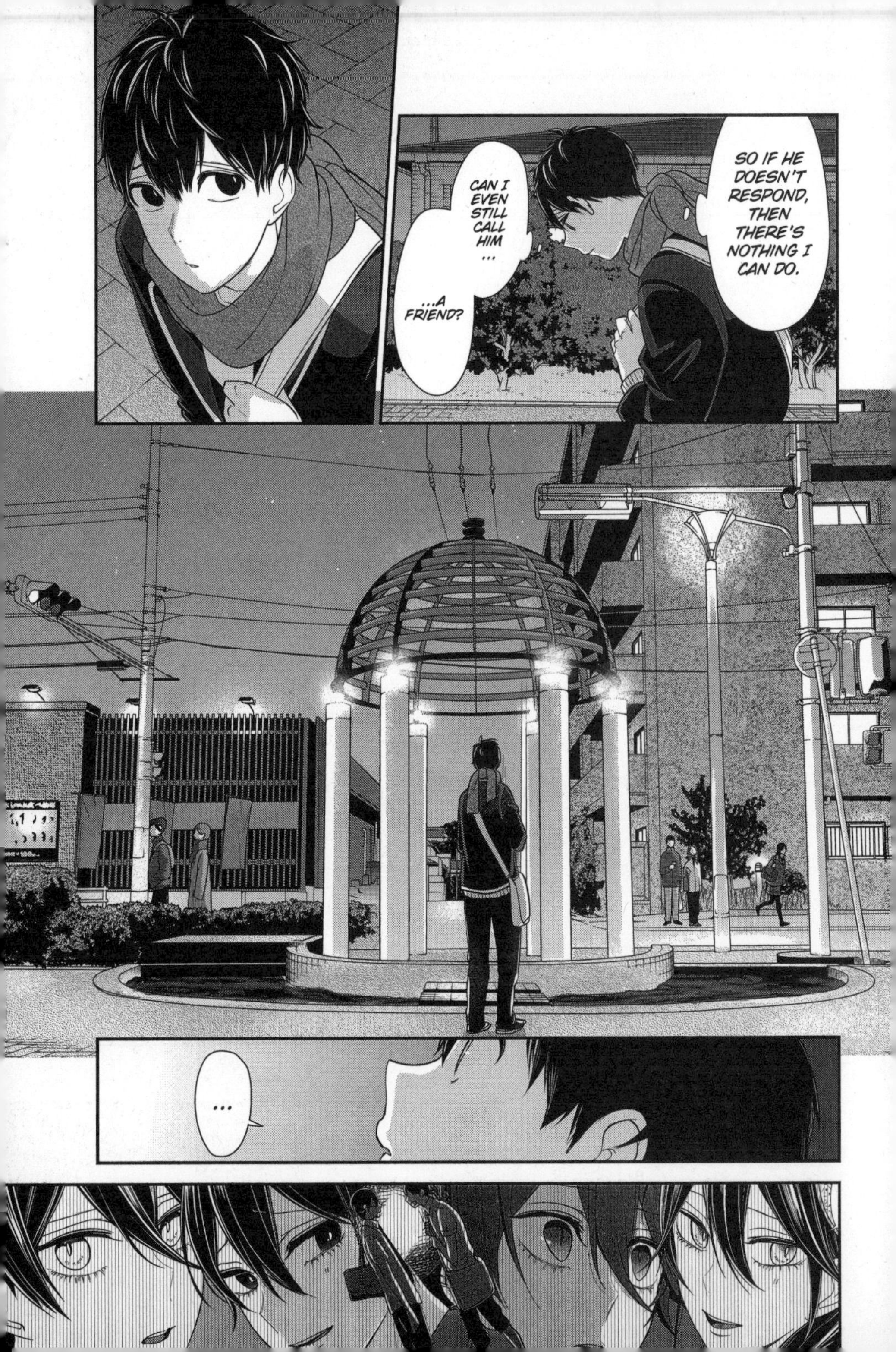
SO IF HE DOESN'T RESPOND, THEN THERE'S NOTHING I CAN DO.
CAN I EVEN STILL CALL HIM ...
...A FRIEND?
...

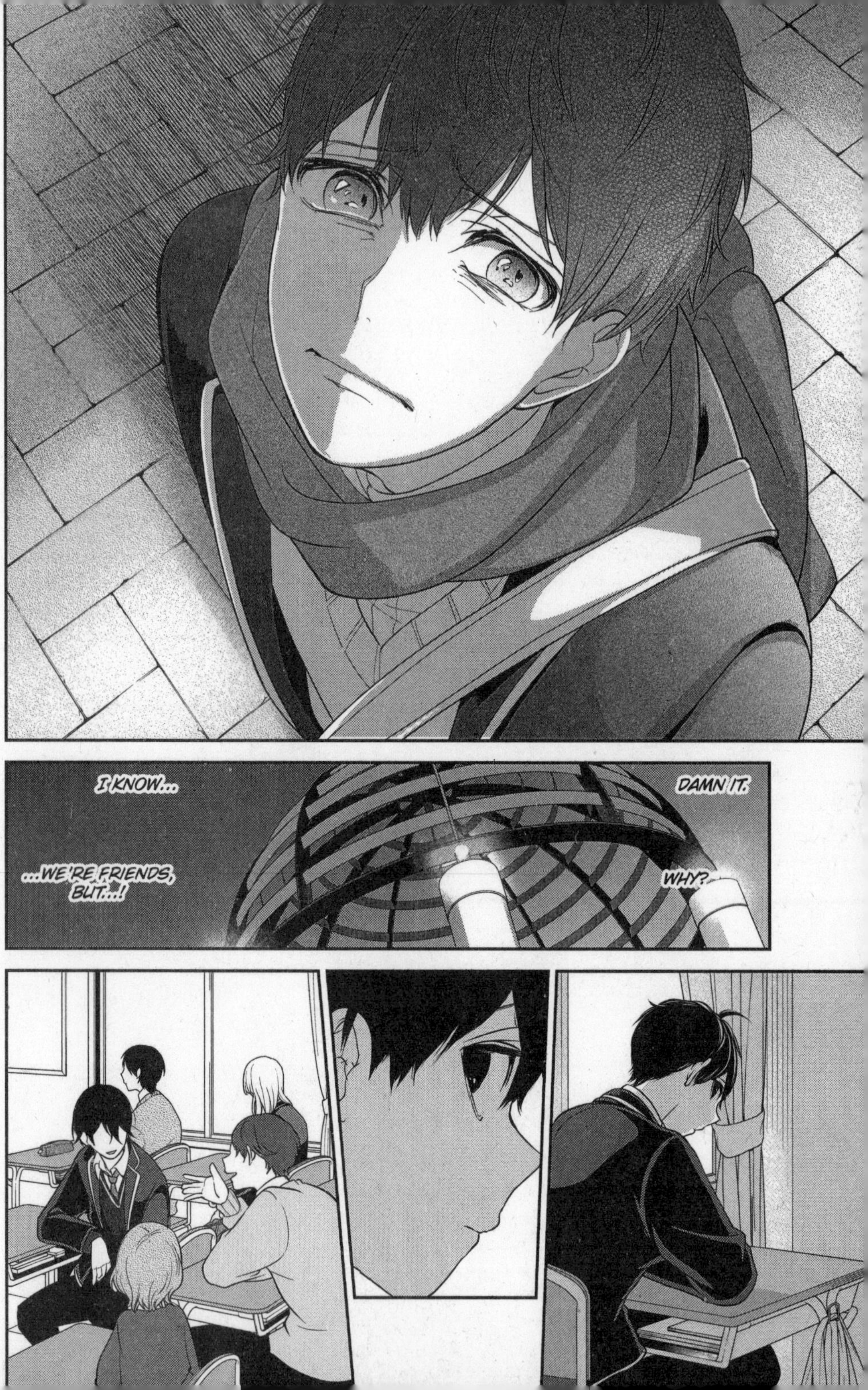
DAMN IT.
WHY?
I KNOW...
...WE'RE FRIENDS, BUT...!

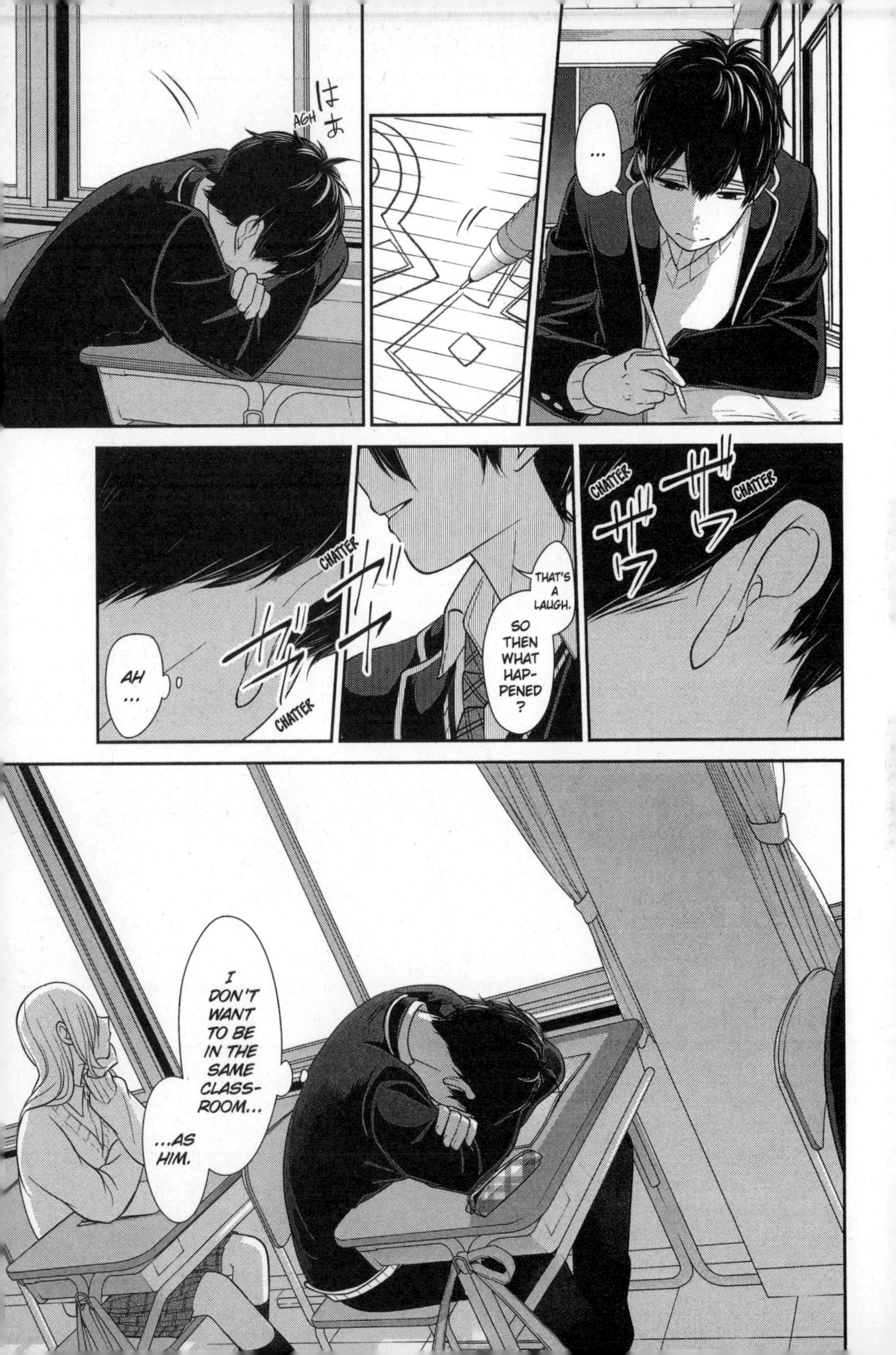
...
はぁ
AGH
CHATTER
ザワ
ザワ
CHATTER
THAT'S A LAUGH.
SO THEN WHAT HAPPENED?
CHATTER
ザワ
ザワ
CHATTER
AH...
I DON'T WANT TO BE IN THE SAME CLASSROOM...
...AS HIM.

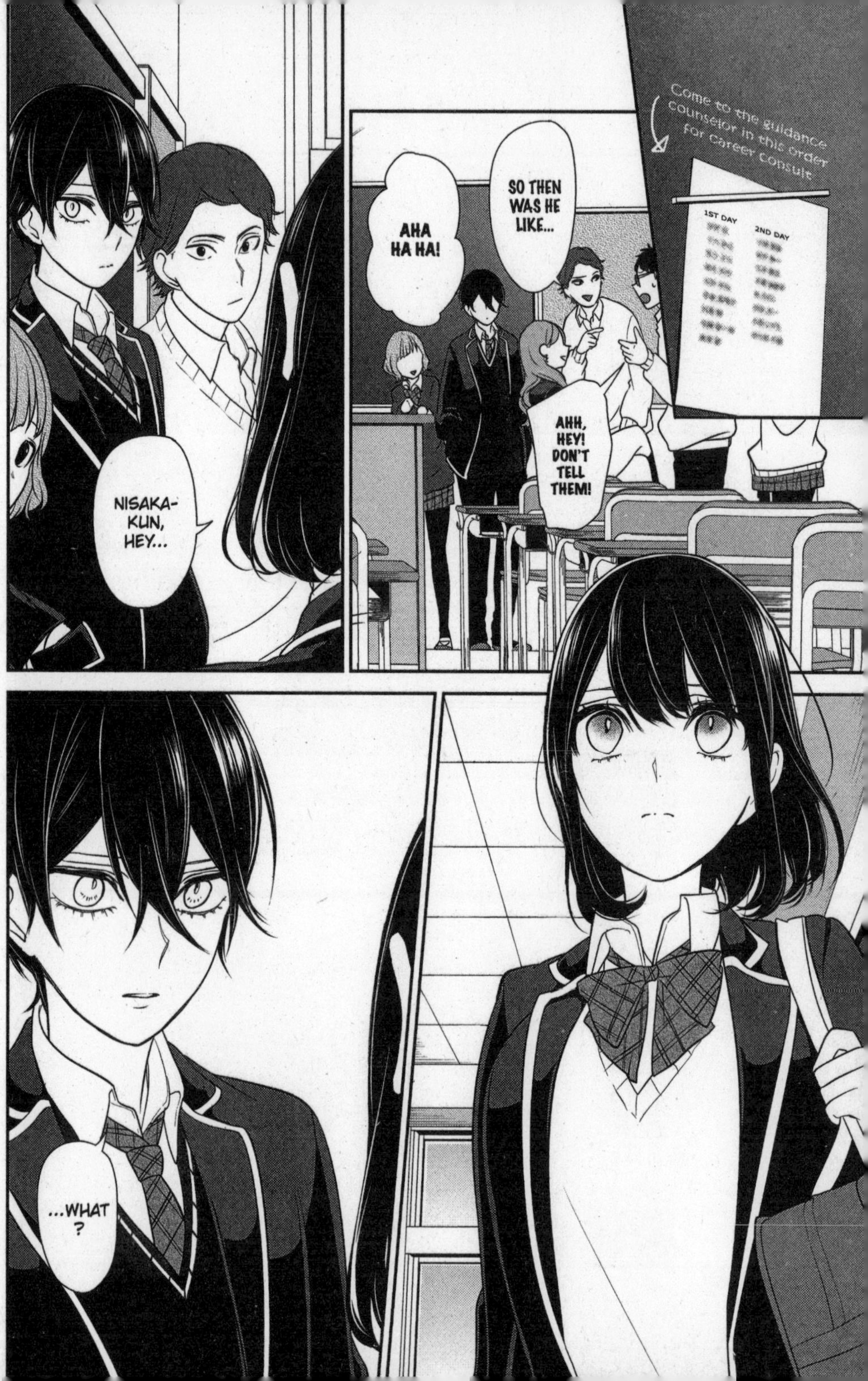

Come to the guidance counselor in this order for career consult
1ST DAY
2ND DAY
SO THEN WAS HE LIKE...
AHA HA HA!
AHH, HEY! DON'T TELL THEM!
NISAKA-KUN, HEY...
...WHAT?

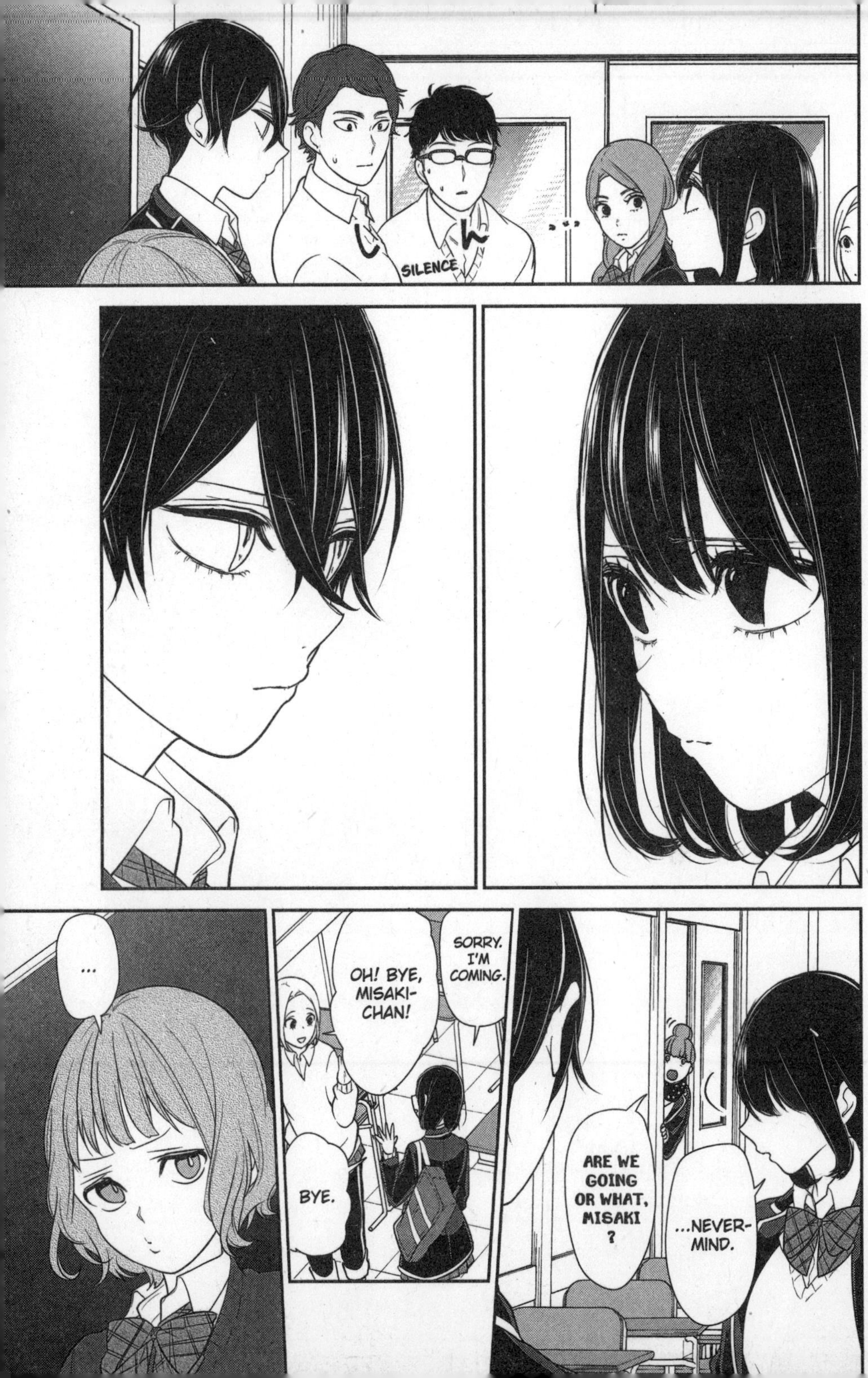

...
じん
SILENCE
...NEVER-MIND.
ARE WE GOING OR WHAT, MISAKI ?
SORRY. I'M COMING.
OH! BYE, MISAKI-CHAN!
BYE.
...

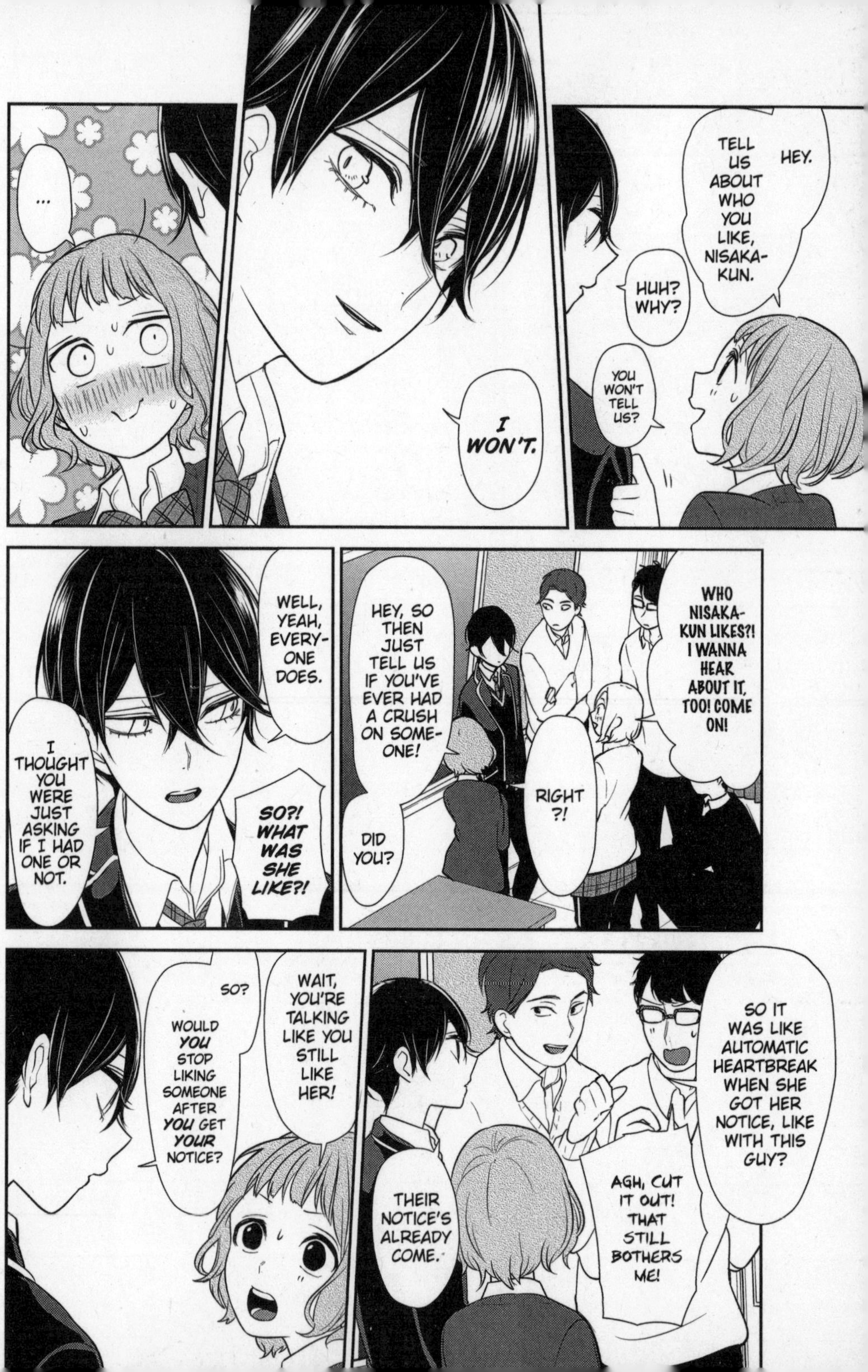

HEY.
TELL US ABOUT WHO YOU LIKE, NISAKA-KUN.
HUH? WHY?
YOU WON'T TELL US?
I WON'T.
...
WHO NISAKA-KUN LIKES?! I WANNA HEAR ABOUT IT, TOO! COME ON!
HEY, SO THEN JUST TELL US IF YOU'VE EVER HAD A CRUSH ON SOMEONE!
RIGHT?!
DID YOU?
WELL, YEAH, EVERYONE DOES.
SO?! WHAT WAS SHE LIKE?!
I THOUGHT YOU WERE JUST ASKING IF I HAD ONE OR NOT.
SO IT WAS LIKE AUTOMATIC HEARTBREAK WHEN SHE GOT HER NOTICE, LIKE WITH THIS GUY?
AGH, CUT IT OUT! THAT STILL BOTHERS ME!
THEIR NOTICE'S ALREADY COME.
WAIT, YOU'RE TALKING LIKE YOU STILL LIKE HER!
SO?
WOULD YOU STOP LIKING SOMEONE AFTER YOU GET YOUR NOTICE?

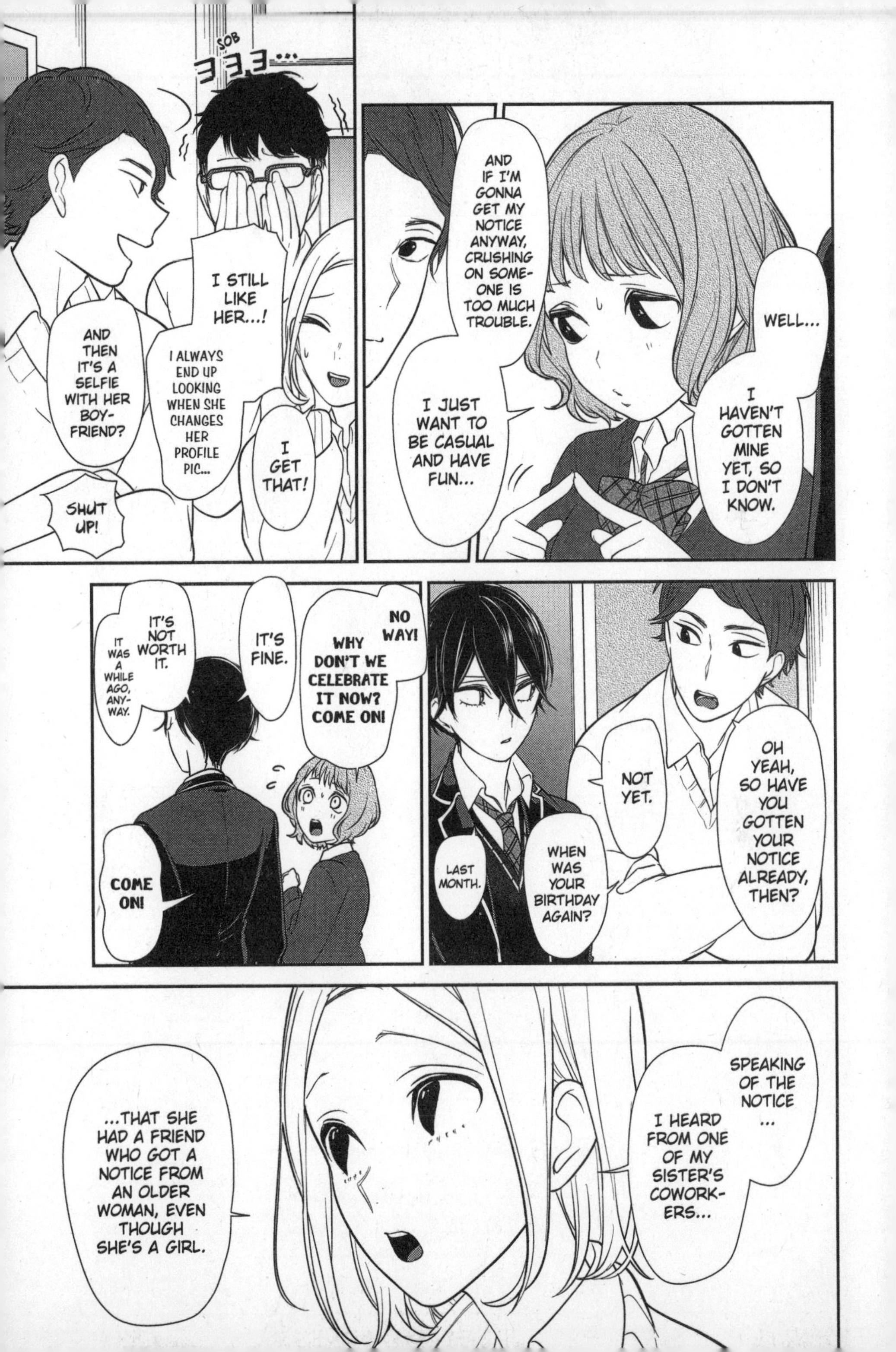
WELL...
I HAVEN'T GOTTEN MINE YET, SO I DON'T KNOW.
AND IF I'M GONNA GET MY NOTICE ANYWAY, CRUSHING ON SOME-ONE IS TOO MUCH TROUBLE.
I JUST WANT TO BE CASUAL AND HAVE FUN...
SOB
ヨヨヨ...
I STILL LIKE HER...!
I GET THAT!
I ALWAYS END UP LOOKING WHEN SHE CHANGES HER PROFILE PIC...
AND THEN IT'S A SELFIE WITH HER BOY-FRIEND?
SHUT UP!
OH YEAH, SO HAVE YOU GOTTEN YOUR NOTICE ALREADY, THEN?
NOT YET.
WHEN WAS YOUR BIRTHDAY AGAIN?
LAST MONTH.
NO WAY!
WHY DON'T WE CELEBRATE IT NOW? COME ON!
IT'S FINE.
IT'S NOT WORTH IT.
IT WAS A WHILE AGO, ANY-WAY.
COME ON!
SPEAKING OF THE NOTICE...
I HEARD FROM ONE OF MY SISTER'S COWORK-ERS...
...THAT SHE HAD A FRIEND WHO GOT A NOTICE FROM AN OLDER WOMAN, EVEN THOUGH SHE'S A GIRL.

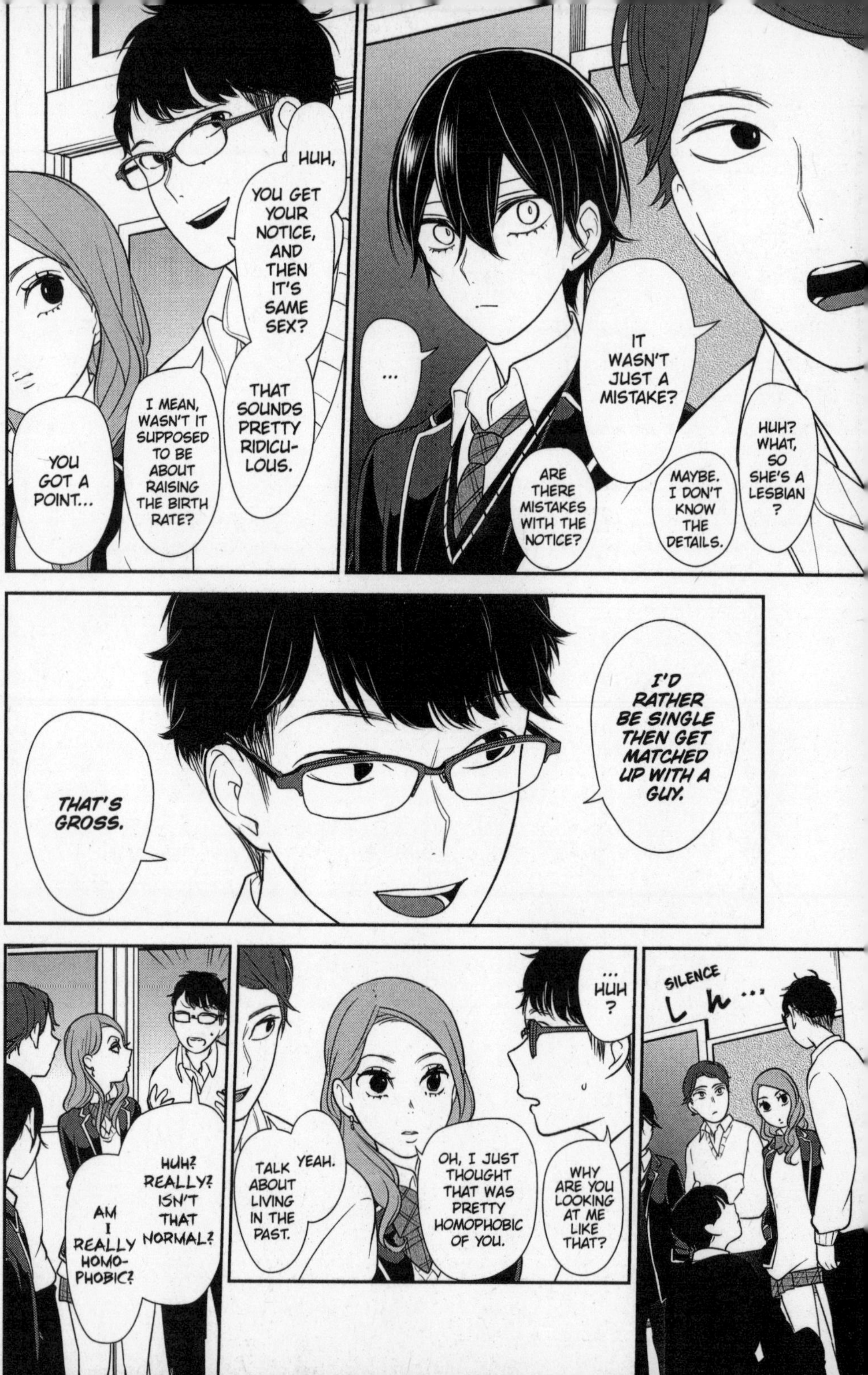
HUH? WHAT, SO SHE'S A LESBIAN?
MAYBE. I DON'T KNOW THE DETAILS.
IT WASN'T JUST A MISTAKE?
ARE THERE MISTAKES WITH THE NOTICE?
...
HUH, YOU GET YOUR NOTICE, AND THEN IT'S SAME SEX?
THAT SOUNDS PRETTY RIDICULOUS.
I MEAN, WASN'T IT SUPPOSED TO BE ABOUT RAISING THE BIRTH RATE?
YOU GOT A POINT...
I'D RATHER BE SINGLE THEN GET MATCHED UP WITH A GUY.
THAT'S GROSS.
SILENCE
しん...
...HUH?
WHY ARE YOU LOOKING AT ME LIKE THAT?
OH, I JUST THOUGHT THAT WAS PRETTY HOMOPHOBIC OF YOU.
YEAH.
TALK ABOUT LIVING IN THE PAST.
HUH? REALLY? ISN'T THAT NORMAL?
AM I REALLY HOMOPHOBIC?

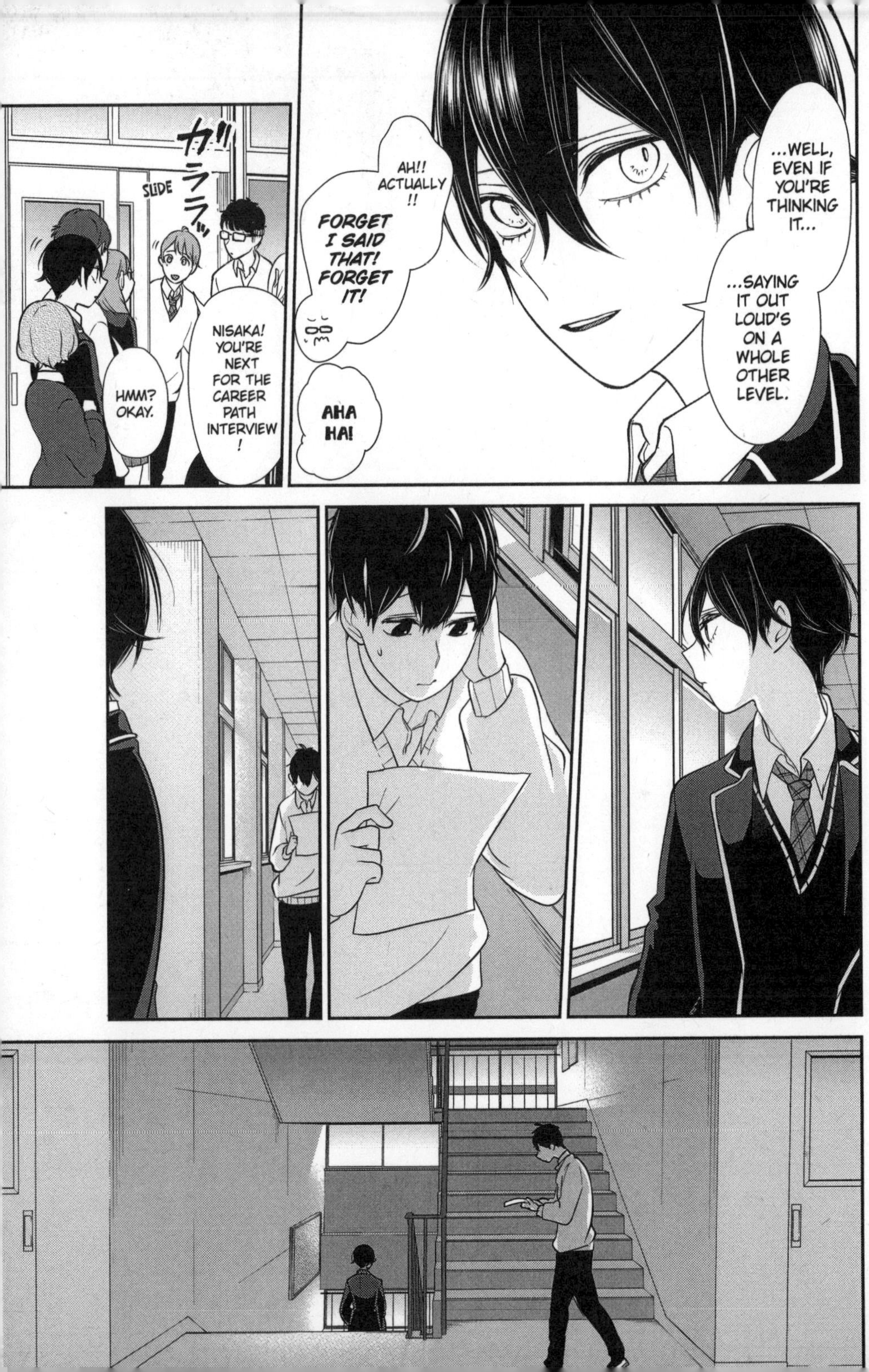
...WELL, EVEN IF YOU'RE THINKING IT...
...SAYING IT OUT LOUD'S ON A WHOLE OTHER LEVEL.
AH!! ACTUALLY !!
FORGET I SAID THAT! FORGET IT!
AHA HA!
ガラララッ
SLIDE
NISAKA! YOU'RE NEXT FOR THE CAREER PATH INTERVIEW!
HMM? OKAY.

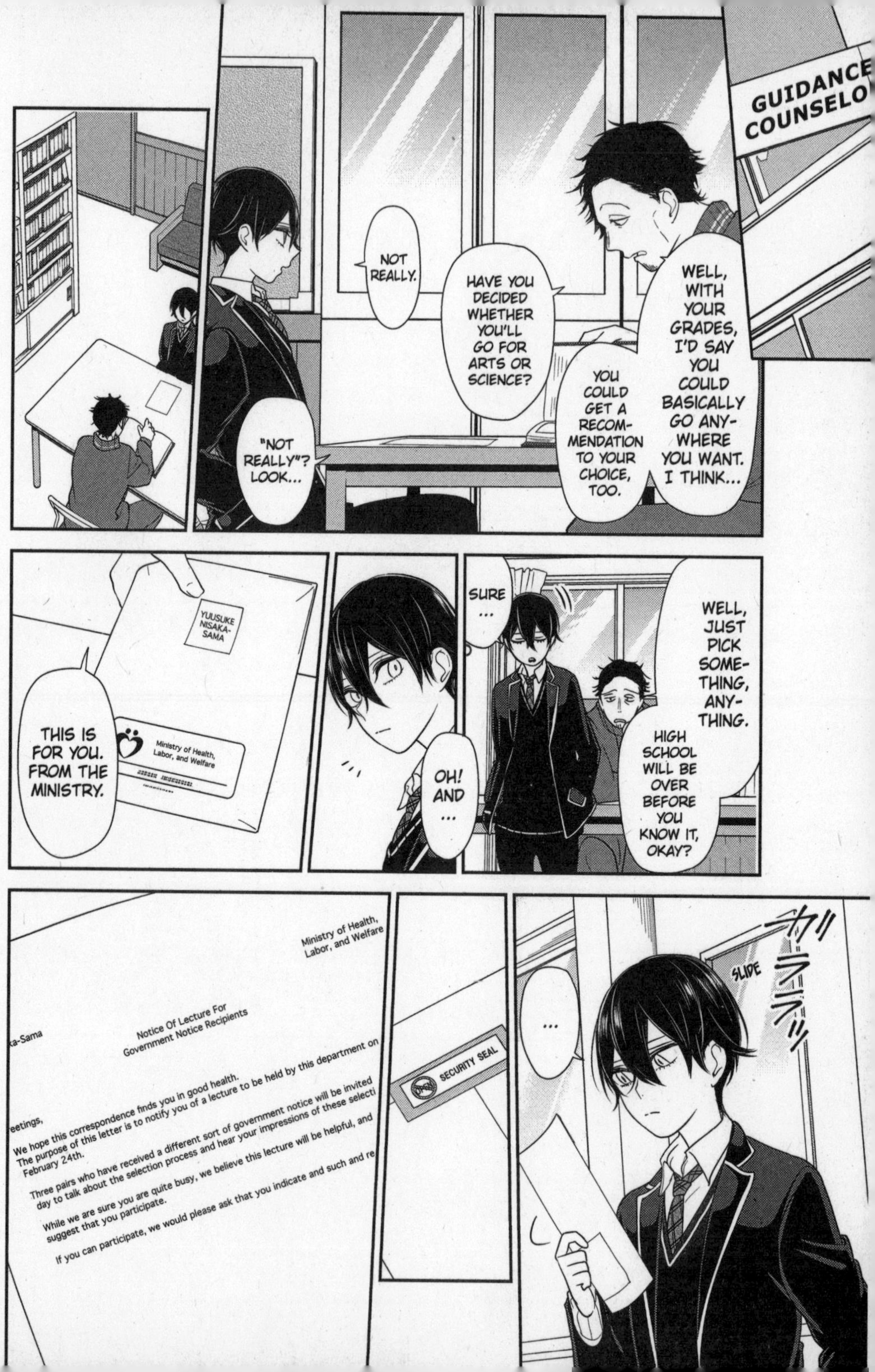
GUIDANCE COUNSELO
WELL, WITH YOUR GRADES, I'D SAY YOU COULD BASICALLY GO ANY-WHERE YOU WANT. I THINK...
YOU COULD GET A RECOM-MENDATION TO YOUR CHOICE, TOO.
HAVE YOU DECIDED WHETHER YOU'LL GO FOR ARTS OR SCIENCE?
NOT REALLY.
"NOT REALLY"? LOOK...
WELL, JUST PICK SOME-THING, ANY-THING.
HIGH SCHOOL WILL BE OVER BEFORE YOU KNOW IT, OKAY?
SURE...
OH! AND...
YUUSUKE NISAKA-SAMA
Ministry of Health, Labor, and Welfare
THIS IS FOR YOU. FROM THE MINISTRY.
SLIDE
...
SECURITY SEAL
Ministry of Health, Labor, and Welfare
ka-Sama
Notice Of Lecture For Government Notice Recipients
eetings,
We hope this correspondence finds you in good health.
The purpose of this letter is to notify you of a lecture to be held by this department on February 24th.
Three pairs who have received a different sort of government notice will be invited day to talk about the selection process and hear your impressions of these selecti
While we are sure you are quite busy, we believe this lecture will be helpful, and suggest that you participate.
If you can participate, we would please ask that you indicate and such and re

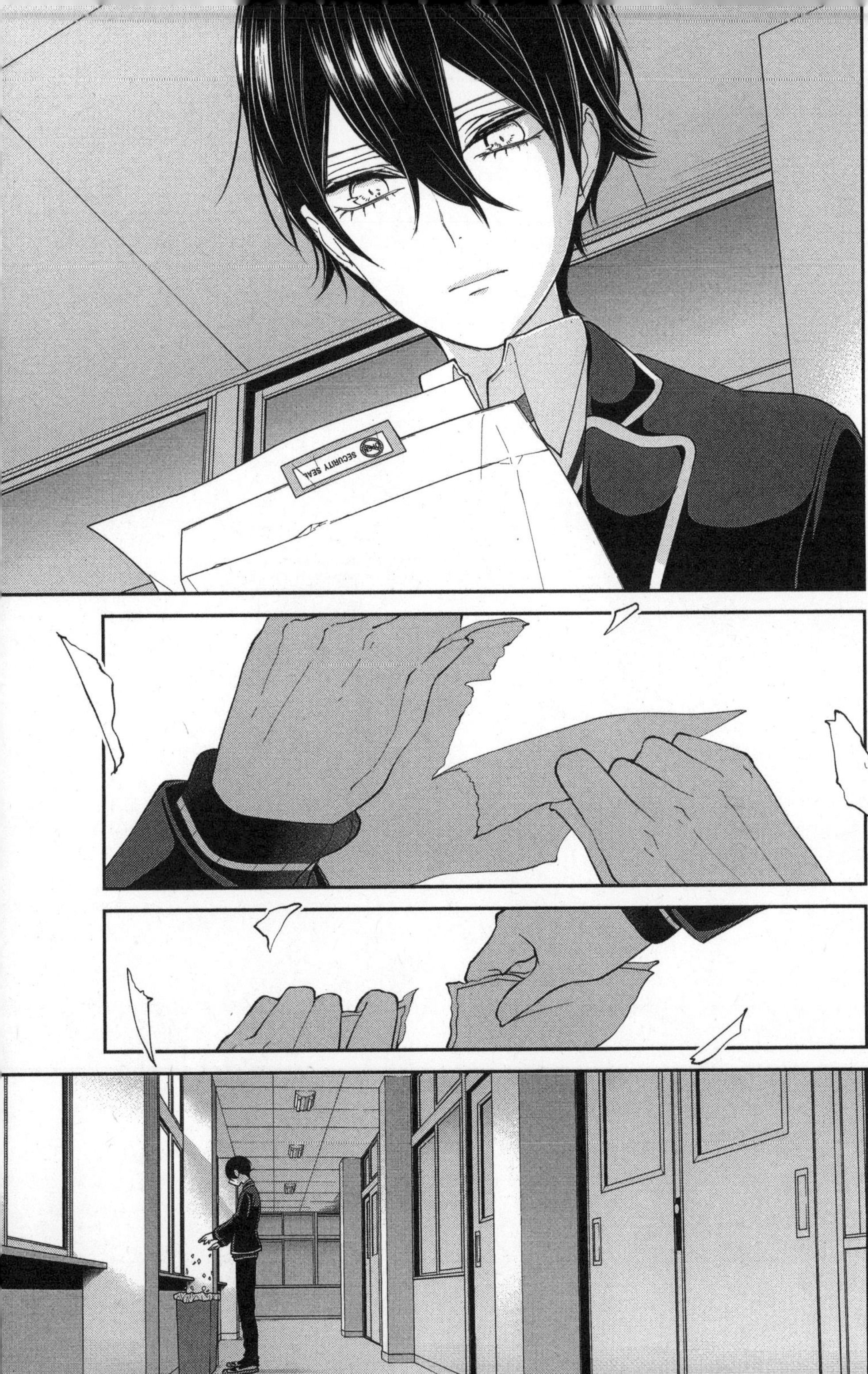
SECURITY SEAL

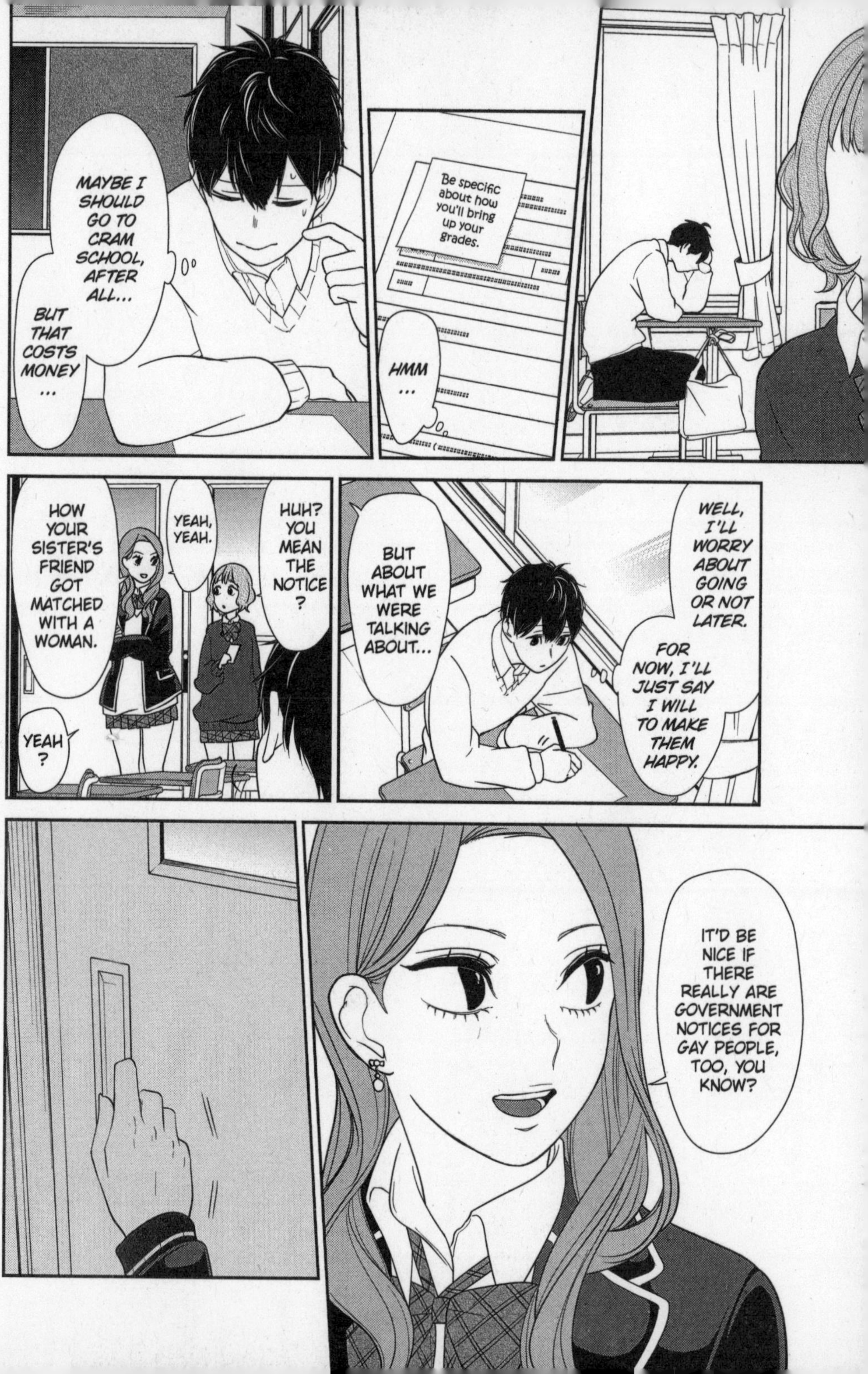
Be specific about how you'll bring up your grades.
HMM...
MAYBE I SHOULD GO TO CRAM SCHOOL, AFTER ALL...
BUT THAT COSTS MONEY...
WELL, I'LL WORRY ABOUT GOING OR NOT LATER.
FOR NOW, I'LL JUST SAY I WILL TO MAKE THEM HAPPY.
BUT ABOUT WHAT WE WERE TALKING ABOUT...
HUH? YOU MEAN THE NOTICE?
YEAH, YEAH.
HOW YOUR SISTER'S FRIEND GOT MATCHED WITH A WOMAN.
YEAH?
IT'D BE NICE IF THERE REALLY ARE GOVERNMENT NOTICES FOR GAY PEOPLE, TOO, YOU KNOW?

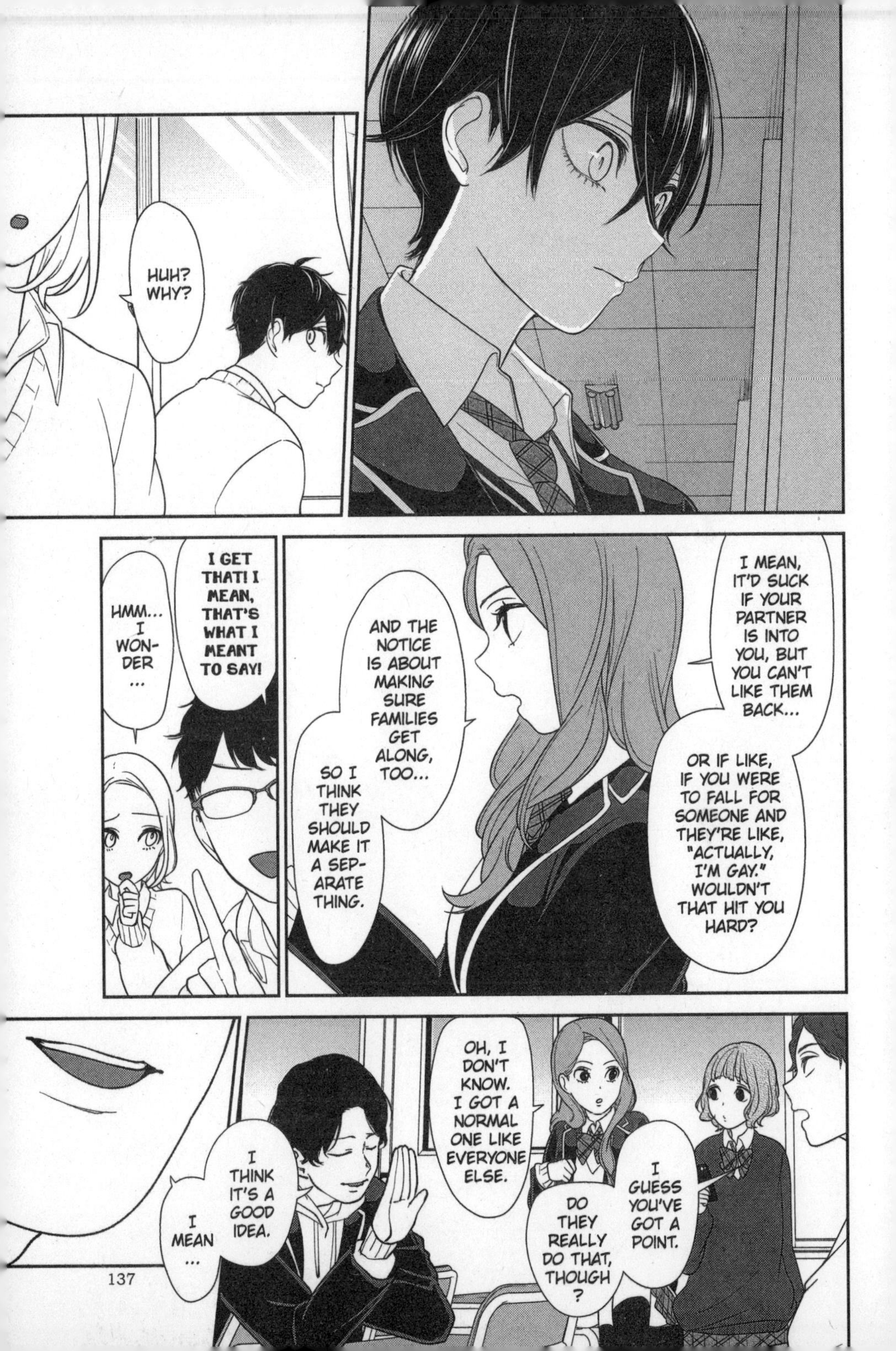
HUH? WHY?
I MEAN, IT'D SUCK IF YOUR PARTNER IS INTO YOU, BUT YOU CAN'T LIKE THEM BACK...
OR IF LIKE, IF YOU WERE TO FALL FOR SOMEONE AND THEY'RE LIKE, "ACTUALLY, I'M GAY." WOULDN'T THAT HIT YOU HARD?
AND THE NOTICE IS ABOUT MAKING SURE FAMILIES GET ALONG, TOO...
SO I THINK THEY SHOULD MAKE IT A SEP-ARATE THING.
I GET THAT! I MEAN, THAT'S WHAT I MEANT TO SAY!
HMM... I WON-DER ...
OH, I DON'T KNOW. I GOT A NORMAL ONE LIKE EVERYONE ELSE.
I GUESS YOU'VE GOT A POINT.
DO THEY REALLY DO THAT, THOUGH ?
I THINK IT'S A GOOD IDEA.
I MEAN ...

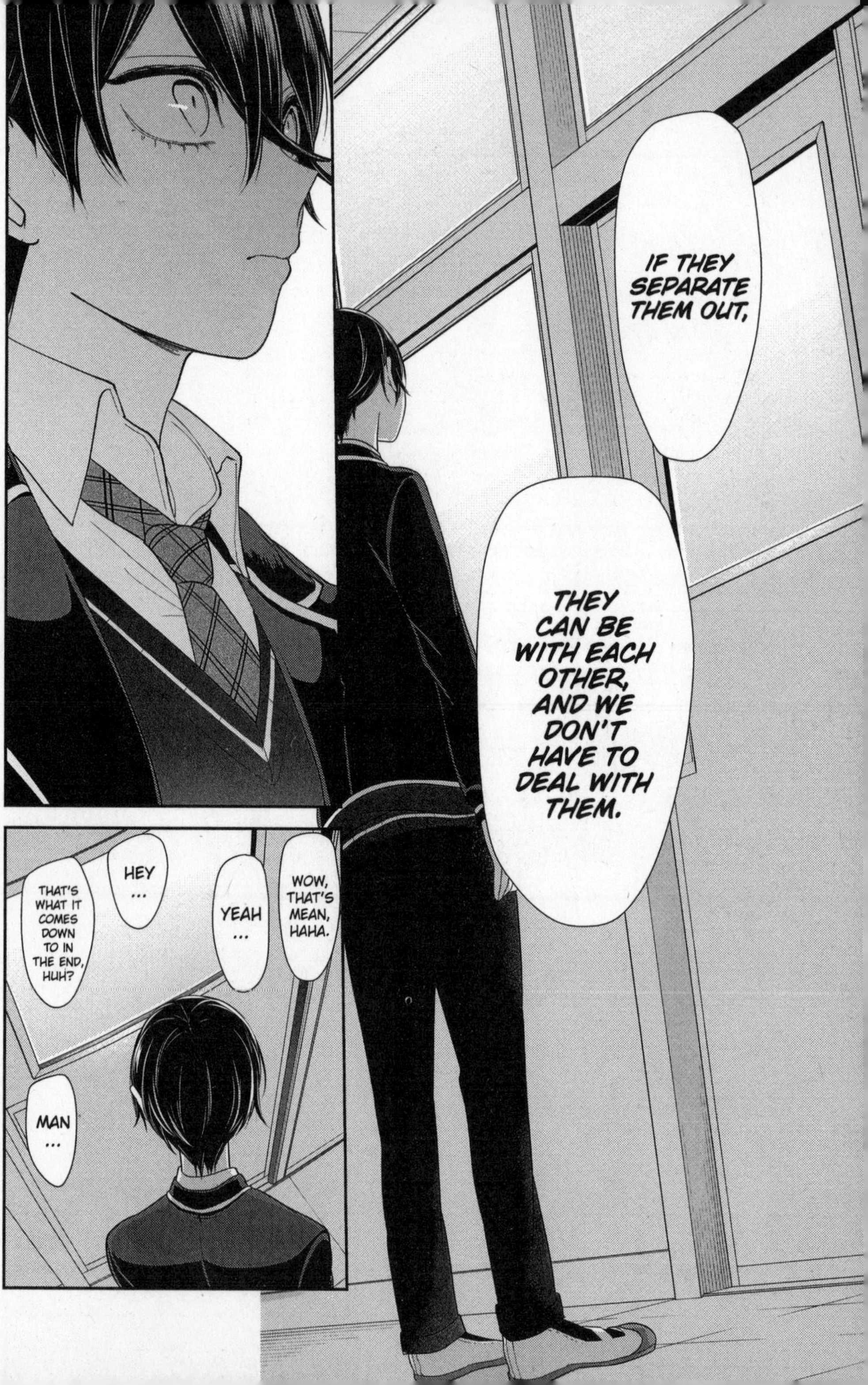
IF THEY SEPARATE THEM OUT,
THEY CAN BE WITH EACH OTHER, AND WE DON'T HAVE TO DEAL WITH THEM.
WOW, THAT'S MEAN, HAHA.
YEAH ...
HEY ...
THAT'S WHAT IT COMES DOWN TO IN THE END, HUH?
MAN ...

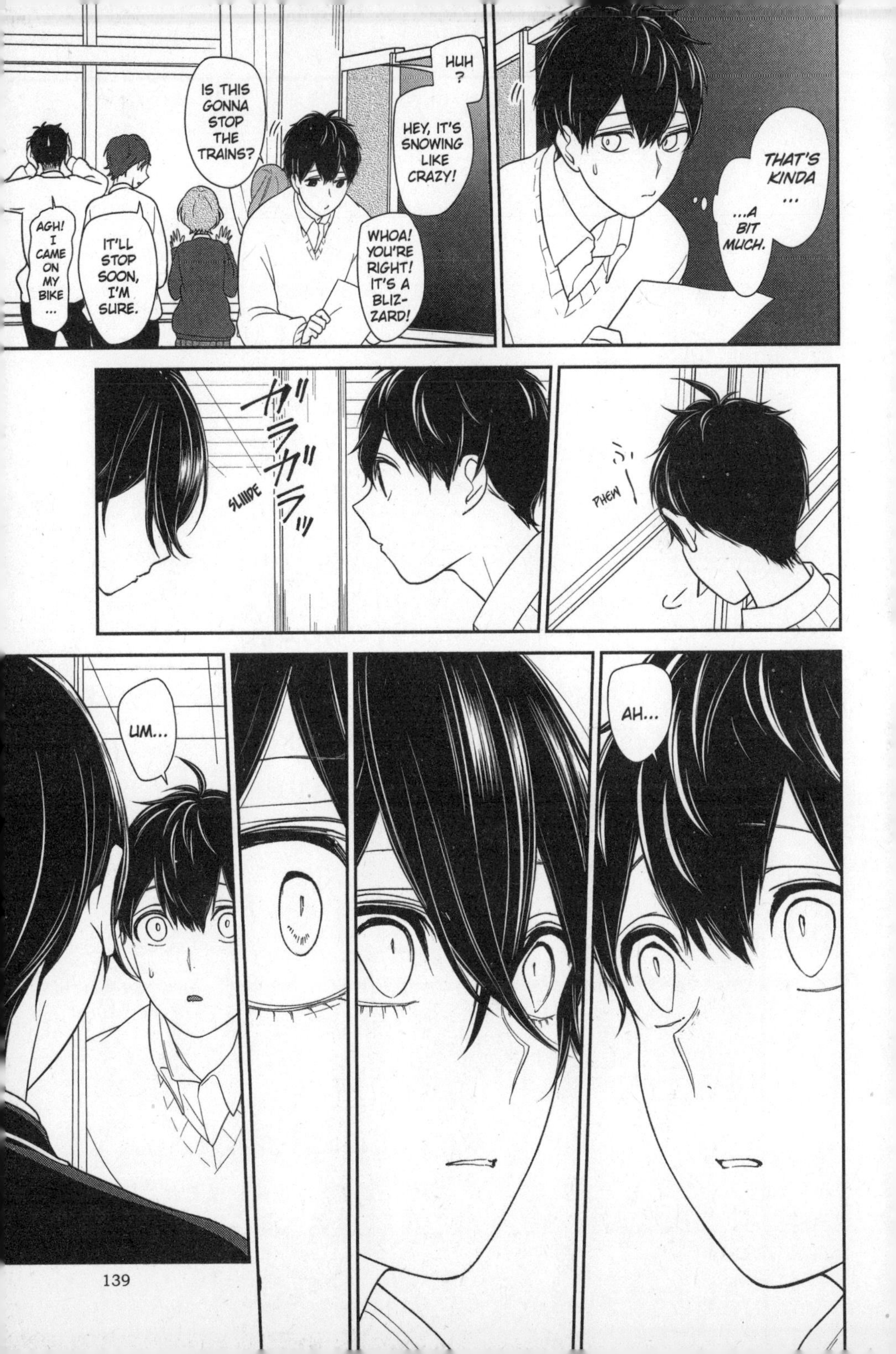

THAT'S KINDA ...
...A BIT MUCH.
HUH ?
HEY, IT'S SNOWING LIKE CRAZY!
WHOA! YOU'RE RIGHT! IT'S A BLIZZARD!
IS THIS GONNA STOP THE TRAINS?
IT'LL STOP SOON, I'M SURE.
AGH! I CAME ON MY BIKE ...
PHEW
ガラガラッ
SLIIIDE
AH...
UM...

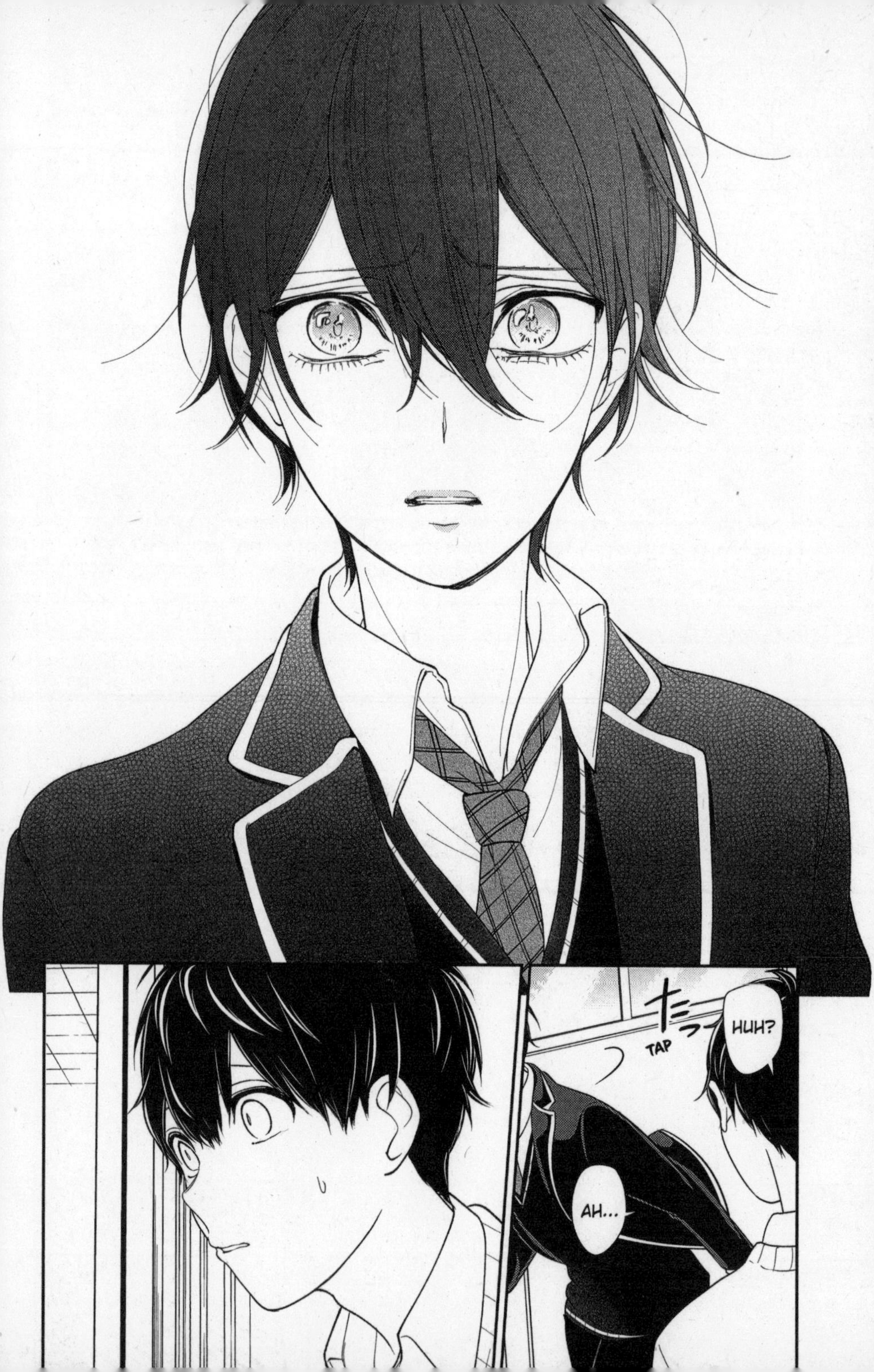
HUH?
TAP
AH...

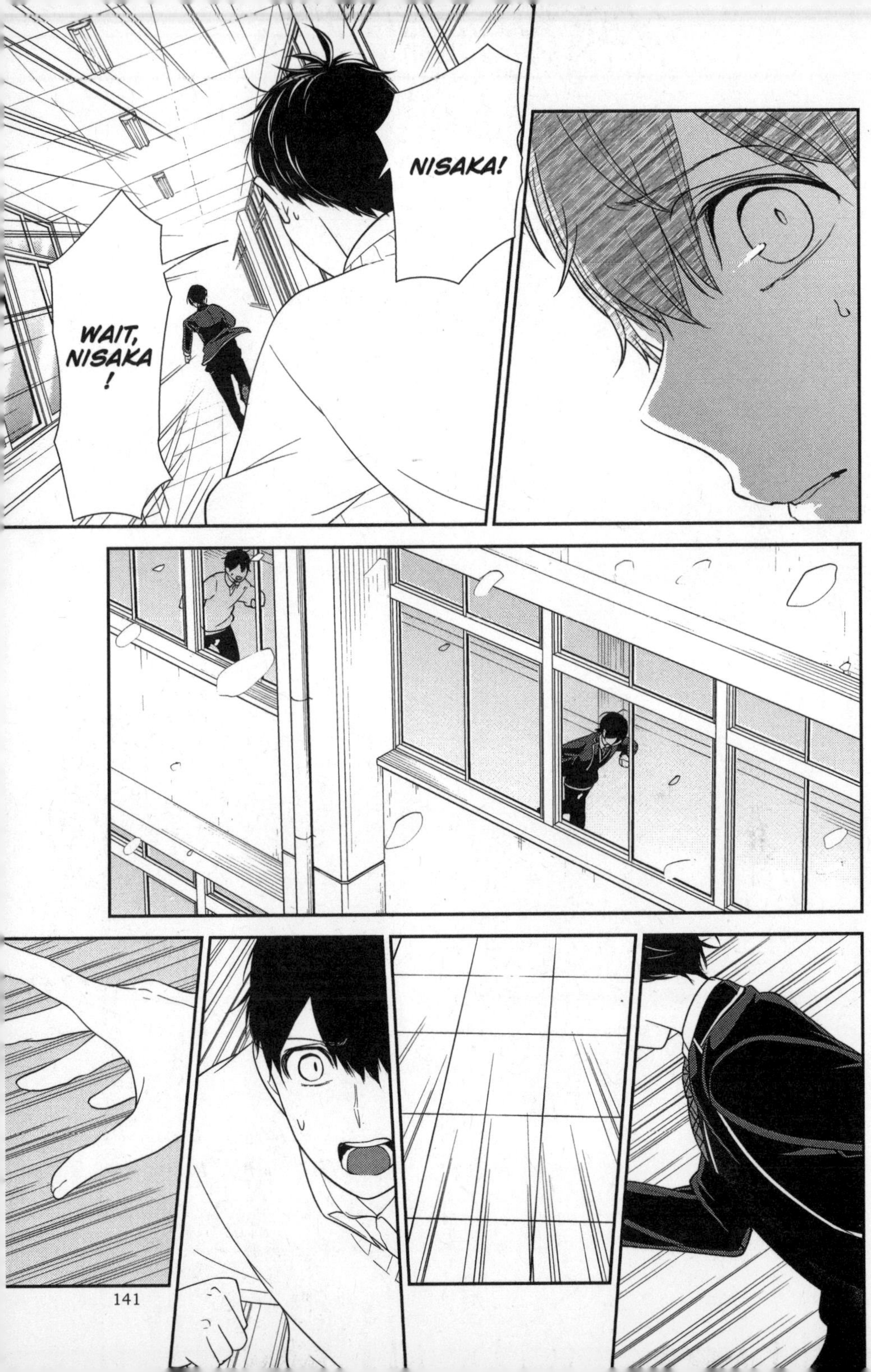
NISAKA!
WAIT, NISAKA!

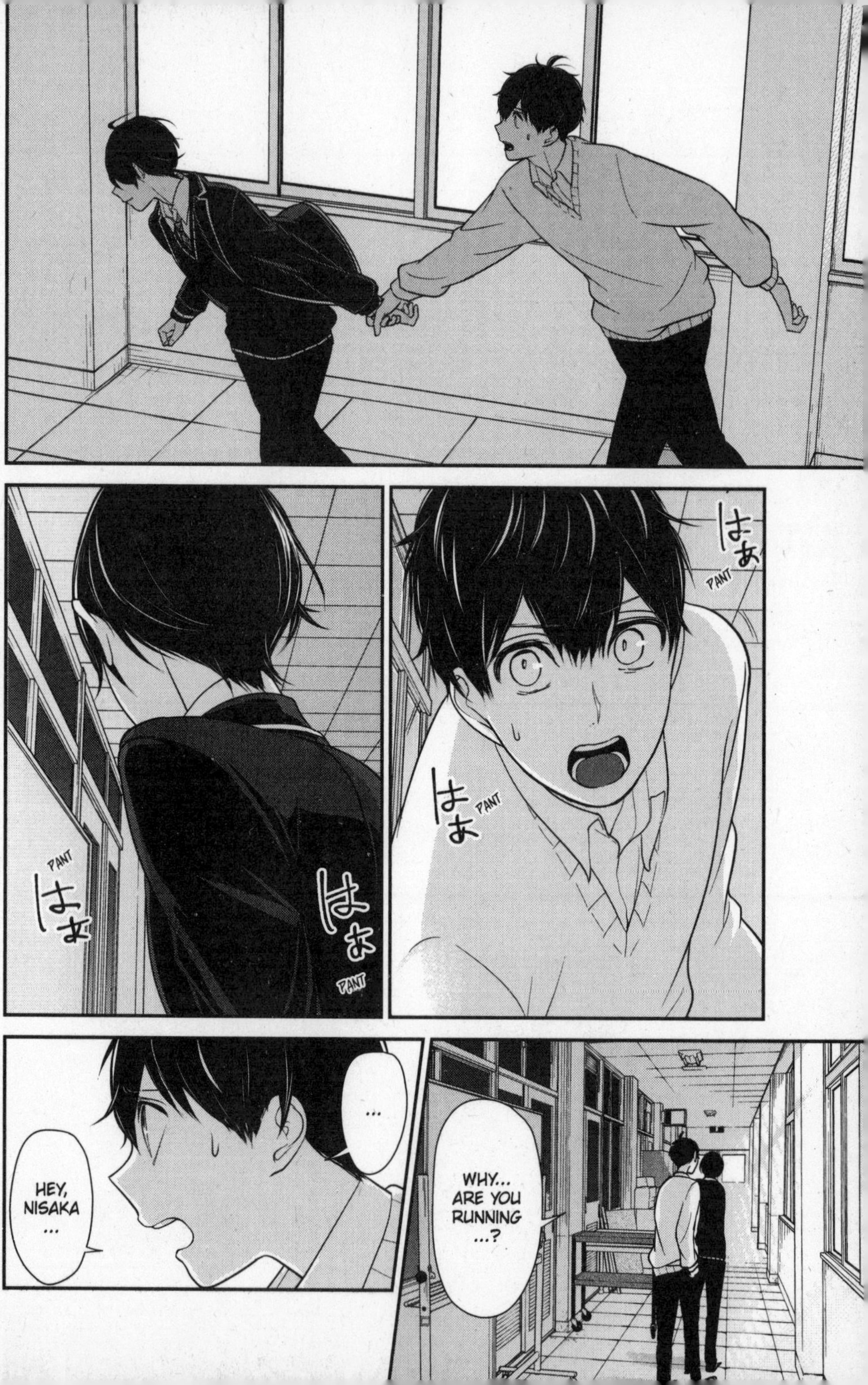
はぁ
PANT
はぁ
PANT
PANT
はぁ
はぁ
PANT
WHY... ARE YOU RUNNING ...?
...
HEY, NISAKA ...

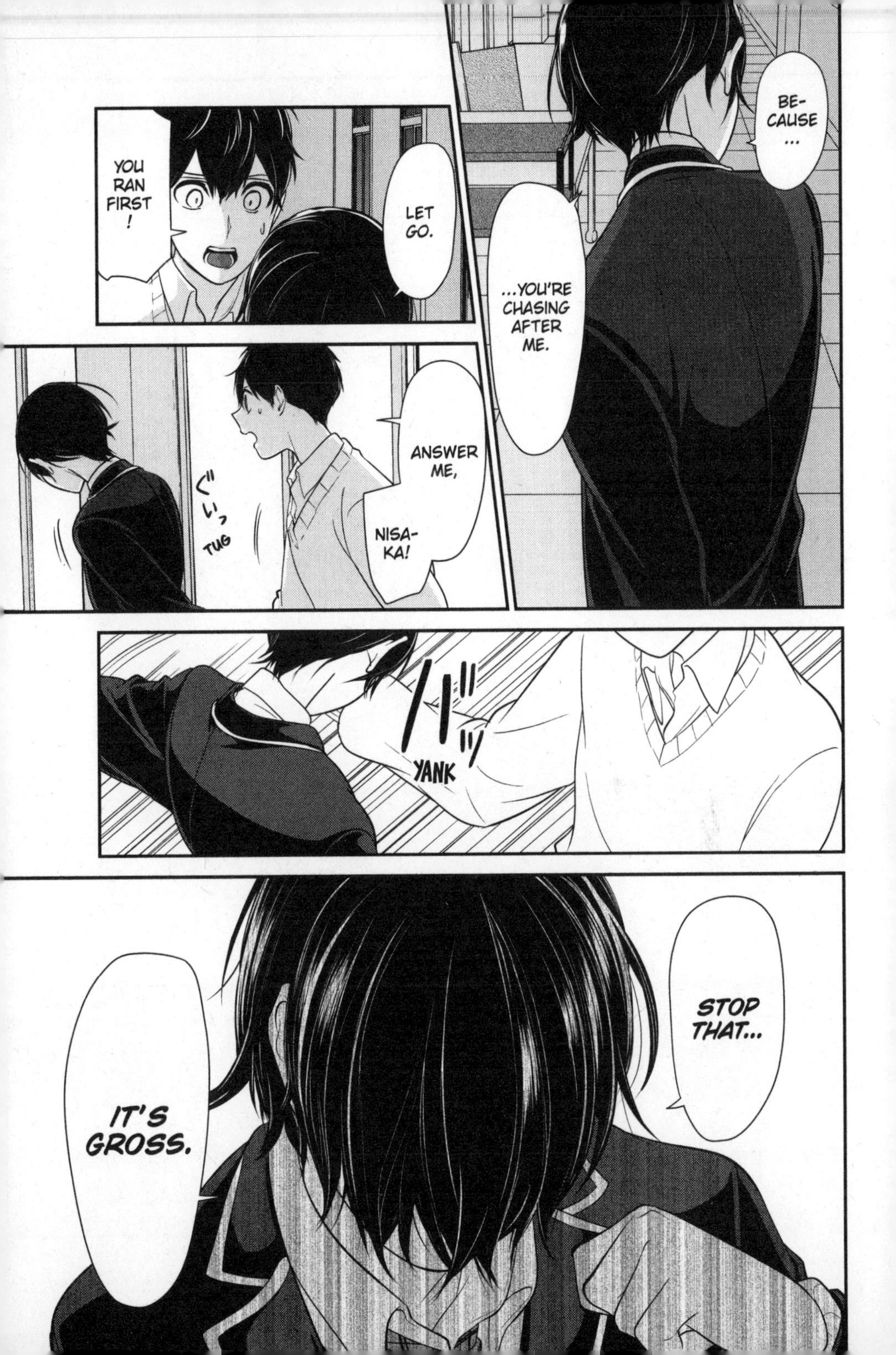
BE-CAUSE...
...YOU'RE CHASING AFTER ME.
LET GO.
YOU RAN FIRST!
ANSWER ME,
NISA-KA!
ぐいっ
TUG
YANK
STOP THAT...
IT'S GROSS.

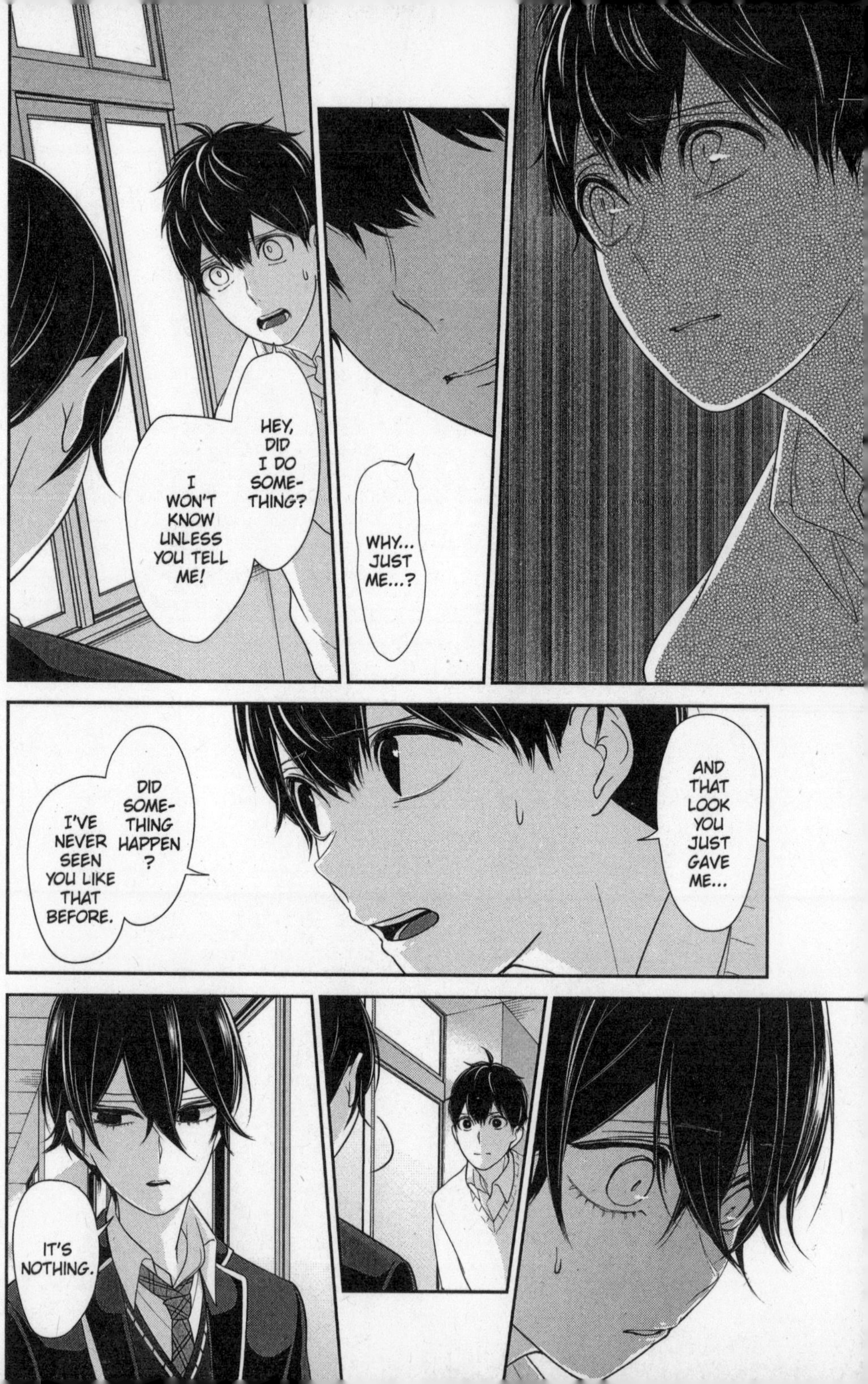
WHY... JUST ME...?
HEY, DID I DO SOMETHING?
I WON'T KNOW UNLESS YOU TELL ME!
AND THAT LOOK YOU JUST GAVE ME...
DID SOMETHING HAPPEN?
I'VE NEVER SEEN YOU LIKE THAT BEFORE.
IT'S NOTHING.

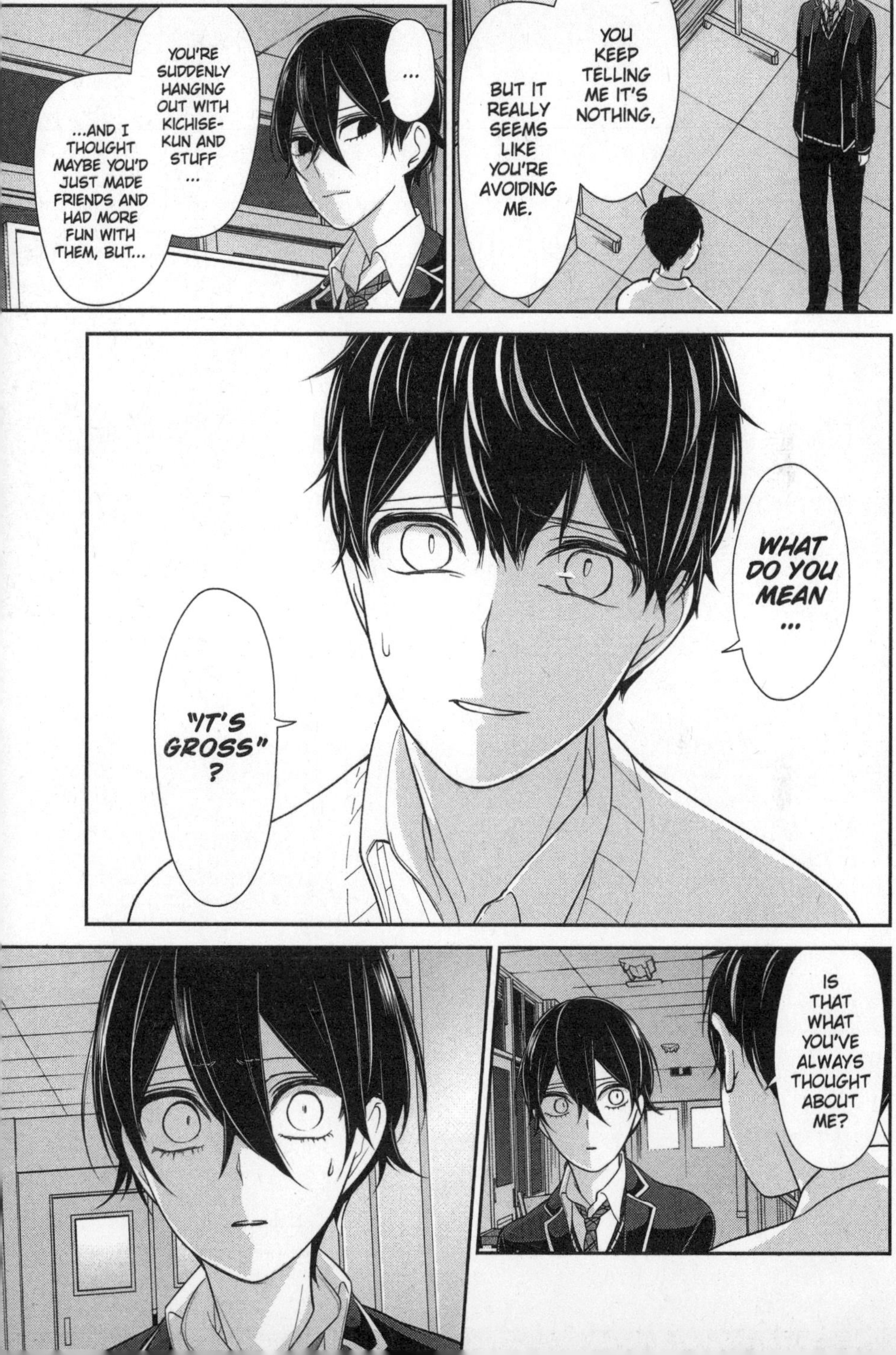
YOU KEEP TELLING ME IT'S NOTHING,
BUT IT REALLY SEEMS LIKE YOU'RE AVOIDING ME.
...
YOU'RE SUDDENLY HANGING OUT WITH KICHISE-KUN AND STUFF...
...AND I THOUGHT MAYBE YOU'D JUST MADE FRIENDS AND HAD MORE FUN WITH THEM, BUT...
WHAT DO YOU MEAN...
"IT'S GROSS"?
IS THAT WHAT YOU'VE ALWAYS THOUGHT ABOUT ME?

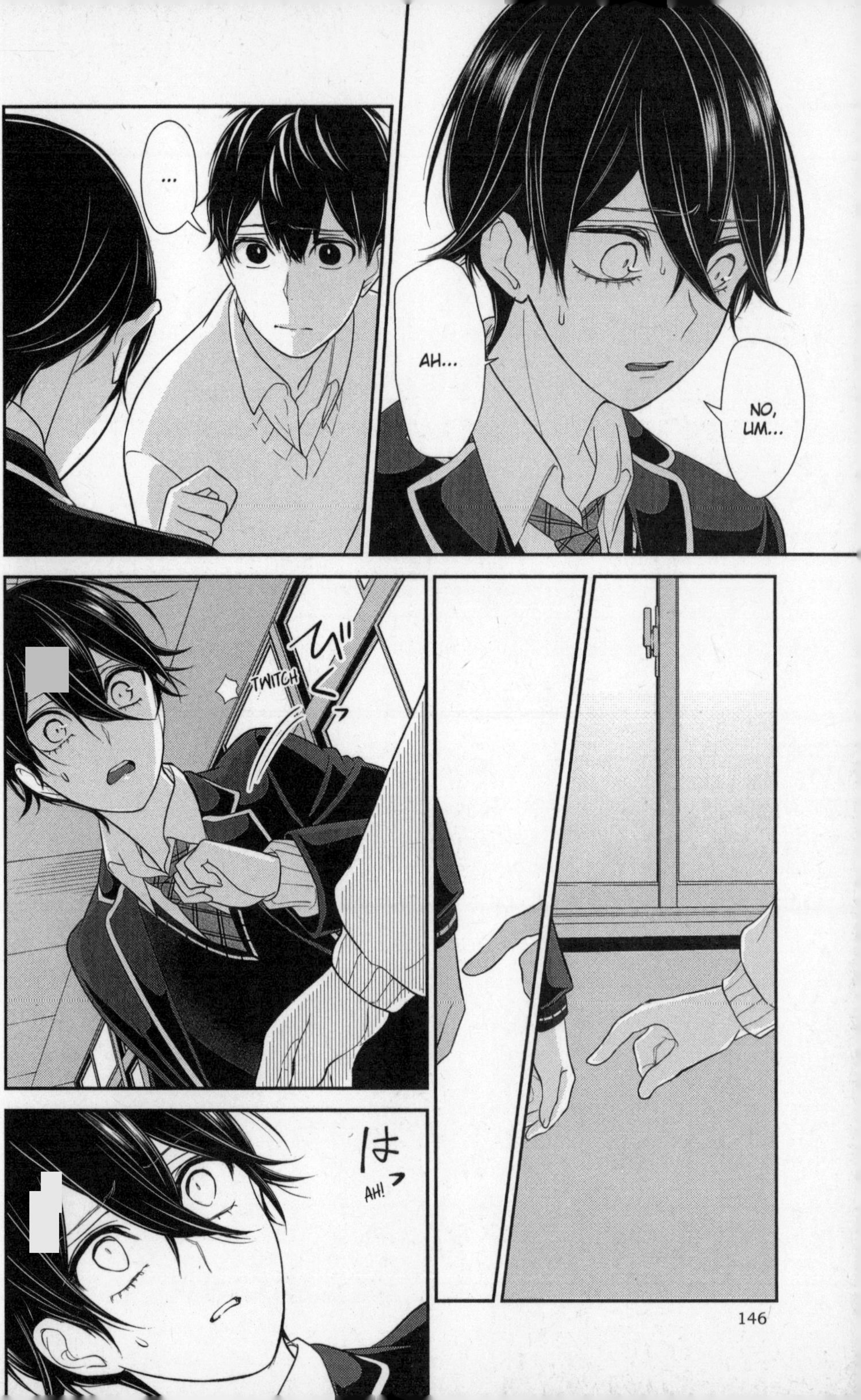
AH...
NO, UM...
...
びくっ
TWITCH
はっ
AH!

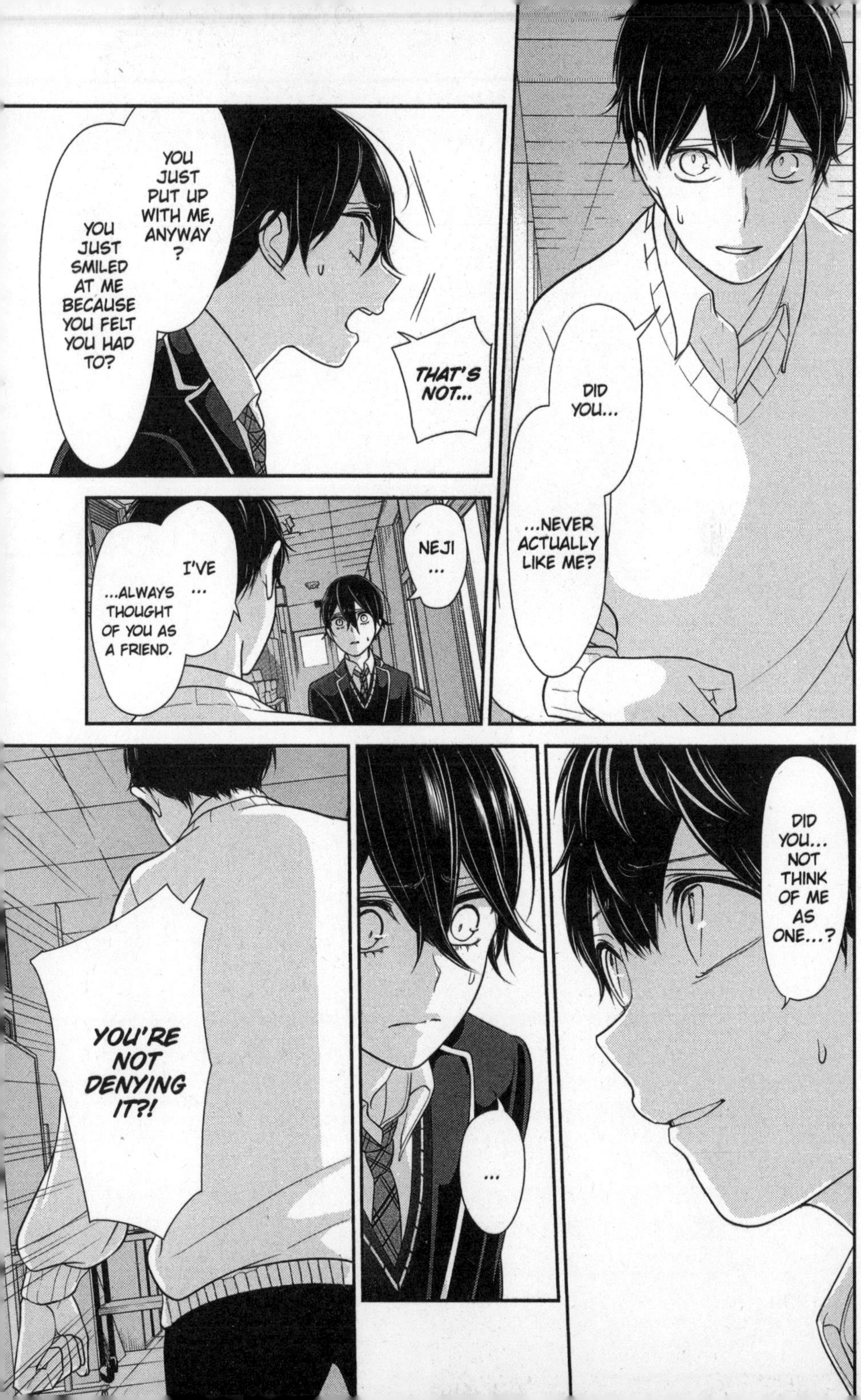
DID YOU...
...NEVER ACTUALLY LIKE ME?
THAT'S NOT...
YOU JUST PUT UP WITH ME, ANYWAY?
YOU JUST SMILED AT ME BECAUSE YOU FELT YOU HAD TO?
NEJI...
I'VE... ...ALWAYS THOUGHT OF YOU AS A FRIEND.
DID YOU... NOT THINK OF ME AS ONE...?
...
YOU'RE NOT DENYING IT?!

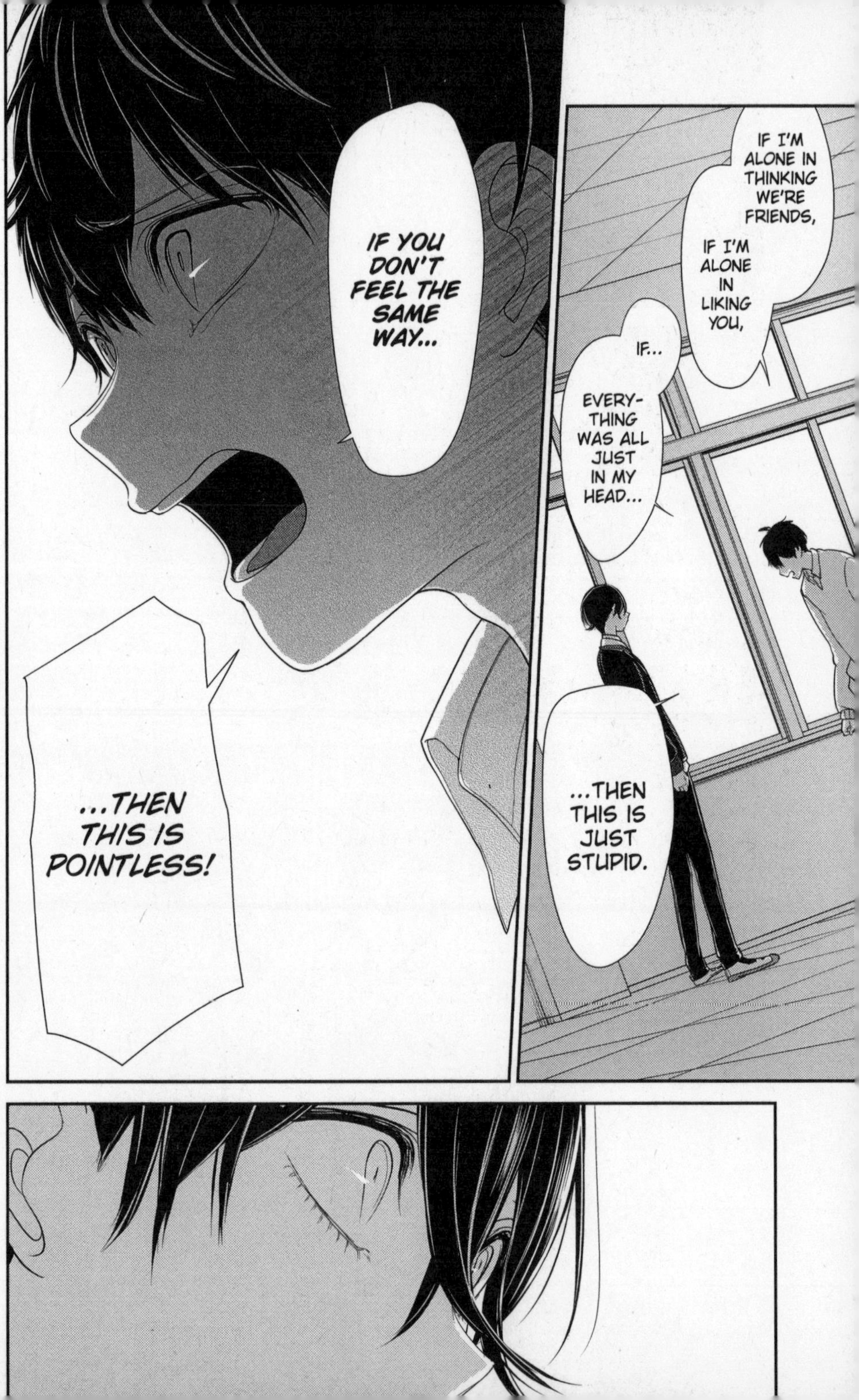
IF I'M ALONE IN THINKING WE'RE FRIENDS,
IF I'M ALONE IN LIKING YOU,
IF...
EVERYTHING WAS ALL JUST IN MY HEAD...
...THEN THIS IS JUST STUPID.
IF YOU DON'T FEEL THE SAME WAY...
...THEN THIS IS POINTLESS!

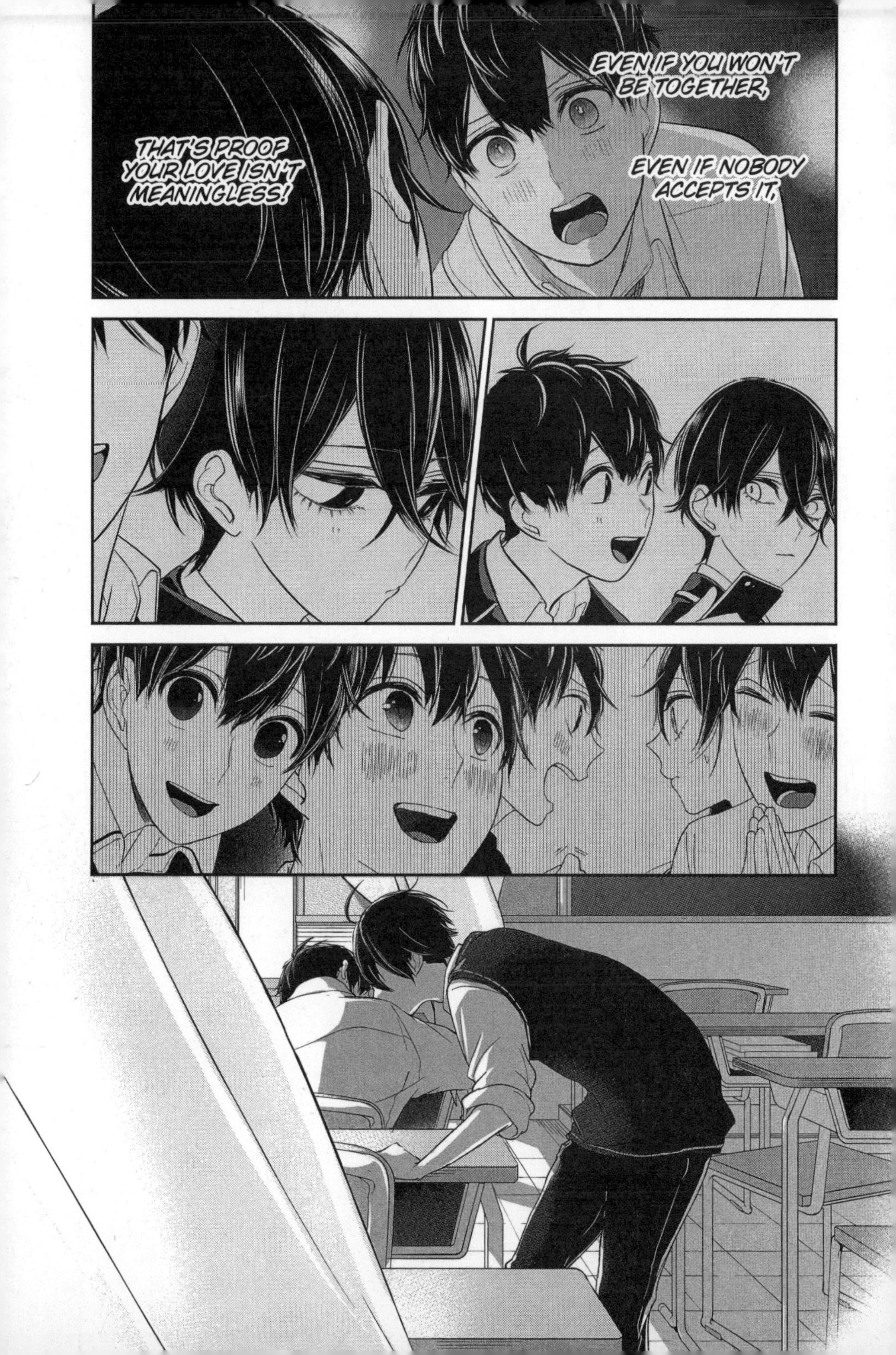
EVEN IF YOU WON'T BE TOGETHER,
EVEN IF NOBODY ACCEPTS IT,
THAT'S PROOF YOUR LOVE ISN'T MEANINGLESS!

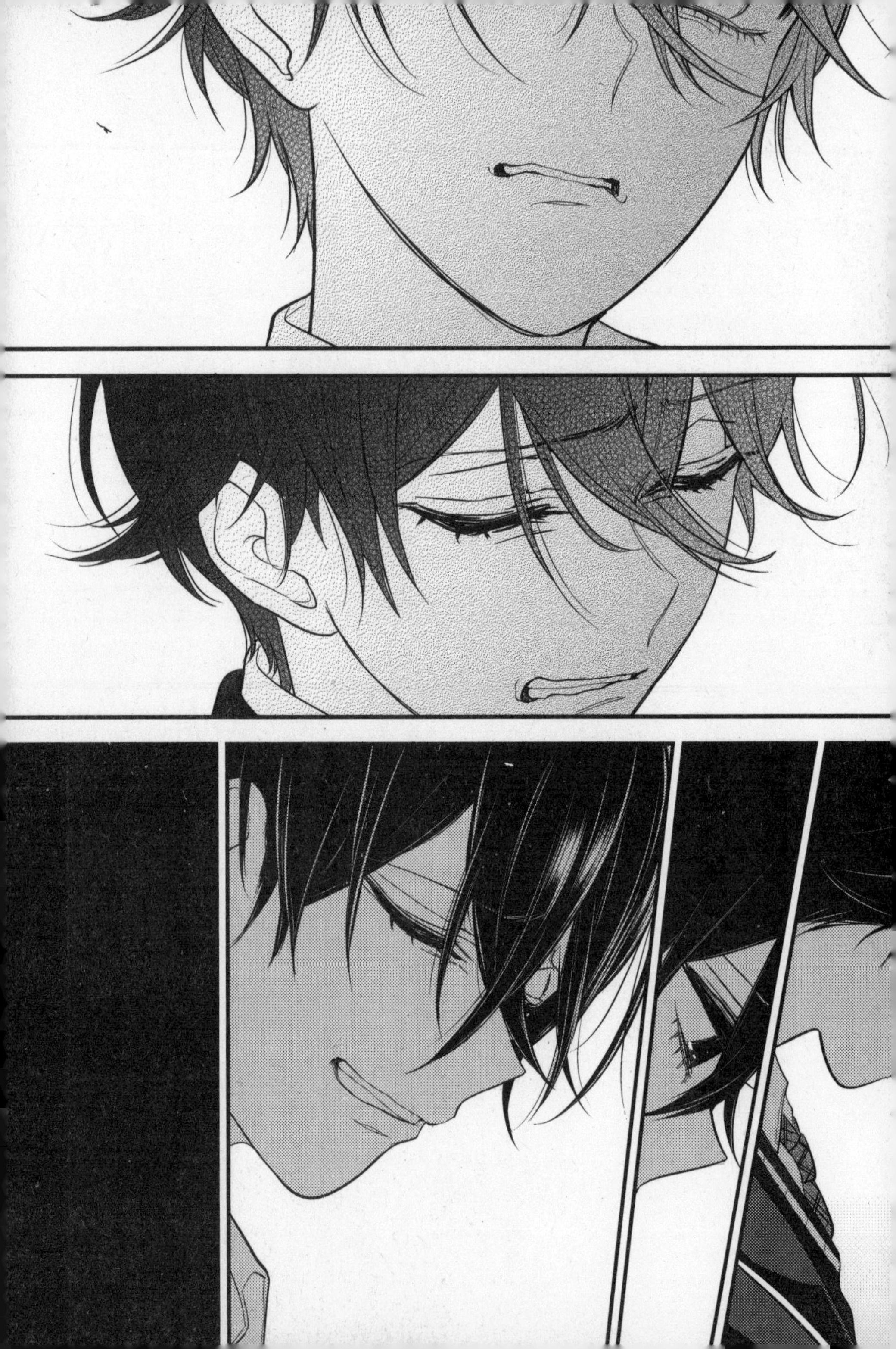

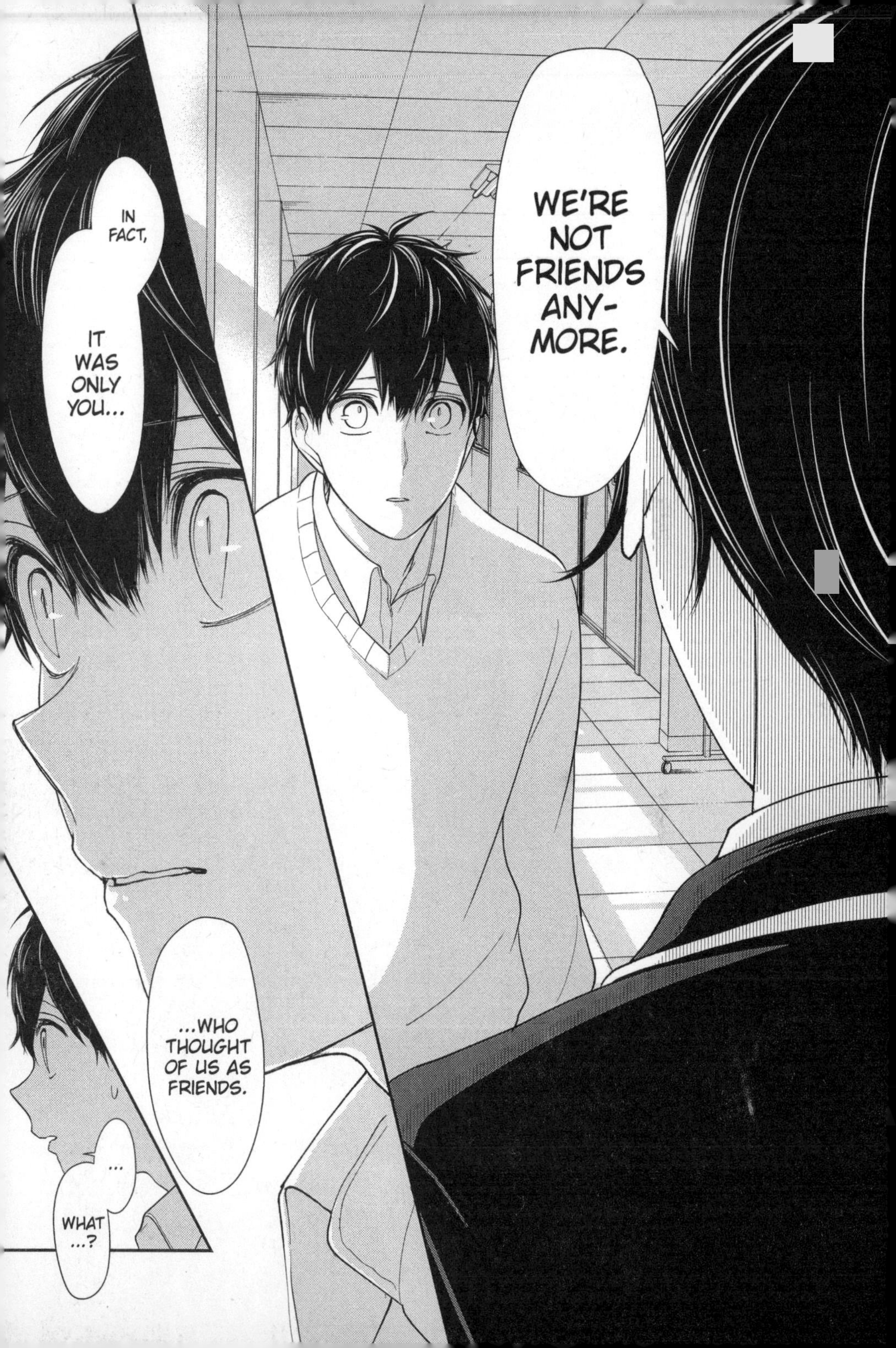
WE'RE NOT FRIENDS ANY-MORE.
IN FACT,
IT WAS ONLY YOU...
...WHO THOUGHT OF US AS FRIENDS.
...
WHAT ...?

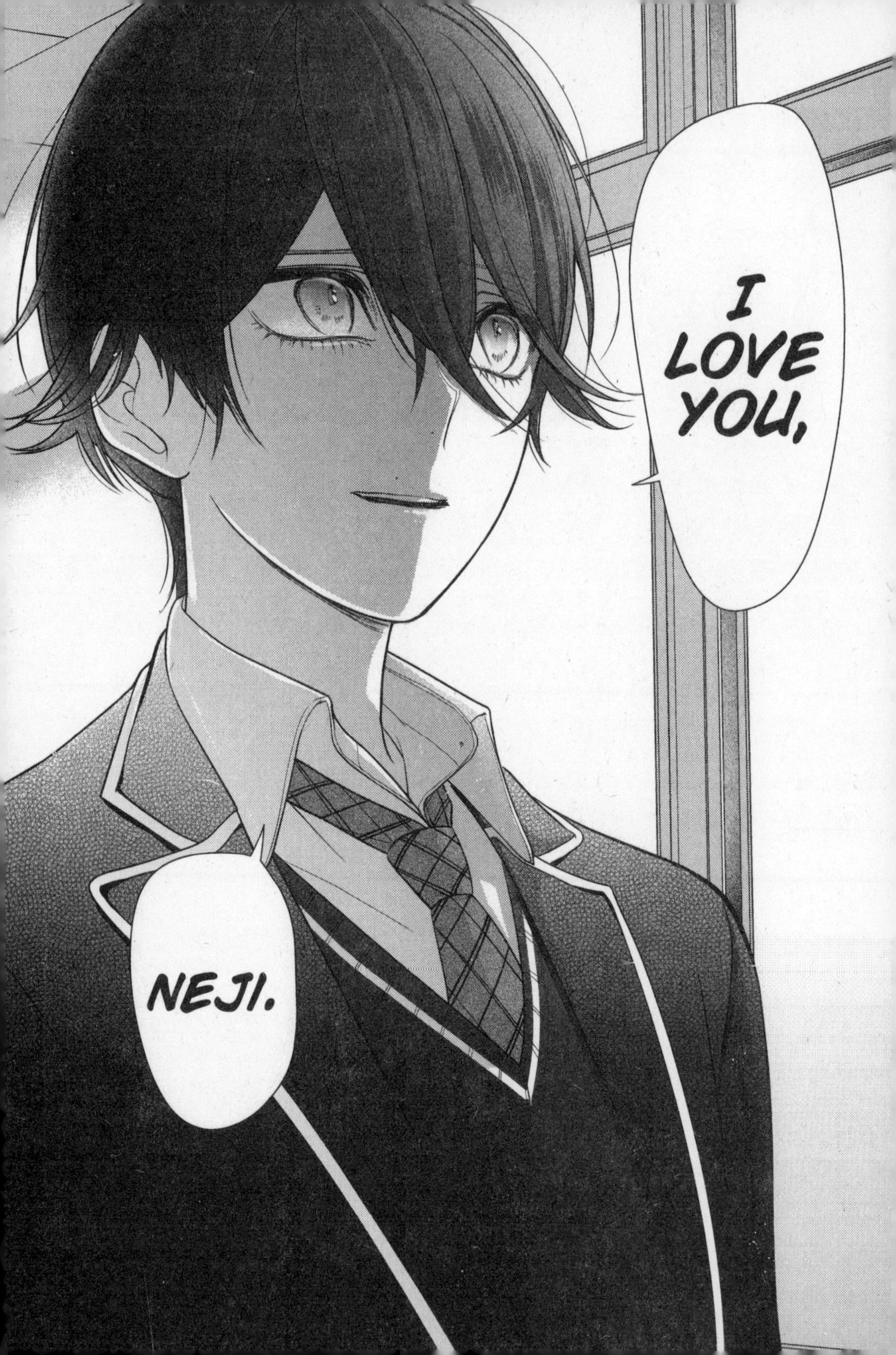
I LOVE YOU,
NEJI.

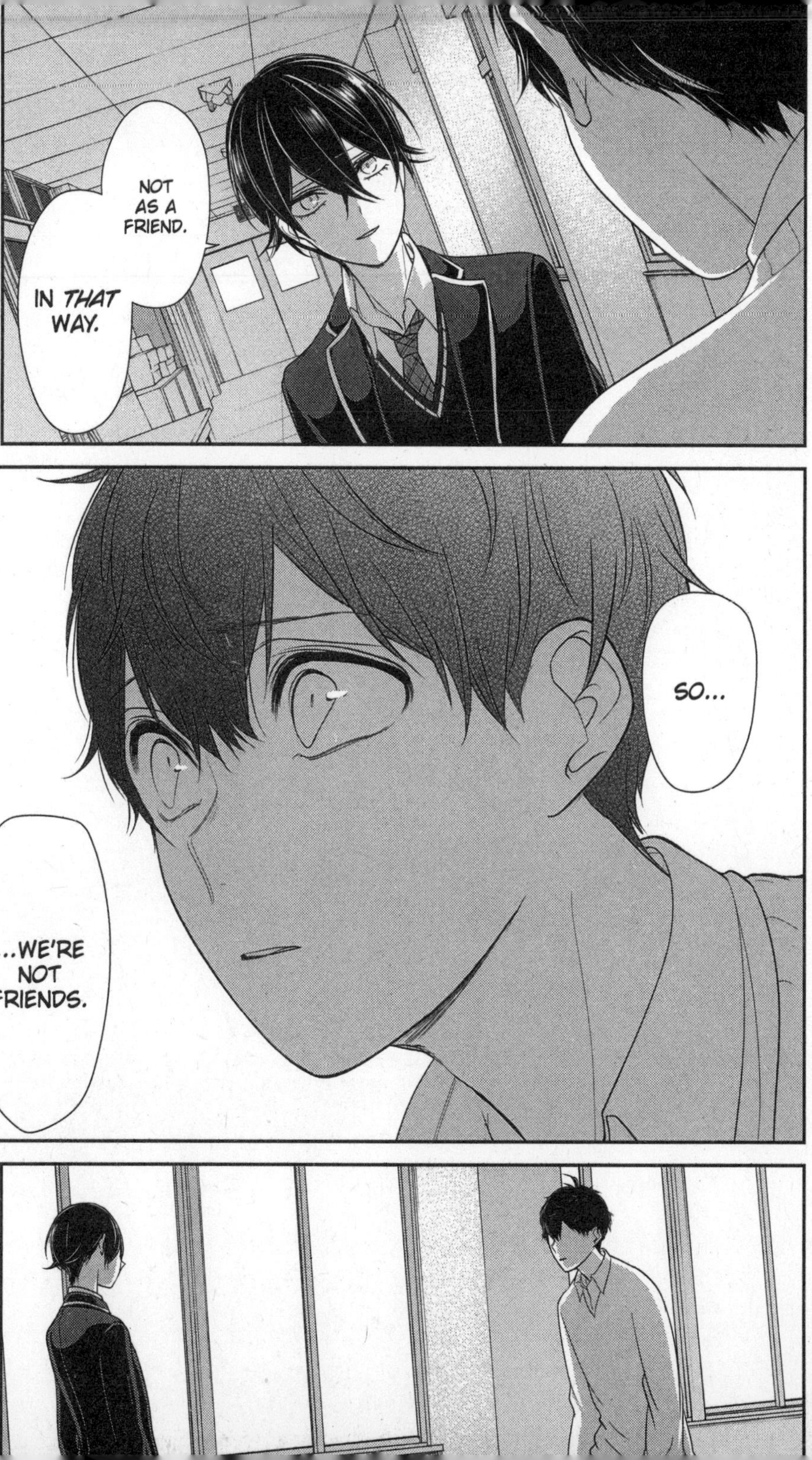
NOT AS A FRIEND.
IN THAT WAY.
SO...
...WE'RE NOT FRIENDS.

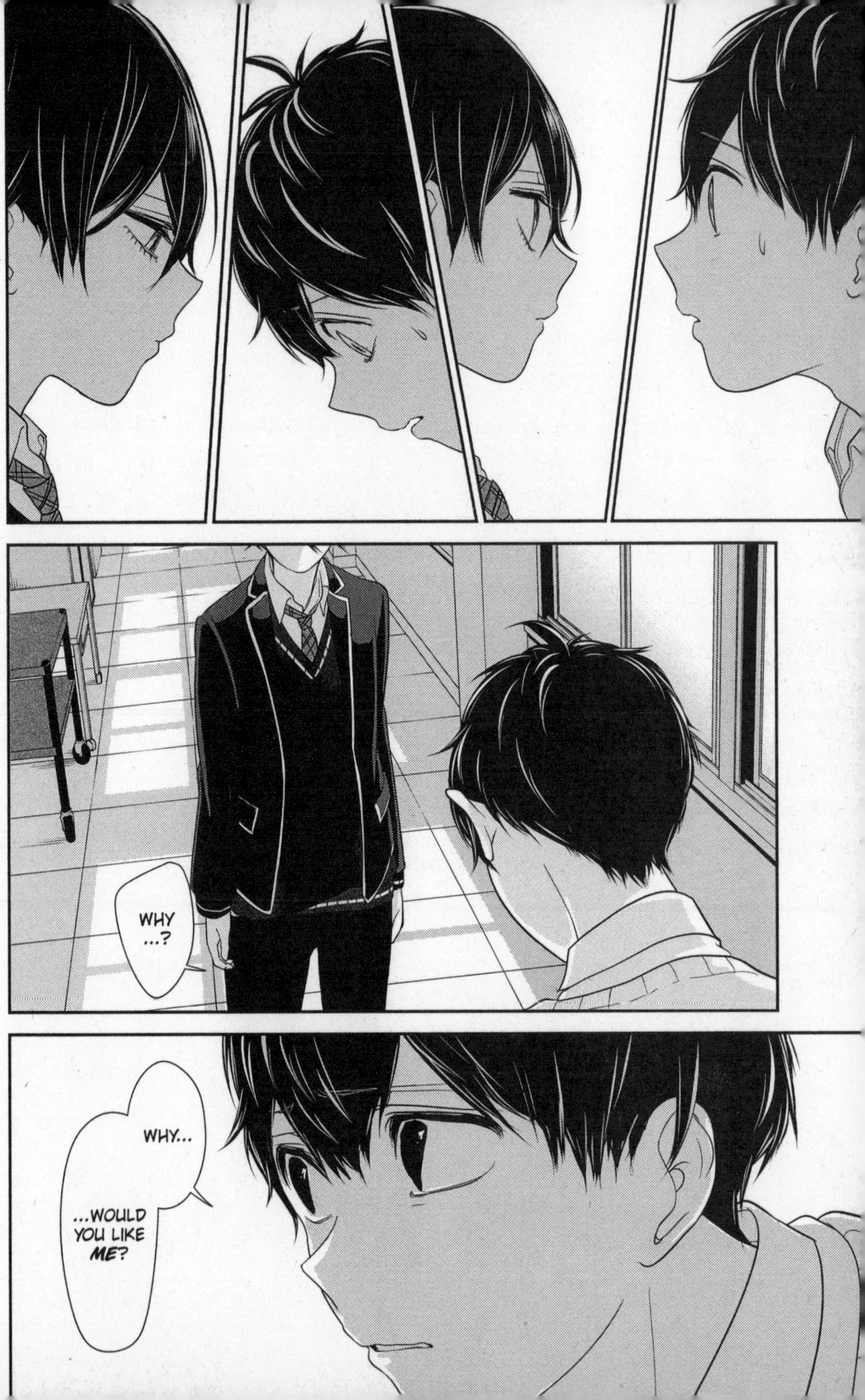
WHY ...?
WHY...
...WOULD YOU LIKE *ME*?

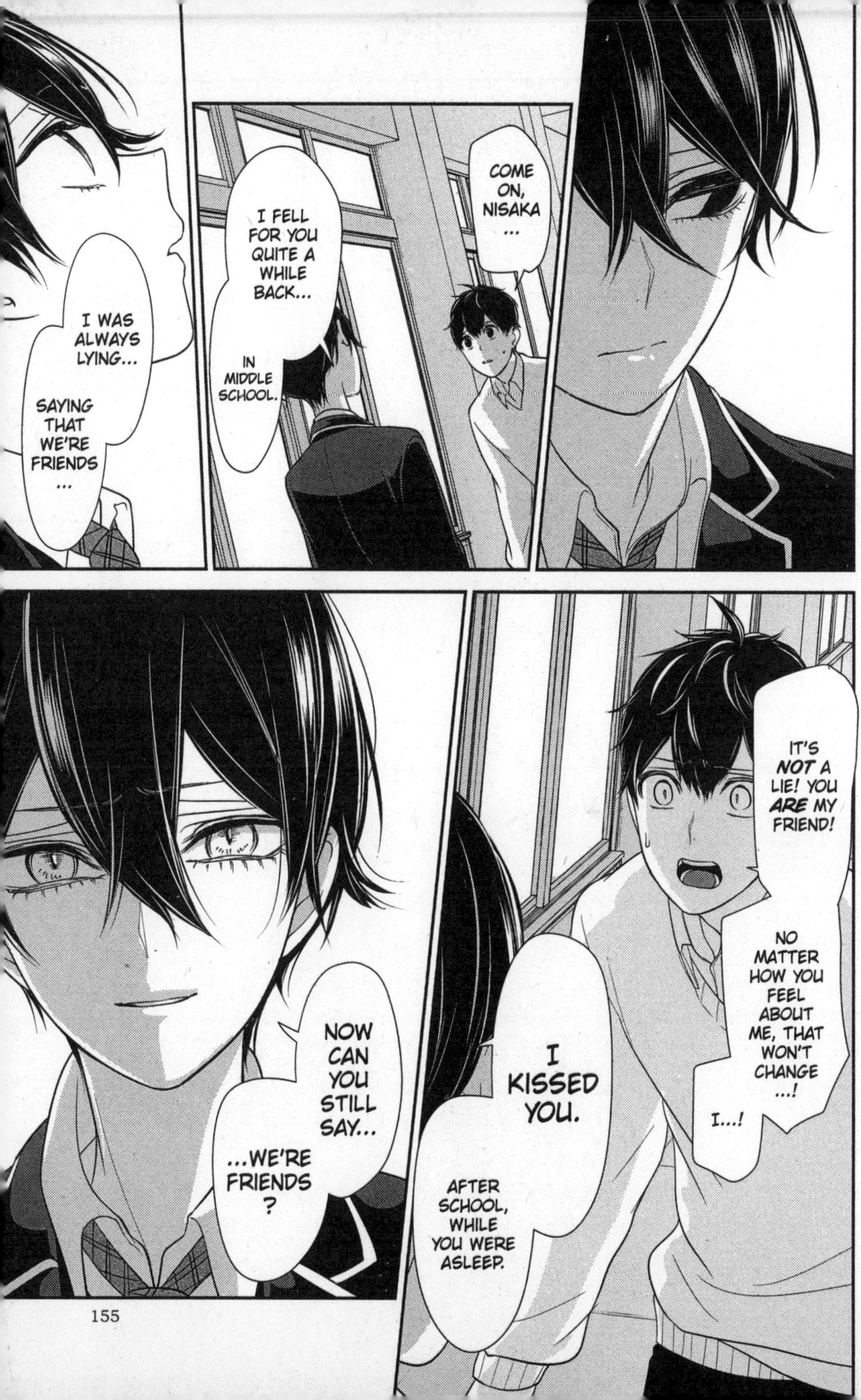
COME ON, NISAKA...
I FELL FOR YOU QUITE A WHILE BACK...
IN MIDDLE SCHOOL.
I WAS ALWAYS LYING...
SAYING THAT WE'RE FRIENDS...
IT'S *NOT* A LIE! YOU *ARE* MY FRIEND!
NO MATTER HOW YOU FEEL ABOUT ME, THAT WON'T CHANGE...!
I...!
I KISSED YOU.
AFTER SCHOOL, WHILE YOU WERE ASLEEP.
NOW CAN YOU STILL SAY...
...WE'RE FRIENDS?

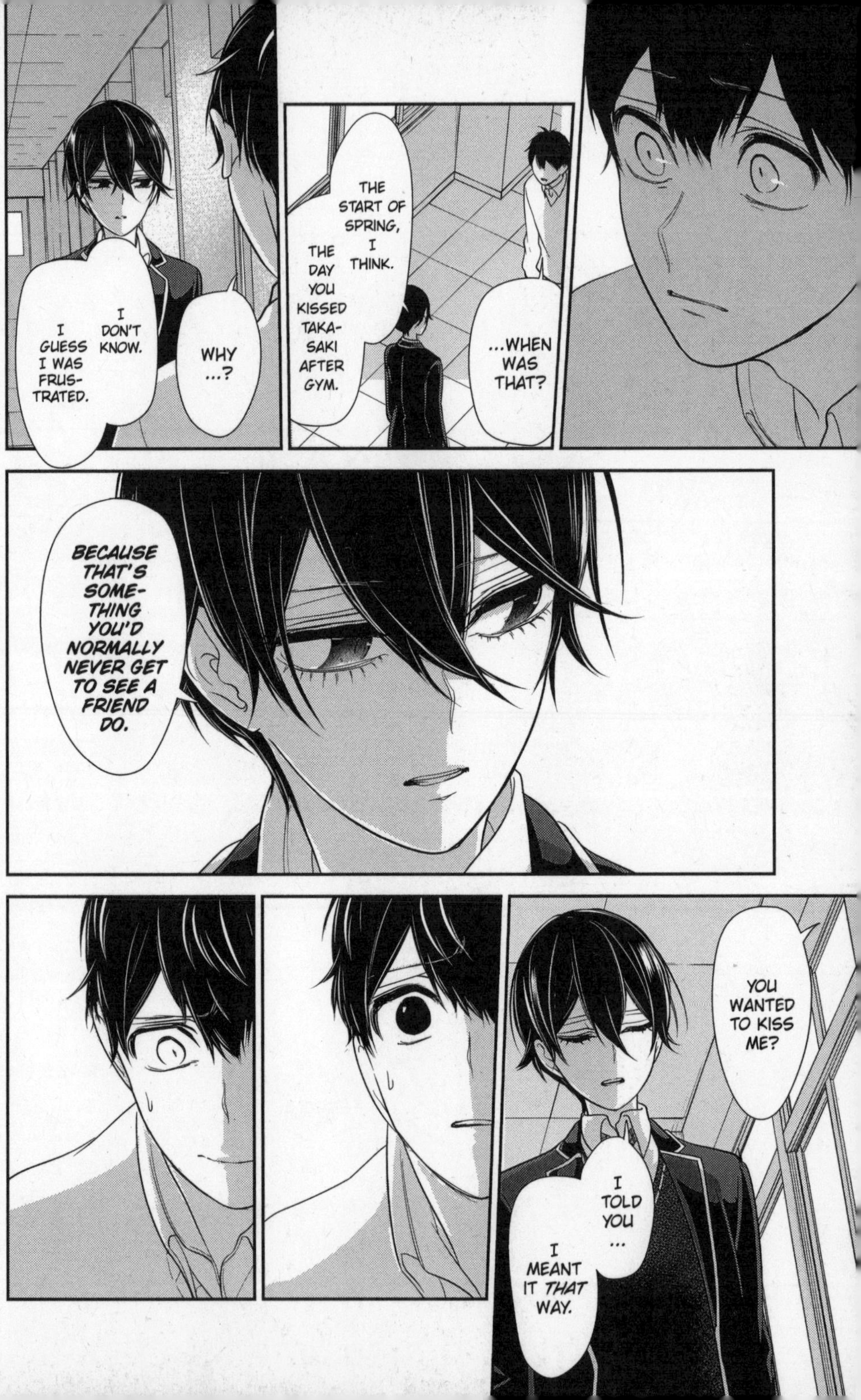
...WHEN WAS THAT?
THE START OF SPRING, I THINK. THE DAY YOU KISSED TAKA-SAKI AFTER GYM.
WHY ...?
I DON'T KNOW. I GUESS I WAS FRUS-TRATED.
BECAUSE THAT'S SOME-THING YOU'D NORMALLY NEVER GET TO SEE A FRIEND DO.
YOU WANTED TO KISS ME?
I TOLD YOU ... I MEANT IT *THAT* WAY.

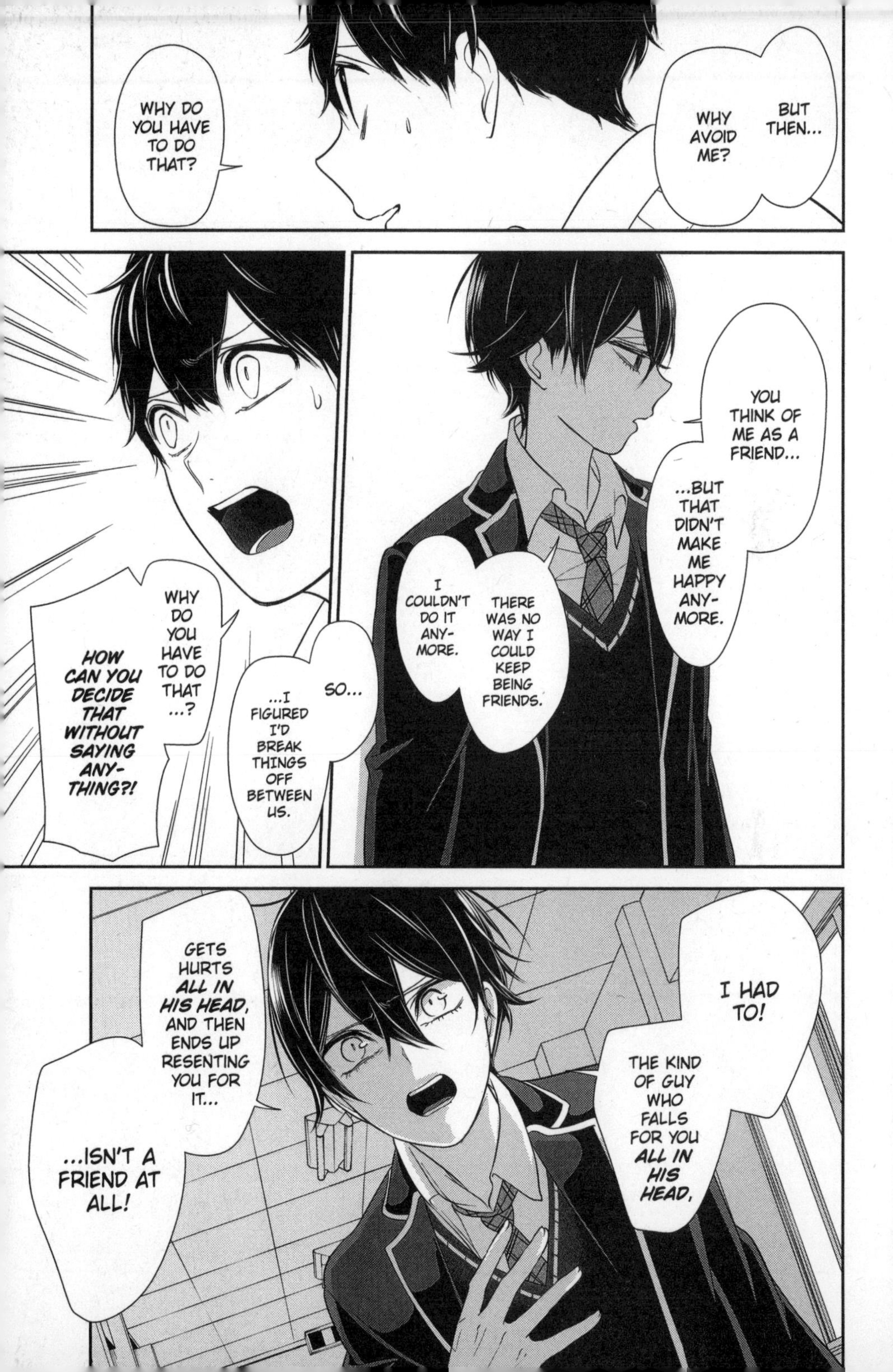
BUT THEN... WHY AVOID ME?
WHY DO YOU HAVE TO DO THAT?
YOU THINK OF ME AS A FRIEND...
...BUT THAT DIDN'T MAKE ME HAPPY ANY-MORE.
THERE WAS NO WAY I COULD KEEP BEING FRIENDS.
I COULDN'T DO IT ANY-MORE.
SO... ...I FIGURED I'D BREAK THINGS OFF BETWEEN US.
WHY DO YOU HAVE TO DO THAT ...? *HOW CAN YOU DECIDE THAT WITHOUT SAYING ANY-THING?!*
I HAD TO!
THE KIND OF GUY WHO FALLS FOR YOU *ALL IN HIS HEAD,*
GETS HURTS *ALL IN HIS HEAD,* AND THEN ENDS UP RESENTING YOU FOR IT...
...ISN'T A FRIEND AT ALL!

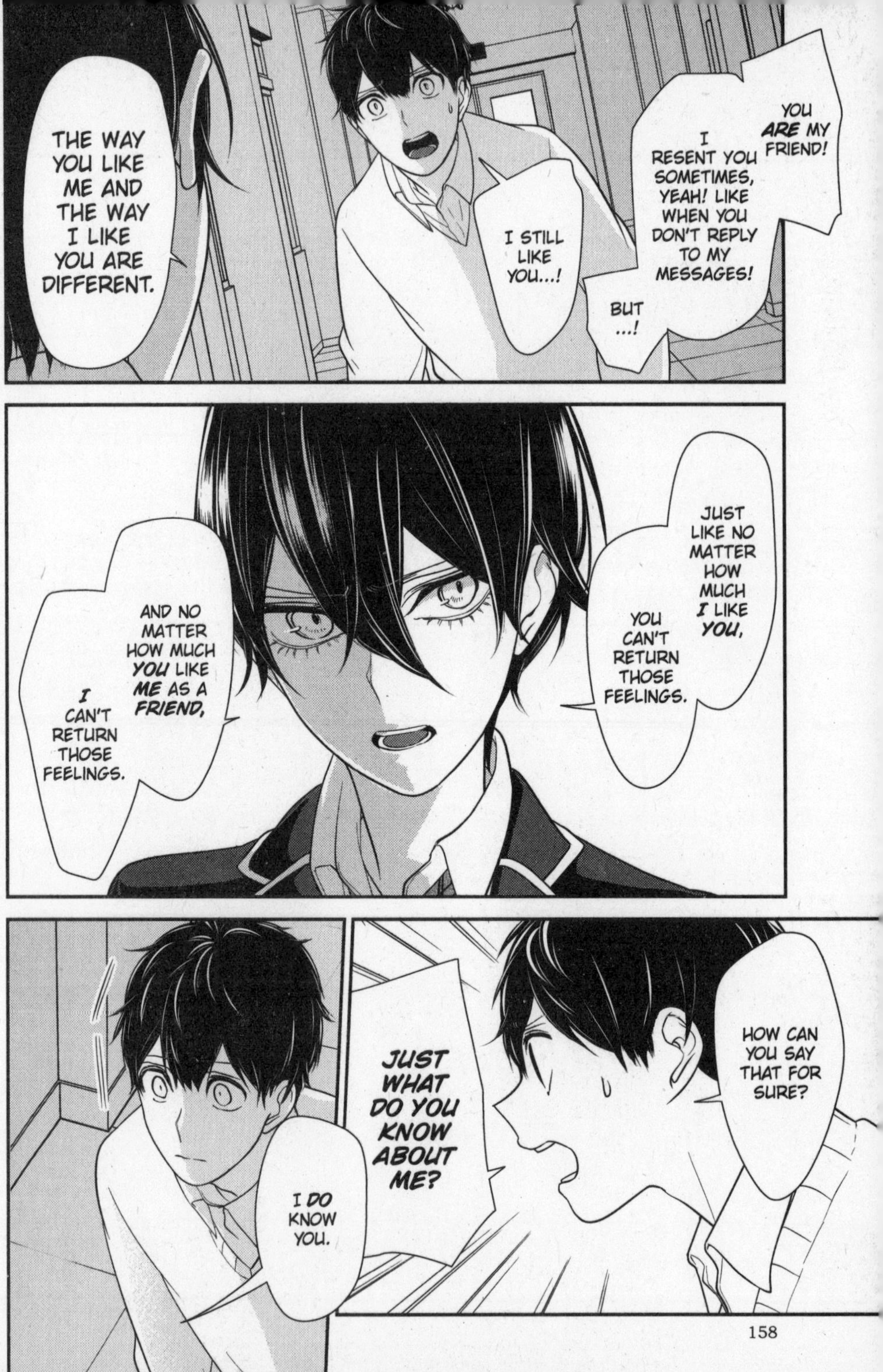
YOU ARE MY FRIEND!
I RESENT YOU SOMETIMES, YEAH! LIKE WHEN YOU DON'T REPLY TO MY MESSAGES!
BUT ...!
I STILL LIKE YOU...!
THE WAY YOU LIKE ME AND THE WAY I LIKE YOU ARE DIFFERENT.
JUST LIKE NO MATTER HOW MUCH I LIKE YOU,
YOU CAN'T RETURN THOSE FEELINGS.
AND NO MATTER HOW MUCH YOU LIKE ME AS A FRIEND,
I CAN'T RETURN THOSE FEELINGS.
HOW CAN YOU SAY THAT FOR SURE?
JUST WHAT DO YOU KNOW ABOUT ME?
I DO KNOW YOU.

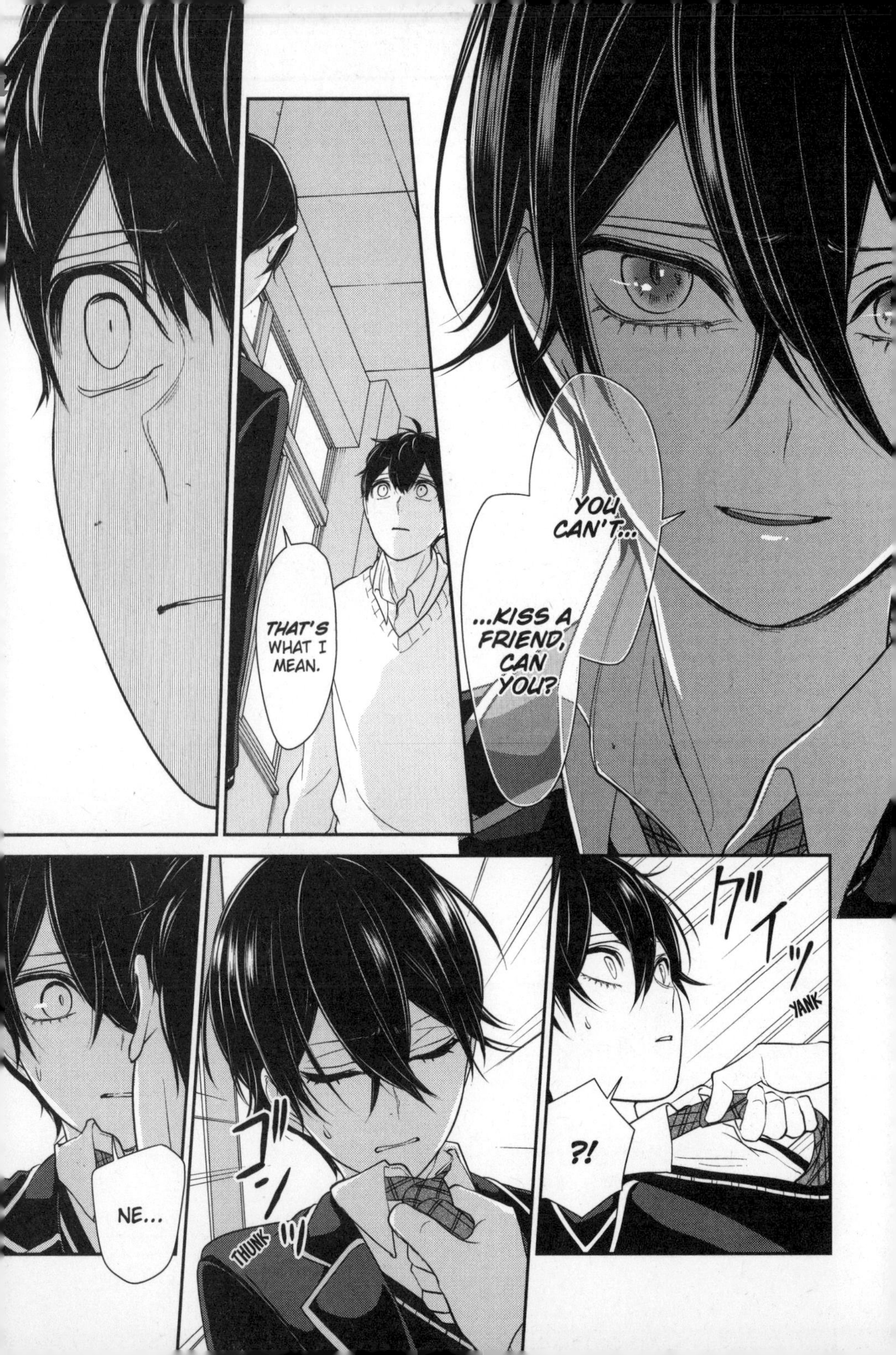
YOU CAN'T...
...KISS A FRIEND, CAN YOU?
THAT'S WHAT I MEAN.
グイッ
YANK
?!
ゴッ
THUNK
NE...

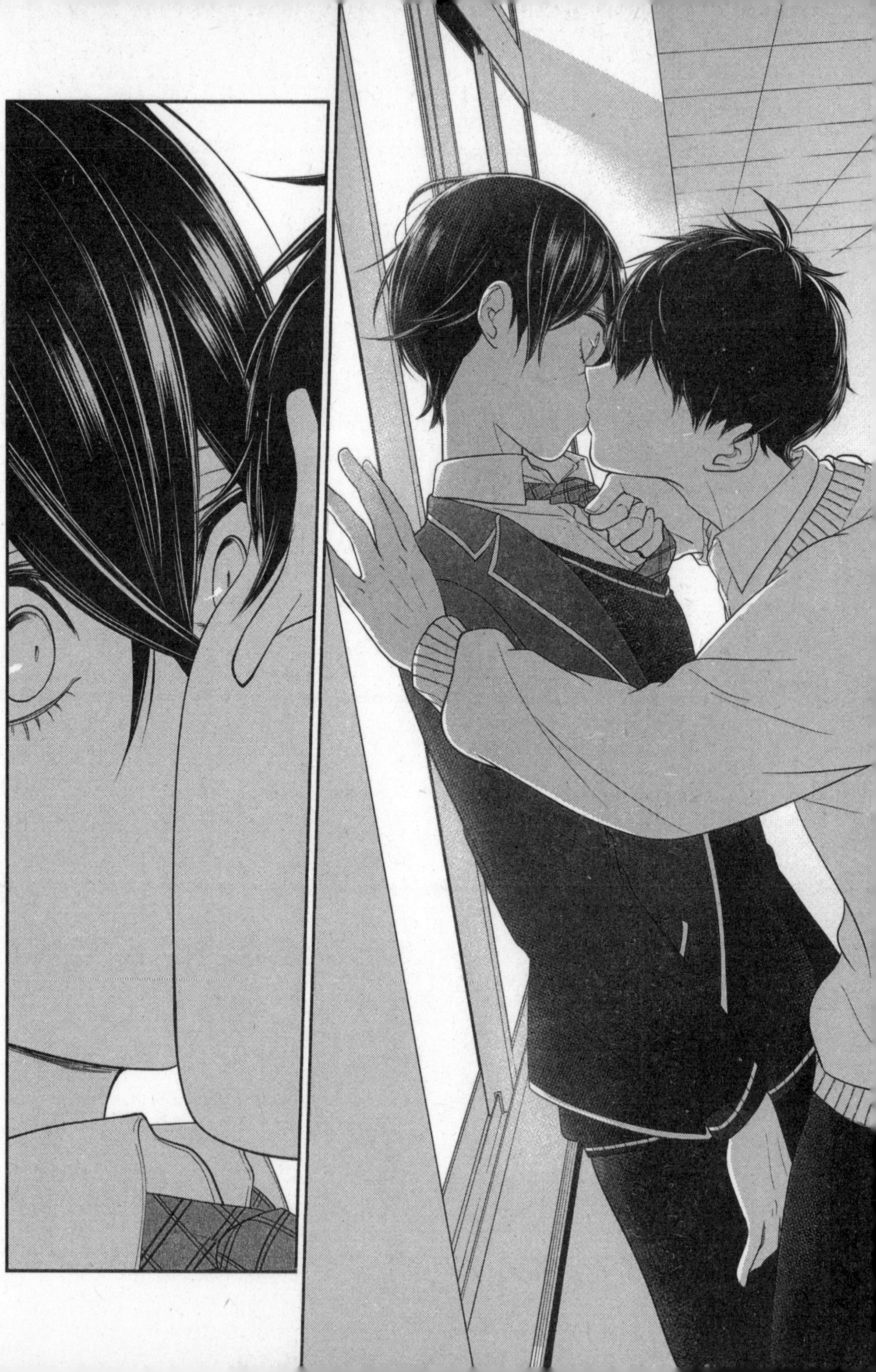

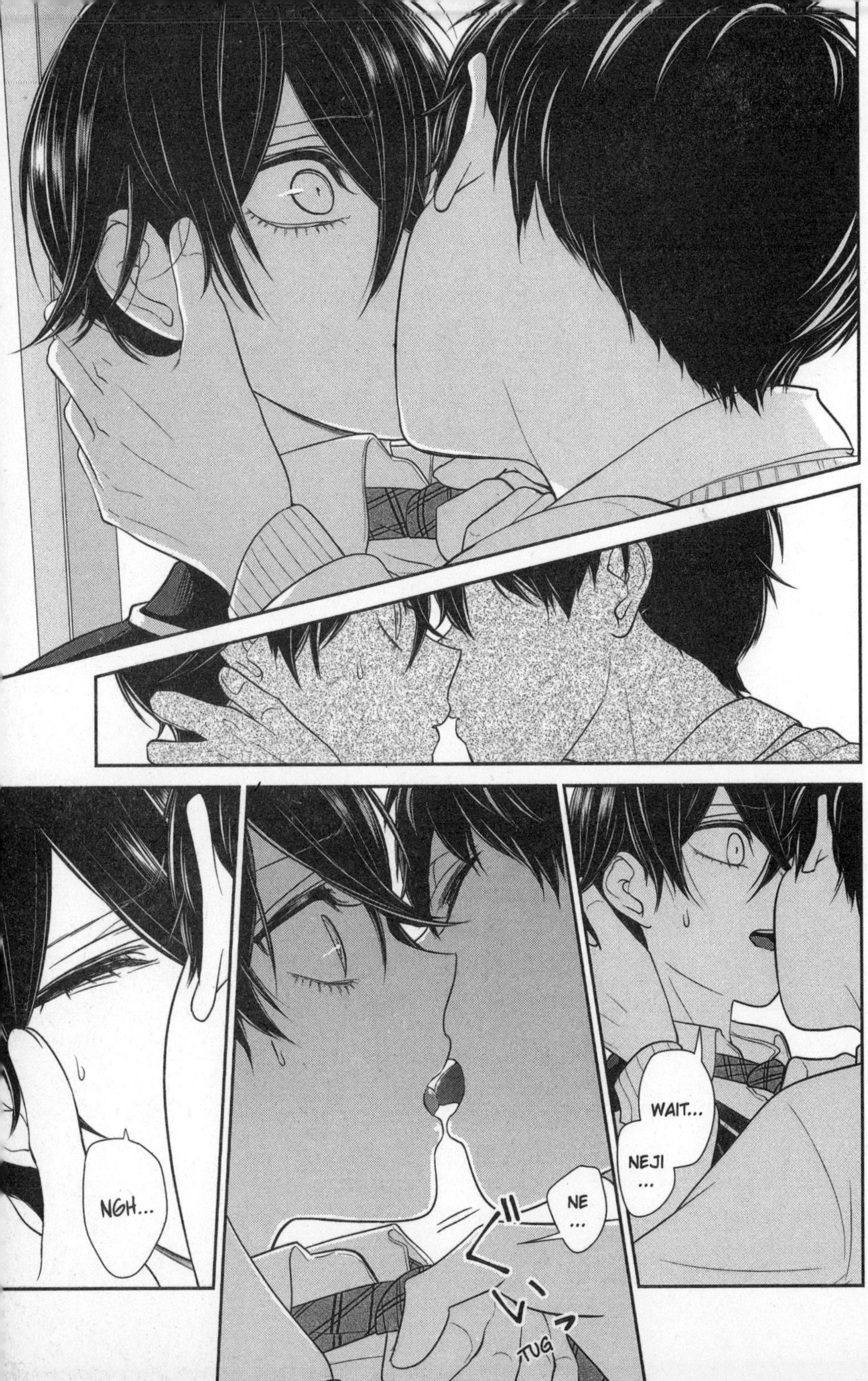
WAIT...
NEJI ...
NE ...
TUG
NGH...

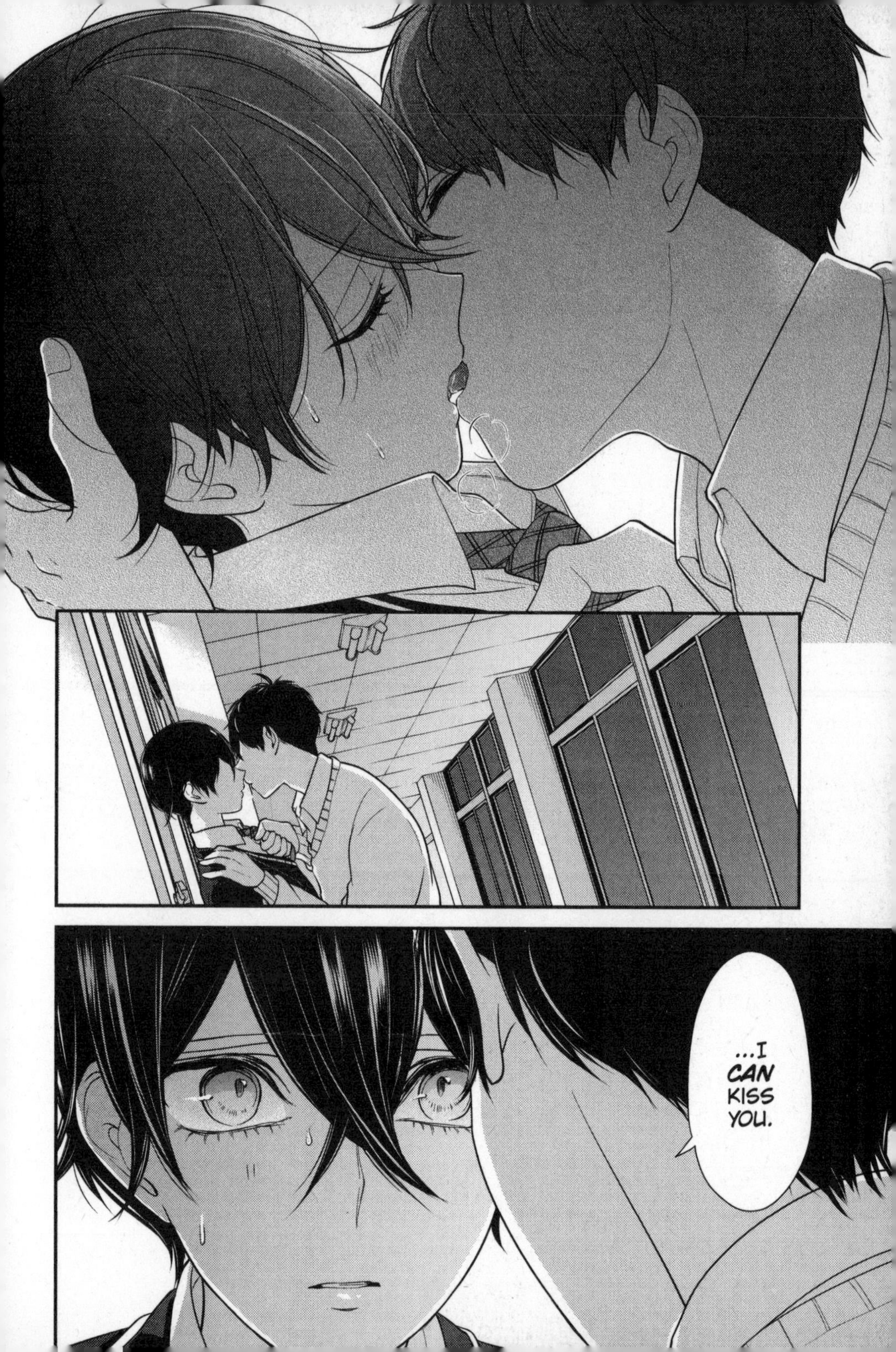
...I CAN KISS YOU.

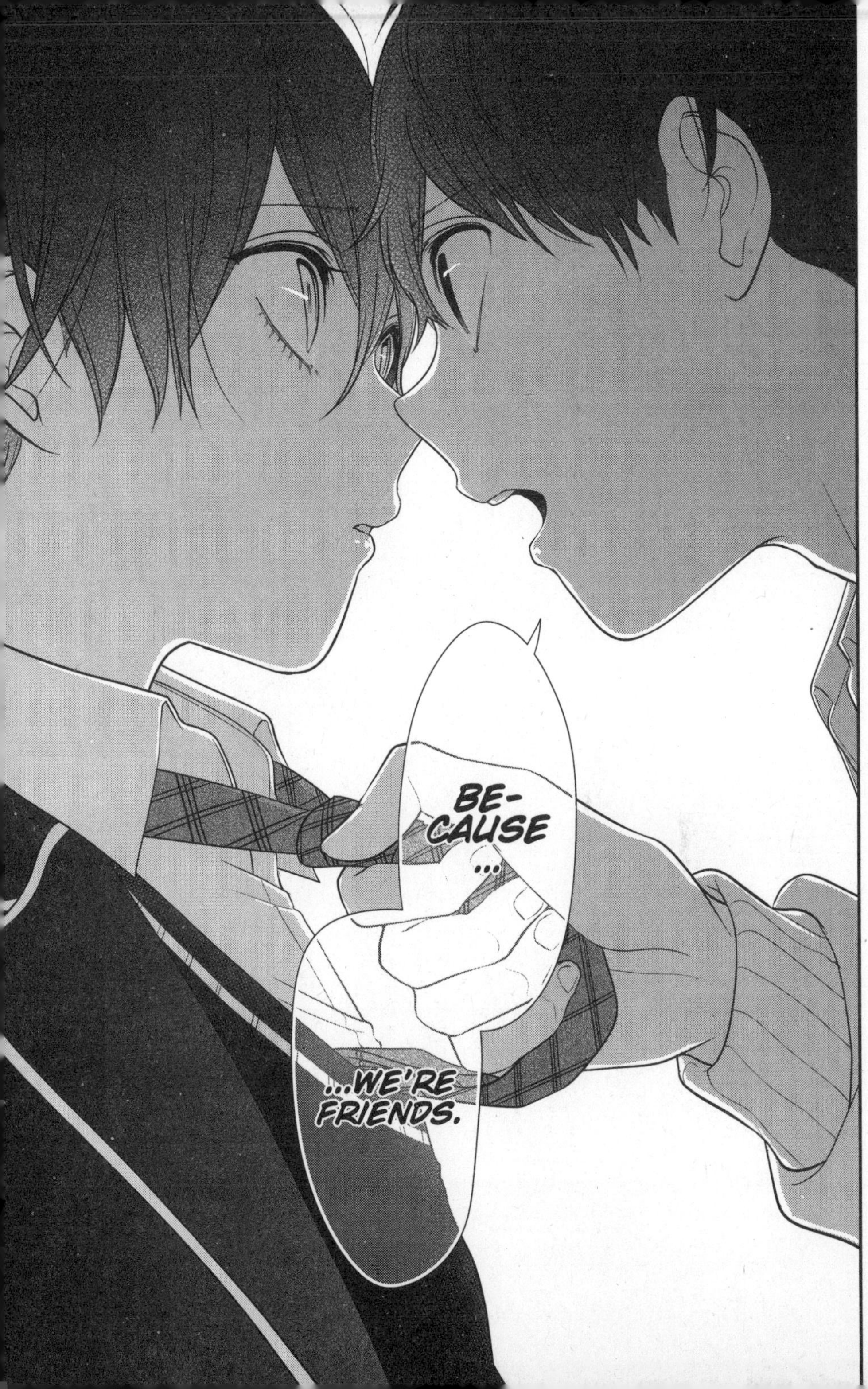
BE-CAUSE ...
...WE'RE FRIENDS.

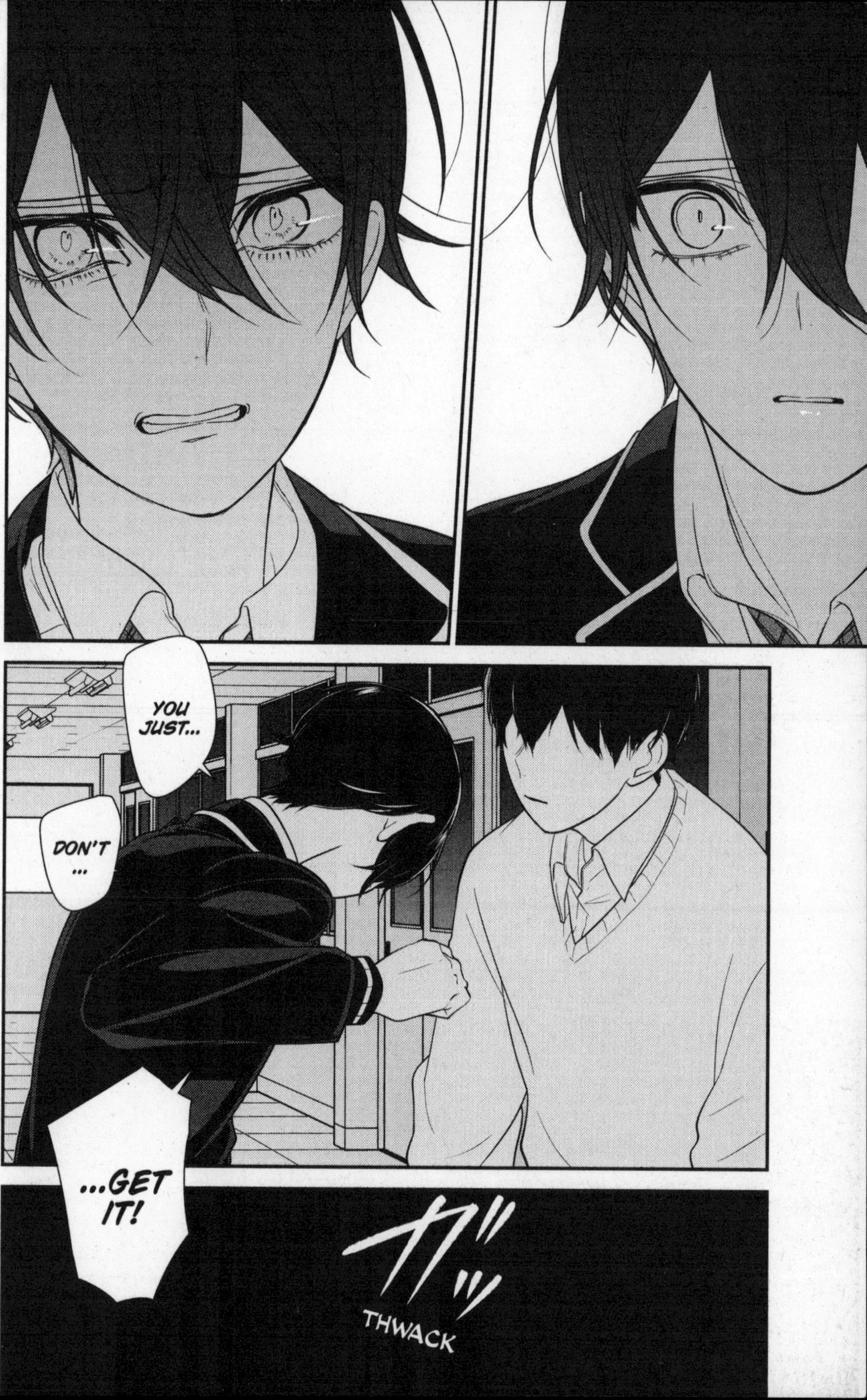
YOU JUST...
DON'T ...
...GET IT!
ガッ
THWACK

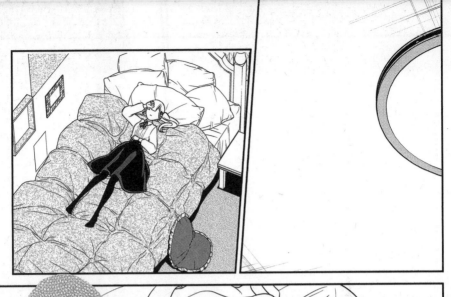

"YOU JUST DON'T GET IT"? LIKE, WHAT DON'T I GET? TELL ME.

...

SO YOU'RE SUPPORTING THEIR RELATIONSHIP?

HUH... WHAT'S THAT SUPPORT EVEN SUPPOSED TO BE, IN THE FIRST PLACE?

IT'S COMMON FOR PEOPLE WHO ARE CHEERING ON THE BENCH TO GO JOIN A SOCCER GAME.

DID YOU THINK "SUPPORT" MEANS YOU'LL NEVER BE INVOLVED YOURSELF?

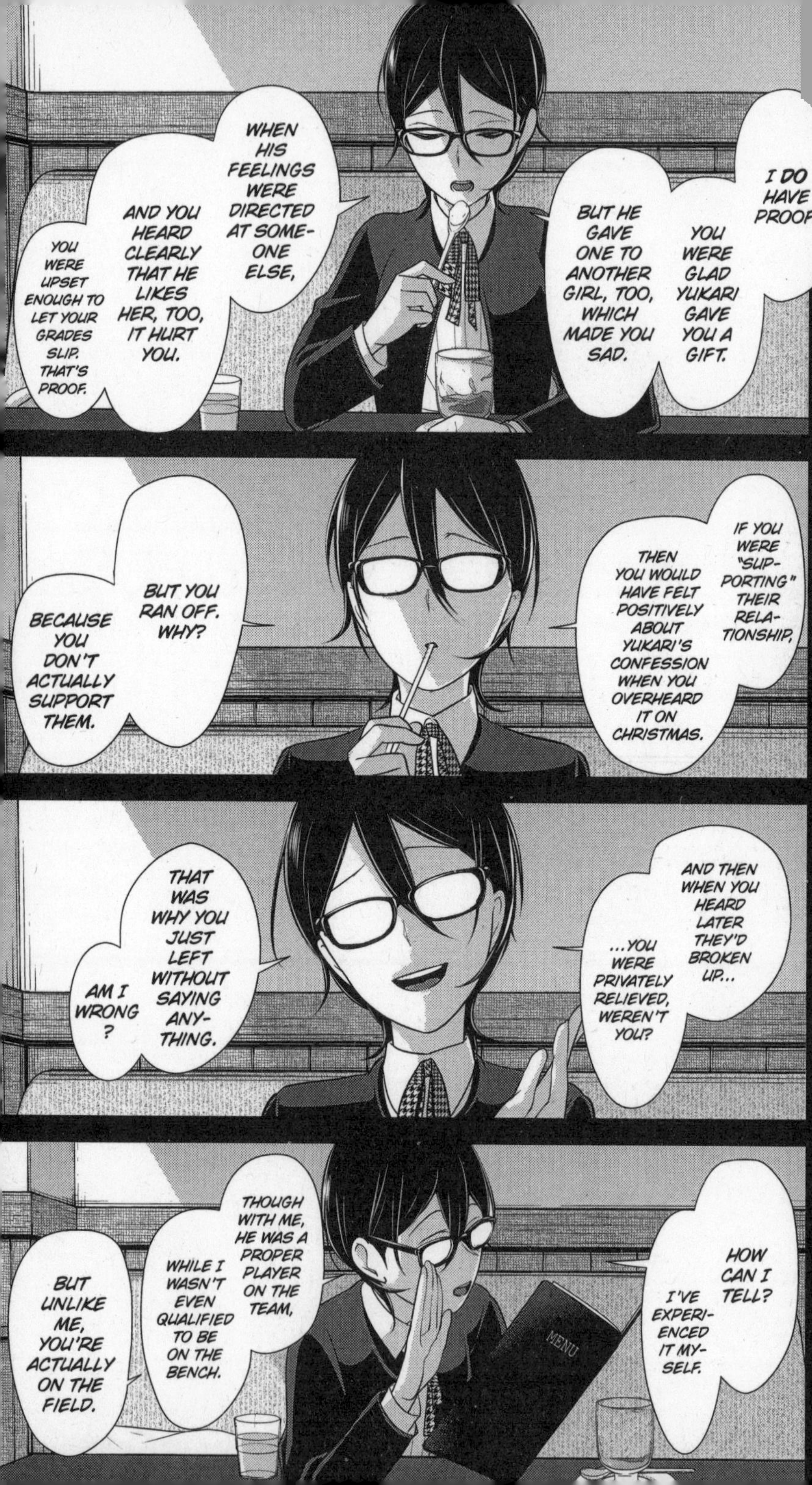
I DO HAVE PROOF.
YOU WERE GLAD YUKARI GAVE YOU A GIFT.
BUT HE GAVE ONE TO ANOTHER GIRL, TOO, WHICH MADE YOU SAD.
WHEN HIS FEELINGS WERE DIRECTED AT SOME-ONE ELSE,
AND YOU HEARD CLEARLY THAT HE LIKES HER, TOO, IT HURT YOU.
YOU WERE UPSET ENOUGH TO LET YOUR GRADES SLIP. THAT'S PROOF.
IF YOU WERE "SUP-PORTING" THEIR RELA-TIONSHIP,
THEN YOU WOULD HAVE FELT POSITIVELY ABOUT YUKARI'S CONFESSION WHEN YOU OVERHEARD IT ON CHRISTMAS.
BUT YOU RAN OFF. WHY?
BECAUSE YOU DON'T ACTUALLY SUPPORT THEM.
AND THEN WHEN YOU HEARD LATER THEY'D BROKEN UP...
...YOU WERE PRIVATELY RELIEVED, WEREN'T YOU?
THAT WAS WHY YOU JUST LEFT WITHOUT SAYING ANY-THING.
AM I WRONG?
HOW CAN I TELL?
I'VE EXPERI-ENCED IT MY-SELF.
THOUGH WITH ME, HE WAS A PROPER PLAYER ON THE TEAM,
WHILE I WASN'T EVEN QUALIFIED TO BE ON THE BENCH.
BUT UNLIKE ME, YOU'RE ACTUALLY ON THE FIELD.
MENU

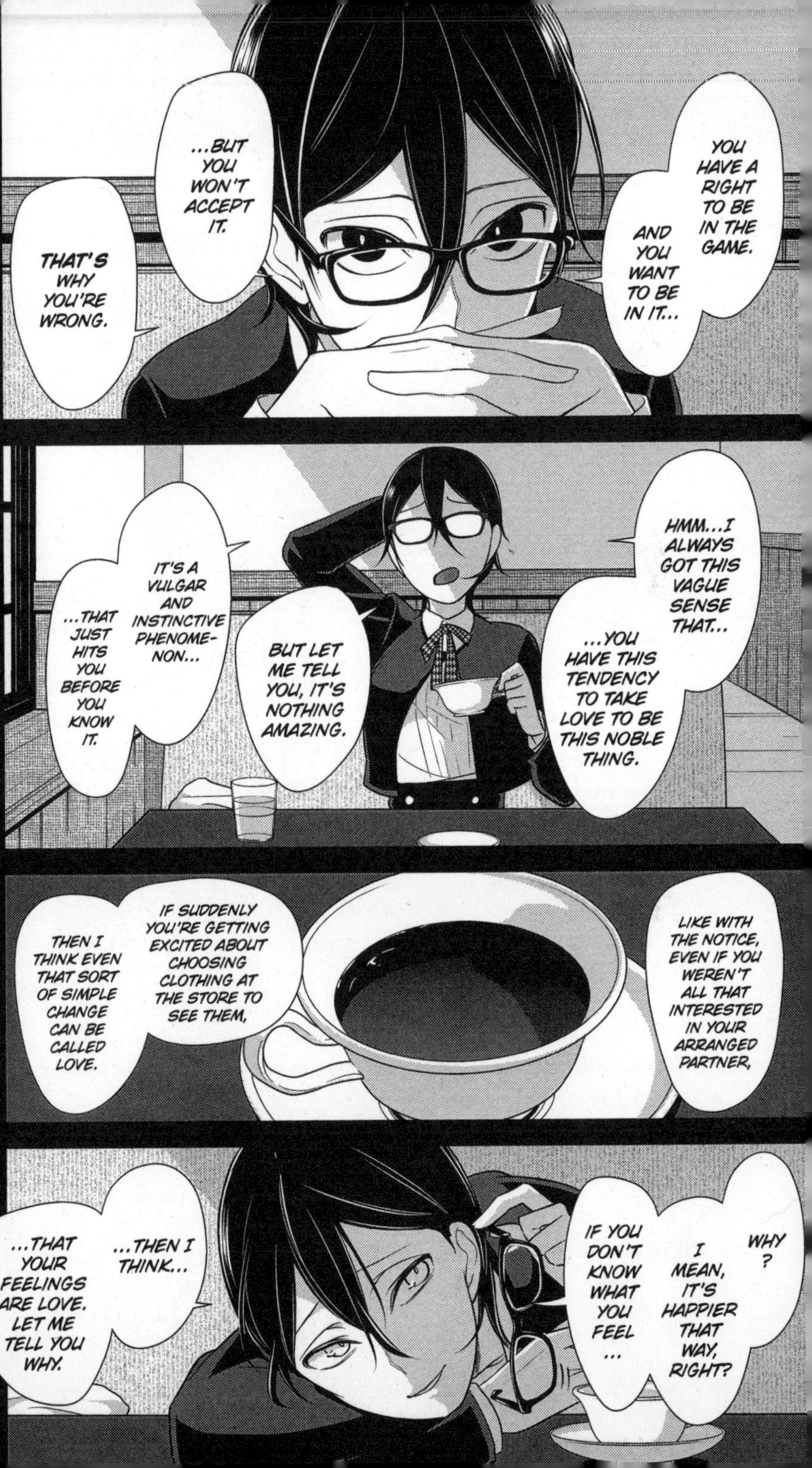
YOU HAVE A RIGHT TO BE IN THE GAME.
AND YOU WANT TO BE IN IT...
...BUT YOU WON'T ACCEPT IT.
THAT'S WHY YOU'RE WRONG.
HMM...I ALWAYS GOT THIS VAGUE SENSE THAT...
...YOU HAVE THIS TENDENCY TO TAKE LOVE TO BE THIS NOBLE THING.
BUT LET ME TELL YOU, IT'S NOTHING AMAZING.
IT'S A VULGAR AND INSTINCTIVE PHENOMENON...
...THAT JUST HITS YOU BEFORE YOU KNOW IT.
LIKE WITH THE NOTICE, EVEN IF YOU WEREN'T ALL THAT INTERESTED IN YOUR ARRANGED PARTNER,
IF SUDDENLY YOU'RE GETTING EXCITED ABOUT CHOOSING CLOTHING AT THE STORE TO SEE THEM,
THEN I THINK EVEN THAT SORT OF SIMPLE CHANGE CAN BE CALLED LOVE.
WHY?
I MEAN, IT'S HAPPIER THAT WAY, RIGHT?
IF YOU DON'T KNOW WHAT YOU FEEL...
...THEN I THINK...
...THAT YOUR FEELINGS ARE LOVE. LET ME TELL YOU WHY.

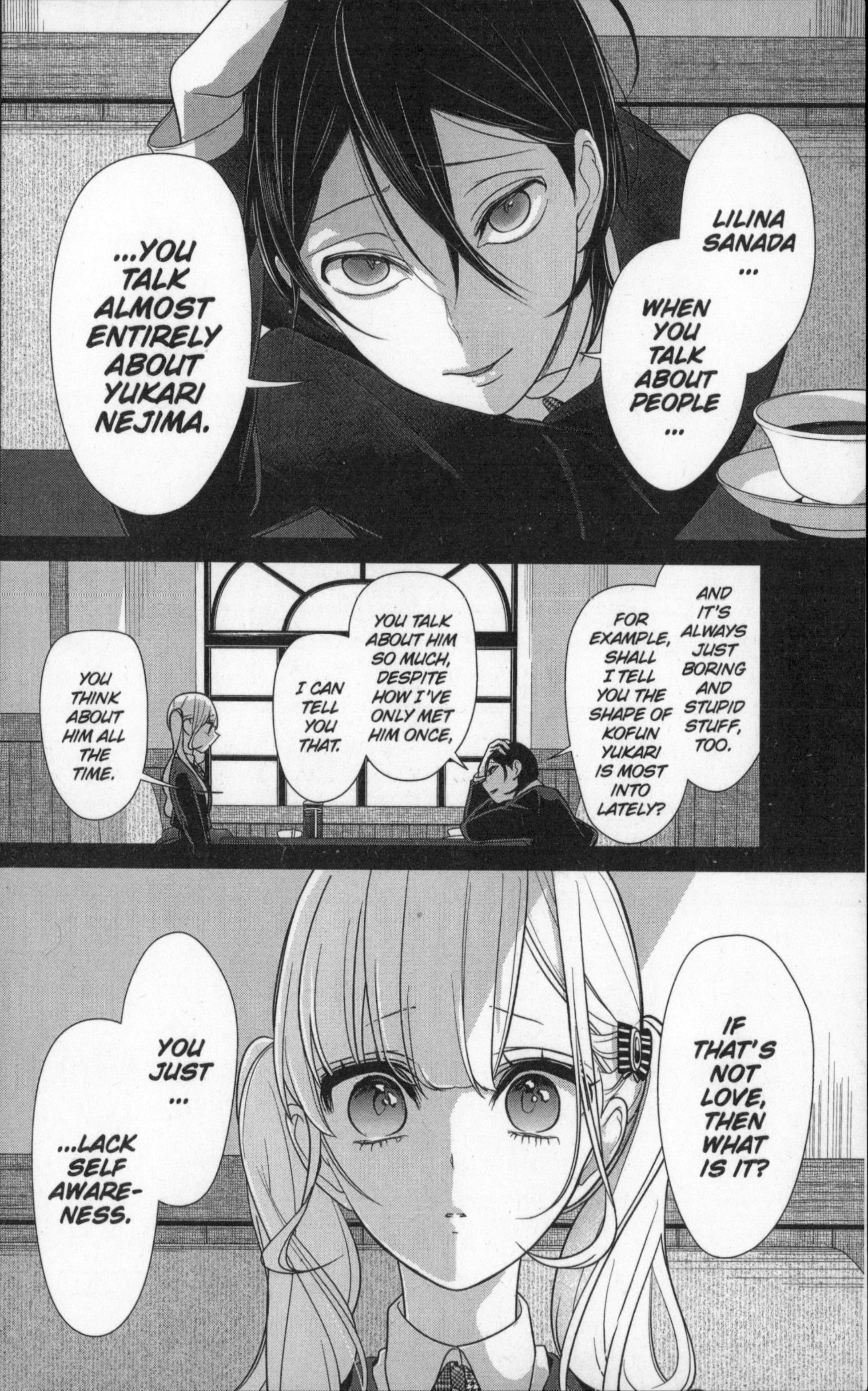
LILINA SANADA ... WHEN YOU TALK ABOUT PEOPLE ...
...YOU TALK ALMOST ENTIRELY ABOUT YUKARI NEJIMA.
AND IT'S ALWAYS JUST BORING AND STUPID STUFF, TOO.
FOR EXAMPLE, SHALL I TELL YOU THE SHAPE OF KOFUN YUKARI IS MOST INTO LATELY?
YOU TALK ABOUT HIM SO MUCH, DESPITE HOW I'VE ONLY MET HIM ONCE,
I CAN TELL YOU THAT.
YOU THINK ABOUT HIM ALL THE TIME.
IF THAT'S NOT LOVE, THEN WHAT IS IT?
YOU JUST ...
...LACK SELF AWARENESS.

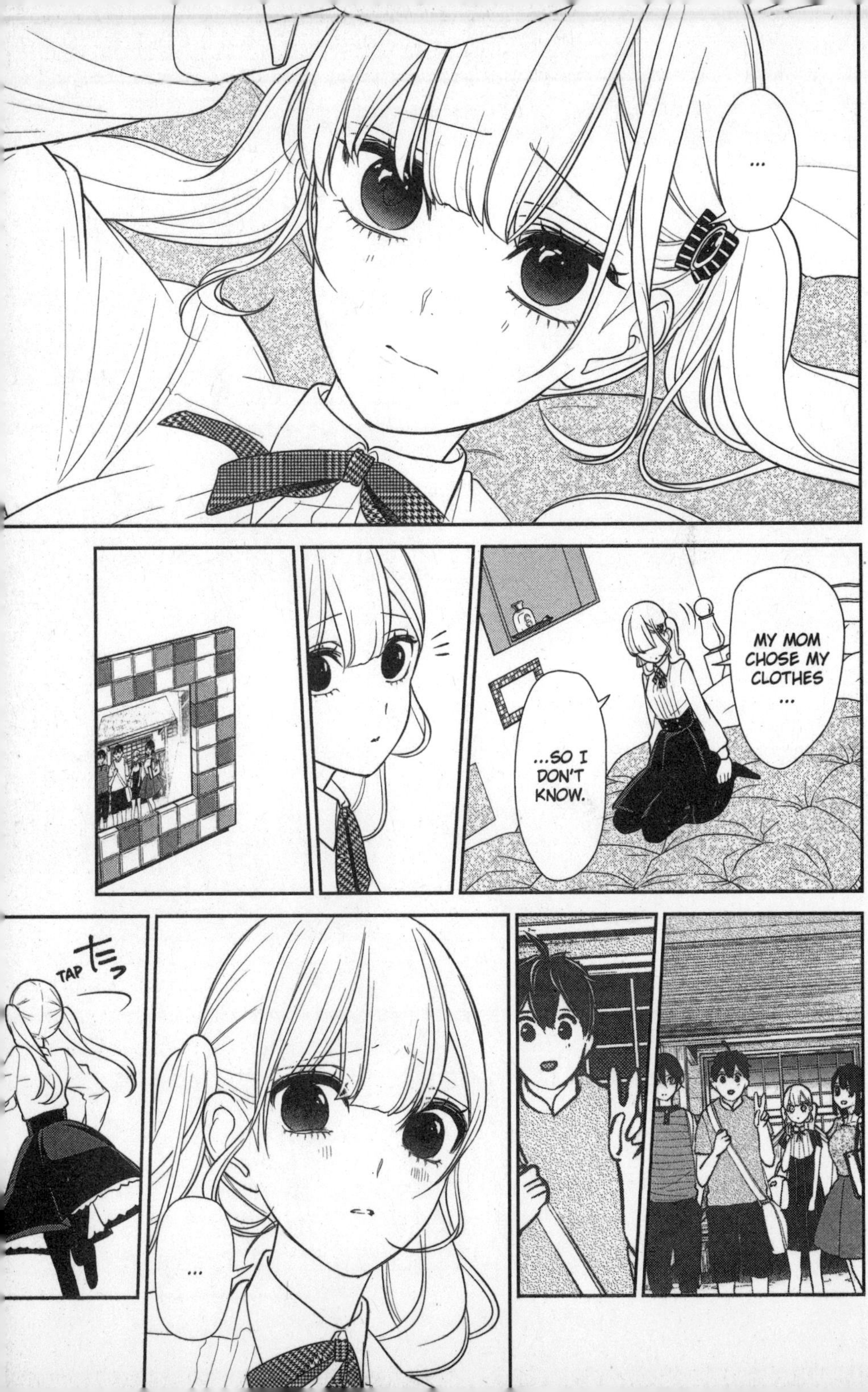
...
MY MOM CHOSE MY CLOTHES ...
...SO I DON'T KNOW.
...
TAP たっ

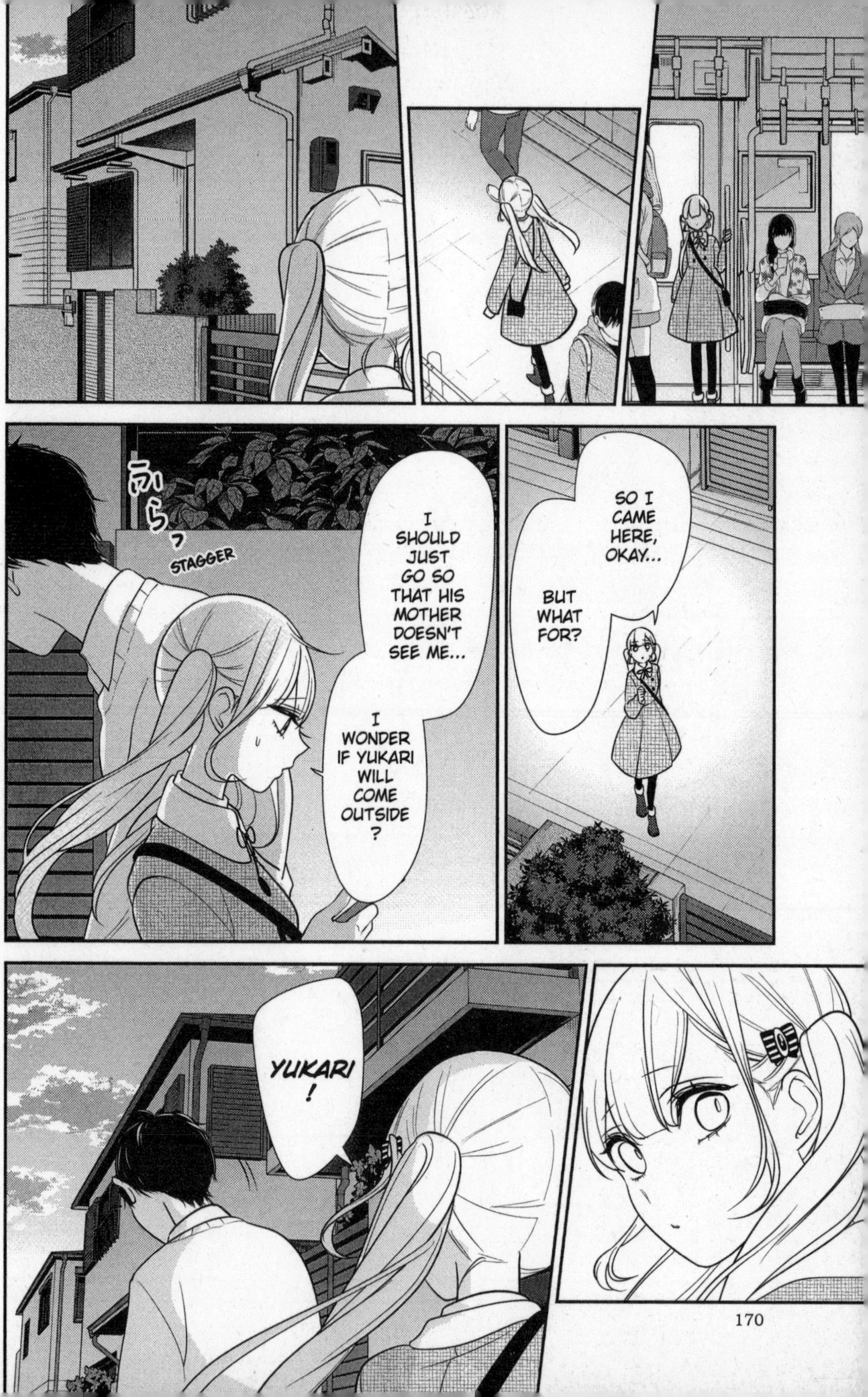
SO I CAME HERE, OKAY...
BUT WHAT FOR?
ふらっ
STAGGER
I SHOULD JUST GO SO THAT HIS MOTHER DOESN'T SEE ME...
I WONDER IF YUKARI WILL COME OUTSIDE?
YUKARI!

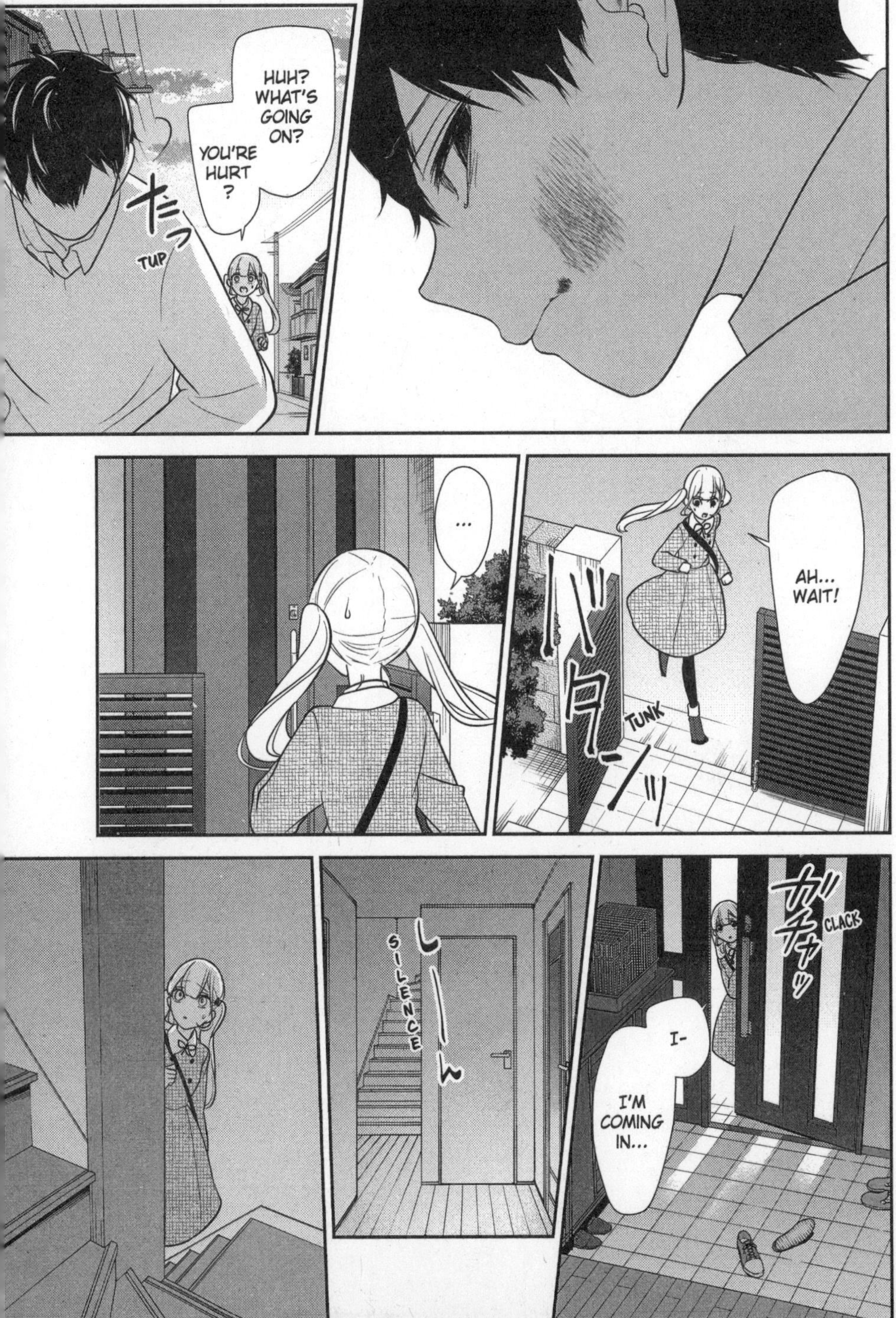
HUH? WHAT'S GOING ON?
YOU'RE HURT?
だっ
TUP
AH... WAIT!
バターン
TUNK
...
ガチャッ
CLACK
I-
I'M COMING IN...
しーん
SILENCE

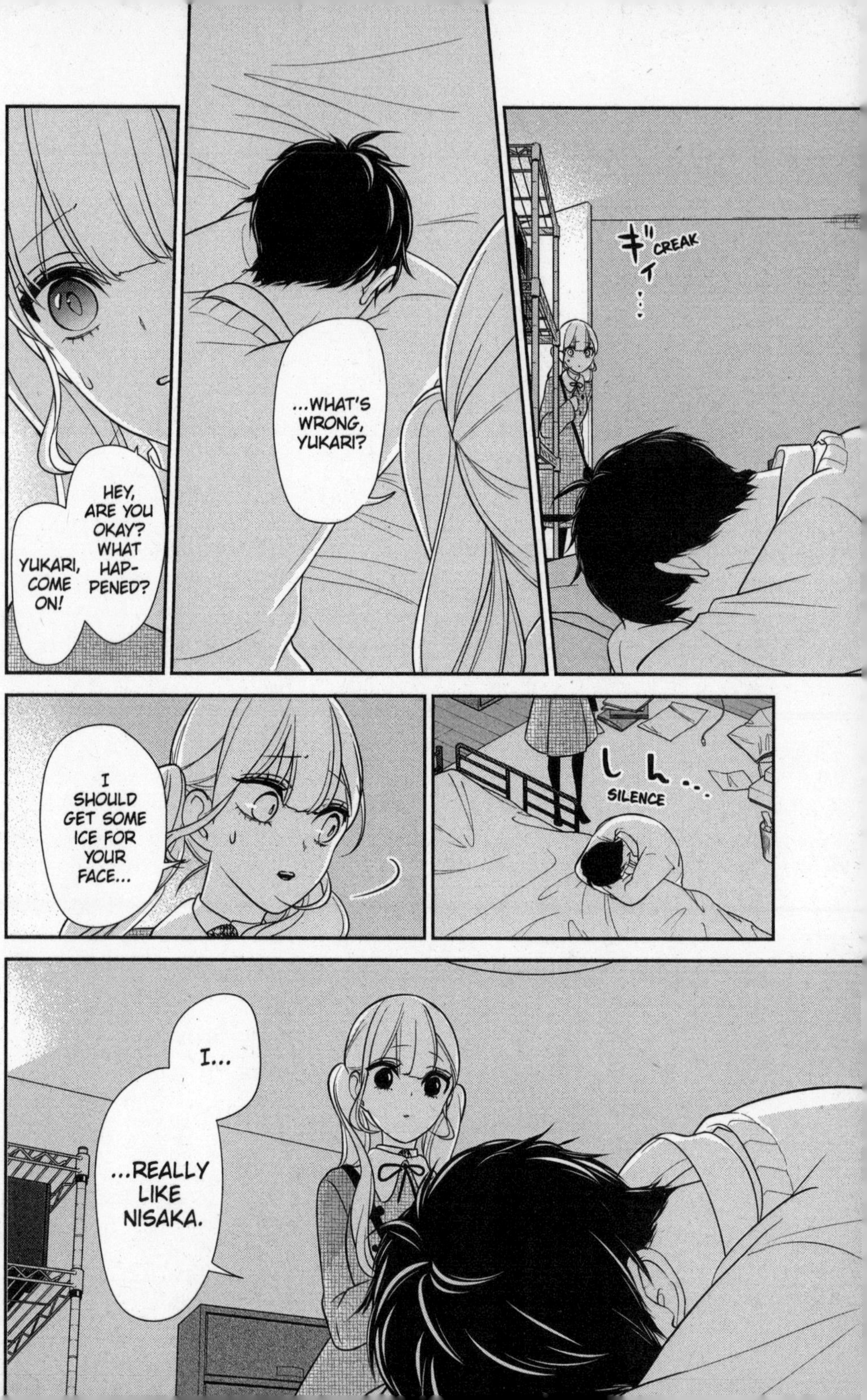
ギィ…
CREAK
...WHAT'S WRONG, YUKARI?
HEY, ARE YOU OKAY? WHAT HAP-PENED?
YUKARI, COME ON!
しん…
SILENCE
I SHOULD GET SOME ICE FOR YOUR FACE...
I...
...REALLY LIKE NISAKA.

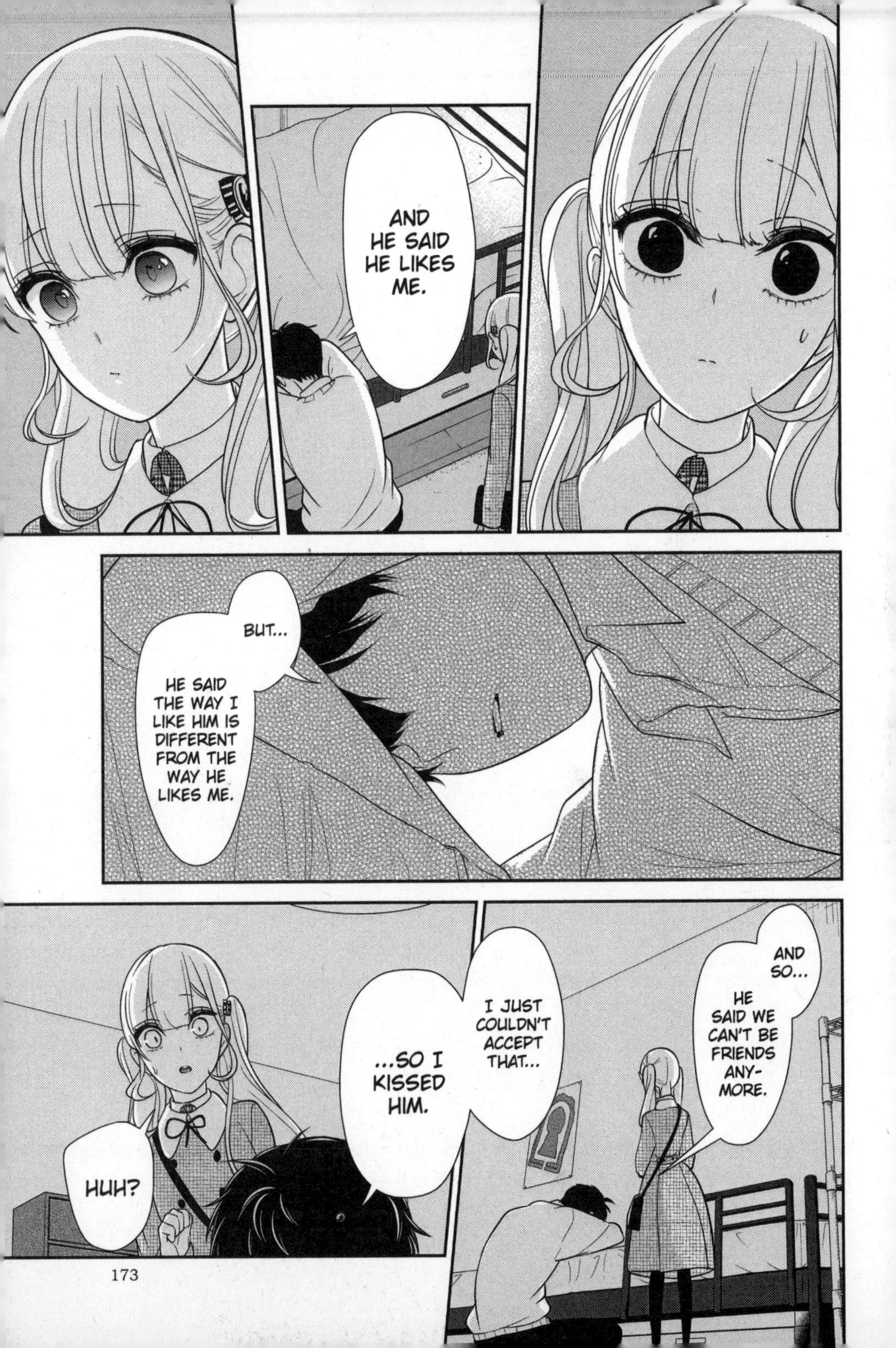
AND HE SAID HE LIKES ME.
BUT...
HE SAID THE WAY I LIKE HIM IS DIFFERENT FROM THE WAY HE LIKES ME.
AND SO...
HE SAID WE CAN'T BE FRIENDS ANY-MORE.
I JUST COULDN'T ACCEPT THAT...
...SO I KISSED HIM.
HUH?

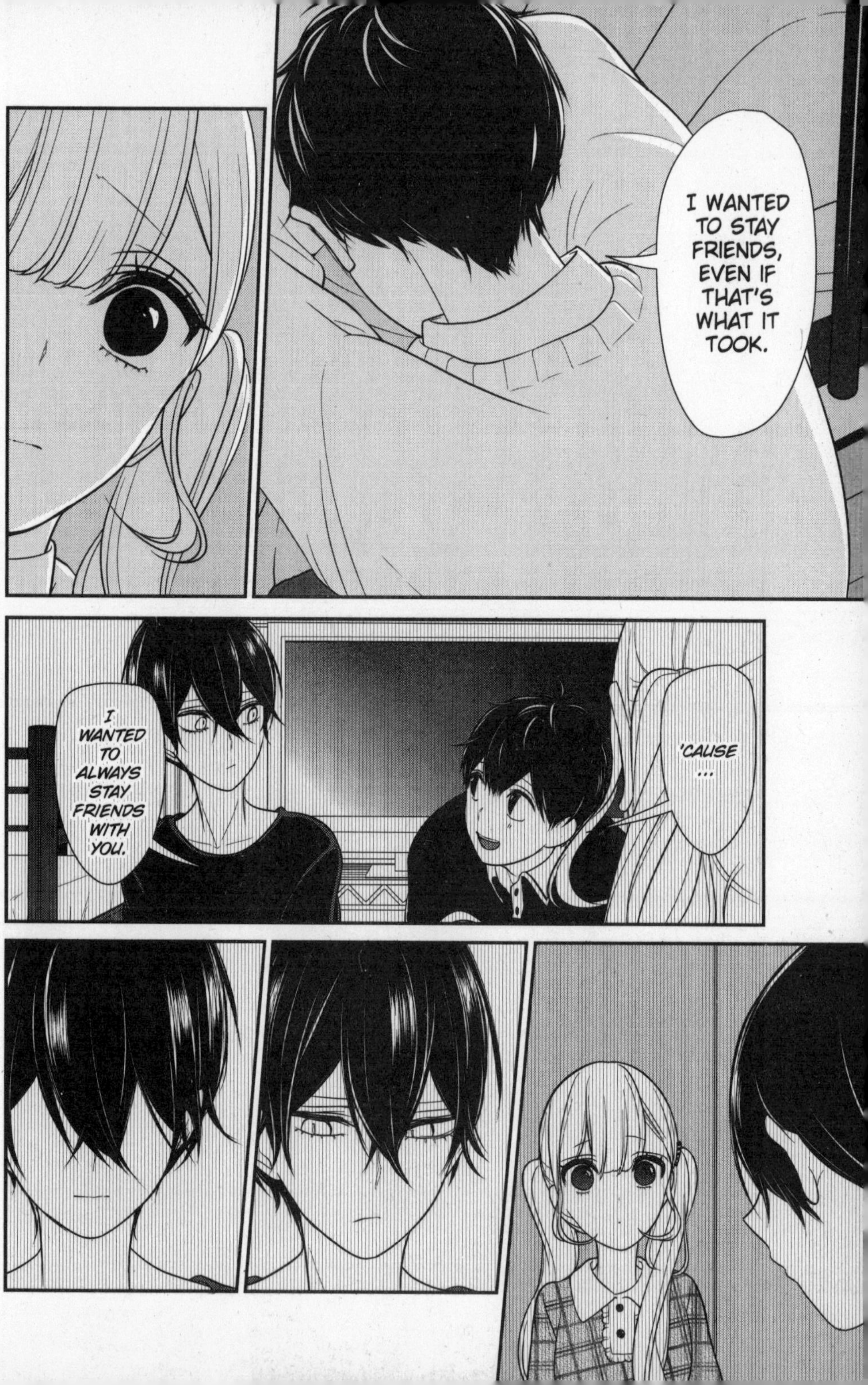
I WANTED TO STAY FRIENDS, EVEN IF THAT'S WHAT IT TOOK.
'CAUSE ...
I WANTED TO ALWAYS STAY FRIENDS WITH YOU.

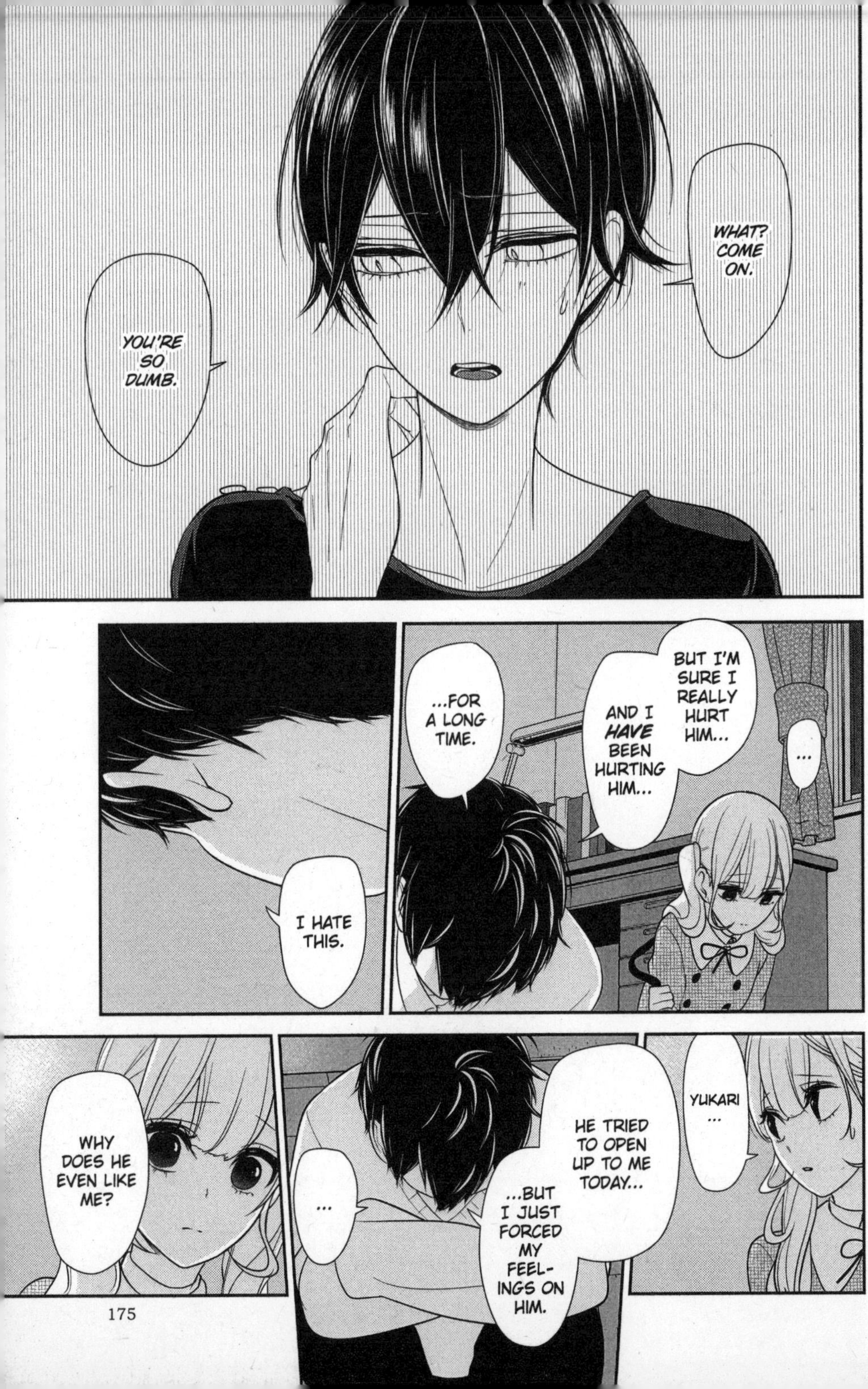
WHAT? COME ON.
YOU'RE SO DUMB.
...
BUT I'M SURE I REALLY HURT HIM...
AND I HAVE BEEN HURTING HIM...
...FOR A LONG TIME.
I HATE THIS.
YUKARI ...
HE TRIED TO OPEN UP TO ME TODAY...
...BUT I JUST FORCED MY FEEL- INGS ON HIM.
...
WHY DOES HE EVEN LIKE ME?

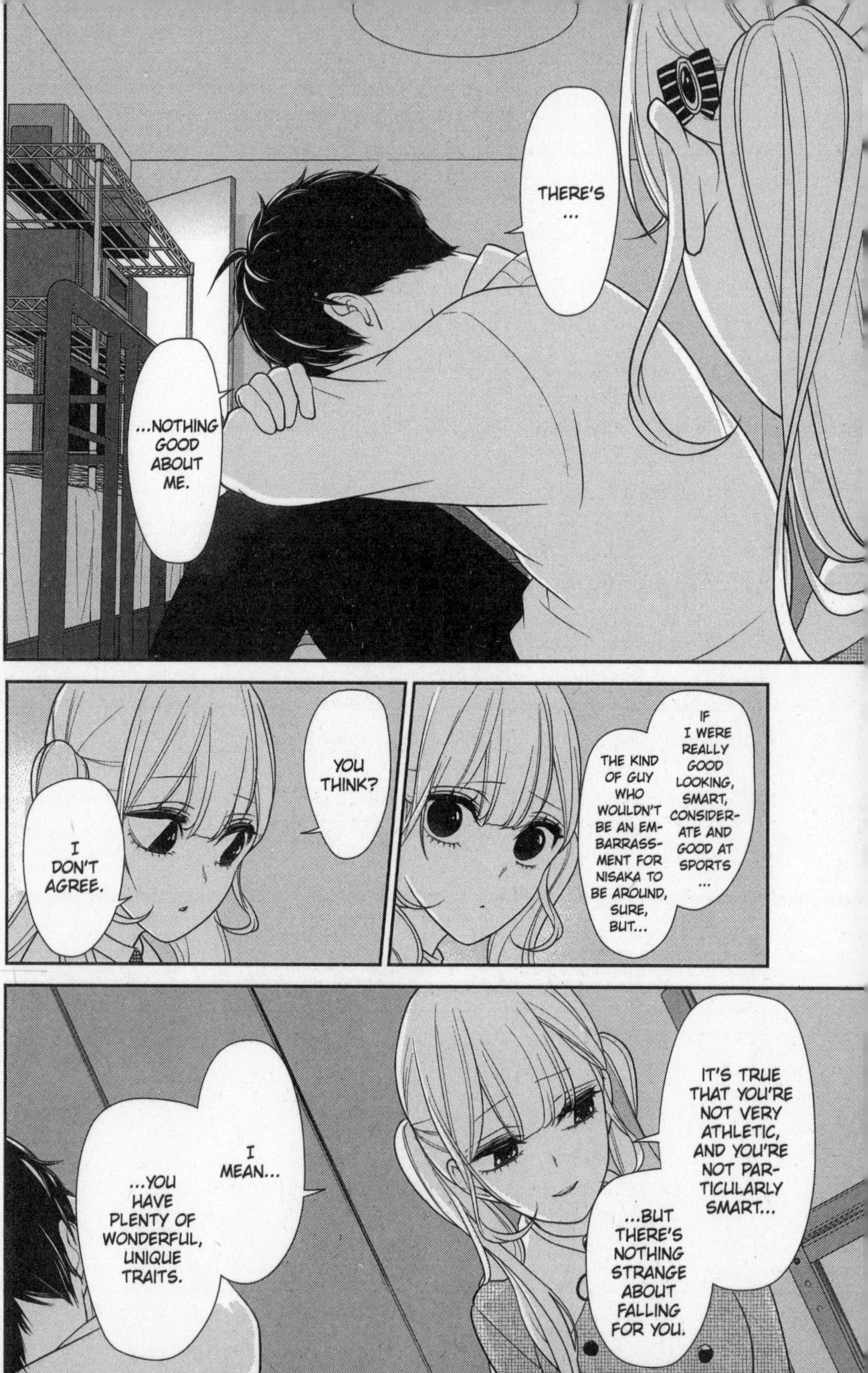
THERE'S ...
...NOTHING GOOD ABOUT ME.
IF I WERE REALLY GOOD LOOKING, SMART, CONSIDER-ATE AND GOOD AT SPORTS ...
THE KIND OF GUY WHO WOULDN'T BE AN EM-BARRASS-MENT FOR NISAKA TO BE AROUND, SURE, BUT...
YOU THINK?
I DON'T AGREE.
IT'S TRUE THAT YOU'RE NOT VERY ATHLETIC, AND YOU'RE NOT PAR-TICULARLY SMART...
...BUT THERE'S NOTHING STRANGE ABOUT FALLING FOR YOU.
I MEAN...
...YOU HAVE PLENTY OF WONDERFUL, UNIQUE TRAITS.

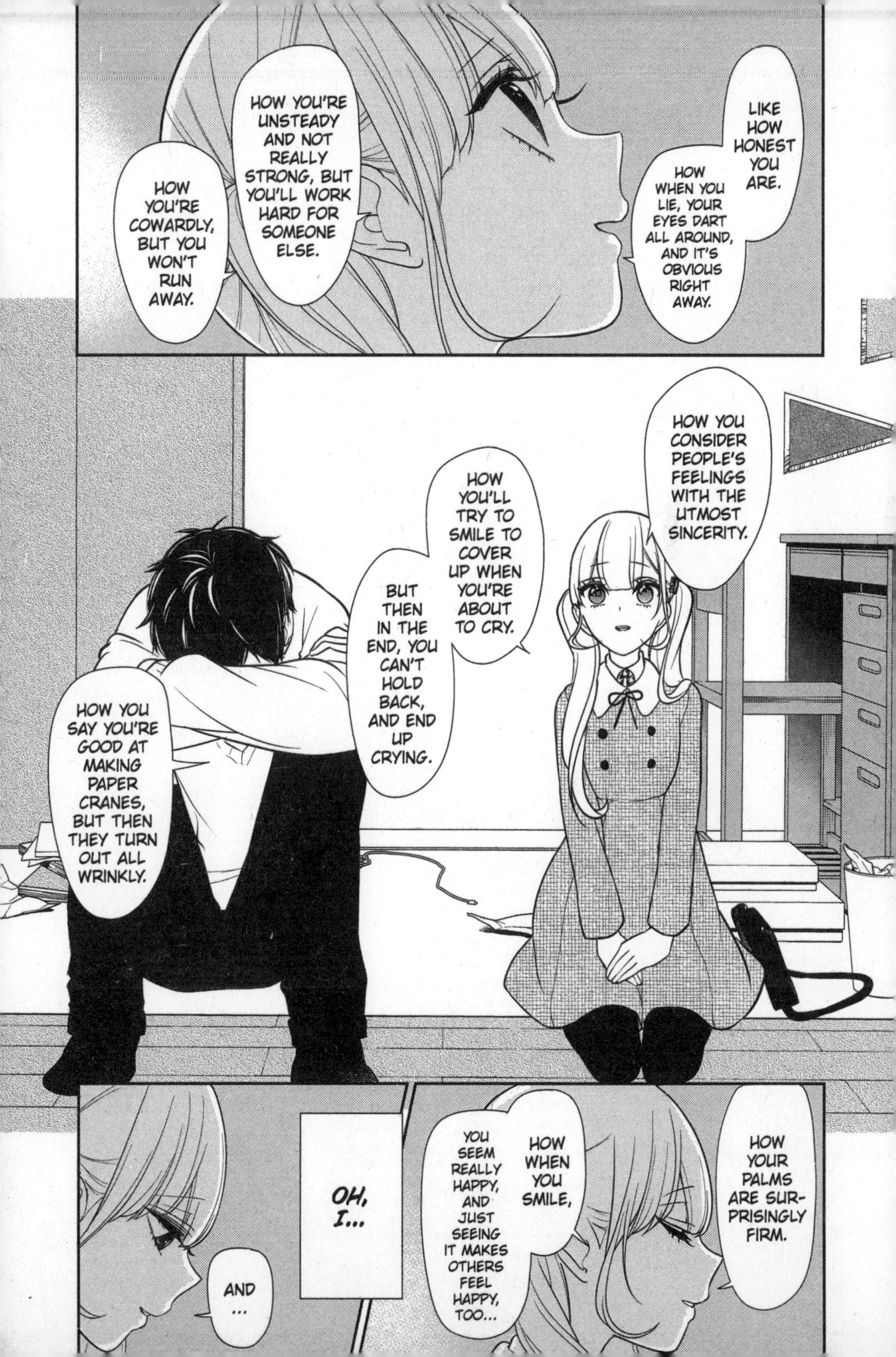

LIKE HOW HONEST YOU ARE.
HOW WHEN YOU LIE, YOUR EYES DART ALL AROUND, AND IT'S OBVIOUS RIGHT AWAY.
HOW YOU'RE UNSTEADY AND NOT REALLY STRONG, BUT YOU'LL WORK HARD FOR SOMEONE ELSE.
HOW YOU'RE COWARDLY, BUT YOU WON'T RUN AWAY.
HOW YOU CONSIDER PEOPLE'S FEELINGS WITH THE UTMOST SINCERITY.
HOW YOU'LL TRY TO SMILE TO COVER UP WHEN YOU'RE ABOUT TO CRY.
BUT THEN IN THE END, YOU CAN'T HOLD BACK, AND END UP CRYING.
HOW YOU SAY YOU'RE GOOD AT MAKING PAPER CRANES, BUT THEN THEY TURN OUT ALL WRINKLY.
HOW YOUR PALMS ARE SUR-PRISINGLY FIRM.
HOW WHEN YOU SMILE,
YOU SEEM REALLY HAPPY, AND JUST SEEING IT MAKES OTHERS FEEL HAPPY, TOO...
OH, I...
AND ...

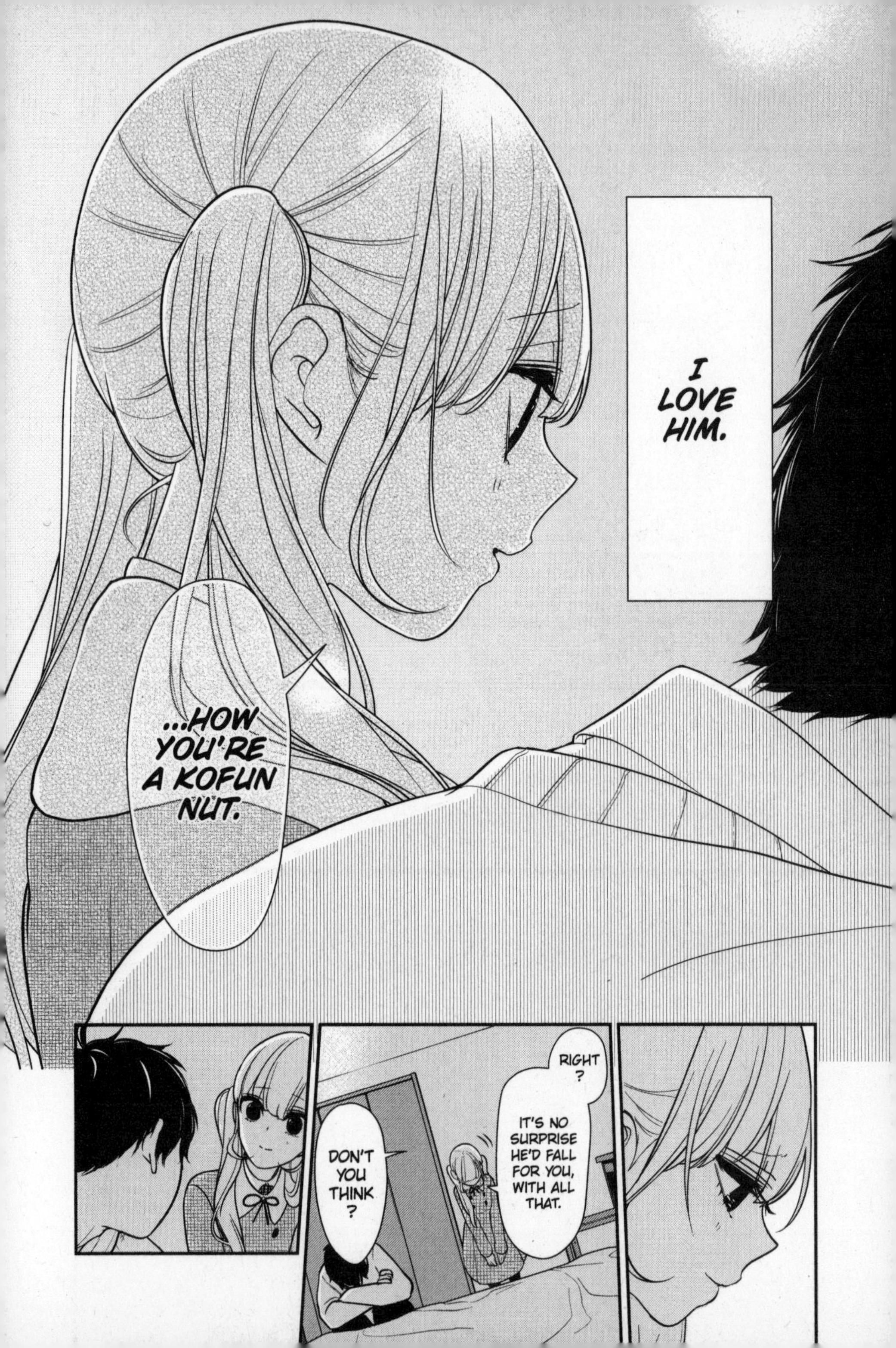
I LOVE HIM.
...HOW YOU'RE A KOFUN NUT.
RIGHT?
IT'S NO SURPRISE HE'D FALL FOR YOU, WITH ALL THAT.
DON'T YOU THINK?

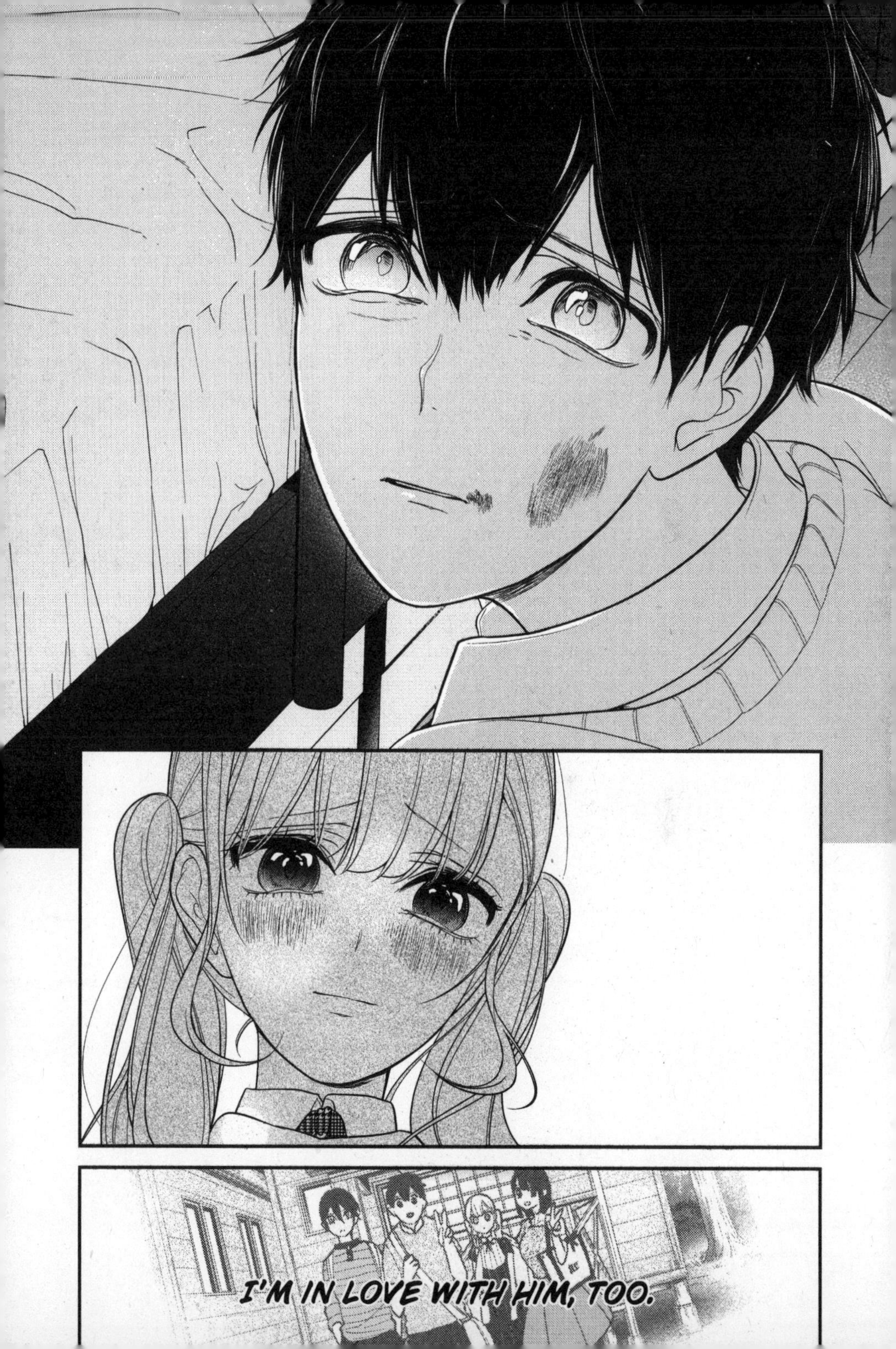
I'M IN LOVE WITH HIM, TOO.

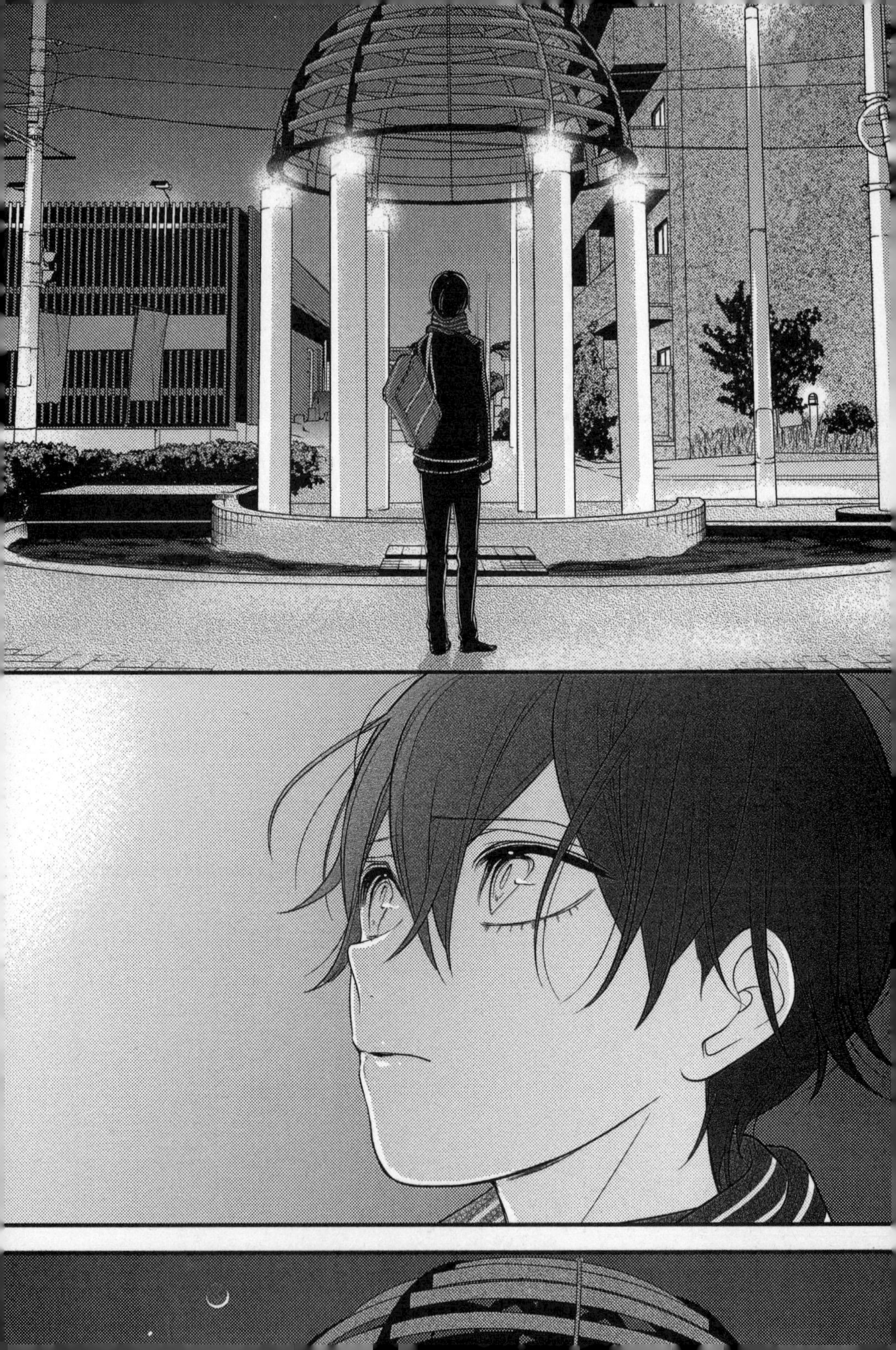

Love & Lies

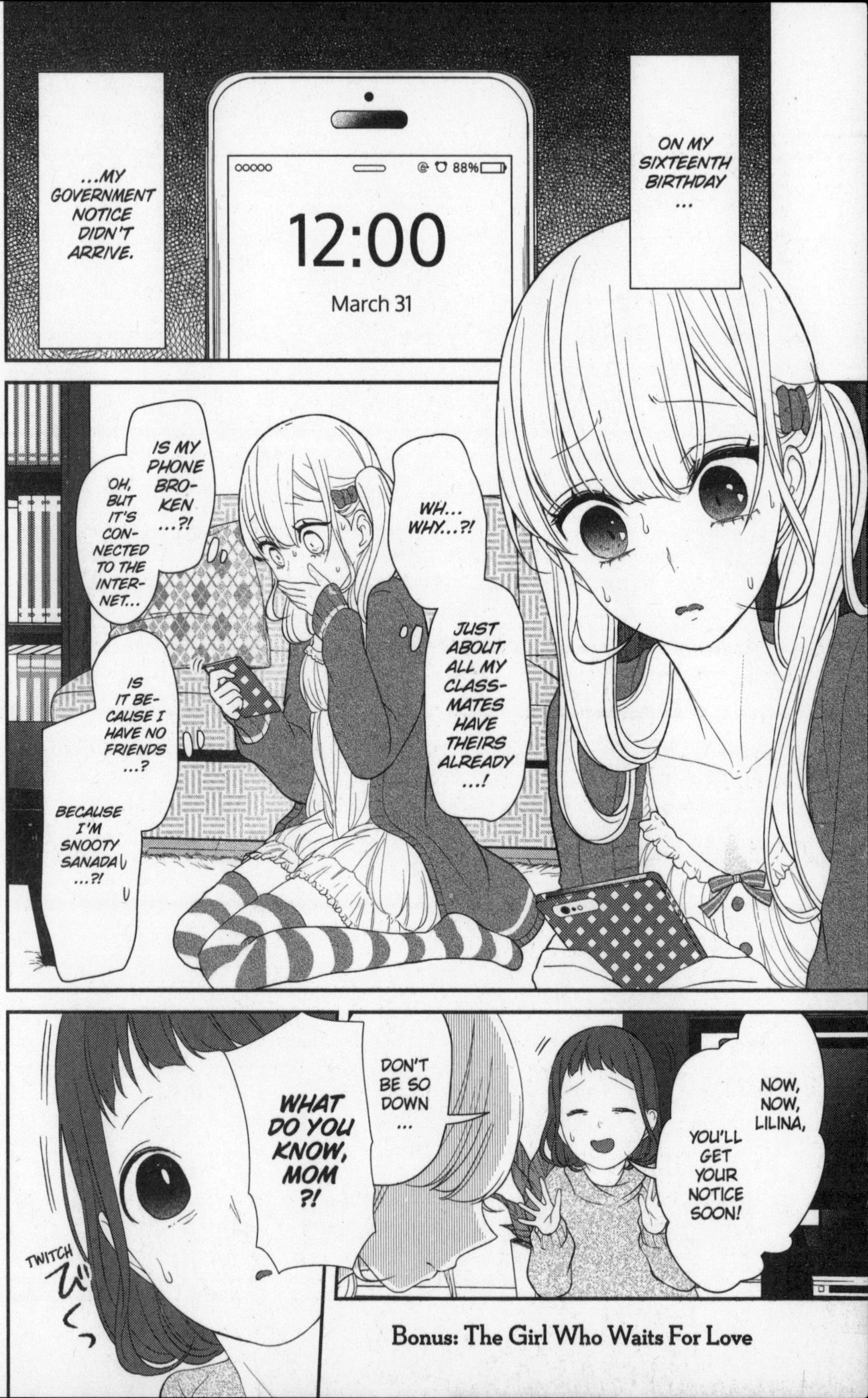
ON MY SIXTEENTH BIRTHDAY...
88%
12:00
March 31
...MY GOVERNMENT NOTICE DIDN'T ARRIVE.
WH... WHY...?!
JUST ABOUT ALL MY CLASSMATES HAVE THEIRS ALREADY...!
IS MY PHONE BRO-KEN...?!
OH, BUT IT'S CON-NECTED TO THE INTER-NET...
IS IT BE-CAUSE I HAVE NO FRIENDS...?
BECAUSE I'M SNOOTY SANADA...?!
NOW, NOW, LILINA,
YOU'LL GET YOUR NOTICE SOON!
DON'T BE SO DOWN...
WHAT DO YOU KNOW, MOM?!
TWITCH

Bonus: The Girl Who Waits For Love

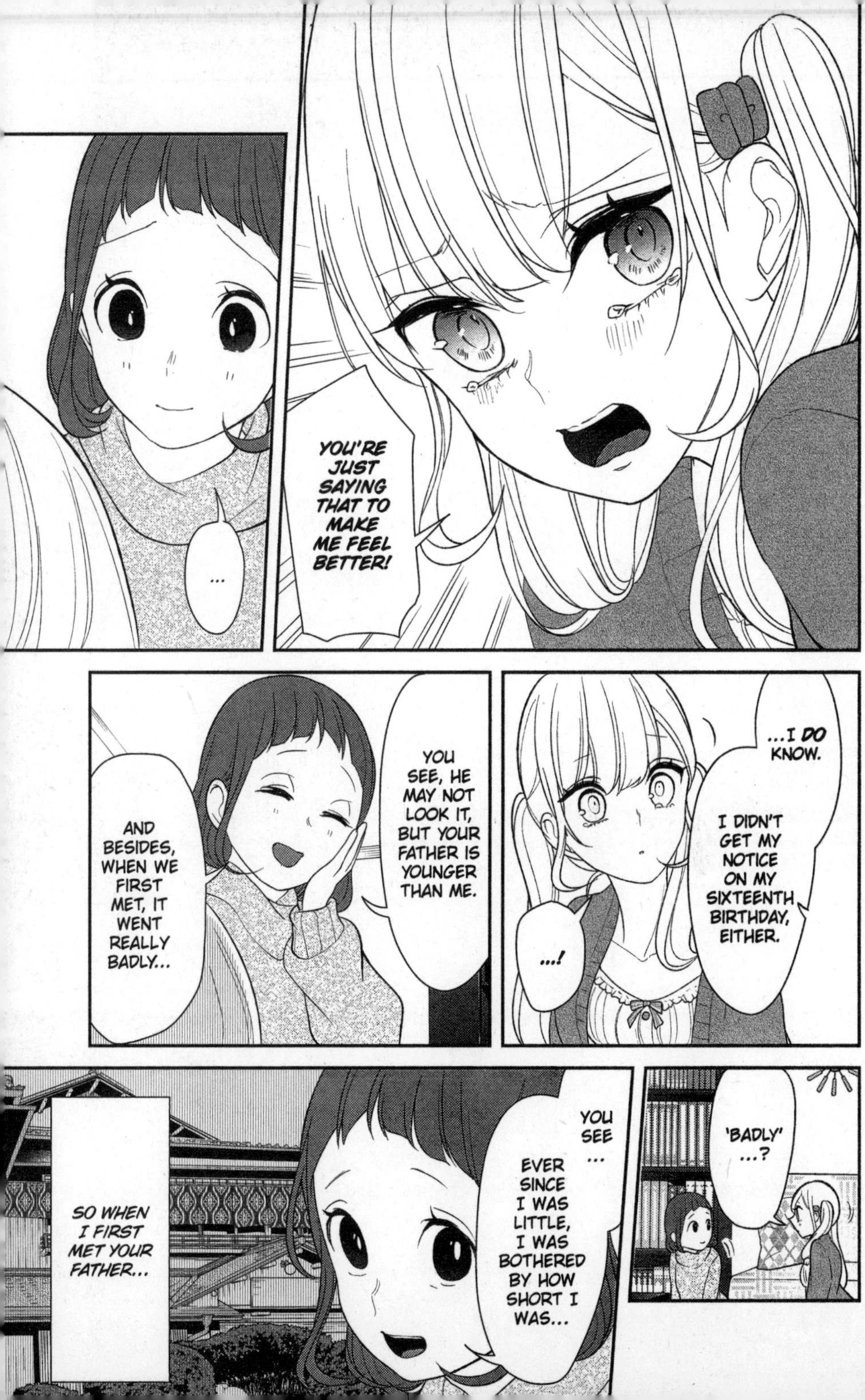
YOU'RE JUST SAYING THAT TO MAKE ME FEEL BETTER!
...
...I DO KNOW.
I DIDN'T GET MY NOTICE ON MY SIXTEENTH BIRTHDAY, EITHER.
...!
YOU SEE, HE MAY NOT LOOK IT, BUT YOUR FATHER IS YOUNGER THAN ME.
AND BESIDES, WHEN WE FIRST MET, IT WENT REALLY BADLY...
'BADLY' ...?
YOU SEE...
EVER SINCE I WAS LITTLE, I WAS BOTHERED BY HOW SHORT I WAS...
SO WHEN I FIRST MET YOUR FATHER...

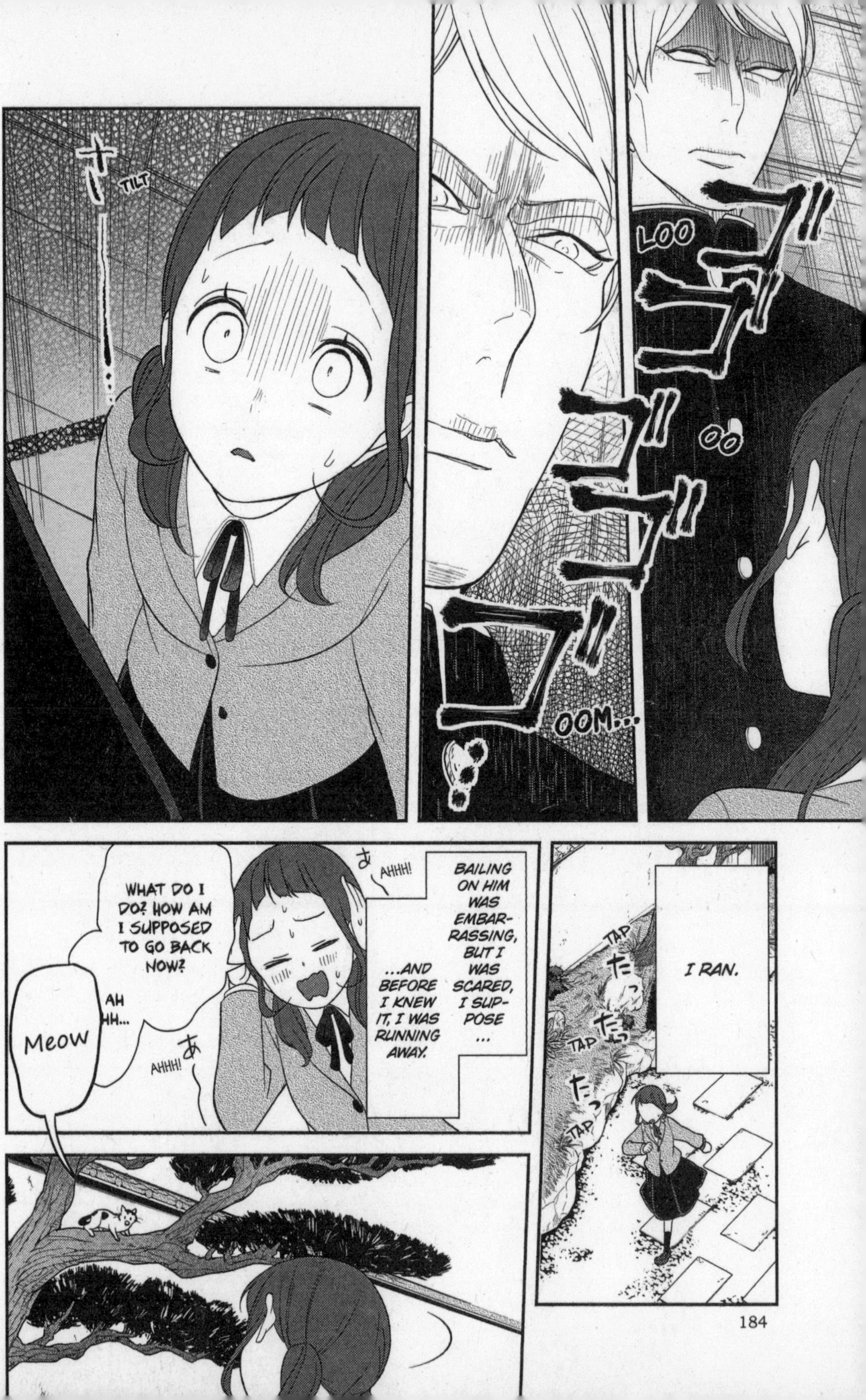
LOO
OO
OOM...
TILT
TAP
TAP
TAP
I RAN.
BAILING ON HIM WAS EMBARRASSING, BUT I WAS SCARED, I SUPPOSE...
...AND BEFORE I KNEW IT, I WAS RUNNING AWAY.
AHHH!
WHAT DO I DO? HOW AM I SUPPOSED TO GO BACK NOW?
AH HH...
AHHH!
Meow

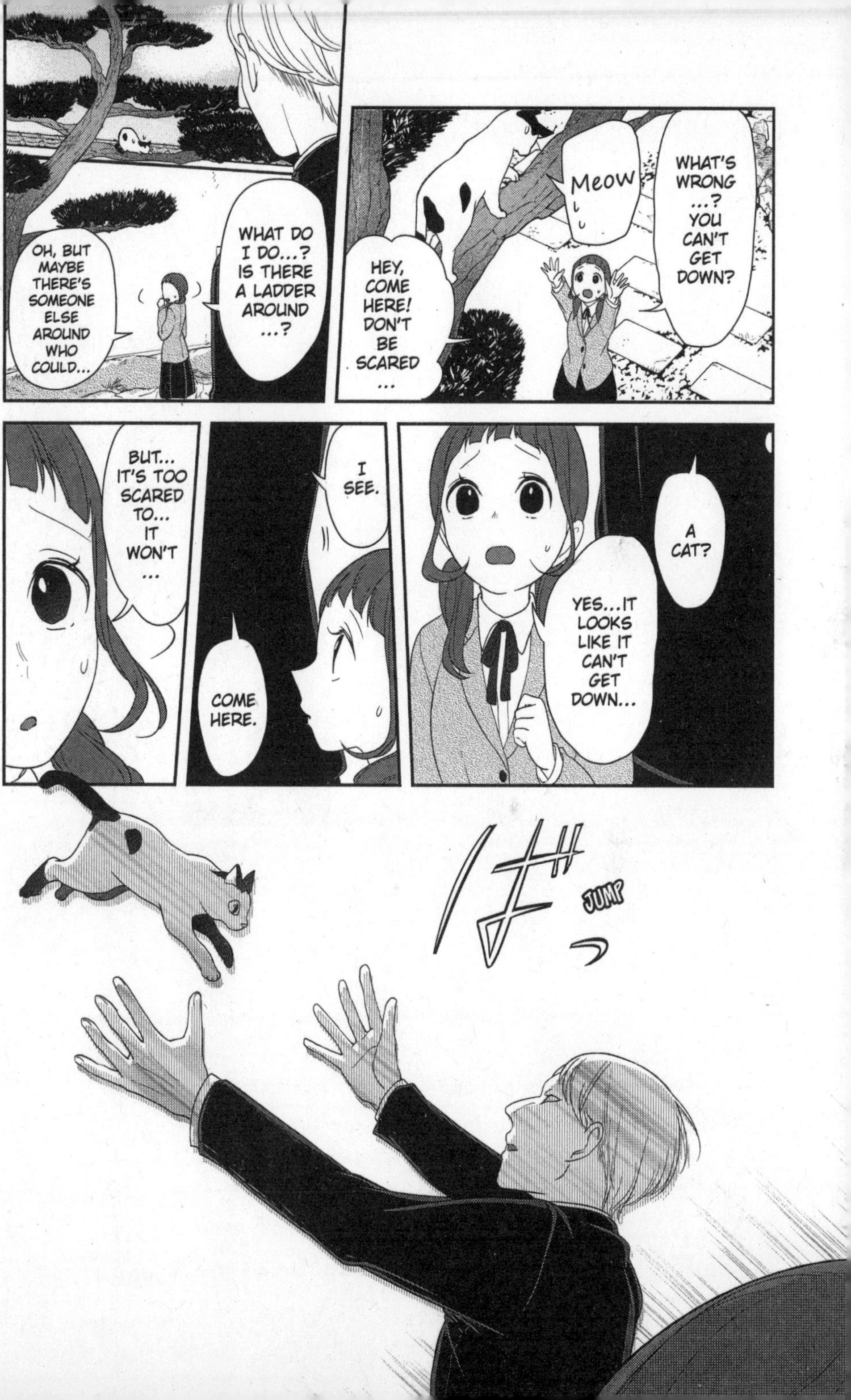
WHAT'S WRONG ...? YOU CAN'T GET DOWN?
Meow
HEY, COME HERE! DON'T BE SCARED ...
WHAT DO I DO...? IS THERE A LADDER AROUND ...?
OH, BUT MAYBE THERE'S SOMEONE ELSE AROUND WHO COULD...
A CAT?
YES...IT LOOKS LIKE IT CAN'T GET DOWN...
I SEE.
COME HERE.
BUT... IT'S TOO SCARED TO... IT WON'T ...
JUMP

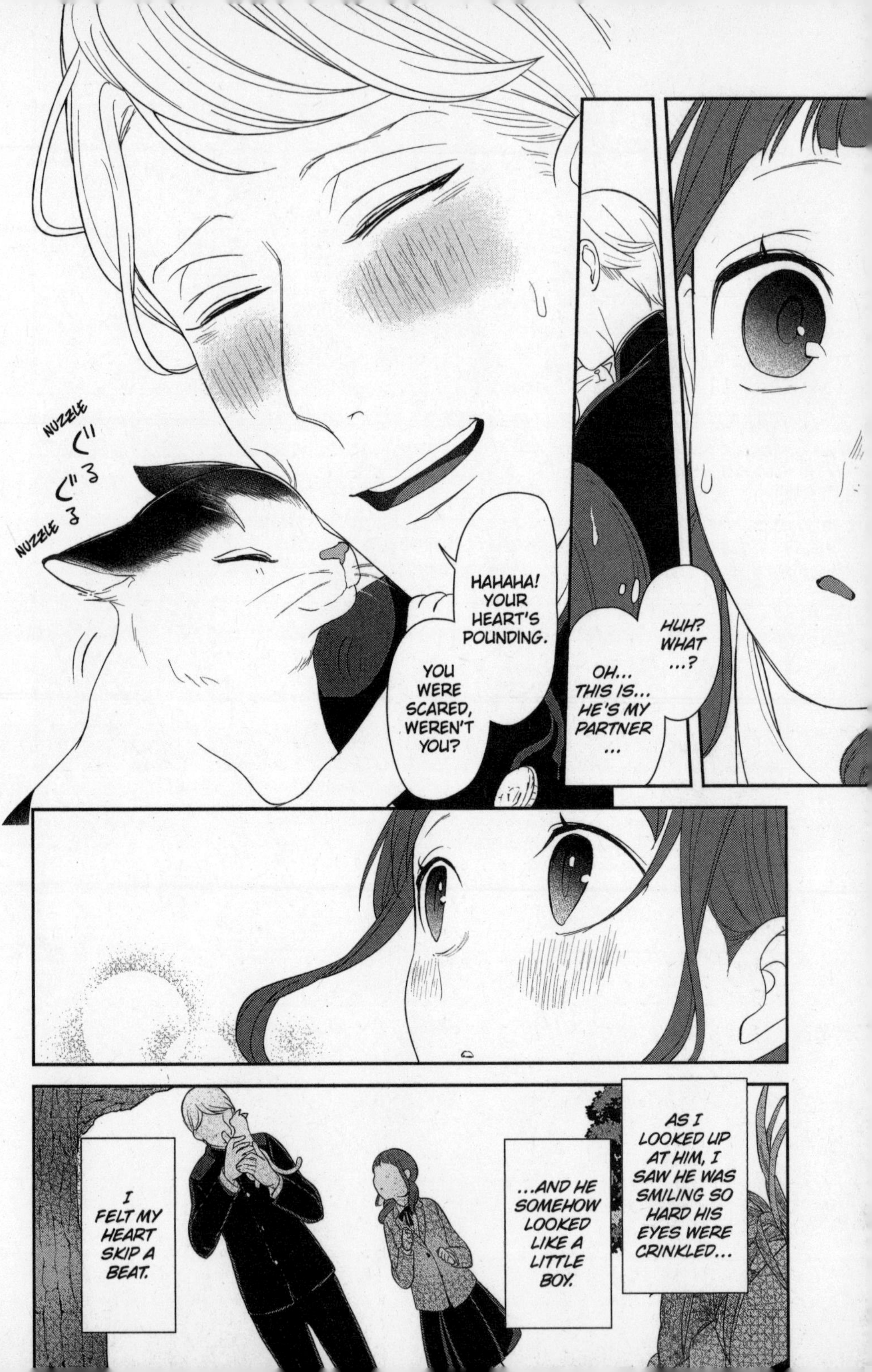
HUH? WHAT ...?
OH... THIS IS... HE'S MY PARTNER ...
HAHAHA! YOUR HEART'S POUNDING.
YOU WERE SCARED, WEREN'T YOU?
NUZZLE
NUZZLE
AS I LOOKED UP AT HIM, I SAW HE WAS SMILING SO HARD HIS EYES WERE CRINKLED...
...AND HE SOMEHOW LOOKED LIKE A LITTLE BOY.
I FELT MY HEART SKIP A BEAT.

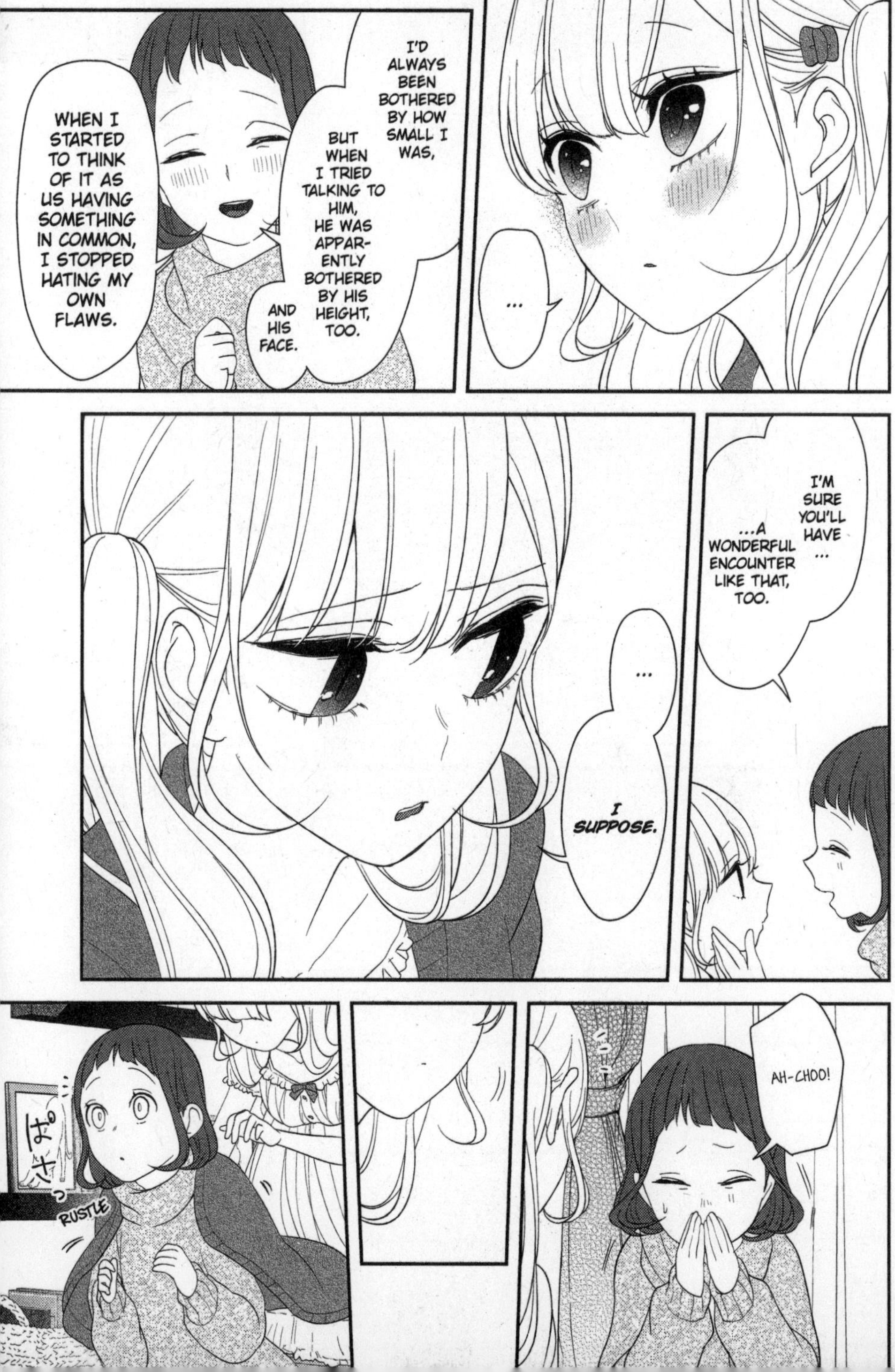
...
I'D ALWAYS BEEN BOTHERED BY HOW SMALL I WAS,
BUT WHEN I TRIED TALKING TO HIM, HE WAS APPARENTLY BOTHERED BY HIS HEIGHT, TOO.
AND HIS FACE.
WHEN I STARTED TO THINK OF IT AS US HAVING SOMETHING IN COMMON, I STOPPED HATING MY OWN FLAWS.
I'M SURE YOU'LL HAVE ...
...A WONDERFUL ENCOUNTER LIKE THAT, TOO.
...
I SUPPOSE.
AH-CHOO!
ぱさっ
RUSTLE

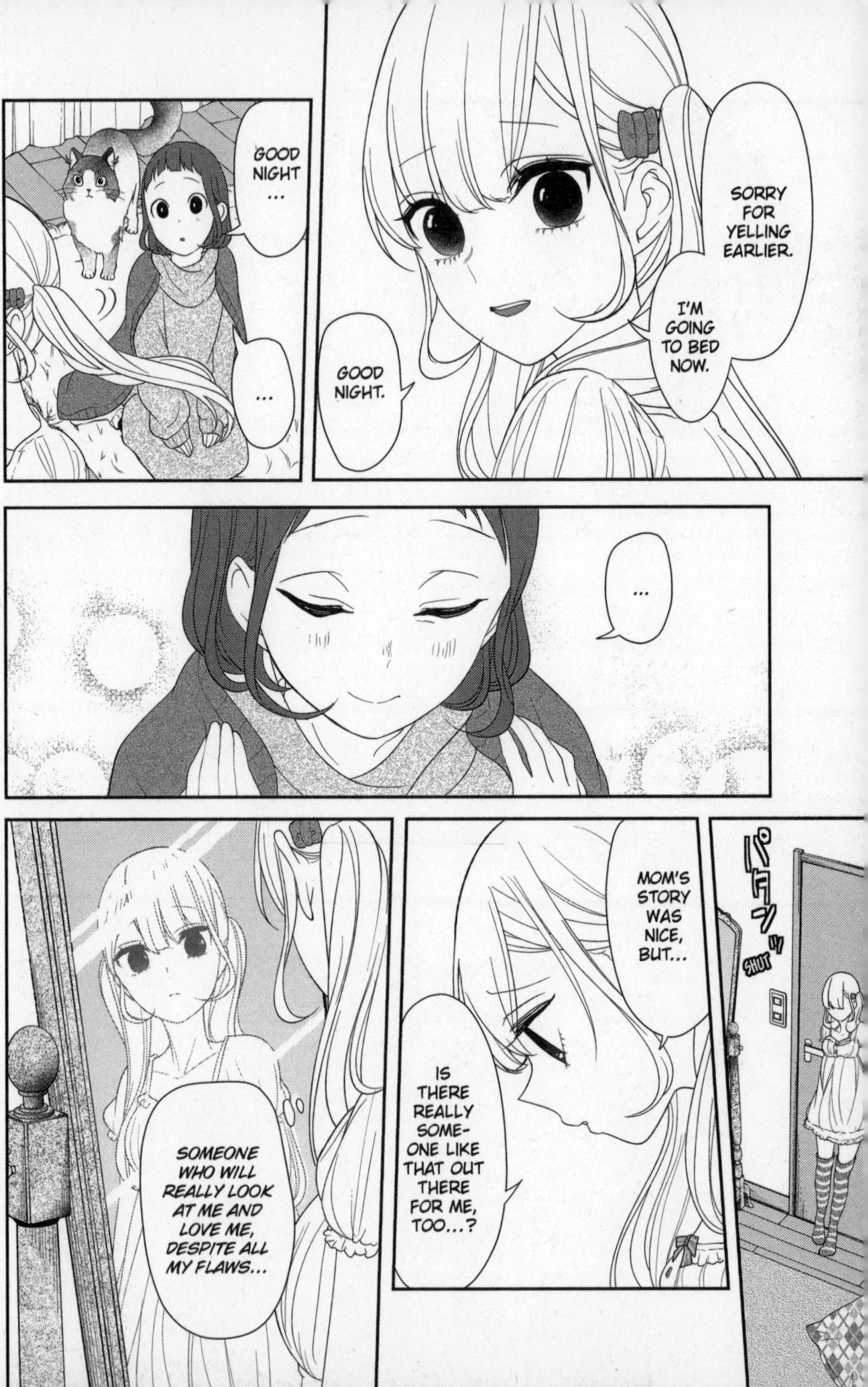
SORRY FOR YELLING EARLIER.
I'M GOING TO BED NOW.
GOOD NIGHT.
GOOD NIGHT...
...
...
パタンッ
SHUT
MOM'S STORY WAS NICE, BUT...
IS THERE REALLY SOME-ONE LIKE THAT OUT THERE FOR ME, TOO...?
SOMEONE WHO WILL REALLY LOOK AT ME AND LOVE ME, DESPITE ALL MY FLAWS...

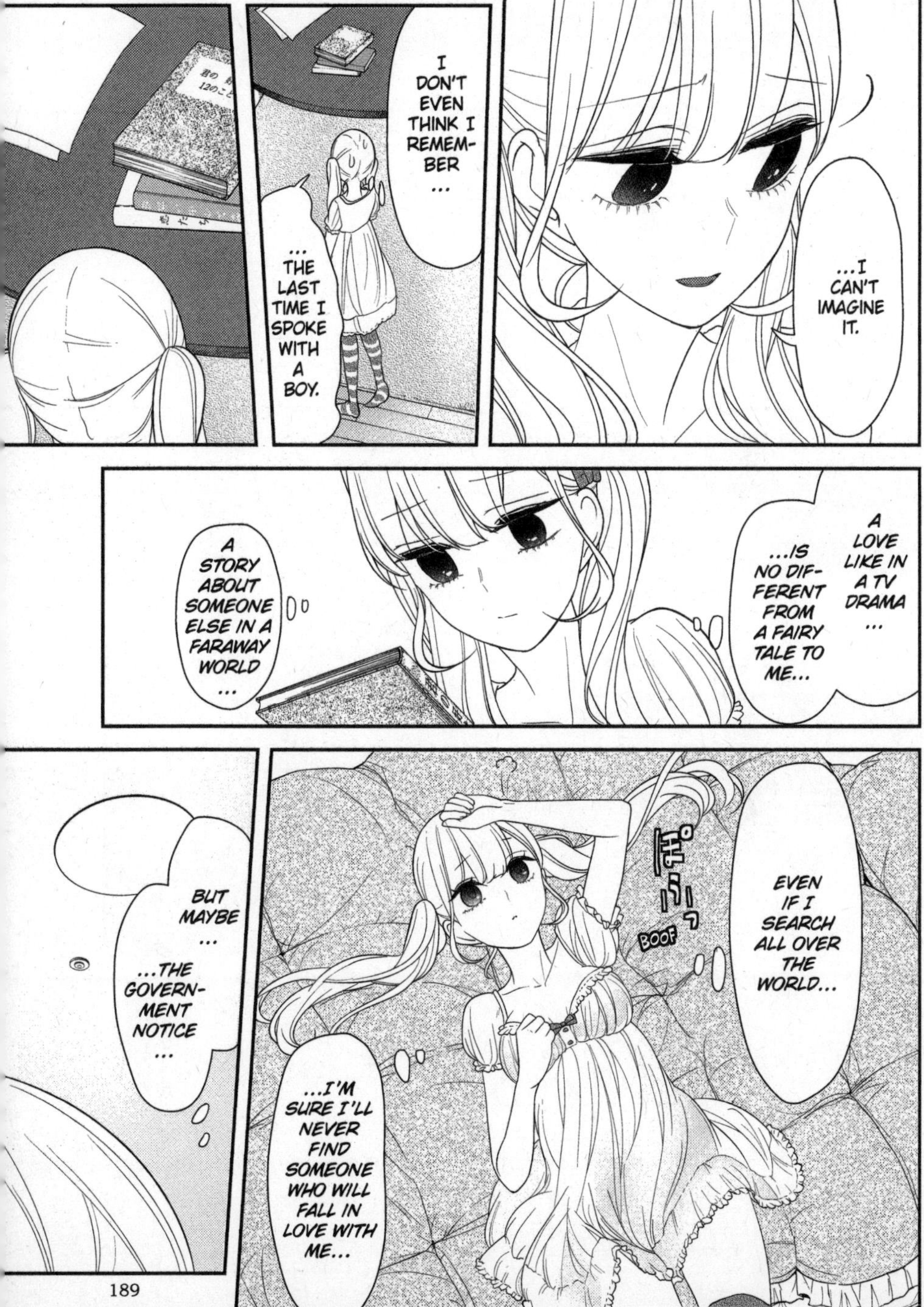
...I CAN'T IMAGINE IT.
I DON'T EVEN THINK I REMEMBER...
...THE LAST TIME I SPOKE WITH A BOY.
A LOVE LIKE IN A TV DRAMA...
...IS NO DIFFERENT FROM A FAIRY TALE TO ME...
A STORY ABOUT SOMEONE ELSE IN A FARAWAY WORLD...
EVEN IF I SEARCH ALL OVER THE WORLD...
ポフッ
BOOF
...I'M SURE I'LL NEVER FIND SOMEONE WHO WILL FALL IN LOVE WITH ME...
BUT MAYBE...
...THE GOVERNMENT NOTICE...

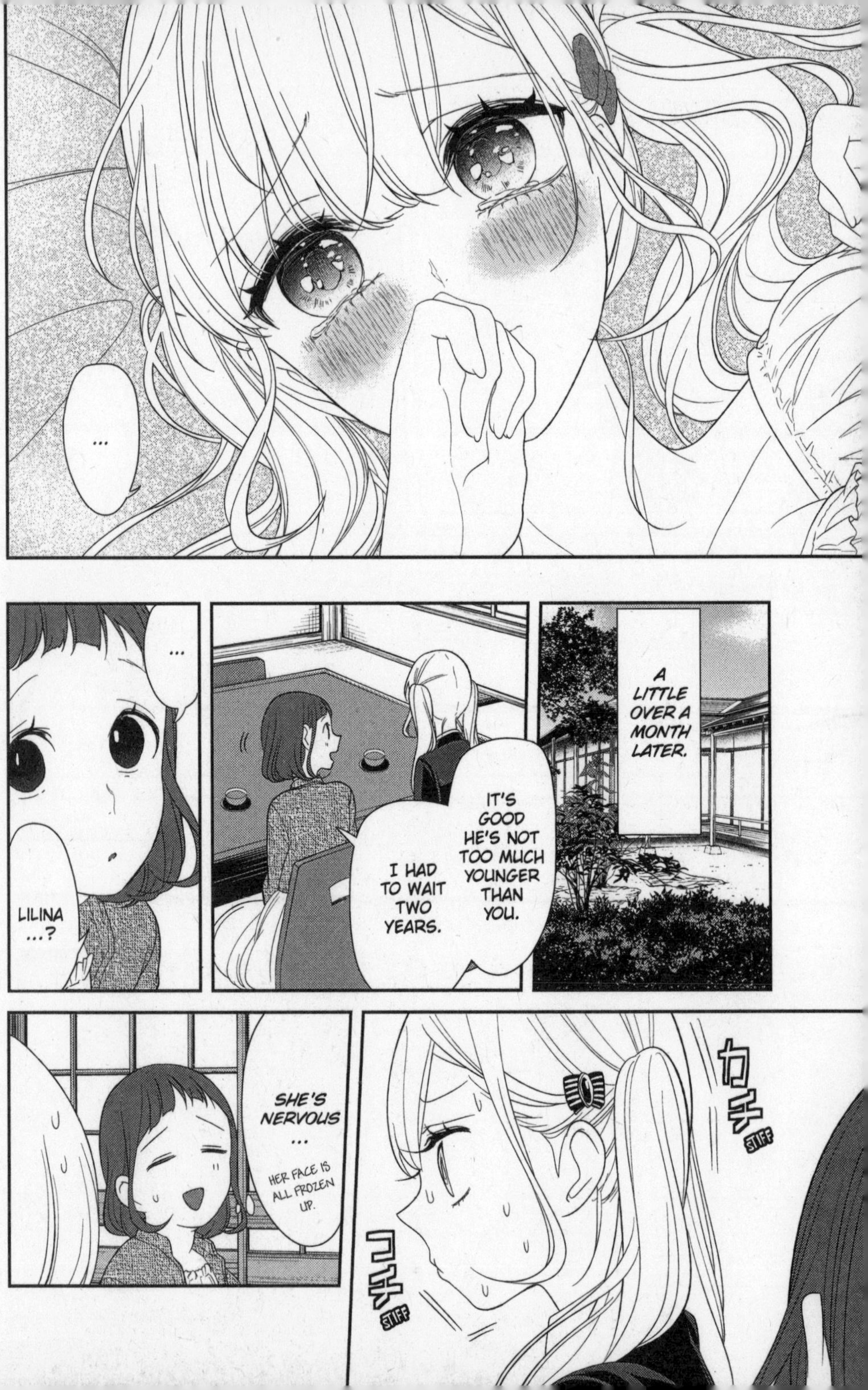
...
A LITTLE OVER A MONTH LATER.
IT'S GOOD HE'S NOT TOO MUCH YOUNGER THAN YOU.
I HAD TO WAIT TWO YEARS.
...
LILINA ...?
カチ
STIFF
コチ
STIFF
SHE'S NERVOUS ...
HER FACE IS ALL FROZEN UP.

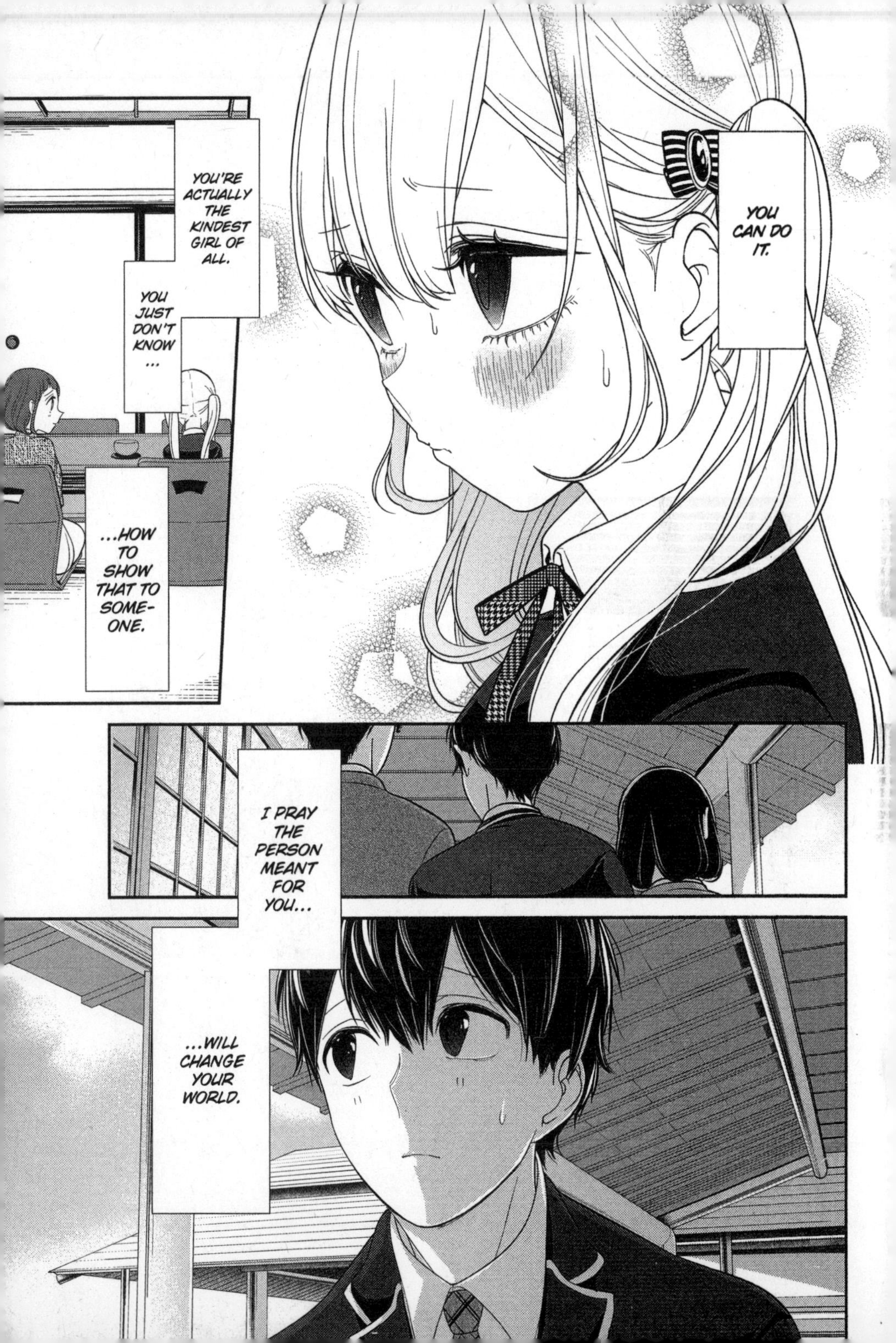
YOU CAN DO IT.
YOU'RE ACTUALLY THE KINDEST GIRL OF ALL.
YOU JUST DON'T KNOW...
...HOW TO SHOW THAT TO SOME-ONE.
I PRAY THE PERSON MEANT FOR YOU...
...WILL CHANGE YOUR WORLD.

A Kodansha Comics Trade Paperback Original.

Love and Lies volume 8 copyright © 2018 Musawo
English translation copyright © 2019 Musawo

All rights reserved.

Published in the United States by Kodansha Comics, an imprint of Kodansha USA Publishing, LLC, New York.

Publication rights for this English edition arranged through Kodansha Ltd., Tokyo.

First published in Japan in 2018 by Kodansha Ltd., Tokyo, as *Koi to Uso* volume 8.

ISBN 978-1-63236-675-7

Printed in the United States of America.

www.kodanshacomics.com

9 8 7 6 5 4 3 2 1

Translator: Jennifer Ward
Lettering: Daniel CY
Editing: Tiff Ferentini
Kodansha Comics edition cover design by Phil Balsman